BUSINESS STATISTICS AND ACCOUNTING
Made Simple

The Made Simple series
has been created
primarily for self-education
but can equally well
be used as
an aid to group study.
However complex the subject,
the reader is taken
step by step,
clearly and methodically,
through the course. Each volume
has been prepared by experts,
using throughout the
Made Simple technique of teaching.
Consequently the gaining
of knowledge now becomes
an experience to be enjoyed.

In the same series

Accounting
Acting and Stagecraft
Additional Mathematics
Advertising
Anthropology
Applied Economics
Applied Mathematics
Applied Mechanics
Art Appreciation
Art of Speaking
Art of Writing
Biology
Book-keeping
British Constitution
Business and Administrative Organisation
Business Statistics and Accounting
Calculus
Chemistry
Childcare
Commerce
Company Administration
Company Law
Computer Programming
Cookery
Cost and Management Accounting
Data Processing
Dressmaking
Economic History
Economic and Social Geography
Economics
Effective Communication
Electricity
Electronic Computers
Electronics
English
English Literature
Export
Financial Management
French
Geology
German
Human Anatomy
Italian
Journalism
Latin
Law
Management
Marketing
Mathematics
Modern Biology
Modern Electronics
Modern European History
New Mathematics
Office Practice
Organic Chemistry
Philosophy
Photography
Physical Geography
Physics
Pottery
Psychology
Rapid Reading
Retailing
Russian
Salesmanship
Secretarial Practice
Social Services
Soft Furnishing
Spanish
Statistics
Transport and Distribution
Twentieth-Century British History
Typing
Woodwork

BUSINESS STATISTICS AND ACCOUNTING
Made Simple

Ken Hoyle, BSc (Econ) and
Geoffrey Whitehead, BSc (Econ)

Made Simple Books
W. H. ALLEN London
A Howard & Wyndham Company

Printed and bound in Great Britain
by Richard Clay (The Chaucer Press), Ltd.,
Bungay, Suffolk
for the publishers W. H. Allen & Company Ltd,
44 Hill Street, London W1X 8LB

ISBN 0 491 02299 9 casebound
ISBN 0 491 02309 X paperbound

Foreword

This book has been written to meet the requirements of modern course specifications which seek to train business and administrative students across wider fields than the traditional subjects. It covers all the elementary aspects of 'Numeracy and Accounting', giving a sound revision in Business Calculations, an introduction to Business Statistics and a complete coverage of the Principles of Accounting to Final Accounts level. In order to meet the needs of the mixed economy the text includes both private sector and public sector aspects of accounting. Thus the book deals with every type of Final Accounts, from the simplest form of club accounts to the Consolidated Fund of the Central Government. It is particularly appropriate for the Business Education Council's compulsory module 'Numeracy and Accounting' and will be of interest to Business Studies students in many other fields.

In writing this book we have received much help from firms and other organisations whose assistance is gratefully acknowledged. We must particularly thank Rex Ingram, Arthur Upson, Sue Bridgeland and Julia Ansell for their painstaking reading of parts of the text, and Robert Postema, the editor of the Made Simple series, for his interest in and encouragement of the project.

KEN HOYLE
GEOFFREY WHITEHEAD

ANSWER BOOK

A booklet is available containing answers to all the Exercises sections in this book, and may be obtained from booksellers (price 95p) or, in the UK, by writing to Made Simple Books, 44 Hill Street, London WIX. 8LB. (Please enclose payment with order.)

Acknowledgements

The firms and organisations listed below have kindly permitted the use of illustrations, statistics, etc. Their help is gratefully acknowledged.

Accountants' Weekly
Burroughs Machines Ltd
The Consumers' Association and the magazine *Which?*
The Controller, Her Majesty's Stationery Office
The County of Cambridgeshire—Finance Department
Economic Progress Report
Finance and Development
Kalamazoo Ltd
George Vyner Ltd

Contents

SECTION 1
INTRODUCTION

1

AN INTRODUCTION TO BUSINESS STATISTICS AND ACCOUNTING

1.1 The Subject-matter of this Book

Business Statistics and Accounting Made Simple covers an extensive range of business activities involving numeracy and accounting. There are really four fields of interest here. They are:

(*a*) Simple business calculations
(*b*) Business statistics
(*c*) Accounting to the Trial Balance level
(*d*) Accounting to the Final Accounts level

A few words about each of these is desirable.

1.2 Simple Business Calculations

Most readers will already have a basic knowledge of business calculations, without which it is impossible to follow the statistical and accounting procedures which form the bulk of the book. For example, it is essential that the reader understands decimal and vulgar fractions, and can solve simple equations. A revision course in these is given in Chapter 2 for the benefit of those who need to brush up their knowledge of simple number work. For those who are very weak at business calculations it is strongly recommended that an introductory course in that subject should be followed first.

Having said this, it remains true that students should not feel worried about the level of work that lies ahead of them as they approach a course in Business Statistics and Accounting. The difficulties are not great, and the coverage given will be sufficiently detailed to enable a serious student to master them.

1.3 Business Statistics

An understanding of statistics is very important to all who propose to enter the business field today. Organised society is increasingly aware of the value of collecting numerical data: individuals are expected to contribute numerical facts to the Inland Revenue, local authority, bank, insurance company, hire-purchase company, etc. It is important that they appreciate the uses to which such data are put. The study of statistics can help here, as it can also in an understanding of modern business operations. Effort at work today may be measured by activity sampling; rewards may be partly decided by reference to the retail price index; pricing policy may be influenced by data collected about the price elasticity of demand, etc. Although these sound difficult matters they are in fact quite simple to follow. The statistics taught on most business studies courses (and certainly those contained within this textbook) require little more than an appreciation of arithmetic and simple mathematics. It is therefore a great pity if students are frightened away from the subject by thoughts of complicated mathematics.

1.4 Accounting to the Trial Balance Level

There are two basic stages in the study of accounting. The reader who scans the advertisements in any evening paper will find many requests for employees who can do 'Book-keeping to the Trial Balance level'. This is the level of routine entries, where documents are entered into books of account called **books of original entry** and are then 'posted' from the book of original entry to the main book of account, which is called the **ledger.** At the end of every month this ledger is balanced to see if any errors have been made. This activity is called a 'trial balance', and hence the name of this section. The reader might like to turn to page 130 where a layout of the elementary accounting processes will show how much is involved in 'Book-keeping to the Trial Balance level'.

A book-keeper who can keep books to the trial balance level knows how to make all the different entries in the books of original entry and how to post them to the ledger without making any mistakes. The result will be that the trial balance balances correctly. Most people can learn this work in two to three weeks (full-time study, i.e. one lesson per day) or in about six weeks to two months of evening classes. It is a very satisfactory level of work to attain, and countless book-keepers throughout the world never learn any more than this level.

1.5 Accounting to Final Accounts Level

As the chart on page 131 shows, the only remaining activity after book-keeping to the trial balance level is the preparation of the 'Final Accounts'. There are only two of these 'Final Accounts': the Trading Account and the Profit and Loss Account.

The Trading Account is used to find the difference between the cost price of goods and their selling price. This is of course the *profit*, but as there are a great many overhead expenses to deduct as well we call the profit found in the Trading Account the **gross profit** or overall profit.

This gross profit is then taken into the Profit and Loss Account, where it is reduced by deducting the various overheads from it—so that the final result is the **net profit**, or clean profit, after all deductions have been made.

Finally a **Balance Sheet** is prepared, which lists the situation at the end of the financial year. What **assets** does the business have and what **liabilities**?

The last stage of accounting seems very simple, and indeed it is—but it is made rather more lengthy because of the different types of business units. We have to do Final Accounts for sole traders, partnerships, limited companies, non-profit-making clubs, public authorities and even for Central Government. This makes accounting a very large body of knowledge, well worthwhile as a major field of study.

1.6 Conclusion

The reader will see from the above that this is not a difficult book. It covers a field of human knowledge which many students have already experienced. At the same time it is comprehensive—there is much to learn, and all of it is well worth learning. Students who master calculations, statistics and accounting have a world of opportunity open to them. They can work in the private sector or the public sector, in almost any country in the world, and will know exactly how the organisation they serve is thriving. Statisticians and accountants take the pulse of Industry, Commerce and the Nation.

SECTION 2
BUSINESS CALCULATIONS

2

BASIC NUMERICAL KNOWLEDGE

2.1 The Importance of Business Calculations

Before proceeding to learn about Business Statistics and Accounting it is essential for the student to have a sound grasp of basic business calculations. Whilst a reasonable knowledge of elementary number work, fractions, decimals and percentages is assumed, the present chapter is intended as a rapid revision course for those who feel they are a trifle 'rusty' in calculations. The reader should work one or two sums from each exercise. (A seperate Answer Book is available – see Foreword.) When confident about a particular aspect he should then proceed to the next section, and so on. Explanations have been kept to a bare minimum because of lack of space.

2.2 Electronic Calculators and Business Calculations

In recent years a wide range of electronic calculators has appeared on the market which have rendered mechanical calculators and comptometers obsolete. Branches of calculations which were formerly performed rather laboriously by logarithms are now performed in fractions of a second. A multiplication sum involving ten digits in both the multiplier and the multiplicand —for example:

$$2\,786\,495\,236 \times 1\,598\,721\,686$$

would be performed in one-fifth of a second. The answers are shown in a display panel or, in the more expensive printing calculators, the machine prints out a record of the calculation and the result on a roll of paper like an ordinary adding-listing machine. The reader may feel as a result that there is no need to do business calculations at all. Unfortunately, it still remains true that one can only use such machines well if one is reasonably familiar with general processes in arithmetic. Since mechanical errors in putting numbers into the machine are quite common, and electronic mis-circuits are not unknown, it is important to have a rough idea what the answer is likely to be so that an obviously incorrect answer is detected. Almost everyone uses these calculators today, and the student who is quite good at business arithmetic, but not used to using calculators, might like to use the exercises in this chapter for familiarising himself with the machine of his choice.

Before purchasing a calculator it is advisable to seek the help of a qualified shop assistant in this field. Many assistants have no idea what the machines they sell are supposed to do. All calculators will add up, subtract, multiply and divide. Most will perform almost all the routine calculations required in business, but some are much more useful than others. For example, a 'clear last entry' facility is very useful if an entry is miskeyed. It removes the last entry without cancelling out any earlier work in the machine. Some calculators cannot be cleared in this way, and a mis-key means the whole calculation must be reworked. Some machines will work out percentages, mark-ups, markdowns and discounts at the touch of a button. In statistical work, where it is frequently necessary to do the same type of calculation on a whole column of different figures, a 'constant factor' facility is a great help. Many of the more expensive calculators will provide intricate scientific and statistical data instantaneously, but they may be more expensive and sophisticated than most students need. Readers of this book should opt for a commercial machine of medium price, with a display panel of 8–10 digits, for personal use. For class use a machine of the type illustrated in Fig. 2.1 would be appropriate.

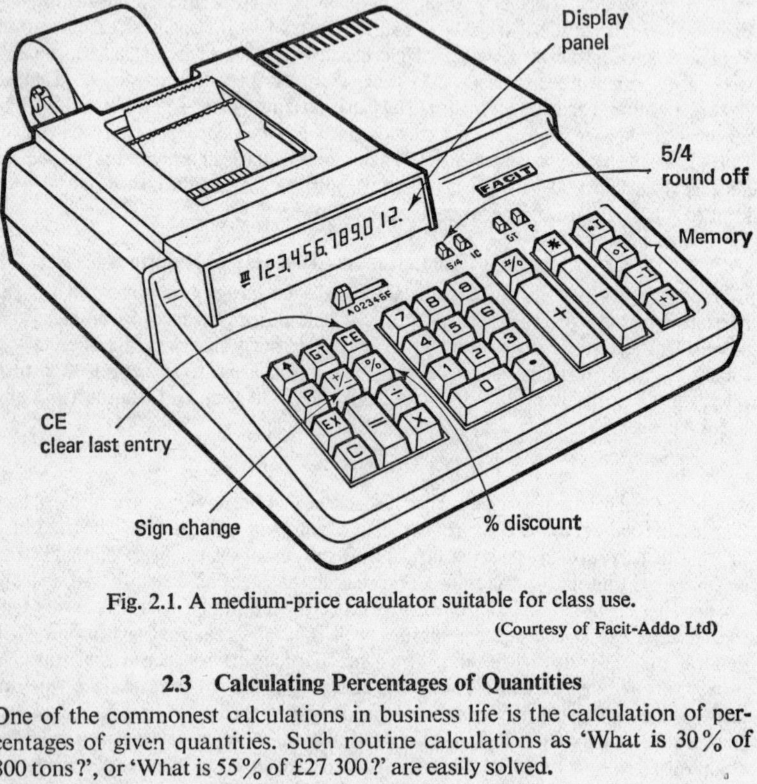

Fig. 2.1. A medium-price calculator suitable for class use.

(Courtesy of Facit-Addo Ltd)

2.3 Calculating Percentages of Quantities

One of the commonest calculations in business life is the calculation of percentages of given quantities. Such routine calculations as 'What is 30% of 800 tons?', or 'What is 55% of £27 300?' are easily solved.

Rule for calculating a percentage of a quantity

(*a*) Write down the required percentage as a fraction, with 100 as the denominator.

(*b*) Multiply this fraction by the full quantity given.

(*c*) Cancel if you can.

(*d*) Finally, multiply out.

Example 2.1. What is 30% of 800 tons?

$$30\% \text{ of } 800 \text{ tons}$$
$$= \frac{30 \times 8\not{0}\not{0}}{1\not{0}\not{0}} \quad \text{(Cancelling by 100)}$$
$$= \underline{\underline{240 \text{ tons}}}$$

Example 2.2. What is 55% of £27 300?

$$55\% \text{ of } £27\,300$$
$$= \frac{55 \times 27\,3\cancel{00}}{1\cancel{00}} \quad \text{(Cancelling by 100)}$$
$$= 55 \times 273$$
$$= £15\,015$$

```
   273
    55
------
 1 365
13 650
------
15 015
```

2.4 Exercises: Calculating Percentages of a Quantity

Calculate the following percentage parts:

1. 35% of £2 800
2. 28% of £4 200
3. 12½% of 3 600 kg
4. 48% of 25 250 kg
5. 65% of 10 500 hectares
6. 88% of £19 250
7. 42% of 76 500 electors
8. 49% of £38 240
9. 82½% of 34 000 members
10. 62% of £7 140

2.5 Calculating Quantities as Percentages of Other Quantities

Frequently statistical calculations require us to state one quantity as a percentage of another. We are all familiar with television personalities who predict the percentage swing required in elections, for example. Similarly, a mailing to consumers might be evaluated on the basis of a percentage response. We might in the planning stages calculate certain percentage responses which we hoped to achieve from particular groups, and then when the responses begin to come in we can compare the actual response with the estimated response. In the latter case, to express the response received as a percentage of the mailing, we proceed as shown below.

Rule for calculating one quantity as a percentage of another

(*a*) Write down the first quantity and rule a line under it.

(*b*) Write down the second quantity underneath the line (thus giving the first quantity as a fraction of the second).

(*c*) Multiply this fraction by 100 to make it a percentage.

Example 2.3. A mailing to 44 000 consumers is planned to achieve a 15% response. In fact 2 560 responses are received. What was the planned objective, and what percentage was in fact achieved?

(*a*) *Planned objective:* 15% of 44 000

$$= \frac{15}{100} \times 44\,000$$
$$= 6\,600 \text{ replies}$$

```
  440
   15
-----
2 200
4 400
-----
6 600
```

(*b*) *Actual response*—2 560 replies.

The fractional response is $\frac{2\,560}{44\,000}$

In percentage terms this is $\frac{2\,560}{44\,000} \times 100$ (Cancelling by 1 000 and then by 4)

$= \frac{64}{11}$

$$11\overline{)64.00} = 5.81$$

$= 5.8\%$

2.6 Exercises: Calculating Quantities as Percentages of Other Quantities

Calculate the first quantity in the sums below, as a percentage of the second quantity (Correct to one decimal place where necessary).

1. 250 as a percentage of 1 750
2. 480 as a percentage of 3 600
3. £520 as a percentage of £18 000
4. £960 as a percentage of £14 400
5. 360 kg as a percentage of 2 tonnes
6. 75 metres as a percentage of 5 kilometres
7. 245 Deutschemarks as a percentage of 5 000 Dm
8. 27 500 votes as a percentage of 75 000 electors
9. 41 500 votes as a percentage of 88 500 votes
10. 7 860 replies as a result of 55 000 questionnaires

2.7 Simple Ratios

We are all familiar with such terms as 2:1 (two to one) or 3:1 or 4:1, used to describe the relationship between two quantities. Thus the sales of 'Junior' models and 'Senior' models of an appliance might be in the ratio of 2:1, meaning that for every two 'Junior' models sold one 'Senior' model is sold. Similarly, we compare speeds of vehicles in this way. If two cars are travelling at speeds of 60 km/h and 30 km/h their speeds are in the ratio of 60:30. This is an inconvenient ratio, because it is not as simple as it could be, and it is usual to express ratios (rather like fractions) in their lowest terms. Thus

$$\begin{aligned} & 60:30 \\ = {} & 6:3 \\ = {} & 2:1 \end{aligned}$$

The cars' speeds are therefore in the ratio of 2:1.

Example 2.4. Two buses are travelling at average speeds of 30 km/h and 75 km/h respectively. What is the ratio between the speeds?

$$\begin{aligned} & 30\text{ km} : 75\text{ km} \\ & 30 : 75 \\ = {} & 6 : 15 \quad \text{(Cancelling by 5)} \\ = {} & 2 : 5 \quad \text{(Cancelling by 3)} \end{aligned}$$

Note that the units used (in this case kilometres) also cancel out from the ratio, since they appear on both sides, and leave us with an answer in numerical terms only.

It is sufficient in many cases to come down to some simple ratio of whole numbers since such a ratio is easily understood. For greater precision we can continue to divide out until one side of the ratio is 1, with the result that the other side will include a fractional part. Continuing Example 2.4 to this point, we have

$$\begin{aligned} &2:5 \\ =\ &1:2.5 \end{aligned}$$

For every kilometre the first bus travels, the second travels 2.5 km.

Example 2.5. What is the ratio between 25 metres and 5 kilometres?

Here we must note that a ratio cannot be cancelled down unless the parts of the ratio are in the same terms. Thus

$$\begin{aligned} &25\text{ m} : 5\text{ km} \\ =\ &25\text{ m} : 5\,000\text{ m} \quad \text{(changing the km to m)} \\ =\ &1 : 200 \end{aligned}$$

2.8 Exercises: Simple Ratios

Express the following ratios as simply as possible.

1. £25 to £100
2. £16 to £64
3. 300 m to 6 m
4. 72 m to 3.6 km
5. 25 km/h to 80 km/h
6. 100 km/h to $12\frac{1}{2}$ km/h
7. 45 seconds to 1 minute 30 seconds
8. 30 minutes to 2 days

In these two questions give your answer in the form 1 : ? (Correct to two decimal places)

9. 24 tonnes to 84 tonnes
10. 19 votes to 27 votes

2.9 The Unitary Method

Many calculations make use of the 'Unitary Method'—that is, a method of calculating through 1.

Example 2.6. Seven spades cost £24.50. What will 12 cost?

The unitary method gives us a calculation which involves three lines of working:

(*a*) The first line is what we know already.

(*b*) The second line is the line where we state what one would cost.

(*c*) The third line tells us what we need to know. The actual calculation is postponed until the third line.

Thus

$$\begin{aligned} &\text{7 spades cost £24.50} \\ &\text{1 spade costs } \frac{\text{£24.50}}{7} \\ &\text{12 spades will therefore cost } \frac{\text{£24.50} \times 12}{7} \\ &= \text{£3.50} \times 12 \text{ (dividing by 7)} \\ &= \text{£42} \qquad \text{(multiplying by 12)} \end{aligned}$$

2.10 Exercises: The Unitary Method

In each of the following calculations do a 'three-line calculation' with the value of one item as the second line of the calculation.

1. 12 shredding machines cost £90. What will 5 cost at the same rate?
2. 500 International Marine shares cost £1 750. What would I pay for 350 at the same rate?
3. A hotel charges £124.60 per week. What will it charge at the same rate for four days?

4. A machine costs £380 to hire for 9 days. What will it cost from July 4th to September 4th inclusive?
5. An airline flight of 3 450 miles costs £264. What will a flight of 8 625 miles cost at the same rate?

2.11 Powers and Roots

When a number is multiplied by itself we say the number has been **squared.** Thus 2 × 2 = 4, and 4 is said to be **the square** of 2; 3 × 3 = 9, so 9 is the square of three. A table of squares could be drawn up as follows:

Numbers	1	2	3	4	5	6	7	8	9	10
Squares of the numbers (1 × 1, etc.)	1	4	9	16	25	36	49	64	81	100

Clearly such a table could be continued indefinitely. We can see from the table what are the squares of the numbers 1, 2, 3, etc. Thus the square of 1 is 1, the square of 2 is 4, the square of 3 is 9, etc. Equally we can see the process the other way round. If we ask ourselves the question 'What number, when multiplied by itself, makes 4?' the answer is clearly 2; 'What number, when multiplied by itself, gives 9?' the answer is clearly 3. We say that 2 is the **square root** of 4, 3 is the square root of 9, 4 is the square root of 16, etc. A square root is written with the number under a square root sign $\sqrt{\ }$. Thus $\sqrt{25}$ means 'What is the square root of 25?', or 'What number, multiplied by itself, makes 25?'. Clearly the answer is 5. Similarly

$$\sqrt{36} = 6$$
$$\sqrt{81} = 9$$
$$\sqrt{100} = 10, \text{etc.}$$

When a number is multiplied by itself three times it is said to be **cubed.** Thus 2 × 2 × 2 = 8, and 8 is the cube of three. A table of cubes would begin as follows:

Numbers	1	2	3	4	5	6
Cubes of the numbers (1 × 1 × 1, etc.)	1	8	27	64	125	216

Clearly, again, such a table could be continued indefinitely and the numbers would get very large. For example, 25 × 25 × 25 = 15 625. Once again we can read off not only the cubes of the numbers 2, 3, 4, etc., but also the **cube roots** of 1, 8, 27, 64, 125, etc. A cube root is written $\sqrt[3]{\ }$, and therefore $\sqrt[3]{125} = 5$, because 5 is the number which when multiplied by itself twice (5 × 5 × 5) gives 125.

If we continue our multiplications beyond three times, the terms 'squared' and 'cubed' have to be replaced by some more mathematical expression, for we have run out of dimensions. We now talk about **powers**, and say that $2 \times 2 \times 2 \times 2$ is 2 raised to the power 4. We write this as 2^4. So

$$2^4 = 2 \times 2 \times 2 \times 2 = 16$$
$$3^5 = 3 \times 3 \times 3 \times 3 \times 3 = 243$$
$$4^6 = 4 \times 4 \times 4 \times 4 \times 4 \times 4 = 4\,096$$

Such terms as 4^6 are read '4 to the 6th power' or more simply as '4 to the 6th'. Thus $10^5 =$ 10 to the fifth, and means 'five tens multiplied together', i.e. $10 \times 10 \times 10 \times 10 \times 10 = 100\,000$. This is called **index notation** and the small raised numbers are called **index numbers** or **indices.**

The **laws of indices**, referred to below, are the basis of that branch of mathematics known as 'logarithms'. Before proceeding to study the laws of indices the reader should try Exercises 2.12 and 2.13 (see page 14).

The Laws of Indices

The laws of indices enable us to do certain things with numbers more easily than would otherwise be possible, but the invention of the electronic calculator has largely robbed these ideas of their former usefulness as far as everyday life is concerned. Thus the multiplication of two numbers like 1.764 and 3.594 would formerly have been carried out by logarithms using the laws of indices, but today a calculator will do it in about a tenth of a second. Similarly, to calculate the square root of 2 781 requires logarithms or a fairly laborious calculation, but a calculator with a $\sqrt{}$ facility will do it instantaneously.

Whilst it would be perfectly possible to explain the laws of indices using ordinary numbers like 2^3, 3^2, 4^5, etc., it is easier to go further into the field of generalised arithmetic, or algebra. Instead of discussing numbers raised to the power, we replace the number with a letter, and discuss the processes of number work in general terms. Thus a^4 means $a \times a \times a \times a$, and b^2 means $b \times b$, but what numbers they actually represent we do not need to know, for any number could be substituted at any time.

The four rules of indices are:

(*a*) When we multiply numbers with indices we add the indices.
(*b*) When we divide numbers with indices we subtract the indices.
(*c*) When we raise numbers with indices to a power we multiply the indices.
(*d*) When we find the root of numbers with indices we divide the indices.

These may be illustrated as follows:

Example of (*a*). Multiply a^2 by a^3.

$$a^2 = a \times a$$
$$a^3 = a \times a \times a$$

So

$$a^2 \times a^3 = a \times a \times a \times a \times a$$
$$= a^5$$

Therefore to multiply $a^2 \times a^3$ all we need to do is to add the indices $(2 + 3)$ and we have the answer a^5.

Similarly, $a^3 \times a^4 = a^7$; $b^2 \times b^4 = b^6$, etc.

Rule: When we multiply numbers with indices we add the indices.

Example of (*b*). Divide a^4 by a^2.

$$a^4 = a \times a \times a \times a$$
$$a^2 = a \times a$$

So
$$a^4 \div a^2 = \frac{a \times a \times a \times a}{a \times a}$$
$$= a \times a \text{ (cancelling two of the terms out)}$$
$$= a^2$$

Therefore to divide a^4 by a^2 all we need to do is to subtract the indices $(4 - 2)$ and we have the answer a^2.

Similarly, $a^4 \div a^3 = a^{4-3} = a^1$, which we write as a. As a further example, $b^5 \div b^3 = b^{5-3} = b^2$.

Rule: When we divide numbers with indices we subtract the indices.

Example of (*c*). What is the square of a^3, i.e. $(a^3)^2$?

$$\text{The square of } a^3 = a^3 \times a^3$$
$$= a^6$$

This is the same as multiplying the indices in $(a^3)^2 = a^6$

Similarly, $(b^4)^2 = b^8$ and $(c^5)^3 = c^{15}$.

Rule: When we raise numbers with indices to a power we multiply the indices.

Example of (*d*). What is the cube root of a^6, i.e. $\sqrt[3]{a^6}$?

The question is 'What number multiplied by itself three times gives a^6?' Dividing the indices, we have $6 \div 3 = 2$ (check: $a^2 \times a^2 \times a^2 = a^6$).

Similarly, $\sqrt{b^4} = b^{\frac{4}{2}} = b^2$ (check: $b^2 \times b^2 = b^4$) and $\sqrt[5]{c^{10}} = c^{\frac{10}{5}} = c^2$ (check: $c^2 \times c^2 \times c^2 \times c^2 \times c^2 = c^{10}$).

The reader should now try Exercise 2.14.

More Complex Powers and Roots

This book is not suitable for students who wish to acquire real facility in calculating and manipulating roots and powers. For this, the reader should turn to *Mathematics Made Simple* and *New Mathematics Made Simple*.

2.12 Exercises: Raising Numbers to a Power

Work out the real value of the following numbers when raised to the power shown:

1. 3^2	4. 17^2	7. 25^2	10. 155^2
2. 4^3	5. 18^3	8. 38^2	11. 165^3
3. 5^4	6. 15^4	9. 72^2	12. 185^4

2.13 Exercises: Square Roots of Numbers

What are the square roots of the following numbers?

1. 1	2. 16	3. 9	4. 36	5. 81
6. 625	7. 64	8. 49	9. 100	10. 10 000

2.14 Exercises: The Laws of Indices

Write down the answers to the following:

1. (*a*) $a^2 \times a^3$;	(*b*) $x^2 \times x^5$;	(*c*) $x^3 \times x^4 \times x^5$
2. (*a*) $m^2 \times m^7$;	(*b*) $p \times p^3 \times p^4$;	(*c*) $t^2 \times t^3 \times t^5 \times t$
3. (*a*) $r^7 \div r^2$;	(*b*) $x^4 \div x^3$;	(*c*) $m^{14} \div m^7$

4. (*a*) $b^5 \div b^3$; (*b*) $c^3 \div c$; (*c*) $d^5 \div d^4$
5. (*a*) $(a^2)^3$; (*b*) $(m^3)^3$; (*c*) $(r^5)^4$
6. (*a*) $\sqrt[5]{a^5}$; (*b*) $\sqrt{c^4}$; (*c*) $\sqrt[4]{b^{16}}$

2.15 Simple Equations

An equation is a mathematical statement that two expressions are equal to one another. Thus $1 + 1 = 2$ is an equation. Many equations are well known because they are rules for finding essential business facts. The student will instantly recognise the following formulae, for example.

$$\text{Circumference of a circle} = \pi D \text{ or } 2\pi r$$

where D is the diameter and r is the radius of the circle. The Greek letter π is a constant and is usually taken as $3\frac{1}{7}$ or 3.14.

$$\text{Area of a circle} = \pi r^2$$

Simple interest may be found by the formula

$$I = \frac{PRT}{100}$$

where I is the interest, P is the principal invested, R is the rate per cent interest and T is the time in years. The 100 in the equation is part of the rate which has to be written as a rate per cent.

Many simple equations can be made up from commonsense principles, and are used to solve problems. Thus if John earns £5 more than Jack per week and Jack earns twice Peter's weekly wage of £55, we can make up a simple equation as follows.

$$\begin{aligned} \text{John's wage} &= \text{Jack's wage} + £5 \\ &= 2 \times \text{Peter's wage} + £5 \\ &= 2 \times £55 + £5 \\ &= \underline{\underline{£115 \text{ per week}}} \end{aligned}$$

The Manipulation of Equations

Any equation can be manipulated into another form by obeying certain rules. For example, the formula for simple interest given above

$$I = \frac{PRT}{100}$$

can be manipulated to enable us to find the principal, the rate of interest, or the number of years the investment was held. The new formulae are

$$P = \frac{100I}{RT} \quad R = \frac{100I}{PT} \quad T = \frac{100I}{PR}$$

What are the rules which enable us to manipulate equations in this way?

There is really only one rule. It says: '*An equation will always remain true if you do the same thing to both sides of the equation.*'

Consider the following examples, which all start from the simple equation $9 = 9$:

Adding the same figure to both sides:

$$9 = 9$$
$$9 + 7 = 9 + 7$$
$$16 = 16$$

Subtracting the same figure from both sides:

$$9 - 3 = 9 - 3$$
$$\text{or } 6 = 6$$

In each of these cases the equation is still true at the end of the process. Similarly:

Multiplying both sides by the same figure:

$$9 \times 3 = 9 \times 3 \qquad \text{or } 27 = 27$$

Dividing both sides by the same figure:

$$9 \div 2 = 9 \div 2 \qquad \text{or } 4\tfrac{1}{2} = 4\tfrac{1}{2}$$

Raising both sides to a power:

$$9^3 = 9^3 \qquad \text{or } 729 = 729$$

Taking the same root of both sides

$$\sqrt{9} = \sqrt{9} \quad \text{or } 3 = 3$$

Consider the application of this rule to the formula given earlier:

$$I = \frac{PRT}{100}$$

We wish to transpose this to find out what the principal is—for example, to answer the following question: What sum of money must be invested to earn £360 in 3 years at 8% per annum?

To change the formula round we need to leave P isolated on one side of the equation. How shall we do this?

$$I = \frac{PRT}{100}$$

To remove the 100 we must multiply both sides by 100

$$100I = \frac{PRT}{100} \times 100 \text{ (The 100s cancel out)}$$
$$100I = PRT$$

To remove R and T we must divide both sides by R and T

$$\frac{100I}{RT} = \frac{PRT}{RT} \text{ (}R\text{ and }T\text{ cancel out on the right-hand side)}$$
$$\frac{100I}{RT} = P$$

Turning the equation round—for any equation can be turned round and it is still true

$$P = \frac{100I}{RT}$$

Substituting in the values given to solve our problem we have

$$P = \frac{100 \times \overset{120^{15}}{\cancel{360}}}{\cancel{8}_1 \times \cancel{3}_1} \text{ (Cancelling by 3 and 8)}$$
$$= £1\,500$$

In many branchcs of statistics we have quite complex equations, but they can be manipulated and adjusted with ease as long as we stick to the basic rule, that we must treat both sides of the equation exactly alike.

Example 2.7. A circle has an area of 154 cm². What is its radius? (Use $\pi = 3\frac{1}{7}$.)

$$\text{area} = \pi r^2 \quad \text{(Rearrange the formula to find } r^2\text{)}$$
$$\frac{\text{area}}{\pi} = r^2 \quad \text{(Now rearrange it to find } r\text{)}$$
$$\sqrt{\frac{\text{area}}{\pi}} = r \quad \text{(We had to take the square root of both sides)}$$
$$r = \sqrt{\frac{\text{area}}{\pi}} \quad \text{(Turning the equation round)}$$
$$= \sqrt{\frac{154}{3\frac{1}{7}}}$$
$$= \sqrt{\frac{154}{\frac{22}{7}}}$$
$$= \sqrt{\frac{154 \times 7}{22}} \quad \text{(Cancelling by 2 and 11)}$$
$$= \sqrt{49}$$
$$= 7 \text{ cm}$$

2.16 Exercises: Simple Equations

1. Find the distance travelled by a bicycle with wheels of diameter 66 cm if the wheels revolve 3 220 times on the journey. (Use circumference $= \pi D$, $\pi = 3\frac{1}{7}$, and give your answer in kilometres correct to one decimal place.)
2. Find the average speed of a train which travels 292.5 km in $4\frac{1}{2}$ hours. (The basic formula for moving vehicles is $d = s \times t$, where d is the distance, s is the speed and t is the time.)
3. What is the area of a ring of paper cut from two concentric circles of 12 cm and 24 cm radius? (The formula for the area of a ring is $\pi(R + r)(R - r)$, where $\pi = 3.14$, and R and r are the bigger radius and the smaller radius respectively.)
4. Find the rate of interest earned if £2 500 earns £656.25 in $3\frac{1}{2}$ years. The basic formula is $I = \frac{PRT}{100}$.
5. Find the final value of an investment of £2 000 at 8 per cent per annum *compound* interest over a period of 4 years. (With compound interest the interest is added to the principal each year and reinvested for the following year.) The formula for the final amount of such an investment is $A = P \times (1 + \frac{R}{100})^n$ where P is the principal, R is the rate and n is the number of years (answer to nearest penny).

SECTION 3
BUSINESS STATISTICS

3
AN INTRODUCTION TO BUSINESS STATISTICS

3.1 The Meaning of 'Statistics'

The word 'statistics' was originally applied to the collection of numerical facts by the State. Such areas as population, tax revenue, government expenditure, and agricultural output were initially covered. More recently the meaning of statistics has broadened to include not only a set of numerical data, but also the processes used in the collection, presentation, analysis, and interpretation of these data.

It is convenient to divide statistics into two parts:

(*a*) Descriptive statistics
(*b*) Analytical statistics

Descriptive Statistics

This term is applied to any statistics which are collected and arranged in some suitable order so that they can be presented in tabular or diagrammatic form to throw light upon the state of affairs in the field under consideration. In dealing with most human, economic or scientific problems it is helpful to know the true situation. How many people are involved? What expenditure is being envisaged? What is the likely cost of present proposals? Who is most affected by the problem? Such matters call for a clear description in statistical form. Hence, a table showing the number of registered unemployed from 1971 to 1980 falls within the field of descriptive statistics.

Analytical Statistics

These attempt to reach conclusions and make pronouncements on the basis of the information made available by descriptive statistics. It may be possible to make statements about *why* the totals of registered unemployed were as they appeared in the 1971–80 table. Measures taken during the decade might be linked to the changes in unemployment in subsequent periods and their effectiveness assessed. The cost of the measures might be set against the benefits to reveal the most cost-effective policies for the future. Such analysis makes use of techniques to be discussed later, such as averages, trends, correlation and other statistical techniques.

3.2 Criticisms of Statistics

We live in a cynical age and it is fashionable to be particularly cynical about statistics. The well-known phrase, attributed to Disraeli, 'There are lies, damned lies, and statistics' may no longer generate amusement, but it is widely believed. Professional statisticians are entitled to be unhappy about this since they take great pains to ensure that the pronouncements they make are as accurate as they possibly can be, given the resources that have been devoted to the exercise. Why then is there such a public distrust of statistics? The answer lies in the difficulties that must be faced in the collection and interpretation of data. In this introductory chapter it is advisable to mention some of the pitfalls facing the statistician, both in the collection of data and their interpretation. You will find it helpful in preparing your own statistical material if you critically appraise all the statistics presented to you, and examine them for the faults listed in the following section. An appreciation of the difficulties others have faced, or the weaknesses they have failed to overcome, will improve your own chances of presenting reliable data and of giving considered reports about any enquiry you are asked to conduct.

Sources

There are a number of points to note about the source of statistics. By the word 'source' we mean the place from which they originated, or the manner in which they were collected. If the source is a published source we should state it—for example, in the form *Source: Monthly Digest of Statistics, January 1980*. For many purposes statistics can be quoted from official sources and a reasonable degree of confidence can be placed upon them. This is because they have been collected using a well-established process by trained statisticians who presumably have used their expertise to avoid the more obvious errors. Even so it may be necessary to turn up the definitions used in the process, which are usually published as a separate booklet. Thus the *Monthly Digest of Statistics* referred to above is a mass of statistics collected by official agencies using definitions published in a Supplement to the Digest called *Monthly Digest of Statistics—Definitions and Explanatory Notes*.

An example of the incorrect use of a source would be to base an argument about the growth in numbers of the family motorcar on statistics for 'road vehicles'. The definitions of 'road vehicles' would almost certainly be much wider than the definition of 'family motorcars' and a quite misleading figure might be used as a result. The careful definition of terms used is essential before any enquiry can begin.

Many sets of official statistics are based upon records collected for quite different purposes. For example, the Inland Revenue records about taxpayers give a vast mass of statistical material which can be used for many other purposes, provided it is used with caution. Since many people do not pay tax at all (perhaps because they have a family to support which removes them from the taxable bracket), the tax statistics would be inadequate for many purposes, particularly enquiries about family expenditure where many of the families under discussion would not be included. Because the costs of the collection of statistics are high, it is economical to use statistics gathered for other purposes, but we must always do so with caution.

If the enquiry is to be pursued by collecting original data—by sending out questionnaires, for example—the enquiry may need to be conducted with a **representative sample** of the population. The choice of a sample is in itself a major statistical exercise, which balances the type of sample against the costs of collection. If the choice of sample is narrowed to keep down the costs it cannot be as representative as a completely random sample. For example, an enquiry about United Kingdom family expenditure based on citizens living in Westminster will be less representative of the total population than one based on citizens of London, or the Home Counties or the entire nation. Interviewing 1 000 citizens in Westminster presents few problems, and even 1 000 Londoners are reasonably accessible, but 1 000 citizens from the Home

Counties, or the entire country, will involve greater travelling costs and much more time.

Sources can be **biased**. This means that instead of the statistics being completely objective, some subjective consideration causes them to lean in a particular direction. Mark Twain tells us that one Fiji islander's abuse of Cain ceased very suddenly when a missionary casually mentioned that Cain was a Fiji islander. The next remark the savage was heard to make was, 'Well, what did Abel have to come fooling around there for anyway?' A survey asking smokers how many cigarettes they smoke daily is likely to understate the level of consumption. A feeling of guilt causes a smaller total than the actual to be put forward.

Bias can occur for a number of reasons, the most common of which is vested interest. Politicians from the two major parties in the United Kingdom have a vested interest in claiming that '90 per cent of the population do not wish to see a change in the electoral system'. If there was to be such a change, their own influence would be diminished.

When examining a source, it is therefore important to know who is supplying the information, why he is supplying it, and how he obtained it. Is it well founded, or is it just a guess? The unreliability of the sources is certainly one reason for the popular distrust of statistics.

False Reasoning

Another reason for the distrust of those who use statistics is the false reasoning which is often applied to statistical information.

Even if there is no bias in the information used, it is relatively easy to arrive at an incorrect conclusion. In order to avoid this, students are urged to be ruthlessly logical. An enquiry may show that there is a 50 per cent increase in the sale of a particular brand of margarine. Would it be right to conclude that each housewife is buying half as much again as previously? Clearly it would not. Perhaps more outlets now stock the brand so that more housewives buy it. The amount bought per housewife might even have diminished. It will frequently be the case that an enquiry will reveal a situation which could have developed in several different ways, or be caused by a combination of factors which have together produced the effects observed.

Statistical reasoning is really a special case of the general scientific method, and needs to be as rigorous as any other branch of scientific reasoning. What is unfortunate though is that since it is largely used to describe human affairs, and particularly economic affairs, it necessarily suffers from the defects inseparable from descriptions of human activity. For example, we cannot predict human activity with the same certainty that we can predict chemical activity, so that the too confident prognostications of statisticians are often proved wrong by events.

3.3 Discrete and Continuous Variables

The things which statisticians seek to measure—height, weight, wages, unemployment, prices, etc.—are known as **variables**. As the term implies, variables are studied because some variation in their value is anticipated. An investigation into the height of all 11-year-old schoolboys in England would not give the result that they were all of the same height. There will be many heights, because the schoolboys studied vary in the heights they have attained.

Variables are divided into two types: **discrete variables** and **continuous variables.** Those variables which are discrete increase or decrease in definite 'units'. For example, if the number of baby rabbits in a litter is the subject of investigation, the numbers recorded will be 1, 2, 3, 4, 5, etc. It is not possible to have 2.75 rabbits or 2.9, 4.86 or 7.72. The units therefore are single rabbits in this example, though in some enquiries the unit might be a group: we count armies in regiments, and military aircraft in squadrons, for example.

Continuous variables do not have a unitary composition. Instead there is a continuous path of increase or decrease. If one is measuring the number of kilometres which a homing pigeon flies before coming to rest any fraction of a kilometre is possible. The pigeon may fly 2.746 km or 28.527 km or even 257.25757 km.

As explained later (see Section 4.6), this distinction between discrete and continuous data is of importance when constructing class limits.

3.4 Collection of Data

Statistics used by investigators are of two types: **primary** and **secondary.** Primary statistics are collected by the investigator when he searches out new information. Secondary statistics are those which an investigator obtains from other sources. Most of these will be published statistics and the Government is an active supplier of information in this form.

Of course, at some stage all statistics have to be collected from original sources. Such collection involves the investigator in a number of decisions. The following are points which have to be considered when about to embark upon an enquiry:

(*a*) What is the precise purpose of the enquiry?

(*b*) What definitions must we lay down if the investigators are to be clear about the classification of the responses they receive?

(*c*) How is the enquiry to be conducted and how can we make it as foolproof as possible? This usually requires the preparation of a questionnaire, and decisions about sampling.

(*a*) *The Nature of the Enquiry.* The first and most obvious point is that a clear statement of the problem must be made. In other words, what is the investigation setting out to probe? Results which emerge from surveys can be rendered useless because investigators did not have a *precise* view of the problem at the heart of the operation. 'Writing maketh an exact man', and the reduction of the purpose of the enquiry to a clear statement in a short paragraph will clarify matters enormously and make the second problem, the definition of terms, easier.

(*b*) *Defining terms.* In any enquiry there will be terms to be defined. A recent report about 'Small Firms' defined them as firms employing fewer than 200 persons. To the sole trader keeping a village shop 200 employees does not sound 'small', but for the purpose of the enquiry it was judged to be appropriate.

In relation to enquiries about unemployment, what is meant by the term 'unemployed'? Does it refer to *everyone* without a job? Is it applicable only to those registered as unemployed? What about housewives? What about the disabled and the sick? Are people receiving training unemployed? All these points need clarification before an investigator has a reasonable chance of working out which questions to ask.

(*c*) *Method of Procedure.* The collection of statistics must be systematic, and to limit costs it should be reduced to a simple procedure so that highly-qualified investigators are not needed. Provided investigators are reasonably alert and persevering there is no need for them to be trained statisticians.

Most statistical information is collected by means of a **questionnaire** and the investigator may favour this method, but there are alternatives. It might be that the researcher will decide to interview personally everyone considered capable of giving information relevant to the enquiry. This has the advantage of giving high-quality information, but has a very small field of coverage. Another method is for interviewing to be delegated to teams of researchers or to agencies which specialise in collecting information. In either case a number of trained personnel take a standardised schedule and specific instructions, often to preselected interviewees. Such a method also gives high-quality information and a fairly wide coverage, but it is very expensive.

The postal questionnaire is popular because it reaches a potentially larger number of respondents and is also relatively cheap. It does, however, have a number of drawbacks, amongst which is the uncertainty of responses. Unless the return is compulsory—as with Government census surveys—a large number of people are likely to ignore the questionnaire altogether. In addition, those who do return the forms duly completed are probably those most interested in the problems with which the survey deals, and are by self-selection therefore biased. There is also no guarantee that respondents have understood the questions asked and replies might be suspect.

Despite these problems, because of coverage and cost, postal questionnaires are still favoured by many investigators.

It is highly unlikely that the investigator will be able to contact every member of the group in which he is interested. Such a group in total is known as the **population.** The word 'population' is used here in a special technical way, and does not have its ordinary meaning of the entire nation. Thus in an enquiry about artists the 'population' would include only those who earned their living in this way. The investigator would probably have to be satisfied with a selection drawn from this population—a **sample.** Such a sample may form a very small proportion of the total population, maybe one in every 5 000, and it is therefore important that the sample is **representative** of the population as a whole.

In order to avoid bias in the sample a technique known as **random sampling** is used. *A random sample is defined as one which ensures that every item within the population has an equal chance of selection for the sample.* One of the easiest ways to do this is to give a numerical value to items and then programme a computer to select some of the numbers in an unbiased fashion.

Ensuring that the sample is free from bias is not just a matter of avoiding obvious leanings. For example, a survey designed to show the educational attainment of the United Kingdom population would not take its sample solely from a number of universities, for it is obvious that this would overstate the degree of achievement. It is also a requirement that bias of an unconscious nature is not included. Thus, conducting a survey by questioning the first 5 000 persons encountered in Oxford Street may not build in known bias, but is unlikely to be representative of the whole population of the United Kingdom. It is to overcome such a problem that random samples are used.

It is important to note that although random sampling will give a method of sample selection which is free from bias it cannot guarantee that the items in the sample itself will be similarly free from bias. Mr Jones, who happens to be selected in a random sample, may have very biased views on the matter in hand.

3.5 Types of Sample

There are some situations in which it may prove impossible to use the technique of random sampling. For example, the total population may not be known, or if known it may be too expensive to contact a widely dispersed random sample. Other types of sample are therefore available. They are:

(*a*) *Quota Sampling*. Instead of having to approach a whole dispersed group in a random sample, the interviewers conducting the survey are often instructed to fill **quotas** of given types. For example, twenty mothers with blue eyes, forty mothers with brown eyes, etc. Once the interviewers have sufficient numbers for one of their types, the quota has been met and that type is not sought out further. Such a method is cheaper than a random sample.

(*b*) *Multi-stage Sampling*. This technique involves frequent subdivision of the population, but on a random basis. For example, a small number of counties may be selected by random sample. Within these counties a further random sample may give a number of district councils and within these district councils yet another random sample may reveal a number of parish council areas. Interviewers can then be sent to these local areas to conduct the survey. Because of the concentration of observations within a few areas, the method is less expensive than random sampling.

(*c*) *Cluster Sampling*. This is used to overcome a particular problem—lack of knowledge of the population. Again, small areas of the country are selected and interviewers sent into them with the object of collecting information from every person who fits a particular description; for example, from every peroxide blonde.

(*d*) *Systematic Sampling*. This method gives a virtual random sample. All the population is listed and then a percentage of the list taken. For example, if the sample is to be 5 per cent, then every twentieth item is taken from the list. Providing that there is no regular variation on each twentieth item, the sample should be almost as good as a random one.

(*e*) *Stratified Sampling*. Unlike the previous methods, stratified sampling is superior to random sampling since it reduces the possibility of bias. A random sample of the school population of the UK *might* be composed entirely of sixth formers, but a stratified sample composed of representatives of each age group at school could not be. The essence of a stratified sample is that it selects at random from the various strata which comprise the total population. It is therefore important to know (*a*) the total population and (*b*) the proportion that each subgroup, or stratum, bears to the total population. For example, if the total population in a survey were 10 000 units and one stratum was 1 000 units, the random selection within the stratum of 1 000 should amount to 10 per cent of the total sample (since 1 000 is 10 per cent of the total population of 10 000).

3.6 Approximation and Error

When statisticians present figures they have collected or calculated, it is usual for such figures to be rounded to a suitable degree of accuracy. If raw data relate to hundreds of thousands of pounds sterling it is inconvenient to record every single penny. Instead, an **approximation** of the value will be given. If the real figure is £2 127 135.20 then a number of alternatives are open to the researcher:

(*a*) The figure can be rounded down to the nearest pound, i.e. to £2 127 135. When rounding in business statistics it is normal to round up for values above 0.5 and down for values below 0.5. Values of exactly 0.5 are rounded to the nearest even number. Thus 4.25 would be rounded to 4.2, but 4.35 would be rounded to 4.4.

(*b*) The figure can be rounded to some other convenient grouping such as £'000, or £'0 000, or £'00 000 or £m. The earlier example would thus become successively

	2 127	(£'000s)
or	213	(£'0 000s)
or	21	(£'00 000s)
or	2	(£m)

(*c*) The figure can be stated in decimal form—for example, £2.1m.

All of these approximations involve instilling small errors into the figures, but if the degree of approximation is adequate to the enquiry in hand the errors are trifling. One thing must be noted, that rounded figures do not necessarily add up exactly. Thus where a table of statistics includes a number of percentages which have been rounded, they may not add up to 100 per cent, and should not be made to do so. If they add up to 99.9 per cent or 100.2 per cent it is clear that the error is a **rounding error** and only to be expected. On average, rounding errors are **compensating errors,** they cancel one another out to a considerable extent, but this may not eliminate all errors in a total.

Some rounding errors, though, are not compensatory in nature. Instead the degree of error in the figures can be compounded by the method of rounding used. For example, if all rounding undertaken with a set of figures is rounding up then all the errors introduced will be positive. When added together the absolute error could be large. Similarly, if all the rounding undertaken is rounding down the negative errors, when taken together, could be equally large. For such reasons statisticians dislike rounding in one direction only.

Calculations can be made which assist statisticians to discover the amount of error which their approximations have introduced into the figures. Such calculations rest upon the ideas of **absolute** and **relative** error.

An **absolute error** is the difference between the true figure and the approximate figure. Where the true figure is known there is no problem. For example, if the true figure is £2 172 and the approximate figure £2 000, then the absolute error is £2 172 − £2 000 = £172.

However, it is often the case that the true figure is not known, and in such circumstances absolute error has to be expressed within sensible boundaries. For example, suppose that the approximate figure is £2 150 to the nearest £50. The absolute error cannot be greater than £25 since the true figure must lie between £2 125 and £2 174.99.

Relative error is the absolute error expressed as a percentage of the approximate figure. For example, if the approximate figure is £2 150 with a maximum absolute error of £25, then the maximum relative error is

$$\frac{25}{2\,150} \times \frac{100}{1} = 1.16\%$$

There are four basic calculations—addition, subtraction, multiplication and division—and each has to take account of the potential error introduced by approximation. Let us consider each in turn.

(*a*) *Addition.* Consider the following example:

Example 3.1. Add up the following numbers, each of which is approximate to the extent shown. What is the possible error on the total?

1 270 (correct to the nearest 10—maximum error ±5)
1 200 (correct to the nearest 100—maximum error ±50)
137 000 (correct to the nearest 1 000—maximum error ±500)

139 470 Total

What is the maximum possible error on the answer? Clearly if all the approximate numbers had the maximum error possible the error in the total would be the sum of the errors. This is ±555. So the sum of the numbers is 139 470 ±555.

When adding approximate numbers the maximum possible error in the answer is found by taking the sum of the maximum possible errors in the original approximate numbers.

(*b*) *Subtraction.* Here the position is the same as with addition. The maximum possible error in the difference is arrived at by adding together all the maximum possible errors of the component parts of the calculation.

Example 3.2. 2 270 ±5 is subtracted from 24 200 ±50. What is the answer? What is the possible error in the answer?

24 200	±50
− 2 270	± 5
21 930	±55

When subtracting approximate numbers the maximum possible error in the difference is the sum of the maximum possible errors in the original numbers.

(*c*) *Multiplication.* The maximum possible error from a multiplication calculation can be found by adding together the *relative errors* of the component parts.

Example 3.3. In a certain enquiry the figure of 60 000 ±5 000 has to be multiplied by another figure 450 ±5. Do the calculations and state the degree of error in the answer.

60 000	Absolute error ±5 000
	Relative error $\frac{5\,000}{60\,000} \times 100 = 8.3\%$
× 450	Absolute error ±5
	Relative error $= \frac{5}{450} \times 100 = 1.1\%$
27 000 000	

The maximum error in the answer is the *sum* of the relative errors = 9.4%. Since 9.4% of 27 000 000 = 2 538 000, the answer is

27 000 000 ± 2 538 000

(*d*) *Division.* Division calculations also involve adding together separate relative errors in order to arrive at the maximum possible error.

Example 3.4. In a certain enquiry one statistic 2 000 ± 5 has to be divided by another 120 ± 5. What is the answer and what is the possible error in it?

2 000 Absolute error ±5

Relative error $\frac{5}{2\,000} \times 100 = 0.25\%$

120 Absolute error ±5

Relative error $\frac{5}{120} \times 100 = 4.17\%$

∴ 2 000 ÷ 120
= 16.67 with a relative error of 4.42%
= 16.67 ± 0.74 (which is 4.42% of 16.67)

Significant Figures

Statisticians often express the results of their calculations in terms of **significant figures.** Significant figures are those digits which convey accurate information. The accuracy of any figure depends upon the extent to which the figures *it was calculated from* were themselves rounded. For example, the figure 47.172153 is not rounded at all and has 8 significant figures. The figure 47.17 has only 4 significant figures even though it may be a summary of 47.172153. Had the degree of accuracy related to only 2 significant figures then 47 would represent this.

When calculating with rounded figures it is important to remember that the results cannot be more accurate that the *least* accurate rounded figure used. Therefore 47.7123 × 10 000 (rounded to the nearest 1 000) cannot be accurate to more than 2 significant figures—*10* 000 in 10 000. The result 477 123 has only 2 significant figures and should be expressed as 480 000. The addition of 274, 1320 and 400 (to the nearest 100) cannot be stated as of greater accuracy than 2 000, i.e. to the nearest 100.

Any attempt to be more specific than the rounded figures in the calculation warrant is known as being 'spuriously accurate'. In the calculation above, the addition would have been spuriously accurate had it claimed 3 or 4 significant figures: 1990 or 1994.

3.7 Simple Mathematical Symbols

Hardly anyone would consider repeatedly writing 'Her Majesty's Stationery Office' in lists of publications. Instead we use the abbreviation HMSO, because it saves time and it is so commonly used that everyone knows what it means. However, people who are happy with HMSO might not understand Σ (pronounced sigma), which merely means the sum of (or total of), and is a convenient shorthand way of saying this.

Σ 8 12 16 means 8 + 12 + 16 = 36

There are other useful symbols of 'mathematical shorthand'; the following are some of those which will appear in this textbook:

$\triangleq$ means an approximate equal, or almost equal.
n means the number of items.
f means the frequency, or the number of times an item occurs.
$\bar{x}$ means 'the arithmetic mean' or 'arithmetic average'.

3.8 Exercises: Introductory Statistical Concepts

1. Explain what is meant by:

   (*a*) Population
   (*b*) Quota sampling
   (*c*) Multi-stage sampling
   (*d*) Random sampling
   (*e*) Stratified sampling?

2. What is bias? How does bias arise, and what can be done to overcome it?

3. Point out the advantages and disadvantages of collecting information by the following methods:

   (*a*) The telephone
   (*b*) Direct observation
   (*c*) Interview
   (*d*) Postal questionnaire

4. What is meant by the term 'rounding off'? Why is rounding off undertaken?

5. Rounding off can be biased or unbiased. What do these terms mean?

6. What is meant by compensating error? Round the following figures to one decimal place in such a way that any error introduced is compensating: 7.33, 6.86, 7.78, 4.33, 5.57.

7. What is the absolute error in the following instances?

	True figure	*Approximate figure*
(*a*)	2 242	2 000
(*b*)	1 726	1 700
(*c*)	6 421	7 000
(*d*)	1 787	1 780

8. How would you express the absolute error inherent in the following figures?

   (*a*) 2 750 correct to nearest 50
   (*b*) 1 600 correct to nearest 100
   (*c*) 7 000 correct to nearest 1 000
   (*d*) 2 765 correct to nearest 5

9. What is meant by relative error? Calculate the relative error for the following (give your answer correct to two decimal places):

   (*a*) 2 100 ± 50
   (*b*) 2 250 ± 25
   (*c*) 1 725 ± 2.5
   (*d*) 10 700 ± 50

10. Add the following sets of figures:

(*a*)	(*b*)
1 370 ± 5	1 575 ± 2.5
1 200 ± 50	1 300 ± 50
147 000 ± 500	1 400 ± 50

11. Subtract from 27 200 ± 50 the following figures:

   (*a*) 2 170 ± 5 (*b*) 2 100 ± 50 (*c*) 1 855 ± 2.5

12. Multiply the following sets of figures:

   (*a*) 40 000 ± 500 × 350 ± 5 (*b*) 2 700 ± 50 × 175 ± 2.5

13. Divide 2 150 ± 25 by the following figures:

   (*a*) 125 ± 2.5 (*b*) 140 ± 5

4

CLASSIFICATION AND TABULATION

4.1 Introduction

The collection of statistics can be justified by the need for a clear picture of some activity. That clear picture, it is hoped, will be given by the figures amassed about it. For example, it is difficult to make any accurate pronouncement about the fishing industry until we have collected some data about the catches made from various ports.

Suppose that figures were collected every day for every boat, from every port involved in fishing. There would soon be so many sheets of statistics, that rather than clarify the situation they would further confuse it. This is certainly a problem with most statistical enquiries—the raw data in their unprocessed form are too bulky to do anything but create confusion. An attempt, therefore, has to be made to arrange the figures collected in such a fashion that they more easily yield the information they contain, and are more suited to further processing.

This processing might involve the extraction from the data of certain **derived statistics**: averages, percentages, etc. With the advent of computers a whole range of data processing can take place once the raw data have been assembled into some manageable form. This chapter deals with the ways in which some clarification can be brought to a mass of figures. There are two problems:

(*a*) To reduce the amount of detail.

(*b*) To bring the data into a form where significant features stand out prominently.

The first problem is solved by classifying the data into groups of similar or related items. The second may be solved in several ways. In this chapter **tabulation**—the drawing up of tables—is explained as a means of displaying information. Later chapters deal with other methods of presentation.

4.2 The Classification of Data

Classification involves bringing together those items of information which have something in common. For example, we might find in our fishing enquiry that, of the fish landed, some were haddock, some cod, some mackerel, some herring, etc. It is useful to know how much of each type of fish has been caught. Therefore it would be in order to classify (i.e. group together) the species of fish caught. This also reduces the number of classes. Instead of each fish being an individual, there are only half-a-dozen or so classes for all the millions of fishes caught. This makes the handling of the information much easier.

When attempting to classify data much will depend upon the nature of the data themselves and upon the purposes of the enquiry. There is no clear cut 'correct' way of classifying and presenting all data. For example, though a census every ten years is sufficient to discover changes in the size of the United Kingdom population, such a time-scale is not a suitable classification for the measure of the United Kingdom rainfall, statistics for which are collected daily. The reader would do well to remember, then, that the nature of the enquiry is important in determining the classification.

This is not to say that there are no general rules available to guide students when they come to construct their own tables, or when they are required to interpret published statistics. There are such rules and the following are amongst the most important:

(*a*) *Categories must be Comprehensive.* The classes or categories chosen must be comprehensive, i.e. all the possible responses must be taken into account. The statistics relating to fish landed in the United Kingdom are incomplete if only the categories, cod, herring, haddock, plaice and mackerel are included. There are many other varieties of fish and at least one additional category, 'Other', is required to make the classes complete.

(*b*) *Categories must not Overlap.* Though the classes must be comprehensive they must not overlap, since this then allows them to be ambiguous. If we are measuring ages and we have classes of 10–20 years, 20–30 years, etc., we clearly have some element of overlap. The observations of 'age 20 years' could fit into both. A more satisfactory and unambiguous classification would be 10 and under 20; 20 and under 30; etc.

(*c*) *Classes should be Few in Number.* The classes chosen should be sufficiently few in number to allow comparison with each other. Nothing is worse than spending a great deal of time classifying information, only to find that there are so many classes available that no conclusions can be arrived at, or comparisons made. A few large classes will damp out fluctuations in the statistics which are irrelevant to the enquiry in hand. Thus it may be of biological interest that there is one subspecies within the general grouping 'haddock', but for a summary of landings of fish in the United Kingdom it is sufficient to consider all haddock as the same species; subdivisions in this instance could confuse and not clarify.

At the same time the number of classes must be large enough to give an impression of the range of information that has been collected. Between 6 and 11 classes are generally considered most suitable for tables and frequency distributions (see Table 4.1 below).

(*d*) *Classes should be Homogeneous.* Where possible, the items included within a class should all have the same characteristics. They should be homogeneous (or alike). If a class contains items which are vastly different from each other, then few general conclusions can be drawn from it. The statements made about it will tend to be unrepresentative of the items within the group.

4.3 The Tabulation of Data

Once the statistician has decided upon the classification to be used, the problem of presentation has to be faced. The **table** has been found to be a most useful means of presentation, and for general tables the following points should be taken into account:

(*a*) The source of the data in the table should always be given—readers should be wary of information which is presented to them with no indication of its origin.

(*b*) If units of measurement are used these should be clearly defined, unless they are in the recognised SI units. (SI units are the standard international units for which the metric system is the basic reference point. The system takes its name from the French, *Système International.*) If information is collected in national units, such as Imperial units or United States units, this should be made clear and the unit's relationship to the SI system should be given.

(*c*) Where columns of figures are to be totalled, place the totals at the bottom of the table, unless particular attention is to be drawn to the totals—when they may be placed at the top.

(*d*) Use rulings to break up the table. Horizontal lines called eye-lines assist the reader's comprehension of the table. Every fifth line should be followed by an eye-line, or in a short table of, say, eight lines one eye-line inserted halfway down is sufficient.

(*e*) If a table is to be printed, italics can be used to pick out important points.

(*f*) If there is a large mass of information which will result in an unwieldy table, try to break it down into two or more tables.

A general plan for the layout of tables is given in Fig. 4.1, and described in the notes below it. Table 4.1 gives an example of such a table.

Table 4.1. Membership of Working-Men's Clubs

Membership	*Number of clubs*
Under 200	68
200–499	185
500–999	1 027
1 000–1 499	130
1 500–1 999	27
Over 2 000	10
Total	1 447

Footnote: Working-men's clubs are those excluding variety clubs.
Source Note: Workers' Gazette, Issue 2079.

4.4 Simple Tables

The rules of tabulation outlined in Section 4.3 above are easily applied to some sets of data, since by its nature it is uncomplicated and easy to handle. For example, the tabulation of the following catches of fish in a United Kingdom port for October 1st–7th does not present any difficulties: Sunday, 187 kg; Monday, 2 008 kg; Tuesday, 2 775 kg; Wednesday, 1 090 kg; Thursday, 2 050 kg; Friday, 1 720 kg: Saturday, 1 928 kg. Table 4.2 below is a simple way of presenting this information more effectively.

Rounding. As already explained (see Section 3.6), a table can be simplified considerably, and yet convey the same information, if the figures are 'rounded off'. For example, the figures for catches in Table 4.2 (p. 35) could be rounded off to the nearest 100 kg without the loss of detail affecting to any serious extent the accuracy of the information conveyed.

When rounding, it is usual to round up or round down to the accuracy required. Thus Sunday's catch of 187 kg would be rounded up to 200 kg since 87 kg is much more than half a hundred kilograms and therefore is closer to 200 kg than 100 kg. Monday's catch of 2 008 kg would be rounded down to 2000 kg and so on. Where the figures to be dropped are exactly half-way, as in 2 050, the convention is to round in such a way as to leave the retained part an even number. So 2 050 kg would be rounded down to 2 000 kg, while a catch of 2 150 would be rounded up to 2 200 kg since 2 100 kg would be an odd number of hundreds.

1. TITLE

2. Class Description	3. Column Headings
4. Row Headings	5. Data
	6. Totals

7. Footnotes

8. Source notes

Fig. 4.1. A general plan for tabular presentation.

Notes

(1) A table should always have a clear title, which states exactly what the information within the table sets out to show.

(2) Unless it is obvious, the left-hand column heading will describe what is listed in the column below. For example, a table of industrial production might indicate at the top 'Type of Industry', and below this heading the various industries would be listed.

(3) The columns of statistics under scrutiny should have clear column headings indicating what the columns represent.

(4) Row headings for the collected data should be listed in the left-hand column.

(5) The data themselves, ordered according to the information which it is desired to extract.

(6) Any totals necessary should be presented.

(7) Footnotes, which explain variations or points of importance, should be given immediately below the table.

(8) Sources should be given where the origin of the table is some other set of published statistics, and acknowledgements should be made if necessary.

Rounding off the figures in Table 4.2 to the nearest hundred kilograms, we now arrive at Table 4.3. The reader should note that a tiny inaccuracy has crept into the figures, for if the total of Table 4.2 was rounded up it would come to 118 lots of 100 kg. The rounding process in Table 4.3 has produced an

Table 4.2. Catches of Fish—October 1st–7th

Day	*Weight caught (kg)*
Sunday	187
Monday	2 008
Tuesday	2 775
Wednesday	1 090
Thursday	2 050
Friday	1 720
Saturday	1 928
Total	11 758

error, but it is insignificant. The general impression gathered from the two tables is the same, and the figures in the table which has been rounded are simpler to understand.

Table 4.3. Catches of Fish—October 1st–7th

Day	*Weight caught (100 kg)*
Sunday	2
Monday	20
Tuesday	28
Wednesday	11
Thursday	20
Friday	17
Saturday	19
Total	117

4.5 Exercises: Simple Tabulation

1. Gas consumption in millions of therms is given as follows in a report of a nationalised body: 1st quarter, 4197; 2nd quarter, 2611; 3rd quarter, 1872; 4th quarter, 3630. Present this information in tabular form to bring out the total annual consumption.
2. The following information from an agricultural research project refers to: (*a*) cows and heifers in milk; (*b*) cows in calf but not in milk; (*c*) heifers in calf with first calf; (*d*) bulls for service; (*e*) all other cattle and calves. Present the data, given in thousands, to show the information in tabular form, and the total of this type of livestock. The figures are: (*a*) 2627; (*b*) 691; (*c*) 455; (*d*) 90; (*e*) 7951.
3. A trade journal gives the following figures for sales of floorcoverings—(*a*) refers to carpets and rugs and (*b*) to linoleum and plastics. You are asked to round off the figures in each case to thousands of square metres, and present them in a table showing the sales of each type, the total quarterly sales and the total annual sales. The figures are: 1st quarter, (*a*) 38 174 353 square metres, (*b*) 19 264 852 square metres; 2nd quarter, (*a*) 37 291 453 square metres, (*b*) 16 458 391 square metres; 3rd quarter, (*a*) 41 284 723 square metres, (*b*) 14 586 948 square metres; 4th quarter, (*a*) 38 516 849 square metres, (*b*) 21 326 724 square metres.
4. Exports are listed in five categories. These are: (*a*) Foods, beverages and tobacco; (*b*) Fuels; (*c*) Industrial materials; (*d*) Finished manufactures; (*e*) Other transactions. You are asked to round the figures off to the nearest £m and present them

in tabular form for Year 1 and Year 2 to bring out the annual totals. The figures are: (*a*) Year 1 £3 094 276 153, Year 2 £4 993 463 218; (*b*) Year 1 £1 724 858 300, Year 2 £5 652 721 494; (*c*) Year 1 £6 239 434 721, Year 2 £8 738 346 829; (*d*) Year 1 £4 174 059 628, Year 2 £6 386 995 240; (*e*) Year 1 £424 736 284, Year 2 £595 106 386.

4.6 Frequency Distributions

Where the information is less simple than that outlined in Section 4.4, it may be necessary to construct a **frequency distribution**. A frequency distribution is merely a table which has values repeated a number of times, and these are grouped together according to how often (or how frequently) they occur. The frequency distribution is a common and important way of arranging data. Its effectiveness can be seen in considering Example 4.1 below, which consists of **raw**, or unprocessed, **data.**

Example 4.1(a). The following were the earnings in pounds (£) of 100 fishermen for one week in October:

28	64	73	64	37	29	39	70	73	37
56	62	48	39	37	37	70	39	28	37
48	73	39	37	37	70	37	37	64	37
32	39	29	62	73	28	48	62	73	70
73	28	64	56	70	32	32	56	64	70
39	70	56	64	39	29	48	64	37	39
37	70	62	56	29	37	32	56	29	28
70	32	37	39	37	46	70	39	39	37
28	48	39	46	64	48	70	46	70	37
32	37	37	28	73	28	28	28	73	64

The random presentation of this mass of data is most confusing. It conveys little in the way of information. However, it is possible to make the understanding of such data a little easier by displaying it in the form of an **array.** An array is a collection of figures listed in order of size, i.e. they run from the smallest to the largest.

Example 4.1(b). Earnings of 100 fishermen for one week in October, in order of size.

28	29	32	37	39	39	48	62	70	70
28	29	37	37	39	39	56	64	70	70
28	29	37	37	39	46	56	64	70	73
28	29	37	37	39	46	56	64	70	73
28	29	37	37	39	46	56	64	70	73
28	32	37	37	39	48	56	64	70	73
28	32	37	37	39	48	56	64	70	73
28	32	37	37	39	48	62	64	70	73
28	32	37	37	39	48	62	64	70	73
28	32	37	37	39	48	62	64	70	73

Even this array is rather formidable and the student will notice that some items occur many times over. Further simplification, therefore, can be achieved by **listing the number of times an item occurs** (the frequency of its occurrence) instead of including it in the table in full each time it appears. Such a summary results in the frequency distribution table shown in Example 4.1(*c*).

The above frequency distribution table is an ungrouped one, i.e. the fre-

Example 4.1(c). The earnings of 100 fishermen for one week in October.

Earnings (£)	*Frequency (number of men)*
28	10
29	5
32	6
37	19
39	12
46	3
48	6
56	6
62	4
64	9
70	12
73	8
Total	100

quencies for different values are kept separate—they are not grouped together. Every observation of value £28 appears in a class with other values of £28, and not with, say, values of £29. But it will be noticed that the frequency distribution is rather lengthy; having 12 classes. Real life surveys of earnings would have even more classes. Therefore, it is convenient to convert this type of ungrouped frequency distribution into a grouped one. This is done by widening the class limits, so that observations of differing (but not random) values can be included. This process is demonstrated in Example 4.2.

Example 4.2. Grouped frequency distribution of earnings of 100 fishermen for one week in October.

Earnings (£)	*Frequency (number of men)*
20 and under 30	15
30 and under 40	37
40 and under 50	9
50 and under 60	6
60 and under 70	13
70 and under 80	20
Total	100

The student will appreciate how much more concise this form of presentation is, and how it makes the information more comprehensible.

Some important points may be listed as follows:

(*a*) Class intervals must be chosen to give a representative view of the information collected. As mentioned in Section 4.2 above, 6–11 groups are usually adequate. The class limits should be unambiguous. A selection of typical methods of expressing class intervals is given in Table 4.4.

(*b*) A frequency distribution must have a total, and the total of frequencies must correspond with the total number of observations—in Example 4.2 this was 100 fishermen.

Table 4.4. Methods of Expressing Class Intervals

A	B	C (*Correct to nearest whole number*)
Under 5	0–	0–4
5 and under 10	5–	5–9
10 and under 15	10–	10–14
15 and under 20	15–	15–19
20 and under 25	20–	20–24
25 and under 30	25–	25–29
30 and under 35	30–	30–34

Notes

(i) In A the class intervals are unambiguous, and in accordance with the rules of classification in Section 4.2, that they should not overlap.

(ii) In B the class intervals are exactly the same as in A. 0– means under 5, 5– means 5 and under 10, etc. When used to refer to ages this method indicates that a child exactly 5 years old would be included in the second group, not the first. The final interval, 30–, is open ended.

(iii) When figures are specified as correct to the nearest whole number as in C a slight difficulty arises. Because of the rules for 'correcting up' and 'correcting down' (which hold that when a number ends in 5 we correct to the nearest even number), 0–4 means that the items in that group might be as large as 4.5, while the 5–9 group includes items greater than 4.5 and up to 9.499—for 9.5 would be rounded up to 10 (the nearest even number).

(*c*) Where the class intervals chosen for some reason do not embrace all the observations, a final class interval must be added to conform with the rule in Section 4.2 calling for comprehensiveness. In frequency distributions this will usually have a description like '30 and over' (in Table 4.4B for example).

Rules for Drawing up Frequency Distributions

Readers might find the following a useful and speedy method of constructing a frequency distribution table:

(*a*) Examine all the data and determine the range. This is the variation in value from the lowest item to the highest item.

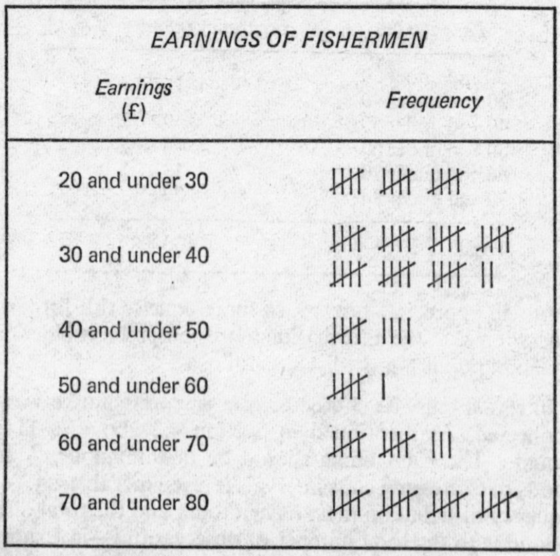

Fig. 4.2. Recording raw data as a frequency distribution.

(*b*) Given the range in (*a*) above, decide upon the number of groups necessary and the class interval which is to be used. (The class interval will not always be the same for all the groups.)

(*c*) Prepare a draft table with class intervals on the left. Sift through the original data and place a mark against the appropriate class on the draft table, each time an item falls into that group. To facilitate the final count-up it is usual to record the items in fives like a five-barred gate. Fig. 4.2 illustrates this, using the data from Example 4.1(a).

4.7 Cumulative Frequency Distributions

This is an *alternative* way of presenting the same information as might appear in a standard frequency distribution. Here, though, all previous frequencies are added to each group in turn; the final frequency shown is thus the total of all the items. Example 4.3 shows such a cumulative frequency distribution.

Example 4.3. Cumulative frequency table of the earnings of 100 fishermen for one week in October.

Earnings (£)	*Normal frequency distribution*	*Cumulative frequency*
20—	15	15
30—	37	52
40—	9	61
50—	6	67
60—	13	80
70—	20	100
Total	100	100

4.8 Exercises: Frequency Distributions

1. Little-but-Good Ltd have 30 employees whose weekly wages are given below. Arrange these in a frequency distribution choosing appropriate class intervals.

Wages. Machine Shop: £56, £62, £84, £48 (earned by four employees), £32 (earned by six apprentices).
Tool Shop: £84, £86, £90 (earned by seven employees), £30 (earned by five apprentices).
Office: £56, £68, £120.

2. Weekly turnover for 40 shops in a pedestrian precinct is found to be as follows. Arrange these in a frequency table with suitable class intervals.

Turnover:

£240	£346	£721	£658	£989	£1 100
£1 370	£1 475	£1 800	£1 250	£5 500	£1 975
£1 650	£1 800	£1 980	£7 500	£5 900	£1 950
£1 880	£1 860	£13 500	£1 350	£1 925	£1 290
£1 450	£1 940	£8 500	£1 820	£1 375	£1 700
£1 224	£25 000	£4 950	£1 840	£32 000	£1 775
£1 960	£1 700	£1 416	£1 790		

3. The wages (in £s) paid to 50 men in a factory in a particular week are given as follows:

£	£	£	£	£
41	42	52	44	72
57	56	48	45	46
69	38	72	49	47
51	28	50	56	44
48	55	44	82	45
49	73	46	74	28
54	48	47	48	72
48	52	49	36	75
66	55	69	52	46
69	53	84	60	56

Group the data into seven classes and present the results in tabular form. Why would it be wrong to specify classes as 30–40, 40–50, 50–60, etc?

4. An earnings survey reveals that earnings per hour in a certain works were as follows. You are asked to present the information as a table grouped into eight classes. Include in your table a cumulative frequency column.

54	73	91	69	100
72	84	93	95	100
62	58	74	67	120
99	81	96	102	120
64	74	99	120	76
86	94	65	75	66
77	82	102	106	130
88	105	124	124	106
79	106	78	130	79
97	106	89	107	89

5

TIME SERIES

5.1 Introduction

Much of Chapter 4 was concerned with an important statistical concept, the frequency distribution. It was stated that frequency distributions are useful where a collection of data *relating to the same period in time* is to be analysed. However, it is often necessary to process data in such a way that comparisons over time are made. There are many examples of such comparisons: the level of registered unemployed, the growth (or contraction) of population, the number of motorcycle registrations, the number of ships built in shipyards—all these can involve the element of time. In circumstances where a comparison over time is important, a frequency distribution is clearly inappropriate; instead a form of presentation known as a **time series** is used. A time series, as the name suggests, relates to figures taken over a period of time.

Table 5.1. Sales of Portland Cement

Year	*Quarter*	*Sales* (£'000)	*Total* (£'000)
1	1	1 084	
	2	1 976	
	3	3 600	
	4	1 654	8 314
2	1	1 179	
	2	2 532	
	3	5 421	
	4	1 965	11 097
3	1	2 021	
	2	3 251	
	3	6 452	
	4	2 348	14 072
Grand Total			33 483

Table 5.1 illustrates a simple time series. Such a form of presentation is useful in itself in that it helps to clarify a mass of figures. However, a time series is chiefly used in an attempt to isolate three main influences upon the data being studied. These are:

(*a*) The trend
(*b*) Seasonal variation
(*c*) Random variation

We must now study these items in greater detail, in particular devoting time to their calculation.

5.2 The Trend

The trend may be defined as the long-term pattern of development of the data; the course which the data have followed over a considerable period. For example, is the number of registered unemployed rising or falling? Is the number of ships built in the shipyards increasing or decreasing? What is the *trend* in motorcycle deaths in recent years? Are fatalities increasing, decreasing or constant?

It might be thought that all one needs to do to arrive at the trend is to look over the available data and make a rough 'guesstimate'. This could even be appropriate when only a few figures are involved and a *very* rough guide is required. However, more reliable indications of the trend involve calculation. The method used when calculating the trend is that of the **moving average.** This involves nothing more than a series of overlapping arithmetic averages. In Statistics an average is often spoken of as a 'mean'. Table 5.2 indicates how a moving average is calculated.

What type of moving average should be used depends upon the statistics in use. For example, monthly figures would require us to calculate a moving average based on 12 monthly periods, and quarterly figures would be appropriately analysed on the basis of four quarterly periods being averaged together. In Table 5.2 the quarterly figures given in Table 5.1 have been used to produce a moving average The method, which is explained in the notes below the table, has to be carried out in two stages. This is because an average over the first four quarters gives a mean figure which is situated at the date June June 30–July 1, i.e. between quarters 2 and 3, and not at the mid-point of a class interval. This happens successively each quarter. To find an average figure which is positioned at the midpoint of the class interval we further have to average each pair of averages. The reader should now consider Table 5.2 and the notes below it.

Once calculated, the effect of smoothing the actual statistics can be illustrated by utilising a graph. This is done in Fig. 5.1, which demonstrates how the smoothed trend line shows the gradual upward movement of the statistics, as opposed to the indented 'peak-trough' variation in the actual data.

5.3 Seasonal Variation

There are many instances where the examination of a time series will have as its object, not the trend, but the level of seasonal variation. Seasonal variation records to what extent a regular upward or downward character is superimposed on the trend as a result of factors which have a seasonal nature: such factors as the increasing level of unemployment in seaside towns in winter, and the increasing sales of building materials in spring and summer, are very largely though not exclusively explained by seasonal events.

It is possible to calculate the degree to which seasonal factors cause distortion from the overall trend. The work proceeds in three stages, which may be listed as follows:

(*a*) Calculating the deviation of actual figures from 'trend' figures.

(*b*) These deviations from trend will partly be caused by seasonal events and partly by random deviations caused by a wide variety of events, such as strikes, natural disasters, changes in taste and fashion, credit availability, etc. To

Table 5.2. Sales of Portland Cement (£'000)

Year (I)	*Quarter* (II)	*Sales* (III)	*Four-quarter moving average* (IV)	*Centred trend* (V)	*Deviation of actual from trend* (VI)
1	1	1 084			
	2	1 976			
			2 078.50		
	3	3 600		2 090.38	+1 509.62
			2 102.25		
	4	1 654		2 171.75	−517.75
			2 241.25		
2	1	1 179		2 468.88	−1 289.88
			2 696.5		
	2	2 532		2 735.38	−203.38
			2 774.25		
	3	5 421		2 879.50	+2 541.5
			2 984.75		
	4	1 965		3 074.62	−1 109.62
			3 164.50		
3	1	2 021		3 293.38	−1 272.38
			3 422.25		
	2	3 251		3 470.12	−219.12
			3 518.00		
	3	6 452		3 532.38	+2 919.62
			3 546.75		
	4	2 348		3 600.62	−1 252.62
			3 654.50		
4	1	2 136		3 667.00	−1531.00
			3 679.50		
	2	3 682		3 788.12	−106.12
			3 896.75		
	3	6 552		4 004.75	+2 547.25
			4 112.75		
	4	3 217		4 168.00	−951.00
			4 223.25		
5	1	3 000		4 238.62	−1 238.62
			4 254.00		
	2	4 124		4 302.00	−178.00
			4 350.00		
	3	6 675			
	4	3 601			

Notes

(i) Column (III) is the quarterly total of sales.

(ii) Column (IV) is the moving average of four quarterly totals. The first of these averages is positioned at the date June 30–July 1 at the division between class intervals 2 and 3. There is no such average therefore on the division between class intervals 1 and 2.

(iii) As the moving average continues down column (IV) it discards the first quarter and picks up the new quarter, so that the average changes all the way down the table. Each of these averages is positioned at the division between two class intervals. This is inconvenient, because it means we cannot compare the actual figure in a class interval (III) with the moving average in (IV). We must therefore find a 'centred' figure for each class interval by averaging the moving averages on either side of the class interval.

(iv) Column (V) shows this 'centred trend' figure. We can now compare the actual figure in the third quarter of year 1 with the trend in the same quarter. Because of high sales in the third quarter the actual sales for that quarter are in excess of the trend.

(v) The effect of calculating a moving average of this sort is to smooth out the set of figures, averaging out the fluctuations. The extent of these fluctuations can then be seen by comparing 'actual' figures with 'trend' figures as explained in (IV) above.

(vi) Column (VI) is explained later (see page 45).

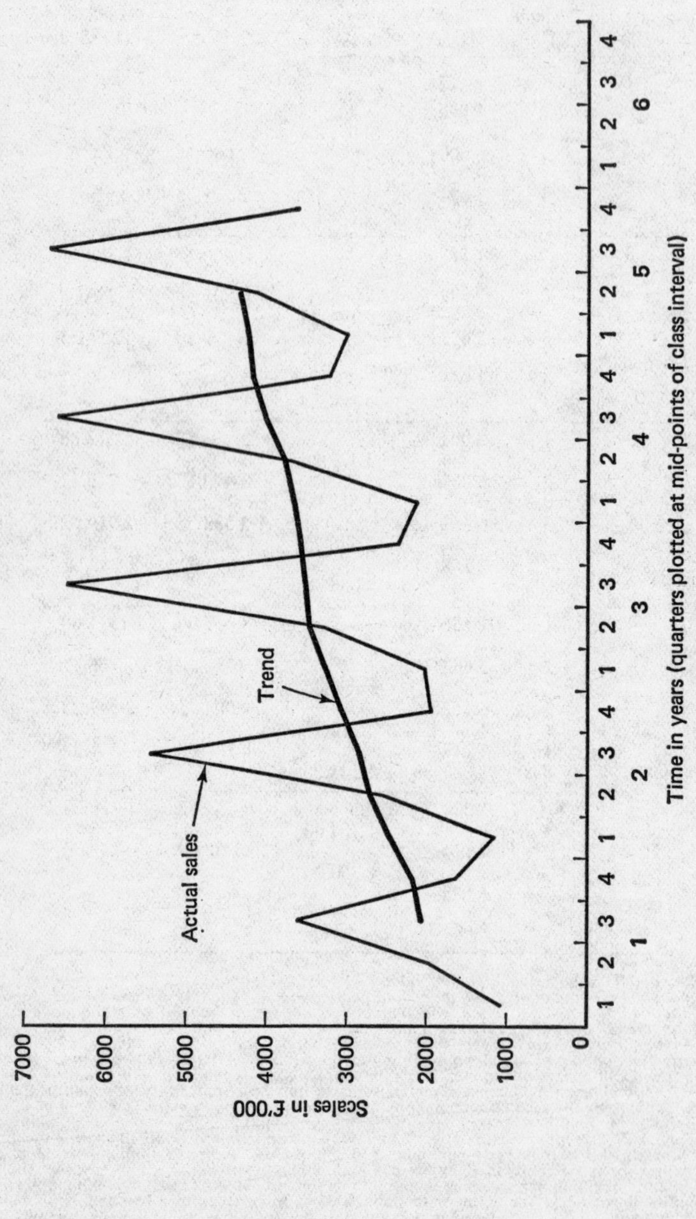

Fig. 5.1. Sales of Portland Cement: actual and trend.

arrive at the best estimate of seasonal influences we *average over the years of the enquiry the seasonal influences for each period.* This is stage (*b*).

(*c*) These seasonal fluctuations should, for reasons explained below, cancel one another out. If they do not they must be adjusted until they do. The result will be a 'corrected' seasonal influence which is the best estimate of seasonal variation at which we can arrive.

Such a seasonal variation might be of enormous importance in planning, for example, port activities, transport availability, stock levels required, etc.

Let us now look at each of these stages in turn.

Stage (*a*). *Calculating the Deviation of Actual Data from the Trend*

It is first necessary to find by how much the actual recorded data deviate from the calculated trend. This is shown in column (VI) of Table 5.2 (see page 43). The difference may be positive (actual figures greater than the trend) or negative (actual figures less than the trend figures). Thus for quarter 3 of year 1 the trend is 2 090.38, which must be subtracted from the actual sales figures of 3 600, to arrive at the deviation from trend: +1 509.62 (£'000).

Stage (*b*). *Averaging the Seasonal Influences for each Period*

The next stage is to calculate the mean deviation from trend for each of the time periods (in our case for each of the quarters). To do this we take the deviation from trend figures for the first quarter of each year, add them together, and divide by the total number of years in which the quarters fall. The process is then repeated for the second, third and fourth quarters. Table 5.3 illustrates this method.

Table 5.3. Seasonal Variation

Year	*Quarter 1*	*Quarter 2*	*Quarter 3*	*Quarter 4*
1	—	—	+1 509.62	−517.75
2	−1 289.88	−203.38	+2 541.50	−1 109.62
3	−1 272.38	−219.12	+2 919.62	−1 252.62
4	−1 531.00	−106.12	+2 547.25	−951.00
5	−1 238.62	−178.00		
Totals	−5 331.88	−706.62	+9 517.99	−3 830.99
Mean of quarterly deviation	−1 332.97	−176.66	+2 379.50	−957.75

(Continued on page 46)

Stage (*c*). *Correcting Seasonal Deviation*

The reader might reasonably conclude that the mean of quarterly deviations can be taken as the figure representing seasonal variation for each quarter in the period covered. However, this is not exactly the case. Some error has in fact entered into our calculations. This error is caused by irregular fluctuations which cannot be eliminated by the 'moving average' process. Since the moving average must average whatever figures are there, a succession of years in which seasonal output was steady will be adequately 'smoothed' but a succession of years which were subject to wild fluctuations due to natural events such as floods might be less well smoothed in the moving average process. The trend will not be a smooth line, but will have 'humps' and 'hollows'.

That an error does exist can easily be proved because the four averages of quarterly deviation listed in Table 5.3 should altogether come to zero. The reader who finds this point difficult to follow should make a simple calculation which will demonstrate that the figures on either side of an arithmetic mean will sum to zero. For example, take the average of 22 + 14, $\frac{22 + 14}{2} = 18$: 18 is 4 below 22 (−4) and 4 above 14 (+4); −4 and +4 when added together = 0. In Table 5.3 the position is:

+ items	− items
+2 379.50 (Quarter 3)	−1 332.97 (Quarter 1)
	− 176.66 (Quarter 2)
	− 957.75 (Quarter 4)
	−2 467.38

Difference = +2 379.50 −2 467.38
= −87.88

Dividing this by four, we have that each quarterly deviation is wrong by −22.00. The **correction factor** is therefore +22.00. Since the negative column in the calculation is larger, giving us a final result of −22.00 per quarterly deviation, we have to add +22.00 to each quarter to make the result come to zero.

Our final calculation of seasonal deviation is therefore as follows:

Table 5.3. (continued)

	Quarter 1	*Quarter 2*	*Quarter 3*	*Quarter 4*
Mean of quarterly deviation	−1 332.97	−176.66	+2 379.50	−957.75
Correction factor	+22.00	+22.00	+ 22.00	+ 22.00
Seasonal Variation	−1 310.97	−154.66	+2 401.50	−935.75

Check: −1 310.97 and −154.66 and −935.75 when added together give −2 401.38. The tiny error here is due to rounding.

The seasonal variation figures from Table 5.3 above can now be used to de-seasonalise the data and assist us in calculating random variation.

5.4 Random Variations and the De-seasonalising of Data

We have already calculated the trend and also found the degree to which the actual data deviate from the trend. We have seen that these deviations from trend can be due to seasonal variations or other variations termed 'random'.

We must now de-seasonalise the deviations from trend. This means we must subtract the seasonal variations from the deviations from the trend. Any remaining deviation must be explained by random variations. Table 5.4 shows how this is done, and is fully explained in the notes below the table.

Table 5.4. Finding the Random Variation

Year	*Quarter*	*Sales (£'000)*	*Trend*	*Deviation from trend*	*Seasonal variation*	*Random variation*
1	1	1 084	—			
	2	1 976	—			
	3	3 600	2 090.38	+1 509.62	+2 401.50	−891.88
	4	1 654	2 171.75	−517.75	−935.75	+418.00
2	1	1 179	2 468.88	−1 289.88	−1 310.97	+21.09
	2	2 532	2 735.38	−203.38	−154.66	−48.72
	3	5 421	2 879.50	+2 541.50	+2 401.50	+140.00
	4	1 965	3 074.62	−1 109.62	−935.75	−173.87
3	1	2 021	3 293.38	−1 272.38	−1 310.97	+38.59
	2	3 251	3 470.12	−219.12	−154.66	−64.46
	3	6 452	3 532.38	+2 919.62	+2 401.50	+518.12
	4	2 348	3 600.62	−1 252.62	−935.75	−316.87
4	1	2 136	3 667.00	−1 531.00	−1 310.97	−220.03
	2	3 682	3 788.12	−106.12	−154.66	+48.54
	3	6 552	4 004.75	+2 547.25	+2 401.50	+145.75
	4	3 217	4 168.00	−951.00	−935.75	−15.25
5	1	3 000	4 238.62	−1 238.62	−1 310.97	+72.35
	2	4 124	4 302.00	−178.00	−154.66	−23.34
	3	6 675				
	4	3 601				

Notes

(i) The seasonal variation has been calculated previously (see Table 5.3) and is the same in all years for each season. Thus the same figures appear in quarter 3 Year 1, quarter 3 Year 2, etc.

(ii) The actual deviation from trend is not the same as the seasonal deviation. This shows that other types of random deviations have crept into the statistics that were collected.

(iii) It is easy to see that the amount of these random deviations is the difference between the seasonal variations and the deviations from trend. What is not so easy to understand is which sign the random variation will have. The reader will find the best guide to this is as follows:

(*a*) Look at the seasonal variation column. In the season under consideration (say year 1 quarter 3) we would have expected the deviation from trend to be seasonal, i.e. +2 401.5. In fact, it was only +1 509.62. This means that another variation, a random variation, occurred to reduce the seasonal effect. It must therefore have been a negative variation, i.e. −891.88. By contrast in year 2 quarter 3 the actual deviation, instead of being a seasonal +2 401.5, was even larger +2 451.50. So the random variation of 140.0 was positive, +140.0.

(*b*) By the same argument, in year 1 quarter 4 we would have expected the deviation from trend to be a seasonal −935.75. In fact, it was less than this; the actual figure was−517.75. This means that a random variation which was positive crept into the statistics to reduce the deficit, +418. By contrast, in year 2 quarter 4 the seasonal variation we expected of −935.75 was even larger, −1 109.62. This means that a negative variation crept in to make the deficit even greater, −173.87.

The Nature of Random Variation

As its name implies, random variation can arise from a variety of causes, many of which are quite unpredictable. Fate knocks on the door of individuals, businessmen, governments and even nations every day. The death of a salesman, the departure of a chief executive or a vital craftsman can adversely affect sales, or output, or public confidence. Particular events, like a rise in oil prices, can affect countless businesses, some more than others. Analysis of a series of figures which reveals a particularly sudden random variation may be related to a particular event of this sort. These are often called **special variations.**

Another type of variation is **induced variation.** This induced variation arises because of the averaging process over relatively small groups of numbers.

De-seasonalising the Actual Data

It is frequently helpful—for example, in planning business activities—to de-seasonalise the actual data, i.e. to express the actual figures with the variation due to seasonal fluctuation removed. In order to achieve this the actual figures in Table 5.4 (Sales £'000) have seasonal variation added or subtracted. There is some possible confusion over signs here. If the seasonal variation has a positive sign, this signifies that actual figures for that quarter exceed the trend: the seasonal variation is therefore *subtracted.* If the amount

Table 5.5. De-seasonalising Data

Year	*Quarter*	*Sales (£'000)*	*Seasonal variation*	*De-seasonalised data*
1	1	1 084	−1 310.97	2 394.97
	2	1 976	−154.66	2 130.66
	3	3 600	+2 401.50	1 198.50
	4	1 654	−935.75	2 589.75
2	1	1 179	−1 310.97	2 489.97
	2	2 532	−154.66	2 686.66
	3	5 421	+2 401.50	3 019.50
	4	1 965	−935.75	2 900.75
3	1	2 021	−1 310.97	3 331.97
	2	3 251	−154.66	3 405.66
	3	6 452	+2 401.50	4 050.50
	4	2 348	−935.75	3 283.75
4	1	2 136	−1 310.97	3 446.97
	2	3 682	−154.66	3 836.66
	3	6 552	+2 401.50	4 150.50
	4	3 217	−935.75	4 152.75
5	1	3 000	−1 310.97	4 310.97
	2	4 124	−154.66	4 278.66
	3	6 675	+2 401.50	4 273.50
	4	3 601	−935.75	4 536.75

of seasonal variation has a negative sign, then this means that the actual figures are less than trend and seasonal variation is *added.*

If the actual figures of Table 5.4 (Sales £'000) are seasonally adjusted, they give de-seasonalised data as shown in Table 5.5.

5.5 The Uses of Time Series

The main use of time series relates to predicting the future values of the variable in question. This is of obvious use to businesses, governments, and even to individuals. For example, if a manufacturing enterprise can accurately predict demand for its output in, say, five years' time, this will obviously help it to plan investment to produce such an output. It may be able to achieve economies by buying up at favourable prices manufacturing or transport and handling equipment which becomes available and is likely to be needed if the observed trend continues. It may be able to phase out other less profitable work to make capacity available when it is required.

A common way of showing the method of prediction is **extrapolation** of the trend line. This involves carrying over into a future period the calculated trend line. To extrapolate is to carry a graph on into a future period, beyond the points plotted already.

Thus, if the reader refers back to Fig. 5.1, let us consider what may happen in years 6 and 7 (see page 44). Clearly the trend appears likely to continue up towards the upper 4 000 range in Year 6 and the 5 000 range in Year 7. Because we know the seasonal variations now we can anticipate sales and set targets for our salesmen in each season of Year 6 and Year 7.

The reader should realise that extrapolation is a technique which can have dangerous consequences. The trend is only certain within the range already plotted, Years 1–5. This is the portion calculated from actual data. Outside of this period dramatic changes in events can cause the trend line to vary quite significantly from the extrapolated one. We must watch out for such events and take them into our calculations wherever possible.

5.6 Exercises: Time Series

1. Live births in UK ('000s)

Quarter	1	2	3	4
Year 1	210	198	192	186
Year 2	188	188	189	174
Year 3	177	180	176	163
Year 4	175	174	170	156

Source: *Monthly Digest of Statistics*

(*a*) By means of a moving average find the trend and seasonal adjustments.

(*b*) Explain, without doing the actual calculation, how you would forecast the number of births for the first quarter of Year 5. How reliable are such forecasts?

2. Arrange the following data in such a way that you can conveniently calculate:
   (*a*) A moving average which reveals the trend in the statistics.
   (*b*) The seasonal variation from the trend.
   (*c*) The residual variation that exists in the statistics when seasonally adjusted.

Earnings of Hoteliers from Overseas Tourists (£m)

Quarter	1	2	3	4
Year 1	32	47	160	83
Year 2	37	56	174	96
Year 3	57	80	236	126
Year 4	97	132	341	185
Year 5	128	182	397	227

Make the calculations and comment on the trend and the seasonal variations.

3. The following figures relate to the sale of men's pullovers, jumpers and cardigans over a four-year period. You are required:

(*a*) By means of a moving average to find the trend and seasonal variations concealed in the figures.

(*b*) To give the data for Year 4 seasonally adjusted (calculations correct to two decimal places).

Sales of Male Woollen Overgarments (Millions)

Quarter	1	2	3	4
Year 1	1.98	2.30	2.44	3.09
Year 2	1.80	2.01	2.23	3.04
Year 3	1.68	1.96	2.10	3.12
Year 4	1.91	2.25	2.43	2.98

Source: *Monthly Digest of Statistics*

4. *Sales of Tufted Carpets (100 000 m²)*

Quarter	1	2	3	4
Year 1	248	262	230	283
Year 2	249	265	236	278
Year 3	257	266	259	313
Year 4	313	297	295	353

Source: *Monthly Digest of Statistics*

(*a*) Calculate the trend by means of a moving average (correct to two decimal places).

(*b*) Draw a graph showing the trend and the quarterly figures above.

6

PICTORIAL REPRESENTATION OF STATISTICAL DATA

6.1 Introduction

Often when data have been arranged in a table, frequency distribution or time series, the information which the statistics carry becomes clear, especially to those who use figures regularly. However, many people who could benefit from the knowledge contained in a statistical series are unlikely to absorb such knowledge unless it can be presented in a simple visual form.

It is generally accepted that pictures, diagrams, and graphs are convenient methods of conveying simple ideas of a statistical nature, even to those who are largely uninterested in statistics as a science. Frequent use of pictures, diagrams and graphs is made on television, in the press and in magazines to pass on information relating to the cost of living, the level of unemployment, the cost of building society mortgages, etc.

This chapter deals with some of the more regularly used pictures and diagrams, whilst the slightly more complicated matter of graphs forms the subject of Chapter 7. It should be stressed here that neither of these chapters claims to be exhaustive—they are intended as a guide, not a complete record.

6.2 Pictograms

These are the simplest pictorial representations. Simple outline figures are used to represent quantities or values. For example, if the statistics relate to the changing level of unemployment over 10 years, the pictogram could be drawn as a number of human outlines, each one representing a given level of registered unemployed. Similarly, Fig. 6.1 illustrates the population of

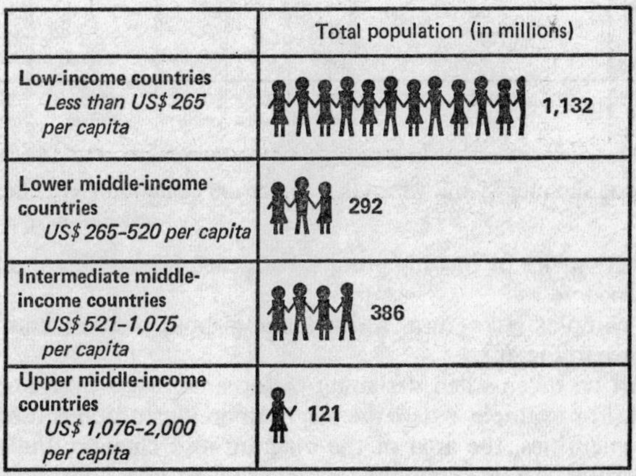

Total population (in millions)
Low-income countries
Less than US$ 265 per capita
1,132
Lower middle-income countries
US$ 265–520 per capita
292
Intermediate middle-income countries
US$ 521–1,075 per capita
386
Upper middle-income countries
US$ 1,076–2,000 per capita
121

Fig. 6.1. Developing countries: population by income groups.

(Reproduced by courtesy of Finance and Development)

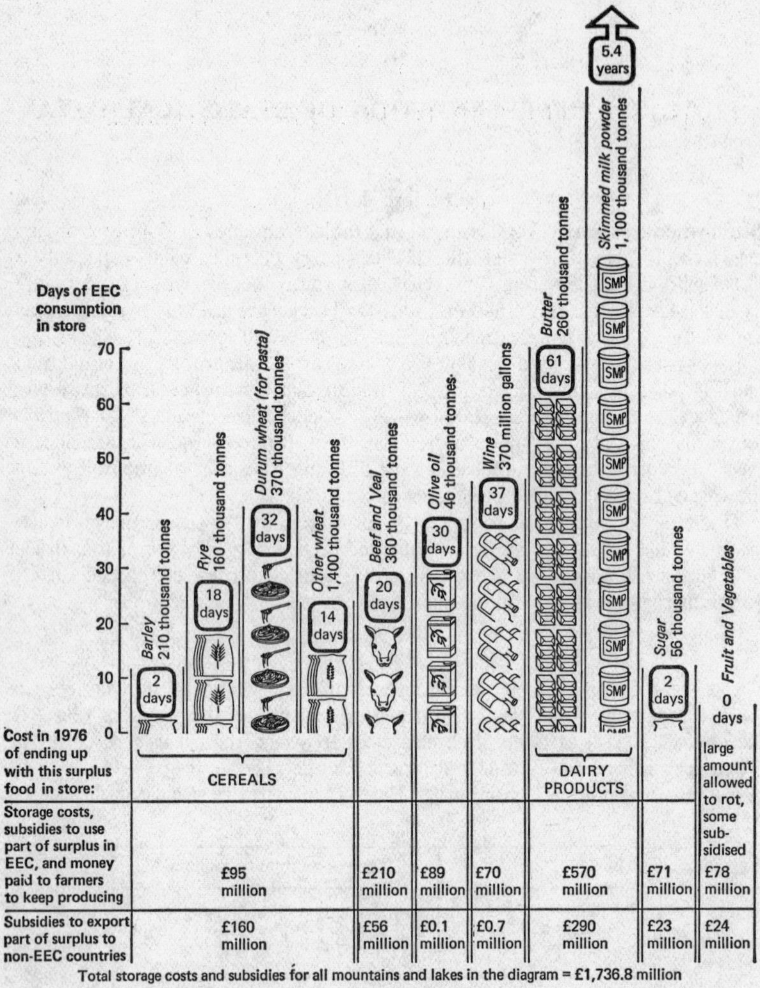

Fig. 6.2. Food mountains and wine lakes under the Common Agricultural Policy.
(Courtesy of *Which?* magazine)

developing countries by income groups, with each human figure representing 100 million people.

A more complex pictogram, which includes both pictures and numerical data, is shown in Fig. 6.2.

Care must be taken when designing pictograms that a false impression is not created. For example, where the height of an illustration is used to depict increasing quantities, the area of the diagram also changes, but not in the same proportion. An unscrupulous presenter might take advantage of this to convey a false impression. Fig. 6.3 illustrates the difficulty, the basket for Year 4 appearing to be much more than twice as large as the basket for Year

1. The tendency of diagrams and graphs to mislead is a problem to which we shall constantly be referring.

6.3 Bar Charts

Bar charts seek to relate information to the horizontal or vertical length of a bar or thick line. They are of two main types, those which compare statistics for a given period of time and those which compare them over a succession of periods of time.

For example, in Fig. 6.4 an ice cream firm has investigated the popularity of different flavours of ice cream by collecting statistics about the value of sales in a given week in one particular seaside resort. The statistics collected and

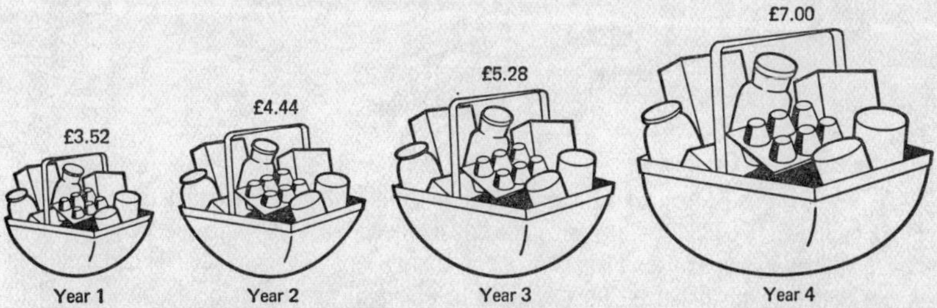

Fig. 6.3. False impressions of the cost of a standard basket of goods, Years 1–4.

presented in a bar chart in this way might lead to a decision to reduce the variety of flavours offered, or to an advertising campaign to promote less popular flavours. The preparation of such a chart presents a few problems. They are:

(*a*) *Scale.* A scale must be chosen which enables the graphics designer to represent the data clearly on the size of paper to be used.

(*b*) *Length of bar.* The length of the bar in each case must be calculated to represent the correct fraction of the full scale chosen. Thus the £1 750 bar in the diagram must be $\frac{1\ 750}{2\ 000} = \frac{7}{8}$ of the length of the longest bar.

(*c*) *Shading, colour. etc.* In some bar charts it might be desirable to pick out the bars in particular cross-hatchings or colours to present a clearer picture.

(*d*) *Title, source details, etc.* A suitable table, explanation of source material and date or dates (if required) should be added to the diagram, and the lettering and layout should be stylish and well-presented.

Where comparisons are being made over a series of time periods the periods should be of equal length. The fact that some years are leap years, and have an extra day, may make an insignificant difference to statistics collected on a yearly basis, but the differing lengths of months can make a significant difference to monthly sales figures. It is quite common for sales figures to be collected in a four-weekly basis, each 'lunar' month thus having 28 days. There will then be 13 months in the year, and a problem of designation arises. What period is actually meant by the seventh four-week period in the year? It requires a calendar to sort out the answer.

In Fig. 6.5 the vertical bar chart shown gives a clear indication of the number of vehicles in use in Great Britain over the given time range.

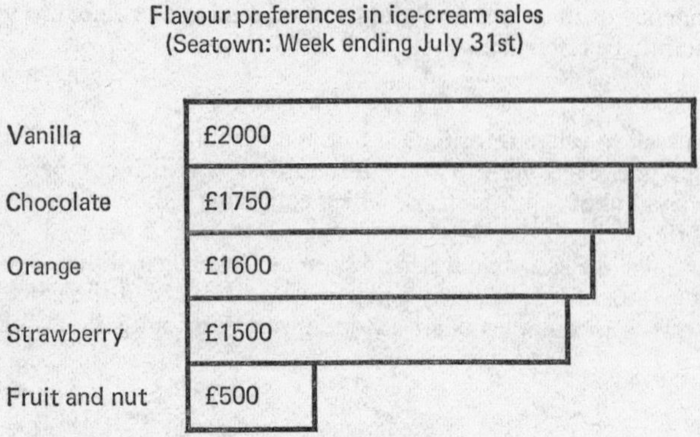

Fig. 6.4. A bar chart.

Percentage Bar Charts

A percentage bar chart is one in which the total body of statistics collected (100 per cent) is divided up into its component parts to show each part as a percentage of the whole. This is most useful where the total set of statistics has some special significance. This special method of presentation is often used in profit statements to show how the profits made have been allocated. For example, taking each £1 of profit it might be that 52 pence went in Corporation Tax, 12 pence to Ordinary Shareholders, 8 pence to Preference Shareholders, 5 pence to Minority Shareholders and 23 pence into General Reserves. Such a set of statistics could be easily displayed using a percentage bar chart.

In Fig. 6.6 the annual expenditure of an average household is broken down into its percentage component elements of expenditure.

6.4 Histograms

These are diagrams which display frequency distributions. Here a vertical block is drawn to represent each class interval. The greater the frequency of

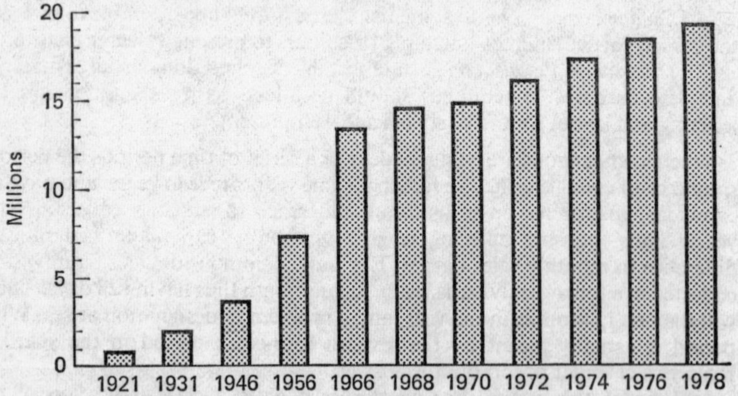

Fig. 6.5. A vertical bar chart. Vehicles in use in Great Britain, 1921–78.

the group, the higher the block. Where class intervals are equal, as in Fig. 6.7, the width of the block is immaterial and may be chosen to suit the space available. The rules for drawing a histogram with uniform class intervals are as follows:

(*a*) Select a width of class interval which is appropriate for the size of paper to be used and the number of rectangles (class intervals) to be drawn. The class intervals will be marked along the horizontal axis and the frequencies up the vertical axis.

(*b*) At the midpoint of each class interval mark in a height above the

Item	£	% (to nearest 0.5%)
Food	1 225	41
Housing	375	12.5
Heat and light	300	10
Transport	300	10
Entertainment	150	5
Clothes	150	5
Other	500	16.5
Total	3 000	100

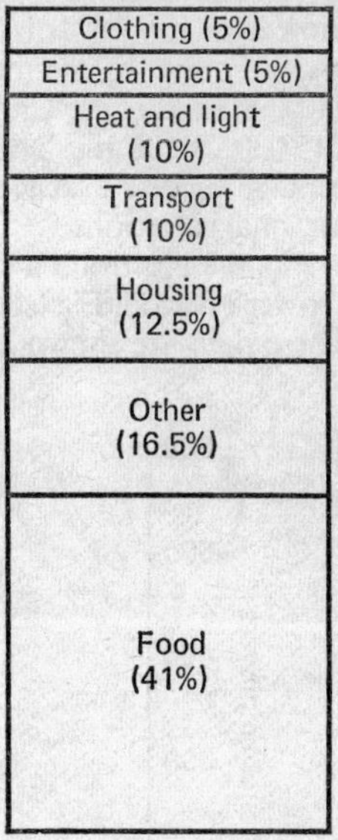

Fig. 6.6. A percentage bar chart. Annual expenditure of an average household.

horizontal axis which is proportional to the frequency of that particular class interval. Draw a horizontal line at this height equal to the width of the class interval.

(*c*) Now draw in the sides of the rectangles by joining up the ends of these lines to the horizontal axis. The result is a series of contiguous rectangles. The heights of the rectangles are proportional to the frequencies of their respective classes, and the total earnings are represented by the total area of the histogram.

Histograms with Unequal Class Intervals

If the class intervals are unequal (which frequently happens when the final class interval is an 'Other items' class), the area of the rectangle becomes the important factor, and must be kept proportional to the class interval multiplied by the frequency of the class. Thus a class of twice the size of a normal class interval would be halved in height providing that the number of frequencies was identical in both cases.

6.5 Gantt Charts

The object of the Gantt chart is to relate actual performance to planned or anticipated performance. The procedure is to mark on the chart a series of equal divisions, say weekly or monthly, each of which represents the planned performance for that period. Against these divisions the actual performance can be plotted in as a thin bar. If the target output, or target sales, is fully achieved the bar will cross from one side of the division to the other. If the target is not fully achieved a gap will be left, while if the target is exceeded a second bar can be started to show the excess. The useful feature of this layout is that although the divisions are equal, the targets to be achieved are not the same each month. It is therefore possible for seasonal variations to be taken into account. A salesman in a slack August period might be set a target of £1 000. In the pre-Christmas rush the October target might be raised to £15 000. Since the 'actual achievement' bar illustrates the salesman's percentage success in reaching the target, there is no problem in accounting for seasonal variations.

Fig. 6.8 illustrates a sales manager's targets for one of his salesmen, over a six-week period. Fig 6.8(*a*) shows the planned and actual sales in tabular form. These data are shown in the form of a Gantt chart in Fig. 6.8(*b*). Here each

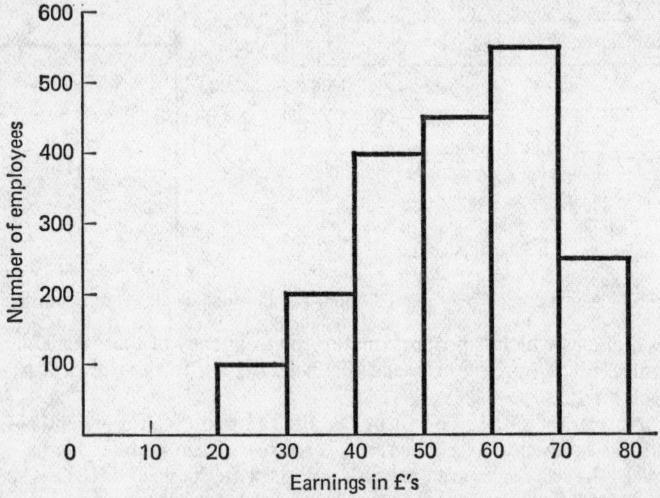

Fig. 6.7. A histogram. Weekly earnings of engineering apprentices and craftsmen.

division (denoted 1, 2, 3, etc.) represents the target performance for one week. The divisions are of equal size, *even though the sales targets are not*. A target is shown as being reached exactly when the horizontal bar *just* fills the division. If it falls short of the division then actual performance is less than planned. If it more than fills the division (shown by the addition of a second bar) then actual performance exceeds that planned. For clarity the actual and planned figures and a percentage success rating can be written in on the chart.

It is also possible to add a further bar below the 'percentage performance' bar which is cumulative, and shows the extent to which targets have been met over a longer period. To illustrate the method this second bar in Fig. 6.8(*b*) has only been marked in for the first four weeks. At the end of this four-week period the cumulative target sales were £5 100, but actual sales were £5 410.

Week	Planned	Actual
1	1 200	1 120
2	1 250	1 180
3	1 300	1 500
4	1 350	1 610
5	1 400	1 820
6	1 450	1 950

(*a*)

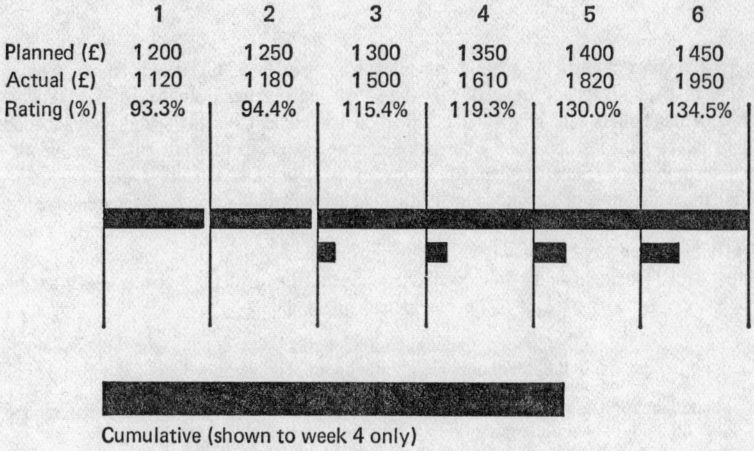

(*b*)

Fig. 6.8. (*a*) Sales—planned and actual. (*b*) A Gantt chart.

This means that £310 of the fifth week's target of £1 400 has already been achieved. This is about 22 per cent of the fifth week's target and the cumulative line at the end of the fourth week therefore goes on to mark in 22 per cent of that division.

6.6 Pie Charts

One of the simplest methods to represent the way in which a whole statistical collection breaks down into its component parts is to use the 'pie' diagram. A pie is a circular culinary delicacy, and we are familiar from childhood with the advantages to be enjoyed by securing a larger slice of pie than other members of the family. The pie chart depicts the component parts of any set of statistical data as slices of pie.

The complete circle represents the whole set of data. Any subdivisions within the set are then shown by subdividing the circle in proportion. In Fig. 6.9, for example, the 'One-person pensioner index' gives a weighting of 442 parts in 1 000 to food. The General index, by contrast, gives food a weighting of 278 parts in 1 000, since food does not form as large a proportion of total expenditure in general households. What share of the pie diagram should be given to 'Food' in these two pie charts? There are 360° in a circle, and therefore the calculations are as follows:

$$\text{Pension index:} \quad \text{Food} = \frac{442}{1000} \times 360^\circ = \underline{\underline{159.1^\circ}}$$

$$\text{General index:} \quad \text{Food} = \frac{278}{1000} \times 360^\circ = \underline{\underline{100.1^\circ}}$$

In Chapter 3, and again in this chapter, reference has been made to the dangers that statistics may be distorted either deliberately or inadvertently. Diagrams, charts and graphs are amongst the easiest of statistical tools to use dishonestly, and since they are more easily understood than other presentations they may therefore delude a larger number of people. Deliberate distortion aside, an enthusiastic individual with a point of view to express which he believes to be in the public interest may unwittingly bring biased, incorrectly presented data forward in the genuine belief that it is correct. The student should appraise all his own work critically, and also the presentations put before him by others, to detect shortcomings.

6.7 Exercises: Diagrammatic Representation

1. The following data have to be displayed in pictorial form. Choose an appropriate symbol and draw a pictogram.

Colour Television Sets in Use in United Kingdom (Thousands)

1966	0
1968	100
1970	500
1972	1 300
1974	6 800
1976	9 500
1978	10 800

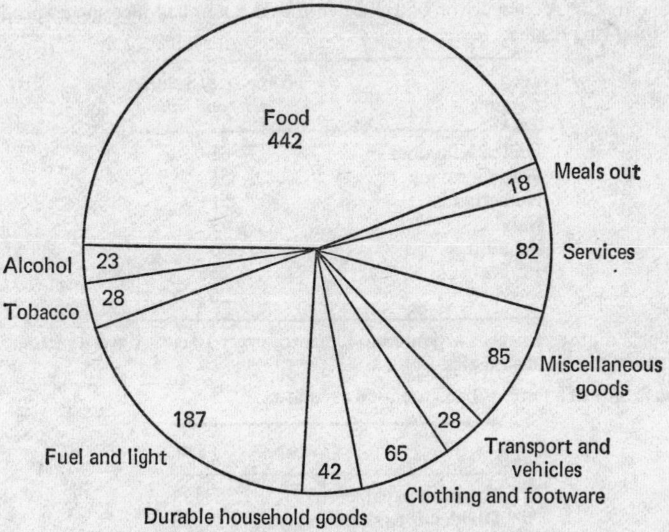

(*a*) Index for one-person pensioner households

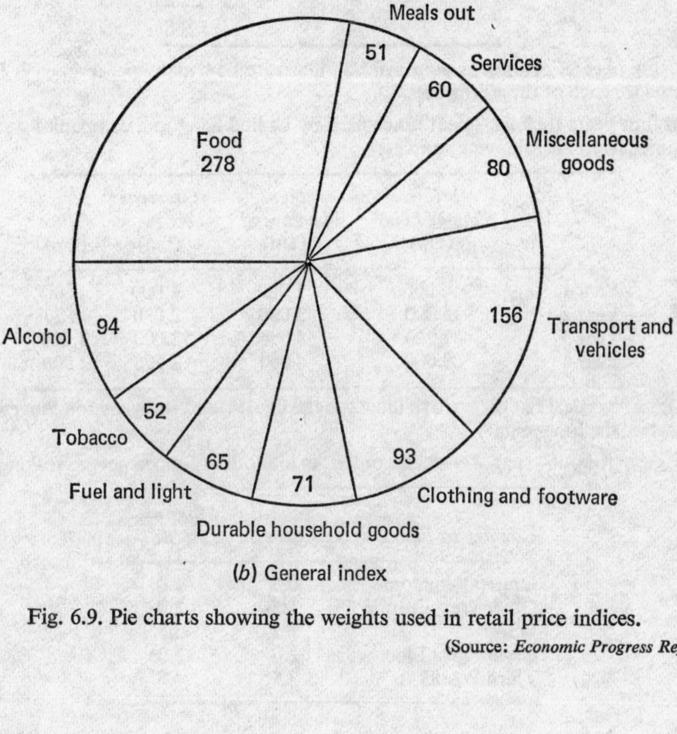

(*b*) General index

Fig. 6.9. Pie charts showing the weights used in retail price indices.

(Source: *Economic Progress Report*)

2. The volume of traffic can be measured by discovering the number of vehicles per mile of roads. A comparison of traffic densities in a number of countries produced the following results:

Country	*Number of vehicles per road-mile*
United Kingdom	61
West Germany	51
Netherlands	51
Italy	49
Belgium	36
France	26
Sweden	20

Using a motor vehicle as a symbol to represent every 10 cars, draw a pictogram to illustrate the set of statistics.

3. The profits of a famous bank are used as follows:

	£m
Taxation payable	133
Dividends to shareholders	23
Minority shareholders	12
Kept in reserves	100
	£268

Using piles of pennies as your symbol, illustrate how many pence in each £1 are used for each of these purposes.

4. In four years the investment funds used by United Kingdom companies were obtained from the following sources:

	Profits ploughed back (£m)	*Bank borrowing* (£m)	*Overseas borrowing* (£m)	*Other* (£m)
Year 1	4 000	1 000	1 000	500
Year 2	5 000	3 000	2 000	500
Year 3	7 000	5 000	3 000	1 000
Year 4	8 000	4 000	3 500	2 000

Draw a vertical bar diagram to illustrate the figures, and show the total invested in each of the four years.

5. Figures for one-year's world fibre output in millions of tonnes were as follows:

Country or bloc	*Natural fibre*	*Man-made fibre*
United Kingdom	0.5	1.0
Other West Europe	1.5	2.0
USA	1.5	3.5
Communist Bloc	2.0	5.0
Third World	3.5	4.5

Draw a bar chart to illustrate these outputs. Use shading or colours to distinguish natural and man-made fibres.

6. Improvements in pupil–teacher ratios are shown in the following table. Draw a bar chart to illustrate the changes.

Pupils per teacher in Primary Schools
(England and Wales only)

Year	*Number of pupils per teacher*
1921	48
1931	43.5
1951	39
1961	36
1971	31.5

7. Employees' wages in the New Town area are shown below for the first week in June. Draw a histogram to illustrate the data.

Class range	*Percentage of population with earnings in the group*
Over £10 and under £30	4.5
£30 and under £40	7.5
£40 and under £50	15.5
£50 and under £60	20.0
£60 and under £70	34.0
£70 and under £80	12.0
£80 and under £90	5.0
£90 and under £100	1.5
	100.0

8. Property values in Seatown were found to be as follows in a survey:

Price range	*Number in class*
£2 000 and under £4 000	154
£4 000 and under £6 000	3 825
£6 000 and under £8 000	4 580
£8 000 and under £10 000	3 580
£10 000 and under £12 000	1 580
£12 000 and under £16 000	75

Draw a histogram to illustrate these statistics.

9. A salesman's sales figures were as follows for the four-week period commencing April 5th. Draw a Gantt chart to illustrate the data, on both a weekly and a cumulative basis.

Week commencing	*Target Sales (£)*	*Actual Sales (£)*
April 5	£2 500	£1 150
April 12	£3 000	£2 450
April 19	£4 000	£3 000
April 26	£5 000	£6 250

10. Draw a pie chart to illustrate the following set of statistics, which is taken from *Social Trends:*

Families in Great Britain, 19. .

	Percentages
All families	100
Families with no dependent children	51.9
1 child	20.5
2 children	16.5
3 children	6.9
4 or more children	4.2

11. Consumers' expenditure in 19. . is given as follows, in £ million.

Food	12 500
Drink and tobacco	7 500
Housing, fuel and light	8 300
Clothing	5 100
Cars and motor cycles	6 500
Durable household goods	3 600
Other goods	4 500
Other services	3 000
	51 000

Draw a pie diagram to illustrate the figures provided.

7

GRAPHS

7.1 Introduction

Chapter 6 illustrated a number of ways of presenting information in a form which the eye could easily assimilate. This chapter continues that process.

Essentially a graph is a diagram which shows the relationship between two variable quantities each measured along one of a pair of axes, at right-angles to one another. Graphs are frequently drawn on squared paper, which assists the 'plotting' of the observed data as a number of points which may then be joined up by a line. In any pair of variables—say, sales during the months of the year—one variable is usually dependent upon the other. Thus the sales vary as the months follow one another. The months may therefore be said to be the independent variable and the sales in the various months are the dependent variable. The sale of Easter bonnets depends upon the closeness of the month to Easter, while the sale of fireworks varies with the approach of various festivals as the year passes.

7.2 Constructing a Graph

The following principles form a useful guide when drawing graphs:

(*a*) Two lines, known as the **axes**, are used as a framework for the graph. One of these is horizontal, and is known as the x-axis (or abscissa). This is used to plot the independent variable. The other is vertical and is known as the y-axis (or ordinate); it carries the dependent variable. The origin of a graph is at the point 0 on the x-axis and 0 on the y-axis. If the full range of the graph is shown this will be the point where the axes intersect.

(*b*) A **scale** must be chosen for each axis which not only enables the data to be plotted over the full range, but also displays the information in the best way possible. Thus the same horizontal axis could be made to show up to 50 000 tons of chemical demanded or 50 000 000 tons, but the scale chosen would need to be different. The scale should present the data as large as possible, using the full width of the page, so that it is easy to plot the points and to 'interpolate' as necessary. The meaning of 'interpolate' and 'extrapolate' is explained later (see page 68). The axes should be clearly labelled, both with the name of the variable (for example, 'Price') and with the units in which the variable is measured (for example '£s').

(*c*) **Points are plotted** on the graph by using the values given in the table supplied, or found in the statistical enquiry which is being carried out. Each pair of related facts, such as the fact that at a price of £100 per tonne 50 000 tonnes of peas are demanded, gives a unique point on the graph. The point may be marked by a tiny dot, but preferably by a small cross made by two short lines intersecting at the exact spot. In such graphs the points are clearly picked out, and the curves joining up the points may be discontinuous to give greater emphasis.

(*d*) The points which have been plotted can now be joined up by a curve. Even where the lines on a graph are straight, convention still refers to them as *curves*. When drawn the curves must be clear and distinct. The purpose of presenting information in this way is to promote understanding. Hence the pattern of the graph and the direction and slope of curves are of vital importance. A large number of lines drawn closely together should be avoided.

We are now ready to consider one or two common types of graph.

7.3 Simple Graphs

The simplest form of graph approximates to the bar diagram of Chapter 6. It merely presents information in pictorial form, so that it can be readily appreciated. Thus a time series may be plotted as a series of points on a graph, which when joined up display the information in a clear visual form. In Fig. 7.1 the sales of an electrical gadget over the course of a year are displayed, so that peak sales periods are pinpointed and troughs of business actively brought out.

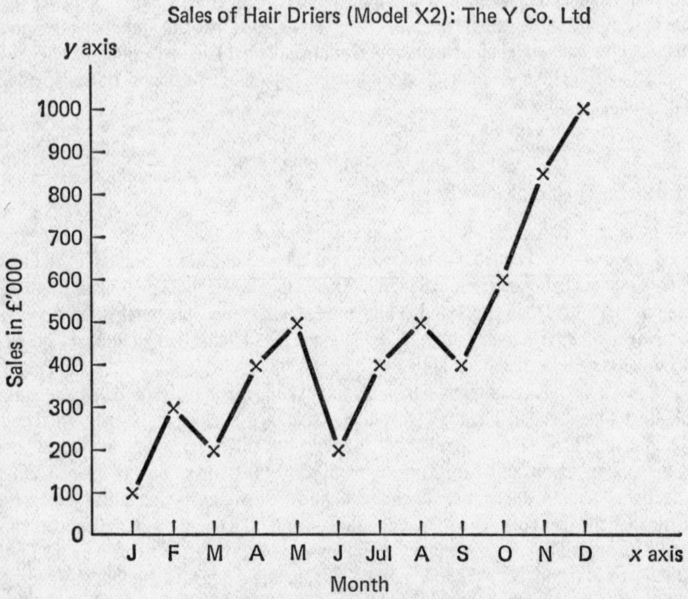

Fig. 7.1. A simple graph.

7.4 The Z Chart

A Z chart is so-called because when completed it looks like a capital Z. The chart is designed to show up three aspects on the same diagram:

(*a*) Current figures—for example, current sales or current output.

(*b*) Cumulative figures—for example, total sales or output to date this year.

(*c*) A moving annual total—which shows the total for the previous year.

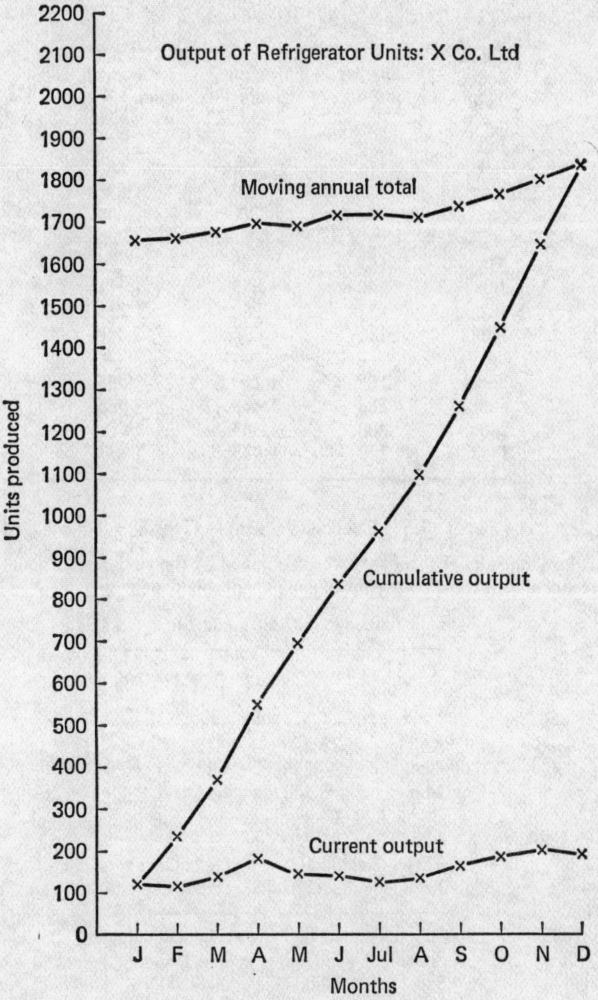

Fig. 7.2. A Z chart.

Each month the total is increased by the current month's sales and reduced by deducting the sales of the same month a year ago. A typical set of figures is shown in Example 7.1 and the Z chart is drawn in Fig. 7.2.

Example 7.1. Output of Refrigerator Units: X Co. Ltd.

Month	*Monthly output*	*Cumulative output*	*Moving annual output*
Jan.	120	120	1 655
Feb.	115	235	1 660
Mar.	135	370	1 675
Apr.	180	550	1 695
May	145	695	1 690
Jun.	140	835	1 715
Jul.	125	960	1 715
Aug.	135	1 095	1 710
Sep.	165	1 260	1 735
Oct.	185	1 445	1 765
Nov.	200	1 645	1 800
Dec.	190	1 835	1 835

7.5 Exercises: Simple Graphs

1. The following sales for the year were achieved by the two departments of a town-centre store. Plot these on a graph, using a suitable scale.

Sales of Supertraders Ltd

	Groceries (£)	*Greengroceries* (£)
Jan.	28 250	12 750
Feb.	24 250	11 500
Mar.	36 500	16 500
Apr.	33 750	14 750
May	34 500	15 500
Jun.	37 250	18 000
Jul.	25 000	13 250
Aug.	28 750	14 500
Sep.	34 000	18 500
Oct.	42 500	20 250
Nov.	43 500	21 000
Dec.	56 000	23 500

2. Mechanical Parts Ltd make two models of a particular machine, the 'Junior' model and the 'Senior' model. Sales during the year are given below. You are asked to record these figures, *and total sales*, on a graph, labelling all parts of the graph as necessary.

Mechanical Parts Ltd: Sales during Year 19..

	Jan. (£)	Feb. (£)	Mar. (£)	Apr. (£)	May (£)	Jun. (£)
Junior	5 000	5 500	7 000	8 000	8 500	9 000
Senior	14 000	13 500	12 000	13 000	11 000	8 000

	Jul. (£)	Aug. (£)	Sep. (£)	Oct. (£)	Nov. (£)	Dec. (£)
Junior	8 500	7 000	9 500	10 000	10 500	12 000
Senior	8 500	3 500	4 000	4 500	4 000	5 000

3. From the following information prepare a Z chart of the sales performance of Alpha Ltd for the present year and comment on the year's results as revealed by the diagram.

Sales (£'000)

	Last year	*This year*
Jan.	56	75
Feb.	54	78
Mar.	58	82
Apr.	62	85
May	66	91
Jun.	66	93
Jul.	71	96
Aug.	73	98
Sep.	75	105
Oct.	78	108
Nov.	80	112
Dec.	81	115

4. From the following figures for output by the Heavy Components Co. Ltd draw up a Z chart showing the present year's production achievements, and comment on the diagram.

Output in Units

	Last year	*This year*
Jan.	27	45
Feb.	24	43
Mar.	28	27
Apr.	40	15
May	42	0
Jun.	44	0
Jul.	33	0
Aug.	35	38
Sep.	46	58
Oct.	48	64
Nov.	50	72
Dec.	51	74

7.6 Straight-line graphs

The simple graph of sales in Fig. 7.1 rose and fell in line with quantity sold—it was a zig-zag line. However, some graphs, where the data are in a special relationship, consist of straight lines. Such a graph arises where one set of data varies directly with changes in the other set of data.

For example, in Fig. 7.3(*a*) the cost of a particular product is plotted against the number of units required, up to a total of 10. Each unit is £3.50, and there is a direct relation between the cost of a particular order and the number of units ordered. The result is a straight-line graph passing through the origin (since when no units are ordered there is nothing to pay).

A straight-line graph of this sort can be used very easily as a ready reckoner. This particular straight-line graph can be used to read off the total cost of any number of units from 1 to 10. To do this we draw a horizontal line across from the number of units required (eight in the diagram) until it intercepts the graph. We then drop a perpendicular from that point on to the price axis, where we find that eight units cost £28 altogether.

Reading off values in this way is called **interpolation**—finding the intermediate terms in the known range of a series from the values already known. If we were to extend the straight line and find values outside the range already given, it would be called **extrapolation.**

Many straight-line graphs pass through the origin, where both variables are zero. For example, in Fig. 7.3(*a*) there is no charge if no units are purchased. This is not always the case, and a straight-line graph may intercept one of the axes at some point. In the break-even chart in Fig. 7.3(*b*) certain fixed costs of an output of a certain product are incurred before any output can be produced at all. This might include costs of jigs and tools to be used in manufacture, or design costs incurred before even a prototype product is produced. The cost of manufacture will therefore start with these fixed costs (£500 in the graph) and the other variable costs which vary directly with output must be borne in addition as output commences. The cost line therefore does not pass through the origin but intercepts the price axis at the £500 mark. By contrast, the proceeds from the sale of the output do start at the origin. Since selling price is fixed at a sufficiently high level to achieve a profit eventually, the 'sales proceeds' line is steeper than the cost line. The two lines therefore intersect at the break-even point. At this point the total costs incurred are covered, and every unit sold after this point will yield a profit.

Drawing Graphs of Simple Functions

In statistics, and mathematics generally, there are many relationships between numbers. For example, one can say that one number y is three times another number x. This can be written $y = 3x$. Such a relationship would be true to the numbers 12 and 4 for 12 is three times four. It would also be true of 9 and 3, or 6 and 2, or 3 and 1, for in each of these cases the first number in the pair is three times the second number in the pair.

Taking another relationship—for example, $y = 2x + 3$—we would draw up a simple table like this:

x	0	1	2	3	4
$y = 2x + 3$	3	5	7	9	11

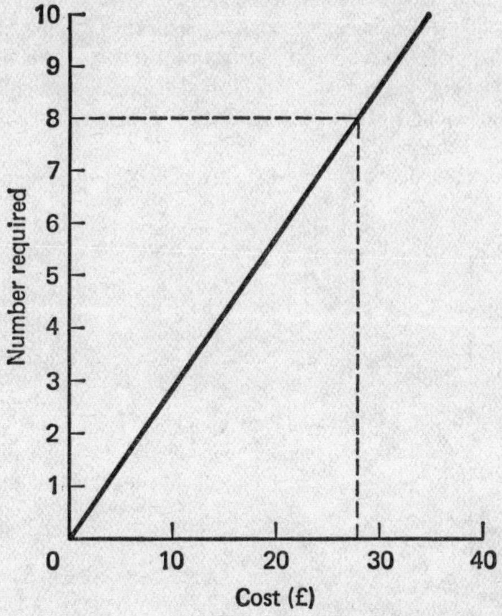

(a)

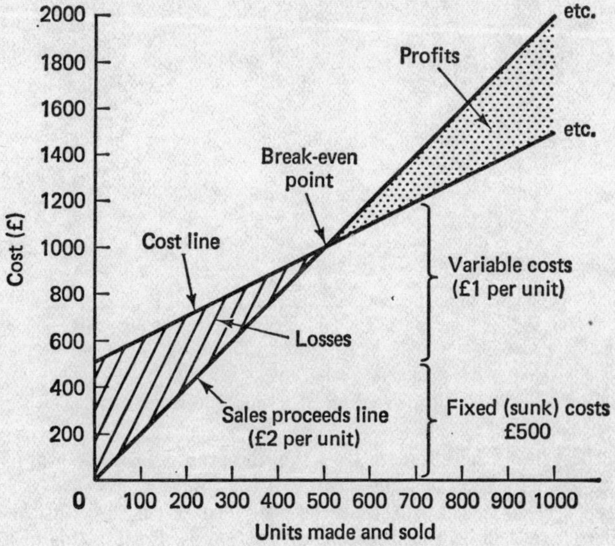

(b)

Fig. 7.3. (*a*) A straight-line graph used as a ready reckoner. (*b*) A break-even chart.

In each case the pairs of numbers 1, 5; 2, 7; etc., are in the same relationship to one another and this relationship is expressed as $y = 2x + 3$. We say that y is a **function** of x and it is easy to draw a graph of such a simple function. In Fig. 7.4 the values of x have been plotted along the x-axis and the values of y along the y-axis. The values of x are called the **independent variables** and the values of y, which depend upon the values of x chosen, are called the **dependent variables.**

The alert reader will note that in graphs like Fig. 7.4 which do not pass

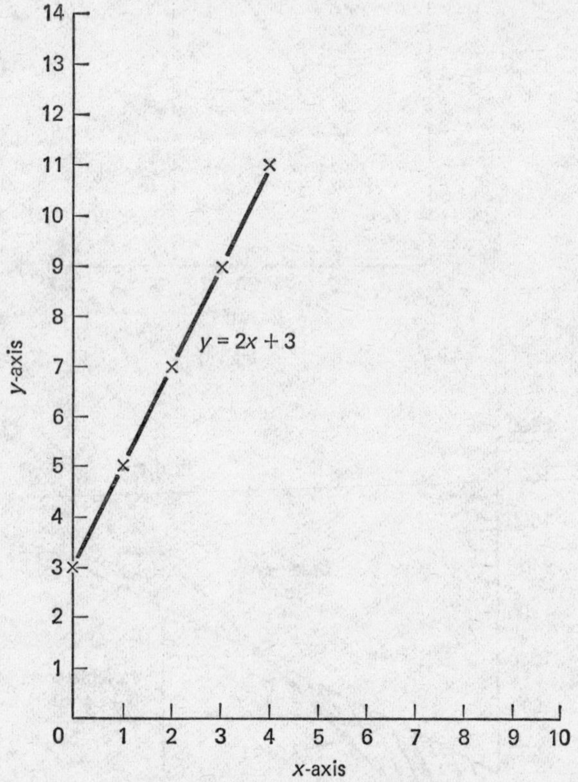

Fig. 7.4. A graph of a simple function.

through the origin, the intercept on y (i.e. the point where the graph cuts the y-axis) is given by the constant term 3 in the function $y = 2x + 3$. At the time when $x = 0$, $2x$ is also 0, and the only term left is the constant term 3, which therefore decides the intercept on the y-axis. Putting this in algebraic terms, if we use the general formula $y = ax + b$, the intercept on the y-axis is always decided by the constant term b, which does not vary with x.

7.7 Exercises: Graphs of Simple Functions

1. Draw the graph of $y = x + 500$, using values of $x = 1\,000$, $x = 2\,000$, $x = 3\,000$ and $x = 4\,000$.
2. Draw the graph of $y = 3x + 4$.
3. Fahrenheit thermometers and Celsius thermometers are connected by the relationship $y = \frac{9}{5}x + 32$. Draw a graph of this function using values of x of 0°, 5°, 10°, 15°, etc., up to 100°. From this graph you should read off: (*a*) the Fahrenheit reading equivalent to 47°C; (*b*) the Celsius reading equivalent to 98°F.
4. The costs of a project are £10 fixed costs and then £2 per unit produced. The proceeds from the sale of the units are £4 per unit. Draw a graph for costs and another for sales on the same diagram, using 0, 5, 10, 15 and 20 units of output and thus determine the break-even point.

7.8 The Frequency Polygon

A frequency polygon is the graphical form of a histogram. Class intervals are marked out along the horizontal axis and values or frequencies along the vertical axis. The points representing the frequency for each group are then plotted as if the frequency occurred at the midpoint of the class interval. Such graphs can only be drawn where class intervals are of equal size.

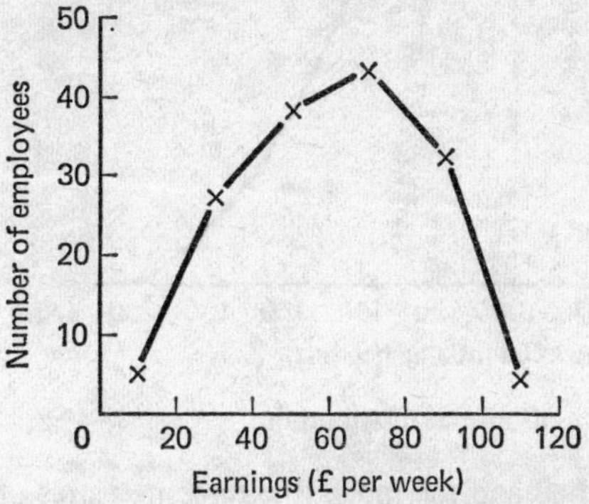

Earnings (£)	Number of employees
0 and under 20	5
20 and under 40	27
40 and under 60	38
60 and under 80	43
80 and under 100	32
100 and under 120	4

Fig. 7.5. A frequency polygon.

In Fig. 7.5 a frequency polygon is drawn to display the earnings of a number of employees shown in the table alongside the graph.

The frequency polygon is often used to illustrate a characteristic of statistical data known as **skewness**. This term is explained below, but before doing so it is first necessary to explain a related term. This is the term 'normal distribution curve'.

The Normal Distribution Curve

Statisticians make use of a fairly complicated mathematical idea known as the normal curve of distribution. If we have an event to which there are only two possible answers, like 'Heads' and 'Tails' when a coin is tossed, we would expect, provided there was no bias introduced (like a badly made coin), that the result would be an equal number of each answer—say 5 heads and 5 tails out of 10. If we repeatedly tossed 10 coins we might occasionally get 5 heads and 5 tails, or 6 heads and 4 tails, or 4 heads and 6 tails, but it would be comparatively rare to get 10 heads and 0 tails, or 0 heads and 10 tails. In fact, the likely frequency of any particular combination, like 8 and 2, or 9 and 1, or 6 and 4, reflects its closeness to the average result 5 and 5. If such a collection of results was plotted as a polygon we would expect the mean result, 5 and 5, to be the most usual result and occur most often, while the result 10 and 0 or 0 and 10 would occur least frequently. Such a polygon would in fact produce a 'curve of normal distribution' like the one shown in Fig. 7.6.

Note that the normal distribution curve is symmetrical, the portion A being an exact mirror image of B. Some collected data, when ranged in a frequency distribution, have this symmetry. One feature of this symmetrical set of

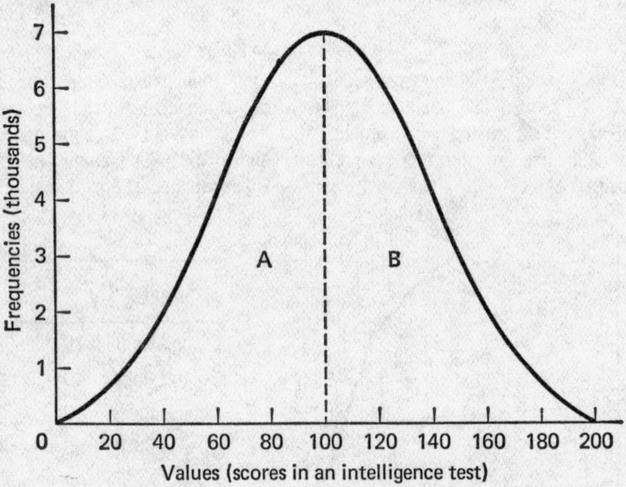

Fig. 7.6. The curve of normal distribution.

statistics is that the mean, the median and the mode (the three measures of 'average' which are explained in Chapter 8) are all to be found in the same place, at the centre of the distribution.

Skewed Distributions

When a sample of data on any particular topic is collected it frequently happens that the data do not follow the normal distribution curve. It would be fairly surprising if they did, for although the normal distribution would be expected if a whole 'population' was being examined, any sample (like any 10 coins tossed) has a good chance of finishing up as a non-normal result (like 6 and 4, 7 and 3, etc.).

Where the frequency occurrence shows a concentration away from the centre and towards one or other of the extremities, the distribution is said to be **skewed**. In such a case the 'average' positions will not all be central. The mean and the mode will be located away from the centre, and the three types of average—the mean, median and mode—will not coincide. Such distributions are shown in Figs 7.7(*a*) and (*b*).

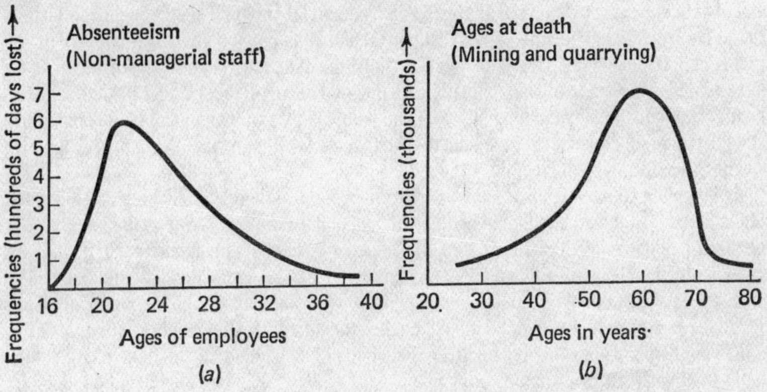

Fig. 7.7. Two examples of skewness.

7.9 Scatter Diagrams

A scatter diagram is a technique for comparing the relationship between two variables. One of the variables is assigned to the horizontal axis, the other to the vertical axis. Observed relationships between the two variables are then plotted as points on the scatter diagram. For example, it might have been observed in an enquiry that a man with a personal income of £7 000 per annum spent £5 500 per annum whilst another with an income of £3 500 spent £2 000 per annum. This might lead us to ask whether there was a **correlation** or link between the two aspects, income and consumption expenditure. If further information is collected, each pair of related facts can then be plotted on a scatter graph such as Fig. 7.8. The spread of scatter may be wide, indicating poor correlation, or narrow, indicating that correlation is fairly close and that people with 'high' incomes do tend to spend more.

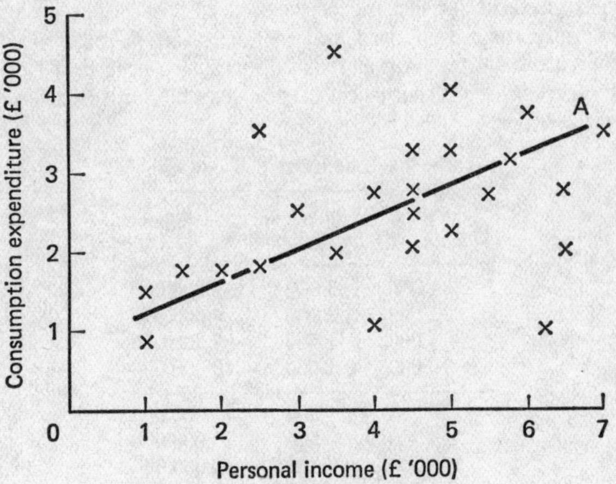

Fig. 7.8. A scatter diagram.

It is then necessary to see if there is any kind of pattern to the points. This is done by inserting the **line of best fit.** Such a line is drawn through the group of points in such a way that the perpendicular distance from the points on one side of the line to the line, total the same as the total perpendicular distances from the points on the other side, to the line. In this position the line represents the pattern of points on the scatter graph as well as possible, and hence the name 'the line of best fit'.

It is easier to see the line of best fit if a piece of stretched thread is held over the scatter diagram and moved about until it occupies what appears to be a central position. By using a piece of thread instead of a ruler scatter points on both sides of the thread can be seen. Line A in Fig. 7.8 is such a line. Since the line of best fit is available it can be used to read off probable values of expenditure against income, or probable incomes if the expenditure level is known. Though such a technique is not exact it gives the best estimate available in the circumstances.

7.10 The Lorenz Curve

It is well known to economists and statisticians that an unequal relationship exists between such items as wealth and population, size of manufacturing plant and percentage of total output, etc. For example, if we were to regard total population in the United Kingdom as 100 per cent, we would not expect to find that *each* 1 per cent owned 1 per cent of the total wealth. Instead we would expect, say, the first 50 per cent of the population to own only 10 per cent of the wealth, and the most prosperous 5 per cent of the population to own, say, 50 per cent of the wealth.

Such relationships involving disparity of proportions can be expressed in a **Lorenz curve.**

To illustrate the Lorenz curve the figures given in Table 7.1, and developed in Table 7.2, may be used. These figures show the incomes earned by the nationals of an imaginary nation, Country A. There are a great many people in the low income group and as the incomes rise the number in successive groups falls. When each income group is worked out as a percentage of the total population, and its income is worked out as a percentage of total national income, these two percentage figures can be plotted against one another to give the Lorenz curve. It is important to note that Lorenz curves compare the *percentage* distribution of one variable with the *percentage* distribution of the other.

Table 7.1. The Income of Nation A

Personal income (£)	*Number of individuals*	*Total income* (£)
1 000	3 000	3 000 000
2 000	2 000	4 000 000
5 000	1 500	7 500 000
10 000	1 000	10 000 000
20 000	800	16 000 000
50 000	500	25 000 000
100 000	300	30 000 000
500 000	100	50 000 000

Table 7.2. Percentages of Income Earned by Various Groups

Number of individuals			*Total income* (£'000s)		
Actual	%	*Cumulative* %	*Actual*	%	*Cumulative* %
3 000	32.6	32.6	3 000	2.1	2.1
2 000	21.7	54.3	4 000	2.7	4.8
1 500	16.3	70.6	7 500	5.2	10.0
1 000	10.9	81.5	10 000	6.9	16.9
800	8.7	90.2	16 000	11.0	27.9
500	5.4	95.6	25 000	17.2	45.1
300	3.3	98.9	30 000	20.6	65.7
100	1.1	100.0	50 000	34.4	100.1
Total 9 200	100.0		145 500	100.1	

Notes
(i) Due to rounding, totals do not necessarily come to 100 per cent.
(ii) Each 'actual' figure is calculated as a percentage of its column total. A cumulative percentage column can then be constructed. Cumulative percentages are then taken in pairs—for example, 32.6 and 2.1; 54.3 and 4.8, etc.—and entered upon the graph, to build up the Lorenz curve.

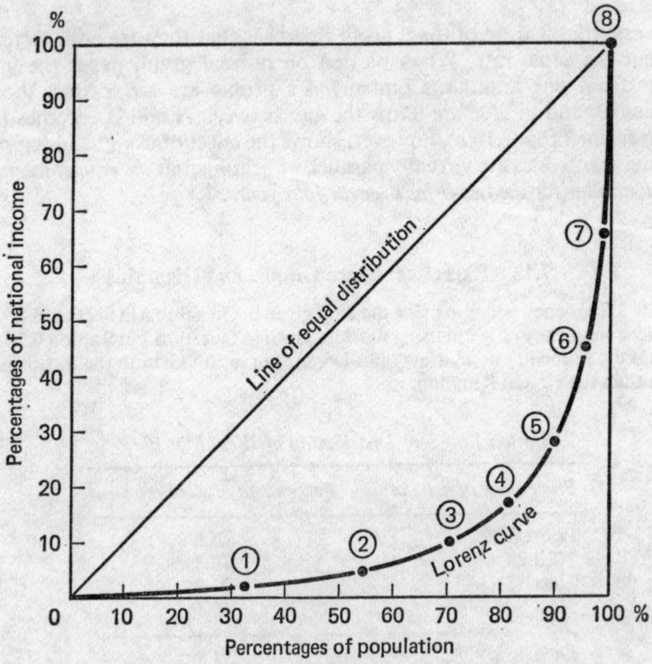

Fig. 7.9. The Lorenz curve.

Notes
A Lorenz curve is composed of two parts:
(i) The line of equal distribution, which shows a 'per cent for per cent' relationship and serves to act as a guide from which to measure the degree of non-proportionality. This per cent for per cent line will be at 45° on the graph and shows therefore the curve that would be plotted if 10 per cent of the population had 10 per cent of the income, 20 per cent had 20 per cent of the income, 30 per cent had 30 per cent of the income, etc.
(ii) The second line, by contrast, shows the true state of affairs, with the large low-income groups first. Thus we can see that the first 70 per cent of the population have only 10 per cent of the income, while the final 5 per cent of the population have 55 per cent of the income.

7.11 Semi-Logarithmic Graphs

The major characteristic of a semi-logarithmic graph is the way in which the *rate of change* takes precedence over absolute changes. The effect of this can be seen in Fig. 7.10, parts (*a*) and (*b*). Fig. 7.10(*a*) shows a graph drawn on normal graph paper. The two graphs plot the profits of two companies. These profits are shown in the table below:

	Co. A (£'000)	Co. B (£'000)
Year 1	92.1	23.9
Year 2	160.0	44.9
Year 3	226.4	67.0
Year 4	284.1	89.0
Year 5	348.7	117.9

The essential feature of these profit figures is that they are both increasing at about the same rate. When plotted on normal graph paper the graphs diverge from one another. Company A's profits are larger than those of company B, and in *absolute* terms the gap between A and B becomes larger still, over time. Fig. 7.10(*b*), however, shows the effect of using semi-log paper. Here the graph lines are virtually parallel, indicating that *the rate of increase in profit is similar for the two firms over the four years.*

7.12 Exercises: More Graphs and Diagrams

1. Draw a frequency polygon using the data given in Question 6 in Section 6.7.
2. Draw a frequency polygon using the data given in Question 7 in Section 6.7.
3. From the following table draw up a Lorenz curve to illustrate the inequalities of wealth in the United Kingdom.

United Kingdom Distribution of Wealth in 19..

Percentage of population	*Percentage of wealth owned*
Poorest 50	8.6
Next 25	18.8
Next 15	21.7
Next 5	12.1
Next 3	11.1
Next 1	5.9
Next 1	21.8

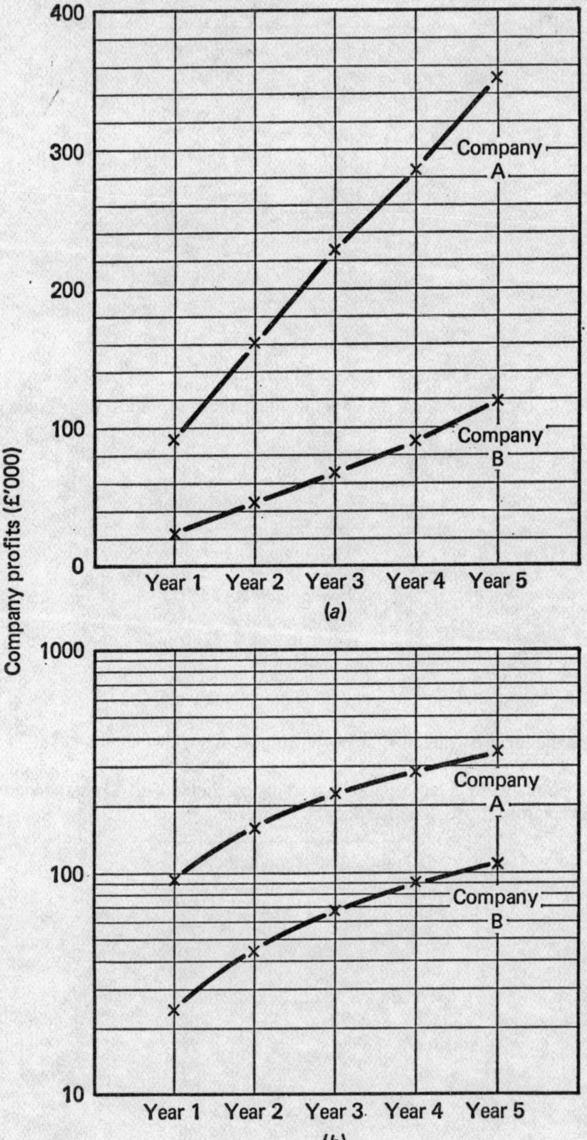

Fig. 7.10. (*a*) Profits growth—linear graph paper showing actual growth. (*b*) Profits growth—semi-log graph paper showing relative growth.

4. The following figures come from the returns of Agro Incorporated, a body which surveys developments in agriculture. They are for the year 19. .

Agricultural units	*Net output (£'000)*
46	1 300
40	2 160
36	3 500
20	2 750
24	3 000
14	4 900
21	18 600
201	36 210

Analyse the table by means of a Lorenz curve.

5. Incomes in Inegalitaria are divided amongst the population as follows in the year 19. .

Number of people (millions)	*Income enjoyed (£ millions)*
26	1 800
16	2 100
9	3 200
4	4 100
0.1	6 100
55.1	17 300

Analyse the table by means of a Lorenz curve.

6. Twelve pupils were given an assessed mark by their tutor. They then sat the end of the year examinations. The marks gained were:

Person	*Assessed*	*Exam*
1	92	85
2	70	72
3	64	70
4	62	50
5	52	62
6	47	70
7	52	77
8	69	92
9	70	62
10	61	60
11	70	47
12	62	60

Construct a scatter diagram of these data and draw the line of best fit.

7. The following is the result of a survey into family expenditures on food and clothing in Commuterville in one year:

Families	*Expenditure on food* (£)	*Expenditure on clothing* (£)
A	500	250
B	520	210
C	590	200
D	420	560
E	650	240
F	1 050	700
G	2 000	820
H	920	1 001
I	540	320
J	520	300
K	560	210
L	510	220

Construct a scatter diagram of these data and draw the line of best fit. What do your findings indicate?

8. The following figures relate to income and expenditure on alcohol of a number of salesmen in the year 19. .

	Income (£)	*Expenditure on alcohol* (£)
Mr A	720	250
Mr B	1 270	260
Mr C	2 400	127
Mr D	2 750	130
Mr E	2 900	100
Mr F	4 520	250
Mr G	6 000	227
Mr H	6 150	127
Mr J	15 000	420
Mr K	21 000	720

Construct a scatter diagram and draw the line of best fit. What conclusions does the graph suggest?

8

MEASURES OF POSITION—THE MEAN, MEDIAN AND MODE

8.1 The Reasons for Measuring Position

Any statistical enquiry results in a mass of data. While each piece of information is of interest, its relation to the whole set of data is more important. Thus, in examining electric light bulbs to see how long they last, the fact that one of them out of 3 000 went 'pop' the moment it was put into the lampholder is interesting, but is it very significant? If the other 2 999 each burnt for more than 500 hours it would seem that this particular bulb was not typical of the whole group. A particular statistic therefore may prove to be of no significance. Similarly, the orderly arrangements of data presented in Section 4.6, while they have many uses, do not summarise the statistics. A more convenient, less detailed form of presentation is sometimes required. It is important, however, that the summary should still be capable of illustrating those points for which the data were initially collected. Hence there are several methods of summarising data and the one chosen will depend upon the objectives of the enquiry.

The most common methods of summary are those which seek to relate the position of a single measurement within a group. Because these operations tend to reduce the significance of extreme values and stress the 'middle' ones, the processes are often referred to as **measures of central tendency**. In everyday life phrases like 'average attendance' or 'average score' are commonly used, and they do give a quick, clear impression of a particular situation. Thus the information that a batsman scored 1, 94, 72, 68, 13, 8, 5, 7, 149, 186, 22 and 145 runs in matches played in the first two months of the cricket season is of great interest, but rather confusing. To say that his average score over 2 months was 64.17 gives a clearer picture of his ability.

Treating data in this fashion can be extremely useful. Where comparison has to be made between different sets of figures, it is more convenient to take a single (representative) figure from each set as the basis of comparison than to utilise every figure available. For example, a comparison of wage rates amongst the four largest United Kingdom car manufacturers would be exceptionally difficult if each worker's wage was included in the presentation. Instead, for comparison, a figure representative of each plant, trade or firm is taken.

The three most commonly used measures of central tendency are:

(*a*) The arithmetic mean
(*b*) The median
(*c*) The mode

Let us consider each of these in turn.

8.2 The Arithmetic Mean

This is the average measure most commonly used in everyday life. Sometimes referred to simply as the **mean** or the **average**, it is what most people would understand when the word 'average' is mentioned. It is found by adding up the values of the variable (the scores in the cricketing example mentioned earlier) and dividing by the number of items (the innings played). A further instance is given in Example 8.1 below. It refers to the earnings of an insurance broker for the first 10 weeks of the financial year. The arithmetic mean is found by adding the set of earnings and dividing by the number in the set.

Example 8.1. Earnings of an insurance broker.

19.. Week		£
Apr.	7	120
	14	100
	21	90
	28	160
May	5	140
	17	100
	19	110
	26	130
June	2	160
	9	110
Number of weeks	10	Total 1 220

Clearly the mean earnings are £1 220 ÷ 10 = £122 per week.

Information of this sort is called 'ungrouped data' to distinguish it from information which has been sorted out into a slightly more coherent form, in groups. Had this information, for example, been sorted out into groups in which the salary earned was recorded in groups of £50 each (£0–49, none; £50–99, 1; £100–159, 7; £150–199, 2) it would have presented different problems in finding the arithmetic mean.

In Business Statistics it is usual to use the sign $\bar{x}$ to represent the arithmetic mean.

For ungrouped data a formula for the arithmetic mean would be

$$\bar{x} = \frac{\Sigma x}{n}$$

where $\bar{x}$ is the arithmetic mean, x is each of the measurements or values, n is the number of measurements or values, and Σ (sigma) means 'the sum of'.

Note: by using Σ the notation $\frac{x_1 + x_2 + x_3 + x_4}{n}$ is avoided.

Using this notation for Example 8.1 we have

$$\bar{x} = \frac{\Sigma x}{n} = \frac{£1\,220}{10} = £122$$

8.3 Exercises: Arithmetic Means of Simple Series

Using the formula given in Section 8.2 above find the arithmetic mean of the following sets of statistics:

1. Electricity consumed during the quarter in a certain factory was as follows:

Jan.	27 284 units
Feb.	35 266 units
Mar.	41 928 units

   Find the mean monthly consumption.
2. The ages of students attending an evening course, to the nearest year, are as follows: 17, 18, 18, 18, 19, 19, 22, 24, 25, 27, 27, 28, 38, 54 and 63. What is the mean age?
3. A library issues books as follows: Monday 742 books, Tuesday 1 529 books, Wednesday 2 472 books, Thursday 495 books and Friday 1 246 books. Only 237 books were issued on Saturday. What is the mean issue per working day? (Answer correct to one decimal place.)
4. Five mills produce the following outputs of cloth in a particular week: 72 856 metres; 49 263 metres; 17 256 metres; 29 254 metres and 86 276 metres. What is the mean output?
5. An experimental crop of wheat from seven plots of land produces the following outputs:

(*a*) 224 kg	(*e*) 495 kg
(*b*) 330 kg	(*f*) 532 kg
(*c*) 75 kg	(*g*) 184 kg
(*d*) 176 kg	

   What was the mean output?

8.4 The Arithmetic Mean from a Frequency Distribution

In a simple series the individual items may occur only once, and the frequency is therefore one. In a mass production world many business statistics involve frequencies greater than one. Thus a garage might sell seven 'Apollo' cars, 15 'Hermes' traveller models and 23 'St Christopher' touring vehicles. With such a frequency distribution the arithmetic mean must take into account not only the value of an item, but also the number of times that item occurs.

The formula must now become

$$\bar{x} = \frac{\Sigma fx}{n}$$

where $\bar{x}$ is the arithmetic mean, x the values of the individual items, f the number of cases of each value, n the total number of item, i.e. the sum of the frequencies, and Σ 'the sum of'. This is illustrated in Example 8.2.

Example 8.2. What is the mean value of the policies sold by the XYZ agency, whose sales are given in the frequency distribution below (answer to nearest penny)?

Value of policy (£)	*Number of policies sold*	*Product* ($f \times x$)
10	165	1 650
20	290	5 800
30	105	3 150
40	92	3 680
	$n = 652$	$\Sigma fx = 14\ 280$

$$\bar{x} = \frac{\Sigma fx}{n}$$

$$= \frac{£14\,280}{652}$$

$$= £21.90$$

8.5 Exercises: The Arithmetic Mean from a Frequency Distribution

1. A fish farm has 120 ponds. Find the mean surface area of the ponds from the following frequency distribution (answer correct to one decimal place).

Surface area (square metres)	*Number of ponds*
65	25
70	40
75	28
80	14
85	13

2. The following table illustrates the annual bonus to be paid by a firm to a number of its employees. What is the mean value of the bonus paid?

Bonus £	*Number of Employees*
900	7
800	15
600	8

3. The weight of timber taken from 43 trees is as shown below. Arrange the information in a frequency distribution and calculate the mean weight of timber (answer to the nearest kg).

Weight of Timber (kg)

1 000	1 200	1 000	1 100	1 400	1 300
1 200	1 000	1 000	1 100	1 100	1 000
1 100	1 200	1 100	1 400	1 300	1 100
1 200	1 300	1 400	1 500	1 000	1 400
1 400	1 100	1 200	1 300	1 400	1 200
1 300	1 200	1 400	1 300	1 100	1 100
1 200	1 300	1 200	1 200	1 100	1 200
1 100	1 200	1 200	1 300	1 300	1 000

4. Below are listed the sums taken at a box office for tickets sold one morning. From the information draw up a frequency distribution and from it find the mean price per ticket sold (correct to the nearest penny).

£1.60	£2.50	£2.50	£3.50
£2.50	£1.60	£3.50	£3.50
£3.50	£2.50	£1.60	£1.00
£5.00	£5.00	£3.50	£3.50
£1.60	£3.50	£3.50	£2.50

8.6 The Arithmetic Mean from Grouped Data

Where data have been grouped, so that data of similar value are put together, the absolute accuracy which is available when every value is known is naturally lost. Thus, if 27 second-hand cars are sold in the £350–400 range we cannot know precisely what the sale price of each car was. It is then necessary to take an assumed value for the group and the mid-point of the group is the most obvious point to choose. The assumption then is that all the items within each group when taken together will have a mean value represented by this mid-point. This method must necessarily be inaccurate but it is nevertheless convenient. Example 8.3 shows how the arithmetic mean is derived from grouped data. The formula is still

$$\bar{x} = \frac{\Sigma fx}{n}$$

where $\bar{x}$ is the arithmetic mean, f the number of cases within the class interval, x the mid-point of each class, n the total number of items, i.e. the sum of the frequencies, and Σ 'the sum of'.

Example 8.3. Earnings of insurance brokers, week ending 30th June, 19..:

Number of brokers (f)	*Class division* (£)	*Mid-points* (x)	*Product* ($f \times x$)
3	50– 59.995	£55	165
7	60– 69.995	£65	455
14	70– 79.995	£75	1 050
18	80– 89.995	£85	1 530
3	90– 99.995	£95	285
1	100–109.995	£105	105
$n = 46$			$\Sigma fx = 3\,590$

$$\bar{x} = \frac{\Sigma fx}{n} = \frac{£3\,590}{46} = £78.04$$

8.7 Exercises: The Arithmetic Mean from Grouped Data

1. The sales achieved by a team of representatives were as shown below. Calculate the mean sales from the data. (Answer to the nearest £100.)

Sales (£'000)	*Number of representatives*
Under 10	4
10 and under 20	12
20 and under 30	15
30 and under 40	18
40 and under 50	14
50 and under 60	3

2. The sales achieved by a team of representatives were as shown below. Calculate the mean sales from the data. (Answer to nearest £100.)

Sales (£'000)	*Number of representatives*
Under 10	8
10 and under 20	12
20 and under 30	10
30 and under 40	8
40 and under 50	6
50 and under 60	4

3. The hourly earnings of male full-time employees in a certain industry are given in the table below. Calculate the mean earnings (to nearest penny).

Hourly earnings (pence)	*Number of employees*
80 but under 90	12
90 but under 100	56
100 but under 110	84
110 but under 120	90
120 but under 130	112
130 but under 140	46
140 but under 150	40

4. The hourly earnings of male full-time employees in a certain industry are given in the table below. Calculate the mean earnings (to nearest penny).

Hourly earnings (pence)	*Number of employees*
80 but under 100	42
100 but under 120	65
120 but under 140	71
140 but under 160	37
160 but under 180	27
180 but under 200	15

8.8 The Arithmetic Mean, Calculated from an Assumed Mean

The methods of finding the arithmetic mean described above are quite satisfactory, but when the values and numbers involved are very large the calculations become tedious, and it is helpful if the figures actually being processed can be made simpler. This is the advantage of calculating from an 'assumed mean'. Usually it is possible to see, from even quite involved sets of figures, roughly where the arithmetic mean will be. If we then take this figure as the 'assumed mean' we have only to find how far away from the 'assumed mean' the 'true mean' is. A simple example will demonstrate the method.

Example 8.4. Find the arithmetic mean of 17, 25 and 36. From a quick inspection of these figures we can see that the average is somewhere above 25. Let us guess 27. This is now the 'assumed mean'.

If we now compare the original numbers with the assumed mean, we find in relation to it, as follows:

$$17 = -10$$
$$25 = -2$$
$$36 = +9$$

These differences add up to -3 ($-12 + 9$).

Dividing by the number of numbers (which is 3), we find that our true mean is -1 from the assumed mean.

$$\therefore \text{ True mean is } 26$$

$$\left(\text{Check: } \frac{17 + 25 + 36}{3} = \frac{78}{3} = 26\right)$$

Let us repeat the method with a more difficult example.

Example 8.5. Earnings of insurance brokers, week ending 30 June, 19. . :

Numbers of brokers (f)	*Class* (£)	*Mid-points*	*Deviation from assumed mean* (*in class intervals*) (d)	*Product* ($f \times d$)
3	50– 59.995	55	−3	−9
7	60– 69.995	65	−2	−14
14	70– 79.995	75	−1	−14
18	80– 89.995	85	0	0
3	90– 99.995	95	+1	+3
1	100–109.995	105	+2	+2
$n = 46$				$\Sigma fd = -32$

Notes

(i) The 'assumed mean' has been taken as 85. Any point may be taken, but the mid-point of a fairly central group is the most sensible, especially if f is large in that group. (In this example $f = 18$.)

(ii) The sum of the deviations from the 'assumed mean' is -32 class intervals. As the class interval is £10, this means the total deviation is $-32 \times 10 = £-320$.

(iii) Dividing by the number of brokers ($n = 46$) we find that the true mean

$$= £-\frac{320}{46} \text{ from the 'assumed mean'.}$$
$$= £-6.96 \text{ from } £85$$
$$= £78.04$$

(iv) Clearly the figures generated using this method are much smaller than those using the other methods, and therefore are more easily handled.

The formula using this short-cut method is

$$\bar{x} = X_0 + \frac{\Sigma fd \times i}{n}$$

where X_0 is the assumed mean (which is the mid-point of the group where the assumed mean is given the value of 0 class intervals), f the number of cases within a group, d the deviation from the assumed mean in class intervals, i the size of the class interval which is normal for the table (see below for abnormal class intervals), n the total number of cases (i.e. the sum of the frequencies), and Σ 'the sum of'.

Difficulties Where the Class Intervals are not Uniform

The table used in Example 8.5 had class intervals which were consistent throughout. However, it is possible for the class intervals in a table to vary. Where this occurs the procedure is to select a 'standard class interval' for the table. In Example 8.6 this 'standard class interval' is 10: a reflection of the majority of intervals. The method is to express any deviation from this in terms of multiples by such a 'standard'.

This approach is shown in Example 8.6. Before we look at this example a further problem must be briefly referred to.

Open-ended Distributions

Sometimes the last interval of a group distribution is open-ended—for example, '100 and over'. This suggests that some items occurred which were well beyond 100. Clearly it is impossible to deal with such an interval unless we make an assumption as to its size. One popular assumption is that this final interval is the same size as the other intervals. A more cautious assumption (and therefore probably better) is to regard this last class interval as twice as big as the other intervals that precede it. Whichever is chosen, the final result can only be approximate, for we can never know the true mean without knowing every item.

Example 8.6. Earnings of insurance brokers, week ending 30 June, 19. . :

Number of brokers (f)	*Class* (£)	*Mid-points*	*Deviations from assumed mean (in standard class intervals)*	*Product* ($f \times d$)
3	50–59.995	55	−3	−9
7	60–69.995	65	−2	−14
14	70–79.995	75	−1	−14
18	80–89.995	85	0	0
4	90–109.995	100	$+1\frac{1}{2}$	+6
$n = 46$				Σfd −31

Once the deviations from the assumed mean have been calculated the working is exactly the same as in Example 8.5. Hence

$$\begin{aligned}\bar{x} &= X + \frac{\Sigma fd \times i}{n}\\ &= 85 + \left(\frac{-31 \times 10}{46}\right)\\ &= 85 + (-6.74)\\ &= 85 - 6.74\\ &= \underline{\underline{£78.26}}\end{aligned}$$

Note. Because of the slight rearrangement of the data to include one non-standard class, the result of the calculations is marginally different from that in Example 8.5. This serves to illustrate the slight inaccuracy of the method. For most practical purposes this inaccuracy is insignificant.

8.9 Exercises: The Arithmetic Mean from an Assumed Mean

1. From the data given below calculate, using the 'assumed mean' method, the mean mortgage granted to members by the XYZ Building Society in 19.. (answer to nearest £100).

Mortgages granted (£)	*Number of members*
£5 000 and under £7 500	381
£7 500 and under £10 000	275
£10 000 and under £12 500	162
£12 500 and under £15 000	35

2. The following table gives the length in centimetres of a number of steel rods. Calculate the mean length of rod, using the 'assumed mean' method.

Length in centimetres	*Number of rods*
20–29.99	4
30–39.99	16
40–49.99	31
50–59.99	64
60–69.99	40
70–79.99	25
80–89.99	15
90–99.99	5

3. Find the arithmetic mean of the information in the table below, which relates to the distances travelled daily by trains in an imaginary region. Use the 'assumed mean' method and give the answer correct to one decimal place.

km	*Frequency*
400 and under 420	13
420 and under 440	27
440 and under 460	34
460 and under 480	24
480 and under 500	15
500 and under 520	8

4. The following table shows the earnings of a group of machinists. Compute the mean earnings, using the 'assumed mean' method, correct to the nearest penny.

Weekly earnings (£)	*Number of employees*
0 and under 10	20
10 and under 20	30
20 and under 30	50
30 and under 40	20
40 and under 60	10

5. The following table shows the length in centimetres of a number of copper pipes used in the construction of a housing estate. Using the 'assumed mean' method, calculate the mean length in centimetres correct to one decimal place.

Length (cm)	*Number of pipes*
Under 30	10
30 and under 60	26
60 and under 90	26
90 and under 120	16
120 and under 150	9
150 and under 180	6
180 and under 240	10

8.10 The Weighted Arithmetic Mean

In some enquiries certain statistics may be relatively more important than others, and are said to carry more 'weight'. Thus if the average householder always buys bread, and only very rarely buys caviare, an enquiry into household expenditure would give more 'weight' to purchases of bread.

It is sometimes necessary to calculate a 'weighted' arithmetic mean where the frequencies, considered in 8.4 above, are replaced by weights. These weights are intended to reflect the relative importance of the various items in the data—the larger the weight (in a given series of weights) the greater the significance of the item bearing it. In the Index of Retail Prices, published in the *Monthly Digest of Statistics*, the total weighting given to all items is 1 000. The subgroup meat and bacon is given a weighting of 63, while fish has a weighting of 8.

When finding 'weighted arithmetic means' the formula used is very similar to that used to find the mean of a frequency distribution, except that the letter w (weight) is substituted for f (frequency)

$$\text{Weighted mean} = \frac{\Sigma wx}{\Sigma w}$$

Note. The total of wx is divided by the sum of the weights—it is important to remember this.

Example 8.7 shows how the formula is used.

Example 8.7. A student's work for a certain course is graded as follows: final examination 62%; homework 70%; classwork 66%. If the weights given each grade are 7, 2 and 1 respectively, calculate the student's weighted grade.

Score % (x)	*Weight (w)*	*wx*
62	7	434
70	2	140
66	1	66
	$\Sigma w = 10$	Σwx 640

$$\text{Weighted mean} = \frac{640}{10} = 64\%$$

Weighted arithmetic means are perhaps met most often in the form of index numbers. Chapter 9 deals with these and shows how the weighted mean is put to use.

8.11 Exercises: Weighted Arithmetic Means

1. In an educational course a weighting of 3 is given to the final examination, a weighting of 2 is given to course work and a weighting of 1 to homework. Calculate the mean score of the following individuals (correct to one decimal place):

   A. Brown, whose final examination total is 54%, whose course work was awarded 84% and whose homework award is 92%;
   C. Dark, whose final examination total is 44%, whose course work was awarded 81% and whose homework award is 68%.

2. In an educational course a weighting of 5 is given to the final examination, a weighting of 3 is given to course work and a weighting of 2 to homework. Work out the mean score of the following individuals:

   M. Lark, whose final examination total is 46%, whose course work was awarded 67% and whose homework award is 58%;
   T. Sparrow, whose final examination total is 64%, whose course work was awarded 94%, and whose homework award is 86%.

3. In a motorcycle three-day event the weighting is as follows:

Care and presentation of machine	4
Reliability in cross-country performance	3
Speed tests	5
Knowledge of road safety	3

   Two competitors scored as follows:

	Mr Y (%)	*Mr Z* (%)
Care and presentation of machine	76	85
Cross-country performance	54	65
Speed tests	84	71
Knowledge of road safety	42	90

   Calculate their weighted mean scores (correct to one decimal place) and hence show which was the better competitor.

4. At a county agricultural show weighting in the animal judging was as follows:

Condition of the animal	3
Special breed characteristics	2
Weight	2

   Each aspect was judged out of 100. The three best in show scored as follows:

	A	*B*	*C*
Condition	84	82	79
Breed characteristics	70	85	90
Weight	78	84	81

   Calculate their weighted mean scores (correct to one decimal place) and hence determine which animal was 'Best in Show'.

8.12 The Median

The median is defined as the value of the middle item of a distribution, when the items are arranged in ascending order of size.

For ungrouped data the method of calculation of the median is very simple. The process is:

(*i*) Arrange the data in order of size, i.e. so that they run from the smallest to the largest. Such an arrangement is called an **array.**

(ii) Find the middle item. The formula for finding the middle item is

$$\frac{n+1}{2}$$

where n is the number of items. Hence where there are seven items

$$\frac{n+1}{2}=\frac{7+1}{2}=4$$

The fourth item would give us the median value. We know this to be the case since in an array of seven there are three items on either side of the fourth one—it is therefore in the middle.

Where the number of items is even it is not possible to isolate an actual item which is the middle one. Thus where there are eight items in an array

$$\frac{n+1}{2}=\frac{8+1}{2}=4\tfrac{1}{2}$$

The middle item is now the $4\frac{1}{2}$th item and it is necessary to find the average of the fourth and fifth items to find the median value.

(iii) Find the value of the middle item.

Note. Statisticians sometimes refer to the 'median' item. Strictly speaking this is not correct. The median is, by definition, the value of the middle item in an array. In an array with an odd number of items the median value will coincide with the middle item in the array. In an array with an even number of items it will be the average of the two middle items. The danger is that a student may say that in an array of 27 numbers, 14 is the median. It is of course the *value* of the fourteenth number in that array that is the median.

Example 8.8. The salaries of seven bank employees (per month) are £178, £220, £230, £150, £280, £275, £270. Find the median salary.

(i) Arrange data in order of value:

1	2	3	4	5	6	7
£150	178	220	230	270	275	280

(ii) Find the middle item. With seven items this is the fourth, $\frac{n+1}{2}$.

(iii) Find the median value. Value of fourth item is £230

$\therefore$ median value = £230

If an extra salary of £290 were added there would be no single median item. It would then be necessary to find the average value of items 4 and 5.

Example 8.9. The monthly salaries of *eight* bank employees are given as £178, £220, £230, £150, £280, £275, £270, £290; find the median salary.

(i) Arrange the data in order of size:

1	2	3	4	5	6	7	8
£150	178	220	230	270	275	280	290

(ii) Find the middle item

$$\frac{n+1}{2} = \frac{9}{2} = 4\tfrac{1}{2}$$

There is no single item: 4 and 5 are 'in the middle'.

(iii) The median value will be the average of these items

$$= \frac{£230 + 270}{2}$$

$$= \frac{£500}{2}$$

$$= £250$$

8.13 Exercises: The Median

1. Calculate the median life of an electric light bulb based on the following nine examples: (*a*) 236 hours, (*b*) 11 hours, (*c*) 248 hours, (*d*) 25 hours, (*e*) 1 294 hours, (*f*) 728 hours, (*g*) 5 hours, (*h*) 1 hour, (*i*) 483 hours.
2. Farmer Brown's hens laid as follows in one year: Lucy 236 eggs; Speckly 426 eggs; Mary 156 eggs; Crooked Leg 184 eggs; Dainty 156 eggs; Brownie 84 eggs; Polynesia 203 eggs; Margaret 225 eggs. Calculate the median output.
3. The orders received from the representatives of Cosmetics Ltd are as follows for the month of July:

	£		£
Mr A	8 540	Mr F	15 230
Mr B	12 720	Miss G	27 460
Mr C	16 230	Mr H	14 250
Mrs D	18 710	Mrs Y	1 850
Miss E	5 950		

Calculate the median value.

4. The orders received from the representatives of Icepack Ltd are as follows for the month of June:

	£		£
Mr A	18 540	Mr F	8 417
Mr B	12 760	Miss G	19 325
Mr C	29 250	Mr H	28 612
Mrs D	13 286	Mrs Y	14 713
Miss E	48 716	Mrs J	8 450

Calculate the median value.

8.14 Calculating the Median from Grouped Data

When dealing with a grouped frequency distribution, finding the median value is slightly more complicated, since the value of the median item may not be known. We do not know the individual values of each occurrence within a group.

It is therefore necessary to make an assumption and then calculate the median value. The assumption is that the items in a group are evenly spread throughout the group—though in fact we cannot be sure of this. They might all be bunched at the lower end, or bunched at the upper end of the group. Having made this assumption we can then tell, if we build up a cumulative frequency table as shown in Example 8.10, which group the median item is in, and how far up the group it is.

Example 8.10. Find the median salary of bank employees from the information given in the following table:

Earnings (£)	*Number of employees*	*Cumulative frequency*
150 and under 170	13	13
170 and under 190	45	58
190 and under 210	209	267
210 and under 230	101	368
230 and under 250	78	446
250 and under 270	42	488
270 and under 290	12	500

With grouped data, for fairly complex reasons, we must use the formula $\frac{n}{2}$ for the median, instead of $\frac{n+1}{2}$. The explanation is that in assuming that the items are evenly spread within the group, with one item in each subdivision, the formula $\frac{n+1}{2}$ finds the upper end of the subdivisions, not the middle of them. We must therefore go back half an interval and use $\frac{n}{2}$, not $\frac{n+1}{2}$. This explanation need not concern the student unduly, but he should use the formula $\frac{n}{2}$ for the median of grouped data. This makes the median item the 250th item.

The median item is clearly located in the £190–210 class interval. In order to find the median item it is necessary to take 192 cases from within the £190–210 class (which when added to the preceding 58, makes 250). Using this information we have:

$$\text{Median} = £190 + \left(\frac{192}{209} \times £20\right)$$

where (*a*) £190 is the bottom of the class interval in which the median is located; (*b*) £20 is the size of the class interval; (*c*) $\frac{192}{209}$ represents the median item—the 192nd item in the £190–210 class. Therefore

$$\begin{aligned}\text{Median item} &= £190 + (0.9186 \times £20)\\ &= £190 + £18.37\\ &= £208.37\end{aligned}$$

Note. The reader should recognise that the result is only an approximation of the true median—an approximation which reflects the assumption we have made about the distribution of the items within the class interval where the median is known to lie.

8.15 Exercises: Medians from Grouped Data

1. From the grouped frequency data given below calculate the median price of cattle for the day.

Prices of cattle at Country Market July 14

Prices (£)	*Number of bargains struck*	*Cumulative frequency*
25–49.99	13	13
50–74.99	38	51
75–99.99	79	130
100–124.99	44	174

2. From the grouped frequency data given below calculate the cumulative frequency and hence the median price of cattle for the day.

Prices of cattle at Country Market July 21

Prices (£)	*Number of bargains struck*	*Cumulative frequency*
25–49.99	9	
50–74.99	59	
75–99.99	168	
100–124.99	34	

3. From the grouped frequency data given below calculate the median passenger load carried on aircraft leaving Cosmo Airport in August:

Passengers carried in August

Groups of passengers	*Number of aircraft*	*Cumulative frequency*
150–199	27	27
200–249	41	68
250–299	56	124
300–349	184	308
350–399	194	502
400–449	127	629
450–499	13	642

4. From the grouped frequency data given below calculate the cumulative frequency and the median cost of operations:

Cost of Operations—County Health Service

Cost per operation (£)	*Number of operations*	*Cumulative frequency*
0–29.99	2 728	
30–59.99	3 856	
60–89.99	4 250	
90–119.99	1 247	
120–149.99	349	
150–179.99	217	
More than 180	584	

8.16 Calculating the Median from a Cumulative Frequency Curve (Ogive)

A relatively simple method of finding the median from a grouped frequency distribution is by the construction of a cumulative frequency curve or **ogive.** This presents the information of the frequency distribution graphically and enables the approximate median value to be 'read off'. This is demonstrated in Example 8.11.

Example 8.11. From the table of bank salaries given below find the median salary.

Monthly Earnings of Bank Employees

Earnings (£)	*Number of employees*	*Cumulative frequency*
150 and under 170	13	13
170 and under 190	45	58
190 and under 210	210	268
210 and under 230	100	368
230 and under 250	78	446
250 and under 270	42	488
270 and under 290	12	500

Procedure

(i) Graph the cumulative frequencies on a cumulative frequency curve (ogive), as in Fig. 8.1.

(ii) Find the median item on the vertical axis. Draw a horizontal line from this item to cut the frequency ogive (Line A).

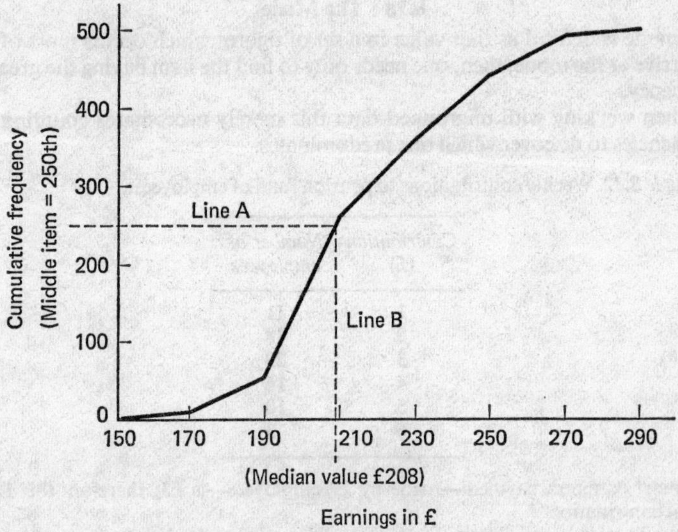

Fig. 8.1. A cumulative frequency ogive.

(iii) Draw a vertical line from the point of intersection of line A and the ogive curve, to the horizontal axis (Line B).

(iv) Read off the value where line B cuts the horizontal axis. This is the median value.

Quartiles, Deciles and Percentiles

Besides reading off the median from a cumulative frequency curve it is possible to read off other measures of position. For example, the **quartiles** divide the series into four parts, and may be read off in Fig. 8.1 from the 125th item (lower quartile or Q_1) and the 375th item (upper quartile or Q_3). The formula for the lower quartile is $\frac{n}{4}$ and for the upper quartile is $\frac{3n}{4}$.

Similarly, the **deciles** (Latin *decem* = 10) divide the series into 10 equal parts and the **percentiles** into 100 equal parts. The formula for any particular decile or percentile is similar to the formula for quartiles. For example, the fourth decile is found by $\frac{4n}{10}$ and the 63rd percentile by $\frac{63n}{100}$.

8.17 Exercises: Calculating the Median from Ogives

1. Use the data given in Exercise 8.15 (No. 1) to draw an ogive and calculate the median price of cattle for the day.
2. Use the data given in Exercise 8.15 (No. 2) to draw an ogive and hence calculate the median price of cattle for the day.
3. Use the data given in Exercise 8.15 (No. 3) to draw an ogive and hence calculate the median passenger load.
4. Use the data given in Exercise 8.15 (No. 4) to draw an ogive and hence calculate the median cost of operations in the County Health Service.

8.18 The Mode

The mode is defined as that value in a set of figures which occurs most often. To arrive at the mode, then, one needs only to find the item having the greatest frequency.

When working with ungrouped data this merely necessitates counting the frequencies to discover which one predominates.

Example 8.12. Weekly contributions to pension fund of employees:

Contribution (£)	*Number of employees*
1	11
2	18
3	29
4	16
5	10
6	3

The most common payment—made by 29 employees—is £3; therefore this is the modal contribution.

Sometimes it is possible to have bi-modal statistics. Had there been 29 people paying £5 per week it would have been a bi-modal series.

Where data are presented in the form of a grouped frequency distribution, the mode can be taken as the mid-point of the class interval with maximum frequency. However, because it is likely that the occurrences within a class interval will not be evenly distributed, finding the mid-point alone will tend towards inaccuracy. In many sets of grouped statistics, for example, the group which occurs most frequently (the modal group) may have below it a group which also has a large number of items, whereas the group above it may have only a few. In such circumstances the mid-point of the modal group would probably be an unsatisfactory mode to pick, for the chances are that there are more items below it than above it, judging from the groups on either side.

To overcome this difficulty two methods can be adopted to find the mode:

(*a*) Calculation
(*b*) Use of a histogram

Since both these methods can give the same result and since the second is much easier to undertake, this is the one demonstrated in Example 8.13 below.

Example 8.13. The earnings of 180 bank employees are as follows. Find the modal salary.

Earnings (£)	*Number of employees*
1 800 and under 2 400	10
2 400 and under 3 000	25
3 000 and under 3 600	40
3 600 and under 4 200	55
4 200 and under 4 800	30
4 800 and under 5 400	20

Method

1. Construct a histogram—as in Fig. 8.2.
2. Find the modal class—this is represented by the tallest rectangle.
3. Join the top left-hand corner of the modal rectangle to the top left-hand corner of the adjacent rectangle as shown, and similarly with the top right-hand corner to the top right-hand corner of the adjacent rectangle, as shown. These lines will intersect.
4. The mode occurs at the intersection.

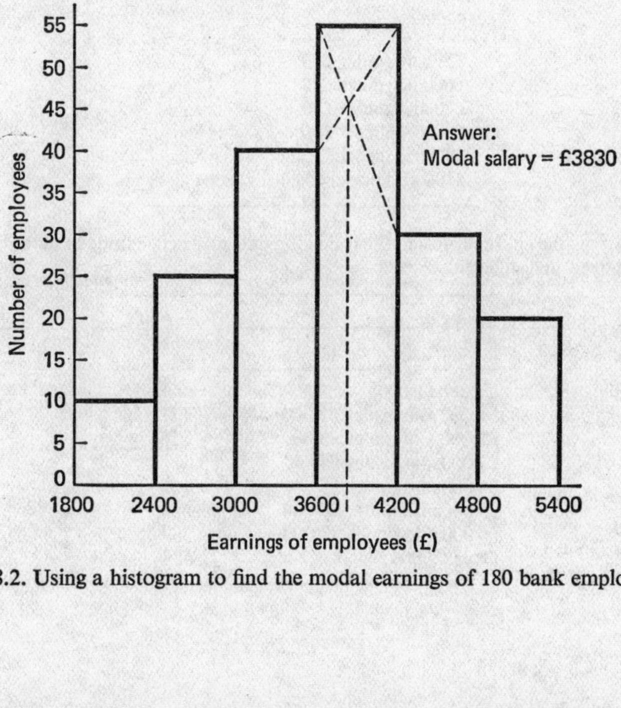

Fig. 8.2. Using a histogram to find the modal earnings of 180 bank employees.

This method clearly demonstrates that the distribution of items within the modal class will probably not be centrally located within that class. Rather there will be a tendency for the maximum distribution of items within the modal class to appear towards the boundary of the adjacent class with more frequencies.

8.19 Exercises: The Mode

1. In the following cricket scores which is the modal score for each batsman?

   Batsman A: 27, 0, 14, 162, 27, 5, 27, 16, 27
   Batsman B: 5, 15, 38, 5, 72, 91, 106, 4, 3, 0, 5
   Batsman C: 27, 14, 36, 7, 21, 9, 19, 36

2. In the following lists of bowling performance which is the modal performance for each bowler?

   Bowler A: Wickets taken 4, 3, 1, 4, 4, 5, 3, 1, 2, 4, 5
   Bowler B: Wickets taken 2, 2, 2, 0, 1, 7, 3, 2, 2, 1, 5
   Bowler C: Wickets taken 5, 1, 4, 7, 1, 1, 3, 2, 3, 3, 4

3. Houses in Newtown have the following number of bedrooms. Which is the modal-sized house?

Number of Rooms	1	2	3	4	5	6
Frequencies	27	272	1 954	825	430	36

4. Draw a histogram to represent the following data and hence find the modal payment:

Commission paid to travellers, January	*Number of salesmen*
£50 and under £60	8
£60 and under £70	13
£70 and under £80	14
£80 and under £90	16
£90 and under £100	5
£100 and under £120	4

5. Draw a histogram to represent the following data and hence find the modal income in the town investigated:

Range of incomes	*Number of families*
Under £1 000	5
£1 000 and under £2 000	127
£2 000 and under £3 000	856
£3 000 and under £4 000	2 327
£4 000 and under £5 000	459
£5 000 and under £6 000	449
£6 000 and under £7 000	389
Over £7 000	484

8.20 Comparison of the Averages

The **arithmetic mean** is the main average used because it is readily understood, fairly easy to calculate, takes into account all the data, and is capable of algebraic manipulation. However, there are certain sets of data for which the arithmetic mean does not fulfil its function of adequate representation. Consider the following illustrations.

(i) Imagine there is an enquiry into the average age of students at a college, classified according to whether they are day-release or evening. The following results might occur: arithmetic average age of day-release students 20 years; arithmetic average age of evening-class students, 20 years. Obviously the mean age is identical but the day-release average may have been computed from a class of 150 students each one aged 20 years, and the evening-class average from a class of 100 students of which 90 were each aged 17 years and 10 each aged 47 years. Clearly, the mean age of 20 is not representative of the evening class but is representative of the day-release group. Therefore if data contain extreme items, the arithmetic mean will tend to distort and incorrectly describe the situation.

(ii) The arithmetic average number of children per household might easily be calculated at 2.2 for Great Britain. Many students might find such a figure unrealistic, since obviously no family actually *has* 2.2 children. The mean number of legs per dog in the United Kingdom may be approximately 3.9, but this conjures up a strange picture of a dog. Clearly the mode conveys the best impression of a dog, and in that enquiry would be the best average to choose.

In the two cases above, to a greater or less extent, the arithmetic mean would appear to be unsatisfactory as a means of description and the **median** would probably be a better choice since:

(i) In the case of data with extreme items the median will not be affected by them and will possibly be more representative. Returning to our two classes of students, the median ages would be 20 for the day-release group and 17 for the evening group—a more accurate picture of the situation.

(ii) The median number of children per household in Great Britain is 2, which is a more realistic indication of the average family than 2.2.

Unfortunately, one of the characteristics of the median which is particularly useful in some circumstances, that of concentrating on the middle item, is a disadvantage in the majority of cases, because, in the main, all data relevant to the problem should be taken into account. Also the median is unsuitable for further mathematical calculation.

The **mode** is of limited use, because although it has some of the advantages and all of the disadvantages associated with the median, there is, in addition, the difficulty of distributions which have no mode or two modes (bi-modal). For example, the data 2, 3, 8, 9, 12 and 13 have no mode; the data 2, 3, 3, 3, 5, 7, 8, 8, 8, 9 and 10 have two modes, 3 and 8.

In summary, it is a good rule-of-thumb guide to use the arithmetic mean in all those cases where it adequately represents the data. Where this is not the case, the median is usually the best alternative.

8.21 Exercises: Comparison of Averages

1. One hundred farmers, taken at random, were asked to submit figures relating to yields of wheat from one hectare on their farms. The results were as follows:

Yield (tonnes)	*Number of plots (each hectare)*
10 and under 12	8
8 and under 10	6
6 and under 8	12
4 and under 6	23
2 and under 4	20
Under 2	31

Calculate the arithmetic mean of the yields (correct to one decimal place). Is the arithmetic mean the best average to use for this distribution of figures? Give reasons for your conclusion.

2. Give a definition of (*a*) the arithmetic mean, (*b*) the median, (*c*) the mode.

Using the following as the basis of a frequency distribution, illustrate the answers given to (*a*), (*b*) and (*c*) above: 11, 16, 4, 7, 6, 13, 2, 5, 8, 10, 6.

3. The following table gives the numbers of those who die as a result of physical attacks in a large city, in a 12-month period, classified by age.

Age	*Number*
Under 1	28
1 but under 5	18
5 but under 10	13
10 but under 20	22
20 but under 35	59
35 but under 50	46
50 but under 70	35
70 but under 85	10

(*a*) Show these figures in the form of a histogram. (*b*) Calculate the mean age at death (correct to the nearest year). (*c*) Are there any other appropriate measures of central tendency? Give reasons for your conclusions.

4. The following data relate to the weekly earnings of 30 insurance brokers:

Earnings (£)	*Number of brokers*
75 and under 85	15
85 and under 95	25
95 and under 105	40
105 and under 115	108
115 and under 125	92
Over 125	20

(*a*) Compute the mean and median earnings of the brokers (correct to one decimal place). (*b*) Which average do you consider to be the most appropriate to represent the data? Give your reasons.

9

INDEX NUMBERS

9.1 What are Index Numbers?

The previous chapter has been concerned with arranging a collection of data in such a way that it becomes easier to interpret. It is suggested there that an array can be cumbersome. A single average figure often conveys the essence of the contents of the array quickly, and in a form which makes possible a comparison with other sets of figures.

Index numbers are, in a sense, a continuation of the process of rendering large masses of figures intelligible In this process they play a special role:

(*a*) They allow the expression of different standards of measures in one figure.

(*b*) They make possible the comparison of information over time.

As an example of (*a*) an index number might reduce to a single statistic the price of a basketful of goods which includes a kilogram of potatoes, 16 litres of petrol, a dozen eggs, 5 metres of curtain material and similar items which do not 'mix' in the ordinary way. As an example of (*b*) we may quote the example of a basketful of goods already referred to, priced on a given date in each year over the period of the enquiry. What did they cost in Year 1, Year 2, etc.?

An index number may be defined as a statistic which indicates the level of prices, wages, outputs and other variables at given dates, relative to their level at an earlier date which is taken as a base or standard.

Before considering index numbers in more detail it is first necessary to explain the special role of the base, and to outline some symbols peculiar to index numbers.

The Base

Since index numbers compare information over a period of time it is usual for one of the points in time to be taken and used as a base. For example, if the price of copper is to be compared in three years (Year 1, Year 2 and Year 3), the price in Year 1 may be assigned the notional value of 100. Then if the price increases by say, 10 per cent from Year 1 to Year 2 and 20 per cent from Year 1 to Year 3, the Year 2 index will be 110 and the Year 3 index 120 (both being based upon the index of 100 for Year 1).

Because most people are familiar with percentages and can easily understand changes in terms of parts of 100, it is almost universal for index numbers to have a base of 100.

Symbols Used in Calculating Index Numbers

The following symbols are used in calculations relating to index numbers:

w = weight (the emphasis or importance given to an item)
q = quantity of individual commodities or items

q_0 = quantity of individual commodities or items in the base year
$q_{1, 2, 3,}$ etc. = as above, but in subsequent years.
p = price of individual commodities or items
p_0 = price of individual commodities or items in the base year
$p_{1, 2, 3,}$ etc. = as above but in subsequent years.

Let us consider the simplest type of index number or price relative.

9.2 A Simple Index or Price Relative

If on the 1st April petrol costs 80p per gallon and on 1st June the same year 88p per gallon this represents a rise in price of 10 per cent. By terming 1st April the base, 100, then the price on 1st June is 110. We have here the basis of a simple index. This is often referred to as a **price relative**, since it shows how the *price* in a *one-item* index changes over time, relative to its price at a base date.

The formula for a simple price index (price relative) is

$$\frac{p_1}{p_0} \times 100$$

Use of this is demonstrated in Example 9.1 below.

Example 9.1. Taking Year 3 as base year, calculate a petrol price index for Years 1–11 inclusive:

The Price of Petrol

Year	*Price*	*Calculation* $\left(\frac{p_1}{p_0} \times \frac{100}{1}\right)$	*Price Index*
Year 1	25	$\frac{25}{33} \times 100$	76
Year 2	30	$\frac{30}{33} \times 100$	91
Year 3	33	$\frac{33}{33} \times 100$	100
Year 4	36	$\frac{36}{33} \times 100$	109
Year 5	38	$\frac{38}{33} \times 100$	115
Year 6	40	$\frac{40}{33} \times 100$	121
Year 7	80	$\frac{80}{33} \times 100$	242
Year 8	90	$\frac{90}{33} \times 100$	273
Year 9	85	$\frac{85}{33} \times 100$	258
Year 10	80	$\frac{80}{33} \times 100$	242
Year 11	82	$\frac{82}{33} \times 100$	248

9.3 Exercises: Simple Index Numbers

1. Over an eight-year period the price of a certain metal per tonne on the London Market averaged out as follows: Year 1 £230; Year 2 £250; Year 3 £320; Year 4 £340; Year 5 £825; Year 6 £900; Year 7 £940; Year 8 £1 000. At the end of Year 4 a civil war broke out in a major producing country, and this caused the sudden rise in prices. Calculate a price index for the metal with Year 4 as 100 (calculations correct to one decimal place).
2. Over a five-year period the price of standard rubber per kilogram on the London Rubber Market was as follows: Year 1 53 pence; Year 2 54 pence; Year 3 47 pence; Year 4 45 pence; Year 5 44 pence. The ending of a cartel agreement in certain countries led to the fall in price in Year 3. Using Year 3 as a base year calculate a price index for Standard Rubber for these five years (calculations correct to one decimal place).
3. The price of wheat on the London markets is quoted as £ per tonne. The prices for September onwards are quoted as follows: September £85.05; October £86.20; November £87.45; December £90.30. Using September as the base month calculate a price index for wheat for the rest of the year (calculations correct to one decimal place).
4. The coffee market quotes prices in £ per tonne. In four successive days prices are as follows: Day 1 £1 180; Day 2 £1 210; Day 3 £1 225; Day 4 £1 272. Using Day 1 as a base calculate a price index for coffee for the period shown (calculations correct to one decimal place).

9.4 Weighted Index Numbers

Although a simple index, as outlined in Example 9.1 above, is easy to calculate, for practical purposes the real value of index numbers is in the comparison of 'unmixables'. For example, how will a rise in the price of synthetic rubber and plastics and a fall in the price of copper affect the price of a family motorcar? The student might think that the answer lies in taking the rise in the prices of synthetic rubber and plastics, adding them together, and then subtracting the fall in price of copper. This would, in fact, be the correct method if all three commodities were used in exactly the same proportions. Consider the information given in Example 9.2 below.

Example 9.2. Raw materials in motor vehicles:

Raw material	*Quantity used per car (kg)*	*Original price per kg (£)*	*Price change per kg*
Synthetic rubber	10	1.60	+£0.20
Plastic	10	1.00	+£0.15
Copper	10	1.80	−£0.10

From the table we can work out that synthetic rubber costs 200p (10 × 20p) more; plastic 150p (10 × 15p) more; and copper 100p less (10 × −10p). The extra cost of producing the vehicle is therefore 200p + 150p − 100p = 250p. A quicker way of finding this would be to take the price increases 20p + 15p = 35p and subtract the decrease −10p. The result, 25p, is then multiplied by the quantities involved (10 kg in each case) to find the over-all price effect, an increase of 250p.

Unfortunately this simple approach has one very serious drawback—it is not realistic. Different commodities are usually used in varying proportions to each other, in the manufacture of outputs. It is to be expected that the quantities of synthetic rubber and plastic would exceed that of copper in the manufacture of a modern motorcar. This will mean that, although copper has fallen in price (Example 9.2), the significance of that price fall will be diminished, since a relatively small amount of the commodity is used. Another example, often quoted in Economics in the study of price elasticity of demand, is from the kitchen: a fall of 5p in the price of a carton of cooking salt will not offset a rise of 5p in the price of a pint of milk. The typical family consumes many more pints of milk in a year than they do cartons of cooking salt!

To overcome this problem **weighting** is used. We have already seen how a weighted arithmetic mean is calculated (see page 89) and the method used to weight index numbers is an extension of this process. The principle of weighting is quite simple—it seeks to give extra emphasis to an item or items because of their greater significance in terms of quantity. If twice as much synthetic rubber as copper is used in the manufacture of a modern motorcar then the weights assigned to each must be in the ratio 2:1. In Example 9.2 above the weights 2:1 would not be appropriate because we still have to accommodate plastic. Assuming that half as much again of plastic compared to copper is used, the weights used could be as shown in Example 9.3, where a weighted index is calculated.

Example 9.3

		Year 1		*Year 2*	
Commodity	*Weight*	*Price per kg (£)*	$p_0 \times w$	*Price per kg (£)*	$p_1 \times w$
Rubber	4	1.60	6.40	1.80	£7.20
Plastic	3	1.00	3.00	1.15	£3.45
Copper	2	1.80	3.60	1.70	£3.40
			£13.00		£14.05

The weighted index number can now be calculated by taking the sum of the Year 1 column and making the base 100. The sum of the Year 2 column can then be expressed as a proportion of the base column.

The formula $\frac{p_1}{p_0} \times 100$ now has to be modified to take account of the weighting, and becomes

$$\text{Index} = \frac{\Sigma\,(p_1 \times w)}{\Sigma\,(p_0 \times w)} \times 100$$
$$= \frac{£14.05}{£13.00} \times 100$$
$$= \underline{\underline{108}}$$

Note. In this calculation the units being used (in other words the £ signs) cancel out and leave us with an index number which is independent of monetary units.

To sum up, then, the method for calculating a weighted index number is as follows:

(*a*) List in a table the constituent items in the basket of goods and their prices.

(*b*) Choose the weights required (see Section 9.8 below).

(*c*) Multiply the prices by their respective weights (this process is known as weighting).

(*d*) Add together these products ($p \times w$) for every item for each year (this process is known as aggregating).

(*e*) Divide the total for the 'new' year by the total for the base year and multiply by 100 to express the new year as an index number of the base year.

9.5 Exercises: Weighted Index Numbers

1. A motor-vehicle component consists of 3 kg ferrous metals, 2 kg non-ferrous metals and 1 kg other materials. In the year the prototype was made the ferrous metals used cost £1.30 per kg, the non-ferrous metals £3.25 per kg and other materials £0.75 per kg. In the following year the prices rose respectively to £1.65, £3.85 and £0.95. Calculate a weighted price index for the component (correct to one decimal place).
2. An aerospace component consists of 50 kg copper, 20 kg aluminium and 30 kg other materials. In the year the prototype was made the copper cost £7.30 per kg, the aluminium £3.20 per kg and other materials £1.20 per kg. In the following year the prices of the copper and the aluminium rose respectively to £8.50 and £3.50. The cost of the other materials fell to £1.00 per kg. Calculate a weighted price index for the component (correct to one decimal place).
3. The average price of wheat, barley and oats per tonne in three successive years is given in the table below. The proportions of these grains being used in cereal products are in the ratios 10 for wheat, 4 for barley and 6 for oats. Take the prices in Year 1 as 100 and calculate a price index for cereal products over the three-year period (correct to one decimal place).

Cereal Grain Prices (£ per tonne)

	Year 1	*Year 2*	*Year 3*
Wheat	83	84.50	89
Barley	75	78	85
Oats	68	78	81

4. A contractor uses a standard mixture which consists of 2 parts ballast, 1 part sand and 1 part cement. Prices per tonne in three years delivered to site were as follows:

	Year 1	*Year 2*	*Year 3*
Ballast	£14	£15	£18
Sand	£18	£20	£22
Cement	£20	£27	£28.50

Compute a price index (correct to one decimal place) for the mixture, using the Year 1 figures as base 100.

9.6 Chain Index Numbers

The indices used so far have all been fixed base ones, i.e. they have all had a particular period (say Year 1) as the point of reference: each year has related back to this one starting point. However, it is possible to construct an index where the base changes annually (or each time period). Such an index uses the previous period as base. There are some advantages with this kind of index:

(*a*) It is a good way of showing the *rate* of change occurring, i.e. whether prices, outputs, etc., are falling, rising or remaining constant.

(*b*) It is possible to incorporate new items into this kind of index without the necessity of recalculating the whole of the previous period's figures. For example, an index started some years ago would not take account of more recent developments. A 1966 retail price index would not have had provision for colour television, and would need recalculation if this item were to be included. Since the chain index is effectively recalculated for each year (time period) this problem is avoided.

Example 9.5 shows how a chain index can be calculated for a single commodity (synthetic rubber).

Example 9.5. A chain index for synthetic rubber prices.

Year	*Price (in pence) per kg*	*Calculation*
Year 1	74	100
Year 2	76	$\frac{76}{74} \times 100 = 102.7$
Year 3	80	$\frac{80}{76} \times 100 = 105.3$
Year 4	100	$\frac{100}{80} \times 100 = 125$
Year 5	130	$\frac{130}{100} \times 100 = 130$
Year 6	160	$\frac{160}{130} \times 100 = 123.1$
Year 7	170	$\frac{170}{160} \times 100 = 106.2$
Year 8	177	$\frac{177}{170} \times 100 = 104.1$

The method here is to:

(*a*) List in a table the price of the commodity each year.

(*b*) Find the price relative for each year using the previous year's price as base.

Question: Why does this particular index number eventually fall even though the price continues to rise?

Answer: Because a chain index brings out the 'rate of change' of prices. Although prices are still rising they are not rising as fast as in the peak year (Year 5) when they rose 30 per cent in the year.

A Weighted Multi-Product Chain Index

It is also possible to construct a chain index which takes into account more than one product, and which can be weighted. Such an index is demonstrated in Example 9.6.

Example 9.6. Finding a Weighted Chain Index of Prices for Commodities (see Table 9.1)

The method here is:

(*a*) List in a table the commodities, their prices for each year and their weights.

Table 9.1. Example 9.6.: Finding a Weighted Chain Index of Prices for Commodities

		Year 1		*Year 2*			*Year 3*		
Commodity	*Weight*	*Price (pence per kg)*	*Base*	*Price (pence per kg)*	*Calculation*	*Index No. × weight*	*Price (pence per kg)*	*Calculation*	*Index No. × weight*
Synthetic rubber	4	180	100	185	$\frac{185}{180} \times 100 \times 4$	411.1	187	$\frac{187}{185} \times 100 \times 4$	404.3
Plastic	3	105	100	111	$\frac{111}{105} \times 100 \times 3$	317.1	115	$\frac{115}{111} \times 100 \times 3$	310.8
Copper	2	180	100	177	$\frac{177}{180} \times 100 \times 2$	196.7	170	$\frac{170}{177} \times 100 \times 2$	192.1
Total	9					924.9 924.9 ÷ 9 = 102.8 on base of Year 1			907.2 907.2 ÷ 9 = 100.8 on base of Year 2

The Index for all commodities is thus 100; 102.8; 100.8 over the period.

(*b*) Give the base year (Year 1 in Example 9.6) the value 100.

(*c*) Find the price relative for each commodity for each year, using the previous year as the base year, and multiply this by its weight.

(*d*) Add together the price relatives × weight for each commodity.

(*e*) Divide the answer, which is the total for all commodities for each year by the sum of the weights, to find the index number.

9.7 Exercises: Chain Index Numbers

1. The price of petrol (in pence per litre) at the pumps over a five-year period was as follows:

	Price
Year 1	12
Year 2	14
Year 3	19
Year 4	23
Year 5	25

Calculate a 'chain' index number for the price of petrol which begins Year 1 = 100, etc. (Calculations correct to one decimal place.)

2. (*a*) The price of tin on the London Metal Exchange over a five-year period was as follows:

	Price in £ per tonne
Year 1	568
Year 2	632
Year 3	988
Year 4	1 362
Year 5	890

Calculate a 'chain' index number for the price of tin which begins with Year 1 = 100 (correct to one decimal place).

(*b*) In Year 1 the price of tin was £568 per tonne and in Year 5 it was £890 per tonne. Explain the index number for Year 5 in the light of these prices.

3. The information given below refers to three commodities used in the manufacture of a popular food product. The weighting is shown, and the price changes for a three-year period. You are asked to calculate a weighted chain index for the food product over the three-year period (correct to one decimal place).

	Weight	*Year 1*	*Year 2*	*Year 3*
Commodity A	4	£1.20	£1.45	£1.95
Commodity B	2	£3.50	£3.35	£3.20
Commodity C	1	£2.20	£2.45	£2.85

4. The information given below refers to three commodities used in the manufacture of a popular food product, the weighting shown, and the price changes for a three-year period. You are asked to calculate a weighted chain index for the food product over the three-year period (correct to one decimal place).

	Weight	*Year 1*	*Year 2*	*Year 3*
Commodity A	4	£1.60	£1.80	£1.95
Commodity B	3	£2.50	£2.65	£3.20
Commodity C	2	£2.40	£2.45	£2.95

9.8 Some Difficulties with Index Numbers

Index numbers can prove enormously useful, and are, in fact, widely used, especially by Government departments. There are series of indices relating to retail prices, wholesale prices, industrial production, import and export of goods, prices of shares on the Stock Exchange, etc.

However, it is important to realise that there are a number of difficulties associated with the construction and use of index numbers. Students should be aware of such difficulties, in order that they may (*a*) avoid errors when constructing their own indices and (*b*) recognise the fact that even official series of indices are largely a compromise between the desired objective and the attainable.

The difficulties most often encountered are:

(*a*) The choice of items.
(*b*) The choice of a base period.
(*c*) The choice of average to be used.
(*d*) The question of 'weighting'.
(*e*) The suitability of a particular index for the enquiry in hand.

(*a*) **Choice of Items.** If our index concerns only a handful of items, it is not difficult to include them all. However, most real-world indices are involved with areas where there may be many thousands of potential items. Clearly all of these cannot be included if the calculations are to be kept reasonably simple. This brings us to the problem of what to put into the index, and what to leave out. An attempt has to be made to choose a selection of items which, though not comprehensive (otherwise all items would be involved), is at least representative of the whole population under investigation. The word 'population' is used to mean the total group of items affected by the enquiry. Thus an index of export prices would perhaps only take account of a relatively small number of types of exports, chosen because they reflect (or it is hoped that they reflect) the complete range of exports.

It has to be admitted that an index number is therefore an indication of variations in data and not a complete record of them. This point can be appreciated by looking at the Retail Price Index. There are many thousands of retail prices, but only a few of these find their way into the Retail Price Index. It is hoped by those who compile the Index that the items they have chosen are a fair reflection of what the 'average' household buys. Preliminary surveys are carried out to determine the pattern of purchases made by different income groups, and the items are then selected to be as representative as possible of the entire population. We have already seen in Chapter 8, however, that there may be no single household which fits the 'average', and many may feel that the items which fall within the Retail Price Index do not reflect their own pattern of purchases.

(*b*) **The Choice of a Base Period.** To have meaning, index numbers must have a base—a point or period at which the representation of information 'starts'. Since the entire index will be related to this base, and will in part be a reflection of it, the choice of base is most important. It is vital to avoid choosing unrepresentative time periods as base, since subsequent calculations will in turn be distorted. For example, suppose a particular year had been bad for growing wheat and yields had been down 50 per cent on the mean of the previous 10 years. To take such a year as base would vastly overstate the increase in the efficiency of growing wheat when in subsequent years wheat yields returned to 'normal'. It is therefore vital to choose as base a time period which does not deviate too far from the observed trend.

(*c*) **The Choice of Average.** Any index number must make use of averages. For example, an index of share prices can only be based on the average prices prevailing on the Stock Exchange, where prices fluctuate from minute to minute in times of crisis. It may make a considerable difference to the index if unweighted averages are used in 'some enquiries': for example, an index of export prices for metal products might need to take account of the extent to which particular metals entered into the export trade. The choice of average (sometimes called the choice of formula) to be used in calculating the index may be very important.

(*d*) **The Choice of Weights.** As we have seen, weights are used to give emphasis to items in order that their contribution to the index number will reflect their relative importance. Weighting is therefore a useful process, but it is essential that weights are chosen which give each item its appropriate importance. For example, a weight of 900 (out of 1 000) for the UK Retail Price Index for food would clearly be misleading—families do not spend nine tenths of their budget on food. (It might, however, be a most appropriate weight for food in a retail price index in a developing country.)

Another problem is whether to keep the weights throughout the life of the index or to change the weights each year or other period. If this is done the index will need to be recalculated each time period. The base-year weighting system—named after *Laspeyre*, its originator—is the one officially favoured, perhaps because it involves less recalculation over a period of years. The current year (or time period) weighting system—termed a *Paasche* system—is hardly used at all in the United Kingdom.

A final problem relating to weights is whether to use volume weights or value weights. So far in this chapter the indices calculated have all used quantity weights—i.e. the significance of items has depended upon *how much* of the item is used. This is not the only way of weighting, however. Some items may be insignificant in quantity terms, but have significant value. It is quite common therefore to find indices weighted by value, and where this is the case a price relative index is often calculated. Such an index is outlined in Section 9.9 below.

(*e*) **The Suitability of a Particular Index for the Enquiry in Hand.** Index numbers are specialised tools and should be used as such. They cannot be expected to yield information accurately on areas for which they were not specifically constructed. For example, it might be thought that the Retail Price Index would be useful in a study to indicate the level of poverty amongst the least affluent 10 per cent of the population. However, it clearly will have limited applicability, since it is highly unlikely that the least affluent families have a pattern of purchases similar to that used to prepare the Index (see Section 9.9 below).

Before making use of an official index, therefore, it is necessary to ensure that it is appropriate for the enquiry at hand. Full details of the salient features of any official index are made available, either in explanatory notes in the official publication in which they appear or in supplements, such as the *Monthly Digest of Statistics Supplement*, 'Definitions and Explanatory Notes'.

9.9 The General Index of Retail Prices

This chapter so far has been concerned with the weighted aggregative type of index—an index which is weighted by volume and which uses the formula

$$\text{Index} = \frac{\Sigma\,(p_1 \times w)}{\Sigma\,(p_0 \times w)} \times 100$$

Some effort has already been made to point out that there are many alternative types of index, and in the United Kingdom one of these in particular deserves more detailed consideration. This is the weighted average of price relatives index, one which is particularly suited to value, as opposed to volume, weighting. It is of importance to us here because the General Index of Retail Prices, probably the best known index in the country, is calculated using this method.

The method of calculation of an index using the weighted average of price relatives is simple. We first have to return to the price relatives we discussed in the early part of this chapter. These are essentially one-item index numbers. If we take a number of these one-item relatives and average them, we effectively have a composite index number. Once again an item's importance in the series can be taken account of by a process of weighting. The following example indicates how the process works.

Example 9.7.

Family Expenditure

Item	*Year 1 (Base Year) Price (£)*	*Year 2 Price (£)*	*One-item price relative* $\frac{p_1}{p_0} \times 100$	*Weight*	*Price relative × Weight*
Fuel and Light	28	36	129	15	1 935
Housing	160	198	124	25	3 100
Food	30	49	163	55	8 965
				100	14 000

$$\therefore \text{ Composite Index Number} = \Sigma\,\frac{\left(\frac{p_1}{p_0} \times 100 \times w\right)}{\Sigma w}$$

$$= \frac{14\,000}{100}$$

$$= 140$$

We must now turn our attention to the General Index of Retail Prices.

The General Index of Retail Prices measures the percentage change, month by month, in the average level of prices of the goods and services purchased by the great majority of households in the United Kingdom. The current index is based on prices at January 1974, and uses weights determined on the Family Expenditure Survey for the previous year. A heavy weighting in the Index reflects heavy expenditure on that item in the Family Expenditure Survey.

The Index is divided into 11 groups, with 1 000 weights. These groups and the weights attached to them are shown in Table 9.2. The index is calculated each month in respect of prices prevailing on a Tuesday near the middle of the month. Table 9.3 shows the index at the time of writing.

Table 9.2. General Index of Retail Prices

Groups of Items	*Weights*
1. Food	247
2. Alcoholic drink	83
3. Tobacco	46
4. Housing	112
5. Fuel and light	58
6. Durable household goods	63
7. Clothing and footwear	82
8. Transport and vehicles	139
9. Miscellaneous goods	71
10. Services	54
11. Meals outside the home	45
All items	1 000

Tab'e 9.3 General Index of Retail Prices (Prices at January 1974 = 100)

Year	*Jan.*	*Feb.*	*Mar.*	*Apr.*	*May*	*Jun.*	*Jul.*	*Aug.*	*Sep.*	*Oct.*	*Nov.*	*Dec.*
1974	100.0	101.7	102.6	106.1	107.6	108.7	109.7	109.8	111.0	113.2	115.2	116.9
1975	119.9	121.9	124.3	129.1	134.5	137.1	138.5	139.3	140.5	142.5	144.2	146.0
1976	147.9	149.8	150.6	153.5	155.2	156.0	156.3	158.5	160.6	163.5	165.8	168.0
1977	172.4	174.1	175.8	180.3	181.7	183.6	183.8	184.7	186.5	186.5	187.4	188.4
1978	189.5	190.6	191.8	194.6	195.7	197.2	198.1	199.4	200.2	201.1	202.5	204.2

9.10 Exercises: Index Numbers

1. Describe the construction and use of the General Index of Retail Prices. To what extent does the General Index of Retail Prices measure changes in the 'Cost of Living'?

2. Calculate the General Index of Retail Prices for all items for Year 3 with January, Year 1 = 100. (Answer correct to one decimal place.)

Group	*Weights*	*Price relatives February, Year 3 (Year 1 = 100)*
Food	228	152.1
Alcoholic drink	81	150.9
Tobacco	46	162.8
Housing	112	135.8
Fuel and light	56	169.4
Durable household goods	75	141.2
Clothing and footwear	84	134.9
Transport and vehicles	140	156.9
Miscellaneous goods	74	154.2
Services	57	154.9
Meals bought and consumed outside home	47	148.3

(RSA Quantitative Methods in Business)

3. Calculate the General Index of Retail Prices for all items for June, Year 4, with January, Year 1 = 100. (Answer correct to one decimal place.)

Group	*Weights*	*Price relatives June, Year 4*
Food	247	193.7
Alcoholic drink	83	184.0
Tobacco	46	216.1
Housing	112	164.3
Fuel and light	58	214.5
Durable household goods	63	166.0
Clothing and footwear	82	155.7
Transport and vehicles	139	193.2
Miscellaneous goods	71	187.8
Services	54	173.3
Meals bought and consumed outside home	45	184.0

4. Calculate the index of industrial production: (*a*) for all industries, (*b*) for manufacturing industries (correct to one decimal place):

Industry	*Weights*	*Index December 1976 1970 = 100*
Mining and quarrying	37	103
Manufacturing		
Food, drink and tobacco	84	105
Chemicals	65	119
Metals	57	74
Engineering	319	98
Textiles	76	94
Other manufacturing	144	100
Construction	146	89
Gas, electricity and water	72	161

Source: *Monthly Digest of Statistics*

10

OFFICIAL SOURCES OF STATISTICS

10.1 The Range of Official Sources of Statistics

Although the enumeration of populations by means of a census is as old as government itself, the systematic collection of statistics is a relatively recent development. The first Census of Population in the United Kingdom was made in 1801 and has continued every 10 years since that date, except for the year 1941 when war intervened. Sample surveys are even more recent, and at first were privately conducted by interested individuals rather than officials. Charles Booth's Victorian enquiry into the *Labour and Life of the People of London* filled 17 volumes. It was followed by another famous enquiry, Seebohm Rowntree's study of poverty amongst the working classes in York, published in 1901. This type of social enquiry continues today in an official way. The Social Survey Division of the Office of Population Censuses and Surveys conducts both standing and *ad hoc* enquiries to meet the needs of Government.

Most official statistics are a by-product of Government and local government activity in the economic, social and cultural fields. Whilst statistics collected for one purpose (for example, the National Health Service) may not be absolutely appropriate for other purposes, there are many cases where they are good enough, and probably more comprehensive than any private enquiry could afford to collect. There are several periodicals containing monthly and quarterly statistics, and others which give annual figures. A further range of publications deals with historical statistics, and with regional data in the four broad regions of England, Scotland, Wales and Northern Ireland. Local authority statistics form a further field. Certain topics, such as education, health, prices and consumer protection, etc., are of wide general interest and detailed analyses of trends and developments are available, whilst more specialised topics, such as weights and measures, industrial safety, distribution, etc., are also well documented.

It is impossible to describe many of these sources in detail in a book of this sort. The Central Statistical Office, which is part of the Cabinet office and was set up in 1941 by Sir Winston Churchill, publishes the *Guide to Official Statistics*, a comprehensive guide to the literature available. The latest edition is in every public library reference section and should be available in every college and school, for it is an invaluable reference work for students.

10.2 Regular Sources of Statistics

For the student the provision of up-to-date statistics is essential and several series of statistics are issued on a regular basis. A word of warning here. Tables for these regular sources are revised and redefined at intervals to suit current needs. This means that tables may not have a long run, especially in inflationary times. Thus a retail price index may have a six-year or eight-year run and then the 'basket of goods and services' on which it is based is reassessed. The new table will not be strictly comparable with the old and a new base year will therefore be designated. Students, particularly those interested in modern history, will find it helpful to keep issues of the *Monthly Digest of Statistics* even if they appear out of date. To throw away such data when—in 10 years' time—it might be of great interest, is unwise.

The chief regular series of statistics are:

(*a*) *Trade and Industry*. This is a weekly publication with a separate statistical section which is updated immediately figures become available. It also includes many 'topic-based' statistics as part of current news items which are very instructive to those seeking to develop a wide appreciation of statistics.

(*b*) *Monthly Digest of Statistics*. This monthly publication is the major source of statistical material for students. It contains about 175 tables covering the main statistical series for which monthly and quarterly figures are available, besides the vital statistics (births, marriages and deaths), social services, entertainment and the weather.

(*c*) *Bank of England Quarterly Bulletin*. This invaluable publication not only includes a statistical section with the most pertinent financial statistics but includes a range of articles and authoritative accounts of the financial scene which are most informative to those studying business subjects.

(*d*) *Annual Abstract of Statistics*. This weighty volume extends the figures available in the *Monthly Digest of Statistics* to cover 400 tables, over a 10-year period. Almost every Government Department contributes to the Abstract, as well as other organisations. Statistics cover area and climate, population and vital statistics, social conditions, education, labour, production, transport and communications, retail distribution and miscellaneous services, external trade, balance of payments, national income and expenditure, etc.

(*e*) *The Blue Book on National Income and Expenditure*. The National Income has been defined as 'the aggregate net product of, and the sole source of payment for, all the factors of production'. If we are to know how much wealth we have created, and how to share it most fairly, we must have reliable data about the National Income. This celebrated 'Blue Book', published annually, gives data under 13 main headings about production, capital investment, private expenditure and public sector expenditure on a rolling 11-year basis. Thus the 1980 edition contains the figures for 1969–79.

(*f*) *The Pink Book on UK Balance of Payments*. Always a topic of enduring interest, the Balance of Payments of the United Kingdom is fully documented in this 'Pink Book'. Published annually, on the same rolling 11-year programme as the Blue Book mentioned above, the statistics are grouped under 14 headings, including Visible Trade, Invisible Services, Investments and Capital Transactions, Official Financing, etc. It is essential reading for all businessmen, and especially for those in the export fields.

(*g*) *Economic Trends*. Published monthly, this publication reviews economic developments as they occur, giving not only the data, but interpretations of them and presentations in diagrammatic form. It is most informative and instructive.

(*h*) *Social Trends*. This is a similar publication, dealing with social developments and giving official analyses of many situations. It is of the very greatest use to those studying sociological aspects of United Kingdom life.

10.3 Occasional Sources of Statistics

Some data, of an historical nature, are not published on a regular basis, though many aspects of updating are in fact covered by regular sources referred to in Section 10.2 above. A more occasional treatment only is necessary. The *Abstract of British Historical Statistics* and the *Second Abstract of British Historical Statistics* give as long a period of statistics as can be made available. Most series start in the nineteenth century, but some start much earlier. The first volume brings data up to 1938, and the second up to 1965.

Lecturers and teachers may find a recent publication, *Using Statistics in Economics*, very helpful. It has been developed by the Central Statistical Office in collaboration with other Government departments and a panel of educational advisers. Purchasers are invited to photocopy any extracts needed for class use, or may order further copies as required. It may be obtained from the Central Statistical Office, Great George St, London, SW1P 3AQ.

10.4 Exercises: Official Statistics

1. Describe in some detail *one* of the following:

   (*a*) The *Monthly Digest of Statistics.*
   (*b*) The *Annual Abstract of Statistics.*
   (*c*) The *Abstract of British Historical Statistics.*

2. Describe in some detail two of the following:

   (*a*) The Census of Production.
   (*b*) The Census of Distribution.
   (*c*) The Census of Population.

3. What is the difference between a census and a survey? In which situations is a census preferable to a survey? Describe in some detail any published census or survey with which you are acquainted.

4. Describe two of the following briefly:

   (*a*) The Blue Book of the National Income.
   (*b*) The Pink Book of the Balance of Payments.
   (*c*) *Economic Trends.*
   (*d*) *Social Trends.*

5. Describe one of the following bodies in some detail:

   (*a*) The Social Survey.
   (*b*) The Central Statistical Office.

SECTION 4

ACCOUNTING TO TRIAL BALANCE LEVEL

11

THE NATURE AND PURPOSE OF ACCOUNTING

11.1 What is Accounting?

Accounting is the process of expressing the economic activities of everyday life in money terms, so that we may estimate the costs of creating goods and services, make decisions about production on the basis of these estimates, compare the actual costs as they occur with the estimates originally made, and adjust the output and prices of goods and services accordingly.

Three of the main sub-divisions of Accounting are financial accounting, cost accounting and management accounting. **Financial accounting** *is concerned with the records of business transactions; with receipts and payments and whether business operations result in a profit or a loss.* **Cost accounting** *is concerned with the expenses incurred in the various cost centres of the business, and attempts to ensure correct pricing of contracts; to discover where actual costs differ from estimates, etc.* **Management accounting** *seeks to control not only the present pattern of business activities but the future pattern, charting the course ahead.*

Although this book is chiefly about elementary financial accounting it is essential even for the beginner to have some idea of the larger framework within which elementary financial accounting operates.

Man is an economic animal. He provides for his daily needs by a complex pattern of economic activities which create goods and services. Since resources are limited, and the demands to be satisfied are enormous, he seeks to produce the greatest possible output of goods and services from the smallest possible input of resources. Accounting enables him to quantify, collect and record the **costs** of the inputs and the **values** of the outputs. Having quantified them, he can then evaluate them using his numerical and statistical abilities, to compare results, estimate trends, improve methods of working, etc.

There are two purposes of accounting:

(*a*) **As a tool for management**
(*b*) **As a record of stewardship**

(*a*) *Accounting as a Tool of Management.* Accounting provides a basic information system on the economic aspects of the provision of goods and services. Whilst the technical problems of building a motorcar, power plant, or a house are enormous the economic problems are important too. Can we build it in such a way that it will be demanded? This means that people will choose to buy it and sacrifice alternative opportunities which they could otherwise enjoy. Accounting will tell us what the costs are, and may lead us to conclude that the project is not viable at all. On the other hand, we may conclude that the project is clearly viable, or viable provided cost reductions can be achieved, either in the short run or the long run. We may be able to calculate a clear **break-even** point, and thus know how long it will be before the project returns to us the value which we have put into it.

The chief tools accountancy provides to managements are **budgets, control ratios** and **decision analyses.**

Budgets enable the costs of future activities to be estimated, recorded and then compared with the costs actually incurred as a project is carried out. Any difference between estimated expenditure and actual expenditure is called a **variance**. By analysing the variance it is possible to tell what it is caused by, and thus to pinpoint favourable or unfavourable developments which can be taken advantage of, or avoided, as the case may be. This type of control is called **budgetary control.**

Control ratios enable management to study the performance of the business. A ratio is, of course, a mathematical concept, which is usually expressed as a percentage or as the number of times one figure contains another. The point about many control ratios is that they should normally remain constant, whatever happens to the business. Any movement away from a constant figure calls for investigation. It does not mean necessarily that anything is wrong; things may actually have improved. Still, the wise accountant wants to know what has happened.

To illustrate the point consider one of the control ratios: the gross profit percentage. This is the percentage of gross profit that we make upon sales, or a better phrase is 'net turnover'. The term net turnover means sales less returns, and the net turnover of the business is itself an important statistic about any enterprise. The formula for the gross profit percentage is therefore

$$\text{Gross profit percentage} = \frac{\text{Gross profit}}{\text{Net turnover}} \times 100$$

Suppose that in a particular business in the first quarter of a year net turnover is £27 500 and gross profit is £12 000. The gross profit percentage from these figures is:

$$\begin{aligned} &\frac{\text{Gross profit}}{\text{Net turnover}} \times 100 \\ &= \frac{12\,000}{27\,500} \times 100 \\ &= \underline{\underline{43.6\%}} \end{aligned}$$

Supposing that next quarter the firm does twice as much business? Would it need to purchase twice as many goods for resale? Would it expect to pay out twice as many expenses? Would it expect to make twice as much profit? Of course we cannot answer 'yes' with absolute confidence to all these questions, but generally speaking the answer will be roughly 'yes'. If we are to sell twice as many goods we would expect to buy twice as many goods. For the sake of this argument we will assume that everything simply doubles. Next year the gross profit percentage works out as follows

$$\begin{aligned} &\frac{\text{Gross profit}}{\text{Net turnover}} \times 100 \\ &= \frac{24\,000}{55\,000} \times 100 \\ &= \underline{\underline{43.6\%}} \end{aligned}$$

You will see that it is the same answer as we had before, and this is the vital thing about the gross profit percentage: it is a constant. It ought to come out the same every year providing our business is running in the same way.

An accountant who found that the gross profit percentage in one quarter had fallen away to 35 per cent would immediately seek an explanation. Perhaps purchase prices have risen and not been passed on to customers by raising selling prices. Perhaps someone is stealing money from the till, so that 'sales' figures are being reduced. Perhaps someone is 'passing out' stock to friends and relatives without taking payment. A tank full of petrol to several good-looking boyfriends soon makes a hole in the gross profit percentage. This type of **performance ratio** therefore detects changes in performance, and enables the accountant to make enquiries about them.

Decision analysis is the examination of proposed policies to discover weaknesses in them, and thus to enable management to choose the best of different alternative policies. Thus with the choice of particular machines it may be necessary to relate their output to the potential demand for the product, and ensure that the machine chosen is the best for the likely volume of output required and the most economic in terms of initial cost, running costs, cash flow generated, etc.

(*b*) *Accounting as a Record of Stewardship.* Since resources have to be employed before any production of goods or services can take place, capital has to be provided to finance any project. Capital enables other resources to be paid for, particularly human resources. Labourers cannot wait for their pay until a project proves profitable but must draw their wages to buy the food, clothing, shelter, etc., which their families need. This means that accounting has a further function to perform. **It must account to the investors, or the organisation which provided the capital, for its stewardship of the funds provided.** It enables the owner or owners of the business to assess the effectiveness with which their capital has been used. In the case of public enterprises Parliament itself, through the Public Accounts Committee, evaluates the uses made of public funds.

There are several different types of owners of businesses. Sole traders and partners are directly involved in the activities of their firms, and are therefore well aware what money is being spent, and why. With limited companies the owners of the business are the 'Ordinary' and 'Preference' shareholders, who play no part at all in the management of the firm (except through their representatives, the directors). For the shareholders the annual accounts represent the Board's record of stewardship of the capital the shareholders have provided, and the Chairman's statement is an explanation of the Board's policy over the past year.

A recent change in attitude concerns the Board's responsibility to the employees. It is held, with some justification, that an employee who contributes his labour to the enterprise is more directly involved than a shareholder who remains essentially external to the everyday working of the firm. Granted, the employee is being rewarded with a wage or salary appropriate to his grade or level of responsibility, but it is claimed that this does not prevent him from having an interest in the firm's activities, particularly as those activities affect his security of employment, pension rights, etc. Therefore, it is held, the Board has a duty of stewardship to the employees as well as to the shareholders, and this is a feeling which is becoming increasingly widespread. Accounting today seeks to explain the firm's true situation to employees, and may present accounts in an appropriately interesting way.

With the many industries and organisations which are socially owned, from the great nationalised industries to the smallest 'school fund' accounts, appropriate records of stewardship must be prepared. There are always managers, governors, councillors or Members of Parliament to receive annual accounts and reports. After considering them they will pass a motion approving them, or bring any breach of regulations to an appropriate disciplinary body.

11.2 The Development of Accounting: Introduction

The origins of accounting are lost in antiquity, but it is no accident that the interpreter of the Linear B Minoan script found that the records so painstakingly kept in Ancient Crete were largely household accounting records. Long before money was invented in the seventh century B.C. records were being kept of goods supplied and taxes paid in kind.

The late Middle Ages saw accounting records developed to a full system of what became known as **double-entry book-keeping**. This is still the basis of all accounting. However complex the activities of computers may become, the system that is being used to keep our records is still the double-entry system of book-keeping. This is explained fully in Chapter 12, but because of the importance of the double-entry principle it is proposed in this chapter to make a detailed explanation of double entry in both ordinary book-keeping and the data processing system. Many business graduates well versed in computer science lament their inability to understand double entry, and consequently their failure to follow the link between routine accounting and data processing. The author hopes to remedy these problems in the next few pages. We must begin by examining Medieval double entry, as it was used until the middle of the nineteenth century.

11.3 Early Double-Entry Book-Keeping

Book-keeping began in the Middle Ages, with two books, a Journal (or Day Book) and a Ledger. The day book was used to record events as they happened in chronological order. Thus if the owner purchased a piece of furniture for £50 from A. Trader, who required to be paid at the end of the month, the **Journal entry** would be made straight away. Later, when time permitted, this Journal entry would be 'posted' into the second book, the Ledger, which may be described as the final destination of all book-keeping entries. The ledger is therefore the main book of account, and all other books are called **subsidiary books**, a term which means 'giving additional help to' the ledger. In the Middle Ages there was only one subsidiary book, the Journal.

Every page in the ledger is called an 'account', and is kept exclusively to record the business's transactions with one person, or thing. Thus A. Trader's account is an account of the transactions with A. Trader, and Postage Account is an account of the sums of money spent on postage only. The Ledger page, as shown in Fig. 11.1, is divided down the middle and the two sides are ruled exactly alike. The left-hand side is called the 'debit side' and the right-hand side is called the 'credit' side. The rules for making entries are as follows:

Debit the account that receives goods, or services, or money. Credit the account that gives goods, or services, or money.

It is at this point that the term 'Double-Entry' comes into use, for every accounting transaction requires two entries, not once. In the transaction referred to earlier Furniture Account receives a piece of furniture worth £50; A. Trader gives a piece of furniture worth £50. Of course, at the end of the month a second transaction will follow, and A. Trader will receive a cheque for £50 from the owner's Bank Account. Until this happens A. Trader will be a creditor of the owner of the business; a person to whom the owner owes money.

The Journal paper is ruled in such a way that the Journal entry shows which

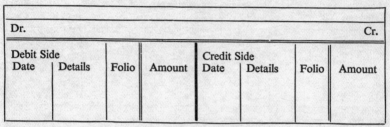

Dr.							Cr.
Debit Side Date	Details	Folio	Amount	Credit Side Date	Details	Folio	Amount

Fig. 11.1. The Ledger.

Notes
(i) The page is divided down the middle.
(ii) The left-hand side is called the debit side, or debtor side, and often has the abbreviation Dr. printed at the top.
(iii) The right-hand side is called the credit side, or creditor side, and often has the abbreviation Cr. printed at the top.
(iv) Columns are drawn on each side for the date, details, folio numbers (to be explained later) and the amount received or given.

account to debit and which account to credit. The account to be debited is named first, and the account to be credited follows. Fig. 11.2 shows this original Journal Entry, and the two ledger accounts which have been posted by the merchant's clerk.

More will be said later about these accounts, and the **principle of double entry**. For the moment let us see what happened in the nineteenth century to improve upon the Medieval system, with its two books: the Day Book (or Journal) and the Ledger (full of accounts).

11.4 Modern Double-Entry Book-Keeping

In the eighteenth and nineteenth centuries businesses grew in size, and difficulties began to appear in the Medieval system, which had always been controlled by one clerk. The Day Book, or Journal, began to have large numbers of entries in it which were very much alike. Instead of selling to one or two firms we might have five or six hundred firms as customers. The Ledger had to have an account for each of these customers and the book was just not large enough to hold them all. Both the Medieval books therefore needed to be divided up into separate parts, with a clerk to look after each part.

The Dividing up of the Journal

If you have only one Journal it is possible for only one book-keeper to use it at a time. The Journal was therefore divided into parts so that several clerks

				J. 1
			£	£
1668 Aug. 17	Furniture Account Dr. A. Trader Account Being purchase of writing desk at this date	L.1 L.2	50.00	 50.00

FURNITURE ACCOUNT — L.1

Dr.							Cr.
1668 Aug. 17	A. Trader	J.1	50.00				

A. TRADER — L.2

Dr.							Cr.
				1668 Aug. 17	Furniture	J.1	50.00

Fig. 11.2. A double entry.

Notes

(i) The two accounts affected, as shown in the Journal Entry, are Furniture Account and A. Trader's Account.

(ii) Each account (page in the ledger) has a reference number written in the top right-hand corner. It is called a 'folio number' (Latin *folium* = leaf).

(iii) When the entries are made it is usual to record the folio number of the other account in the folio column. This tells anyone looking at an account where to find the other half of the double entry, or it may tell him where to find an explanation of the matter concerned—for example, J. 1 means page 1 of the Journal.

(iv) Note that the Furniture Account received value and so it is debited, but A. Trader gave value so his account is credited. Remember the rule: debit the account that receives value, credit the account that gives value.

could work at once. It was found that the work could be divided into two main sections:

(*a*) Transactions that happened repeatedly, because they dealt with 'goods' that the firm could call its 'normal line of business'.

(*b*) Transactions that happened much more rarely—say, once or twice a year.

Section (*a*) was found to consist of the Purchases of Goods, the Sale of Goods, Returns Outwards (i.e. Purchases Returned) or Returns Inwards (Sales Returned by dissatisfied customers). Transactions of this sort took place every day, sometimes many times a day.

Section (*b*) was found to consist of much rarer items, such as the purchasing of assets like furniture, which might last twenty years, or writing off bad debts which might only happen a few times a year.

Larger firms therefore began to divide the Journal, or Day Book, into five parts, and these were called **subsidiary books.** Subsidiary means 'giving additional help to' the **main book,** which is the Ledger.

The five subsidiary books were:

(i) The Purchases Day Book, in which purchases were recorded.
(ii) The Sales Day Book, in which sales were recorded.
(iii) The Purchases Returns Book, in which 'returns outwards' were recorded.
(iv) The Sales Returns Book, in which 'returns inwards' were recorded.
(v) The Journal Proper, containing all the items not to do with 'goods', i.e. the rarer items of section (*b*) above.

The Dividing up of the Ledger

As a business grows the Ledger grows thicker and thicker as more and more customers and creditors enter into business relationships with the firm. Some subdivision of the work becomes necessary as it is impossible for two clerks to work with only one book.

A natural subdivision of the work occurs if we remove from the Ledger the two busiest accounts of all, the **Cash Account** and the **Bank Account.** These two accounts are extremely active. Hardly a day goes by without twenty or thirty items being paid or received by the normal small business, and large businesses may handle hundreds of items daily. It therefore seems sensible to move these two accounts from the ledger and put them into a separate book in the special charge of one person, called the **Cashier.** This gave us the **Cash Book,** as a separate part of the ledger, with only two accounts in it, the Cash Account and the Bank Account. The full story of how the Cash Book developed is given in *Book-keeping Made Simple*, but the point to mention here is that it was soon found easier to put the two accounts side by side on the same page, but with quite separate columns for 'Cash' and 'Bank' items. Later a third column on each side was added for Discount Allowed on one side, and Discount Received on the other. We thus have the **Three-Column Cash Book** as the standard cash book for most purposes.

Another logical division was to remove all the customers' accounts into a separate book (or even a loose-leaf system) and call it the **Sales Ledger** or the **Debtors' Ledger,** whilst all suppliers' accounts were moved into a separate book called the **Purchases Ledger** or **Creditors' Ledger.** This left a small number of accounts only in the rest of the ledger, which became known as the **General Ledger.** Even one or two of these accounts, particularly the **Capital Account** of the sole trader or of the partners in a partnership business, and the **Trading Account** and **Profit and Loss Account,** were taken out and put into a separate ledger called the **Private Ledger.** Only the accountant and the owner would have access to this small ledger.

Before looking at this subdivision of the ledger in diagrammatic form one further point is worth making. The ledger accounts fall into three classes: **Personal Accounts, Real Accounts** and **Nominal Accounts.**

Personal Accounts are the accounts of the persons the business deals with, and there may be hundreds of thousands of them. They will be either debtors or creditors. Debtors are people who owe the business money, usually for the supply of goods or services. Creditors are the people to whom the business owes money, usually because they have supplied goods or services to the business.

Every Personal Account has the name of a person with whom the business deals at the top. These may be sole traders (Tom Jones, for instance), partnerships (Brown and Green) or limited companies (R. Smith & Co. Ltd). Whichever kind of 'person' they are, the account will keep a record of dealings with this person.

Capital Account is a special case of a Personal Account. The value of the proprietor's investment in the business is recorded there; the real assets he brought in are recorded in the Real Accounts.

Real Accounts are accounts where we keep a record of the real things the business owns. Such things are called **assets of the business.** Land, buildings, furniture, equipment, plant and machinery, cash and money-in-the-bank are all examples of real things. You can spend the money, and use the machinery and furniture.

Nominal Accounts are the third type of accounts. They are accounts where we record items which have been gained or lost by the business. Thus the Wages Account records the money paid away to the workers (an expense of the business which becomes a loss on the Profit and Loss Account); the Discount Received Account, to which are posted all the items in the Discount Received column on the Three-Column Cash Book, records all the discounts received, which are profits of the business.

Fig. 11.3 shows the subdivisions of the medieval Journal and Ledger. The reader might like to think about the way in which the ledger has been subdivided, and ask himself where the Personal Accounts, Nominal Accounts and Real Accounts are now to be found in the various parts of the ledger.

11.5 How the Double-Entry System Works

The chart on pages 130–131 (Fig. 11.4) shows clearly how the double-entry system of book-keeping works. This method of keeping books so that the businessman can discover his exact financial position at any time is explained in the diagram, and the student should return to it regularly to discover how each section of his studies fits into the pattern of double entry.

At this stage let us take a very quick look at the diagram to pick up the general framework of book-keeping. The numbers (1) to (5) are guideways through the diagram.

(1) The Original Documents

Every transaction that takes place, whether it is a purchase, a sale, a return, a payment, or some other type of transaction, has an original document. These documents are called invoices, credit notes, statements, receipts, petty cash vouchers, or they may be formal agreements like a hire-purchase document or a legal contract. Even mere letters of complaint require some action to be taken.

(2) The Books of Original Entry

When you have a document you first record it in a book of Original Entry. These books may be Journals—that is, Day Books—or Cash Books like the

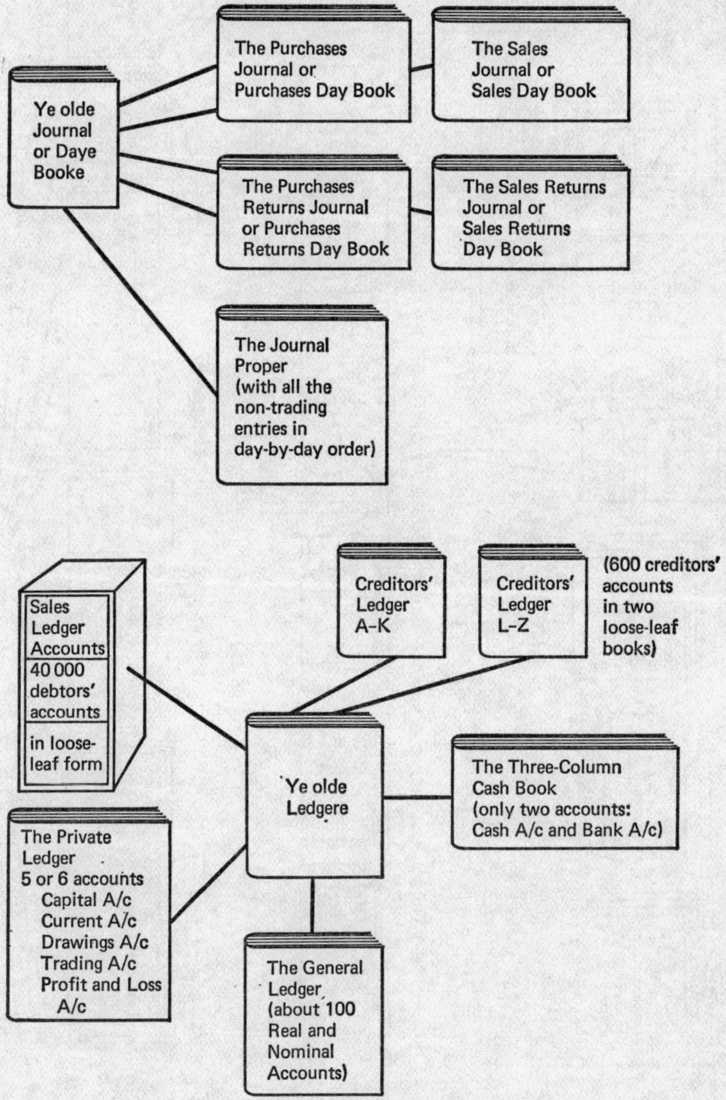

Fig. 11.3. Dividing up the Journal and the Ledger.

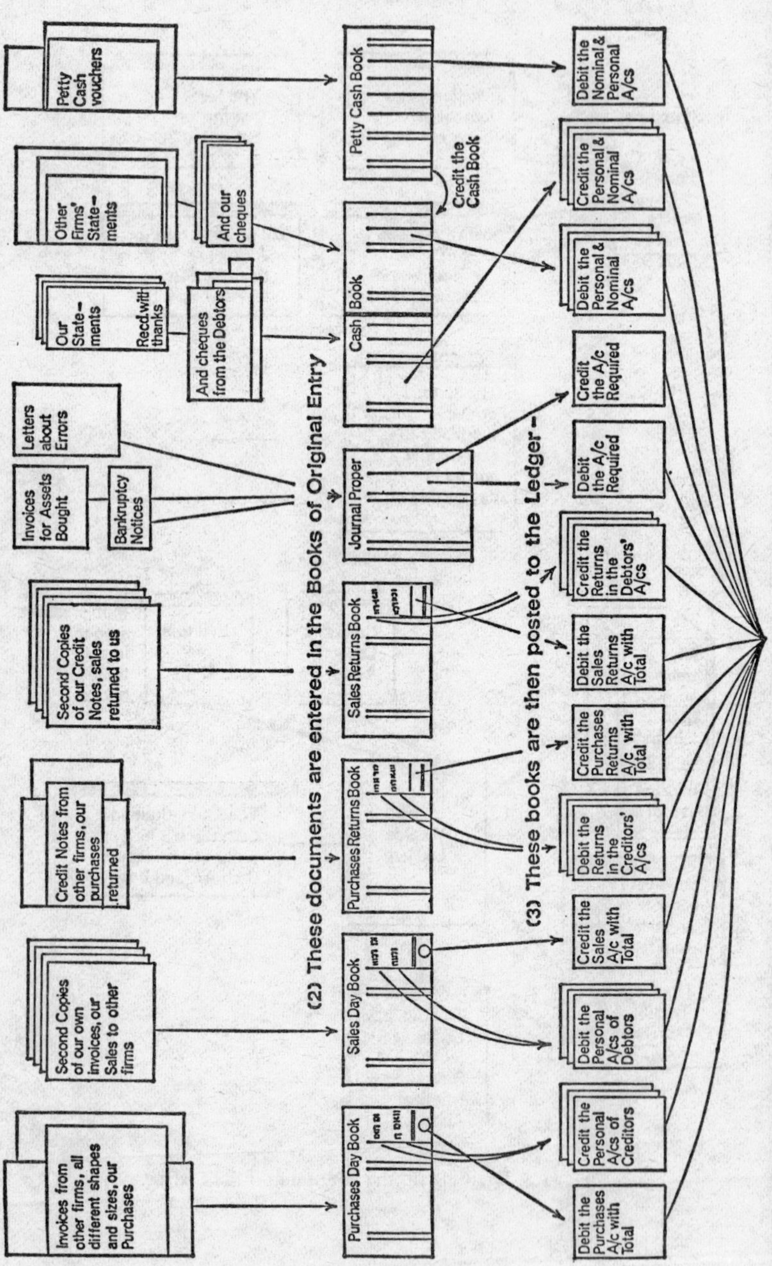
(1) Every transaction has an original Document
Invoices from other firms, all different shapes and sizes, our Purchases
Second Copies of our own invoices, our Sales to other firms
Credit Notes from other firms, our purchases returned
Second Copies of our Credit Notes, sales returned to us
Invoices for Assets Bought
Bankruptcy Notices
Letters about Errors
Our State-ments
Recd. with thanks
And cheques from the Debtors
Other Firms' State-ments
And our cheques
Petty Cash vouchers
(2) These documents are entered in the Books of Original Entry
Purchases Day Book
Sales Day Book
Purchases Returns Book
Sales Returns Book
Journal Proper
Cash Book
Petty Cash Book
Credit the Cash Book
(3) These books are then posted to the Ledger—
Debit the Purchases A/c with Total
Credit the Personal A/cs of Creditors
Debit the Personal A/cs of Debtors
Credit the Sales A/c with Total
Debit the Returns in the Creditors' A/cs
Credit the Purchases Returns A/c with Total
Debit the Sales Returns A/c with Total
Credit the Returns in the Debtors' A/cs
Debit the A/c Required
Credit the A/c Required
Debit the Personal & Nominal A/cs
Credit the Personal & Nominal A/cs
Debit the Nominal & Personal A/cs

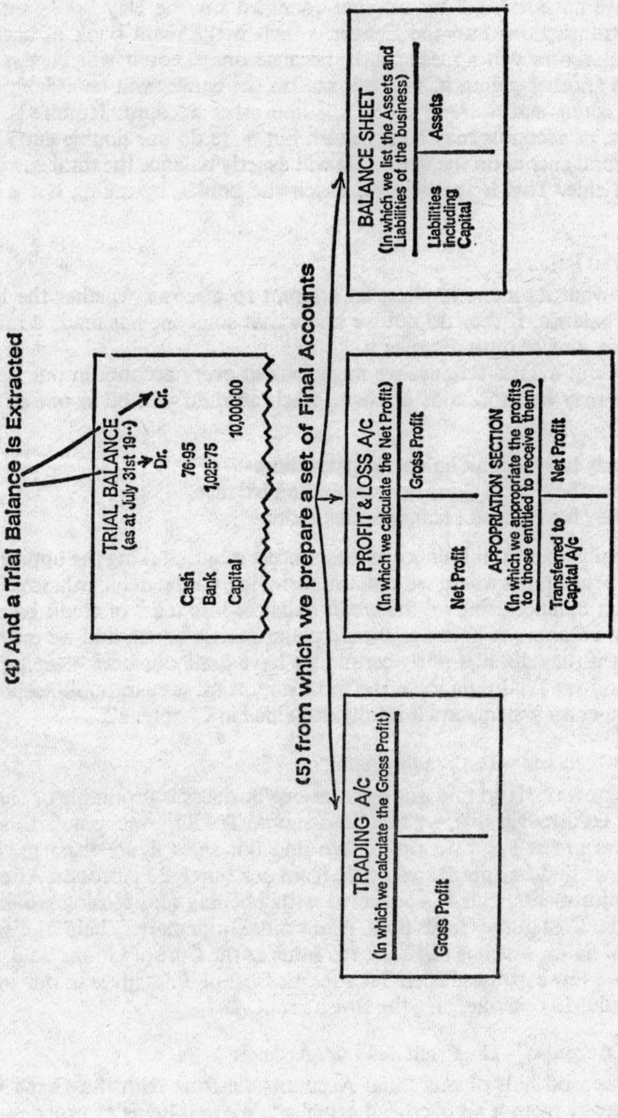
(4) And a Trial Balance is Extracted
TRIAL BALANCE
(as at July 31st 19··)
Dr.
Cr.
Cash 76·95
Bank 1,025·75
Capital 10,000·00
(5) from which we prepare a set of Final Accounts
TRADING A/c
(In which we calculate the Gross Profit)
Gross Profit
PROFIT & LOSS A/c
(In which we calculate the Net Profit)
Net Profit
Gross Profit
APPORIATION SECTION
(In which we appropriate the profits to those entitled to receive them)
Transferred to Capital A/c
Net Profit
BALANCE SHEET
(In which we list the Assets and Liabilities of the business)
Liabilities including Capital
Assets

Fig. 11.4. Double-entry book-keeping.

Three-Column Cash Book or the Petty Cash Book. We also have Bill Books to record Bills of Exchange, and several other books. These Day Books keep a record of the documents received in chronological order, which is a useful record to have.

(3) Posting the Day Books to the Ledger

When we have entered our original documents in the Day Books we then post the transactions into the Ledger, which is the main book of account. Every transaction will appear twice, because one account will be receiving value and another giving it. For this reason the entries will be a debit entry in one account and a credit entry in some other account. Hundreds, even thousands, of accounts may be involved, but if we do our double entry carefully the total entries on the debit side will exactly balance the total entries on the credit side. This is the way we check the books, by taking out a Trial Balance.

(4) The Trial Balance

This is what its name implies, an attempt to discover whether the books really do balance. If they do not we know that someone has made a mistake somewhere, and we must discover it.

To take out a Trial Balance we must look at every account in our Ledger, and there may be thousands of them. Each account will be in one of three positions:

(*a*) It may have a debit balance outstanding.
(*b*) It may be clear, having no outstanding balance.
(*c*) It may have a credit balance outstanding.

We usually do a Trial Balance at least once a month, taking the opportunity to 'tidy up' accounts where we can, and bringing all the debit balances into a list of debit balances, and all the credit balances into a list of credit balances. These two columns of balances should come exactly equal, and we may conclude that if they do, it is fairly certain we have done our book-keeping well. The idea of the Trial Balance is the most important idea in book-keeping by the double-entry system, and it is fully explained in Chapter 12.

(5a) Final Accounts—The Trading Account

We are now ready to find out whether our business is profitable or running at a loss. To discover this, we first do a simple Trading Account. This shows whether we are selling at a profit. We find our sales figure from the Sales Account; we find our purchases figure from our Purchase Account. After one or two adjustments, chiefly connected with opening and closing stocks, we discover the **Cost of the Goods Sold.** A few more little matters help us discover the **Cost of Sales,** which is not quite the same as the Cost of Goods Sold, since it includes a few expenses. Then Sales minus Cost of Sales gives us our overall profit—called in book-keeping the **Gross Profit.**

(5b) Final Accounts—The Profit and Loss Account

In this second half of our Final Accounts we start with the Gross Profit and take away from it all overhead expenses. We add items of profit, such as commission or discounts received. This leads us to the clear profit or clean profit—called in book-keeping **Net Profit.** This Net Profit is the reward of the businessman for his efforts.

With partnership enterprises and with limited companies, the Net Profit has to be shared up between the partners or shareholders. This is done in a section of the Profit and Loss Account called the **Appropriation Account.** We give the profit to the appropriate persons in the appropriate proportions according to the partnership agreement or the resolution passed at the annual general meeting of the company.

(5c) The Balance Sheet

When we have prepared the Final Accounts, discovered the profit (or loss) and allotted it to those entitled to receive (or suffer) it, we have established what degree of success the business has achieved, and all we need to do now is summarise the final position of the business by drawing up a **Balance Sheet** which shows the assets and liabilities of the firm.

This is the general pattern of double-entry book-keeping. To abbreviate it into two sentences: *It is a process of recording documents in books of original entry; posting them from these books into the main book of account; proving the accuracy of the book-keeping by taking out a Trial Balance and from that Trial Balance drawing up a Trading Account and Profit and Loss Account to discover the profit (or loss) of the business. The residue of items left, which carries on into the next financial year, is drawn up into a neat Balance Sheet of assets and liabilities.*

Goethe, perhaps the greatest genius of his age, described book-keeping as 'one of the sublimest creations of the human mind'. What, one wonders, would he have thought of a modern computer, which can add one amount to another 5 000 times in a thousandth of a second, sort 50 000 entries into correct order in one minute, print 12 statement sheets with 30 entries on each in less than two seconds and find the information on 144 different accounts in one second. Even the author of Faust could not have dreamed up such Mephistophelean powers. Fortunately they do not have to be used for evil purposes; instead they work out Trial Balances in the twinkling of an eye.

11.6 The Computerisation of Double-Entry Book-keeping

The Computer Revolution. In the last quarter of a century the development of computers has revolutionised office practices. A program of instructions is fed into the computer which enables it to process any data supplied. Thus the entire debtors' ledger can be stored on a fast computer medium such as disc or magnetic tape, each debtor being given a unique code number which identifies him in the system. The average computer works at a speed of more than a million operations per second. Tedious manual preparation of invoices, credit notes and payments can be performed at electronic speeds, and the accounting entries done simultaneously. Although preparatory work must still be performed—for example, when an order is received—all the operations which follow from that order, e.g. invoicing, accounting records, statements, etc., can be carried out automatically.

Computer Hardware. Whilst a detailed knowledge of computer hardware is not necessary, it is useful to be familiar with the names of the units and the

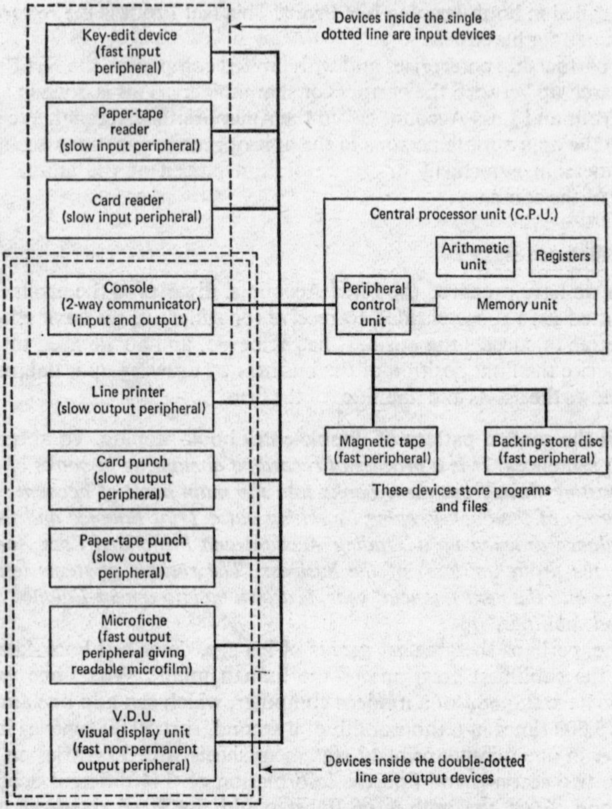

Fig. 11.5. A commercial computer configuration.

Note
It is not intended to imply that all configurations would use all the input and output devices shown. The input devices are alternatives, and only some would be used in any particular configuration. Similarly, the output devices are alternatives to some extent and only some of them would be used to meet the needs of the particular business.

parts they play in meeting the firm's accounting requirements. Fig. 11.5 shows a typical commercial computer configuration.

The three essential elements in computerisation are **inputs, data processing** and **outputs**. We must be able to put data into the computer, which will then process the data and put out the results so that they can be understood. These three elements are provided for in the following ways.

(*a*) *Input Devices.* Some typical input devices are punched-card readers, paper-tape readers, key-edit devices and the console communicator, which is like an electric typewriter. All these devices are relatively slow in the preparation and checking stage. At the time of input the card reader operates at about 160 000 characters per minute; much slower than the computer's million operations per second. The key-edit device is faster, since information is fed onto magnetic tape rather than cards or paper tape. (The term 'edit' refers to the ability of the device to detect when an operator miskeys and feeds an error into the system.) When a collection of documents, such as purchases invoices, is to be put into the computer, the documents are **batched up, coded** with any necessary codes and passed to the punch or key operator. The resulting punched cards, paper tape or magnetic tape can then be used to pass data into the computer. This is called **data transfer**. The data can now be processed according to the programs already stored in the computer.

(*b*) *The Central Processor Unit*. The CPU is the main section of the computer and contained within it are the **memory unit**, the **peripheral control unit or units**, the **arithmetic unit** and the **registers**.

The *memory unit* of the CPU determines the powers of the computer, since it is here that the actual processing of data according to programmed instructions take place.

The *arithmetic unit* is located in the CPU, and here the calculations such as multiplication and division are performed. The answers, and partial answers, to the calculations are stored in the registers temporarily, from where they may be transferred to the memory unit for subsequent output to tape or disc storage.

Peripheral control units are designed to deal with all the ancillary equipment used for input and output of information. Outside components are known as peripherals. The word 'periphery' means 'outside boundary' and the peripherals may be regarded as surrounding the CPU. Note that in some instances the peripheral control units are themselves peripheral to the CPU.

(*c*) *Output Devices*. The chief method of output in the final stage is the **line printer**. This prints out the result of the processed data. It is the computer's most convenient method of communication since it can be read by the human user. Speeds vary with the type of device but an output of 1 300 lines per minute, each line having a maximum of 132 characters, is representative. Other output devices, such as punched cards or paper tape, are less easily understood by the human user. As can be imagined, the production of output information is governed by the printer speed, which is low. To overcome this difficulty matter for printing is **queued** on a fast medium, such as tape or disc, and then printed by a specialist program divorced from the original program. This is known as **'off-line' printing**.

Another method which avoids vast collections of print-out material is the development of **COM (computer output to microfilm)**, which can be produced direct from a magnetic tape file, so that no printing is required. The computer output consists of a succession of microfilm exposures—photographed from a cathode ray tube—which can be read in a microfilm reader.

How Computers have changed Book-keeping. In Fig. 11.4 we have seen how the double-entry book-keeping system works. If we wish to see how computers have modified book-keeping it is useful to redraw this chart, in computerised form, and this is done in Fig. 11.6 (see pages 136–137). The chart is largely self-explanatory.

It is not usual for computers to prepare final accounts, although they can be programmed to do so. The point here is that the cost of a program to make decisions at the final accounts level is greater than the cost of the work saved. Such decisions are most easily made by the accountant. Generally speaking the preparation of final accounts from the print-outs of the ledgers supplied by the computer is a straightforward task easily carried out manually. The reader should now study the chart on pages 136–137.

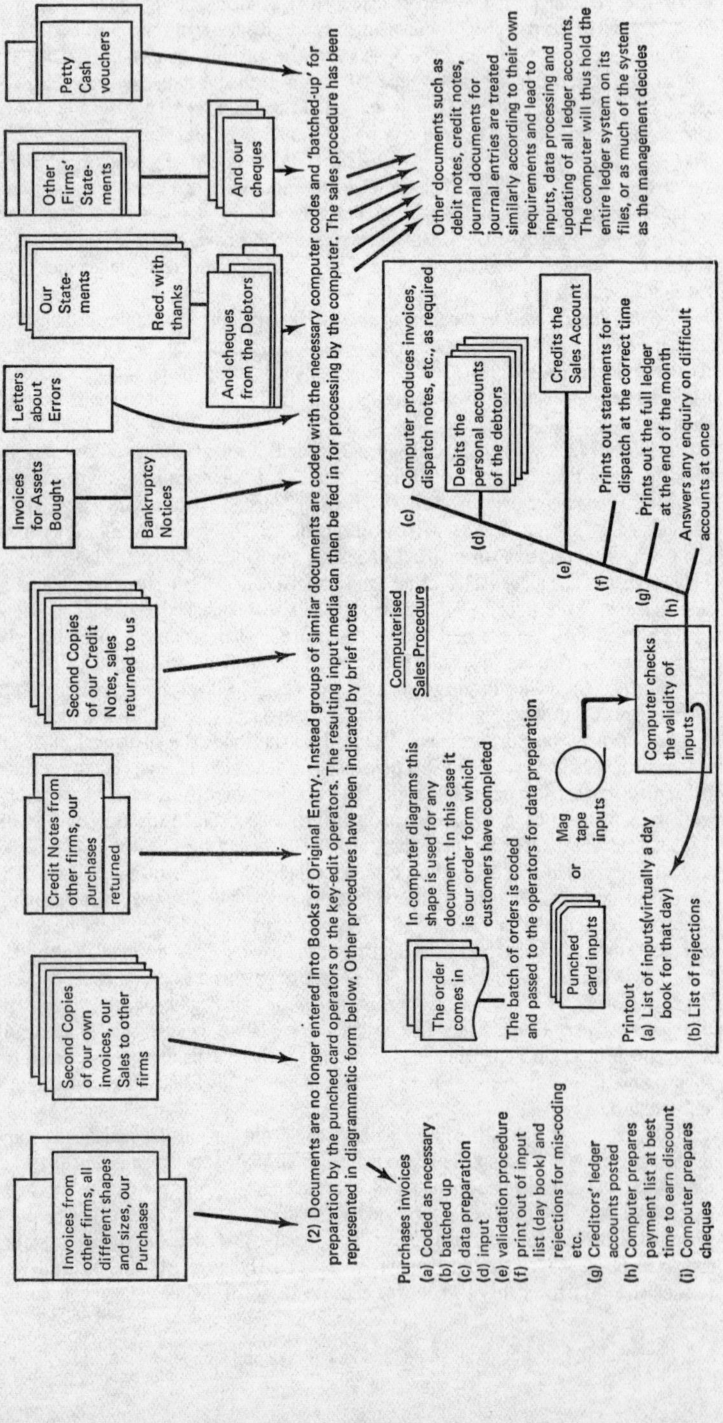
(1) Every transaction has an original document
(but now most of these documents will be produced by the computer automatically instead of manually)
Invoices from other firms, all different shapes and sizes, our Purchases
Second Copies of our own invoices, our Sales to other firms
Credit Notes from other firms, our purchases returned
Second Copies of our Credit Notes, sales returned to us
Invoices for Assets Bought
Bankruptcy Notices
Letters about Errors
Our Statements
Recd. with thanks
And cheques from the Debtors
Other Firms' Statements
And our cheques
Petty Cash vouchers
(2) Documents are no longer entered into Books of Original Entry. Instead groups of similar documents are coded with the necessary computer codes and 'batched-up' for preparation by the punched card operators or the key-edit operators. The resulting input media can then be fed in for processing by the computer. The sales procedure has been represented in diagrammatic form below. Other procedures have been indicated by brief notes
Purchases invoices
(a) Coded as necessary
(b) batched up
(c) data preparation
(d) input
(e) validation procedure
(f) print out of input list (day book) and rejections for mis-coding etc.
(g) Creditors' ledger accounts posted
(h) Computer prepares payment list at best time to earn discount
(i) Computer prepares cheques
Computerised Sales Procedure
The order comes in
In computer diagrams this shape is used for any document. In this case it is our order form which customers have completed
The batch of orders is coded and passed to the operators for data preparation
Punched card inputs
or
Mag tape inputs
Computer checks the validity of inputs
Printout
(a) List of inputs(virtually a day book for that day)
(b) List of rejections
(c) Computer produces invoices, dispatch notes, etc., as required
(d) Debits the personal accounts of the debtors
(e) Credits the Sales Account
(f) Prints out statements for dispatch at the correct time
(g) Prints out the full ledger at the end of the month
(h) Answers any enquiry on difficult accounts at once
Other documents such as debit notes, credit notes, journal documents for journal entries are treated similarly according to their own requirements and lead to inputs, data processing and updating of all ledger accounts. The computer will thus hold the entire ledger system on its files, or as much of the system as the management decides

(3) The computer has already:
(a) accepted all input data
(b) validated it and produced a day-book listing (and listed any rejected items)
(c) produced many documents such as invoices, statements, etc.
(d) posted the entire ledger system
(e) controlled payments outwards and produced the cheques
(f) produced information as required on individual 'enquiries'

(4) The computer will now:
(a) print out the full ledger showing every posting since the previous print-out, in readable form. It will at the same time balance off all the accounts in the computer
(b) produce, if suitably programmed, a wide range of statistical material with great ease, such as an age-of-debtors list, new suppliers' list, control totals for sales areas, etc.

(5) Finally the computer prints out the detailed figures for each chief field of interest which has been computerised

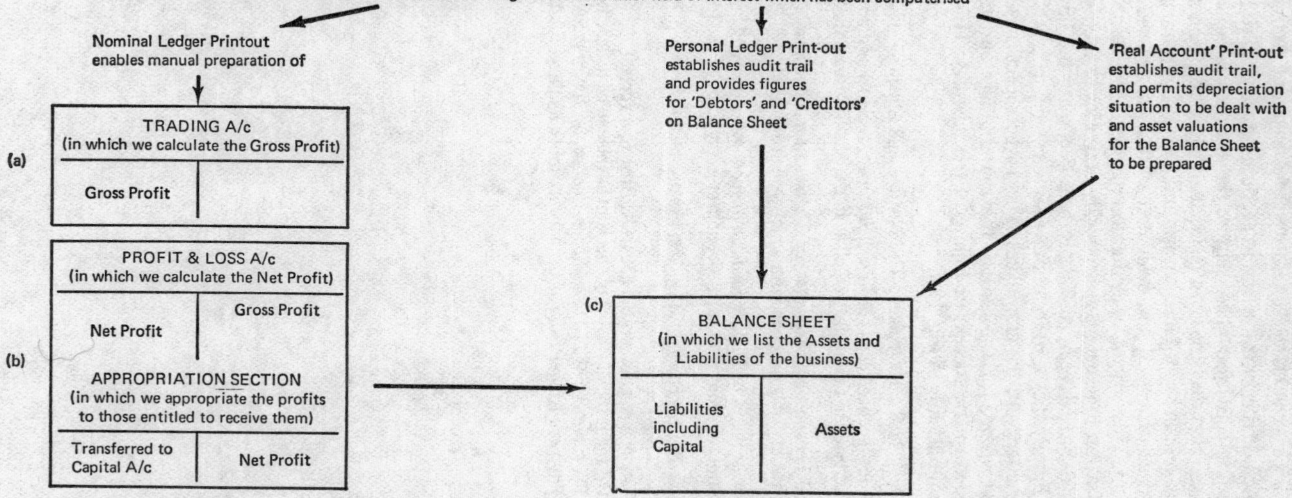

Nominal Ledger Printout enables manual preparation of
(a)
TRADING A/c
(in which we calculate the Gross Profit)
Gross Profit
(b)
PROFIT & LOSS A/c
(in which we calculate the Net Profit)
Net Profit
Gross Profit
APPROPRIATION SECTION
(in which we appropriate the profits to those entitled to receive them)
Transferred to Capital A/c
Net Profit
Personal Ledger Print-out establishes audit trail and provides figures for 'Debtors' and 'Creditors' on Balance Sheet
'Real Account' Print-out establishes audit trail, and permits depreciation situation to be dealt with and asset valuations for the Balance Sheet to be prepared
(c)
BALANCE SHEET
(in which we list the Assets and Liabilities of the business)
Liabilities including Capital
Assets

Fig. 11.6. How double-entry has been computerised.

11.7 The Pattern of Accounting Activities

To conclude this introduction to accounting we need to look at the pattern of accounting activities. These require the estimation, collection and evaluation of data so that decisions can be made, operations planned and monitored and records kept in accordance with sound accounting principles. Then these data have to be processed and evaluated so that we can see quite clearly what is going on. This process of evaluation may lead to a feedback into the business organisation in some way, to modify activities in the light of changes which appear to have developed. This is the aspect of accounting as *a tool of management*. Finally they lead to reports to interested parties, the Inland Revenue, the shareholders and the employees. This is the aspect of accounting as *a record of stewardship*, for the nation, the shareholders and the employees are all interested in the success or failure of the business. This pattern is displayed diagrammatically in Fig. 11.7.

11.8 Exercises: The Nature and Purpose of Accounting

1. 'A book-keeper keeps records of *historical* receipts and payments. An accountant is interested in the future as well as in the past.' Discuss these statements.

2. What is meant by '*Accountancy is a tool of management*'? Explain with reference to a variety of businesses with which you are familiar.

3. What is meant by '*the stewardship of economic resources*'? To whom is the steward accountable, and why is an accountant likely to be of use to him?

4. Define double entry, and explain the double-entry nature of each of the following transactions:
   (*a*) The sale of goods value £50 to R. Brown, on credit.
   (*b*) Payment by R. Brown of this sum at the end of the credit period.
   (*c*) The payment of £10 to a glazier, in cash, for repairs to a window.
   (*d*) Payment to R. Peters of £180 for a month's salary.

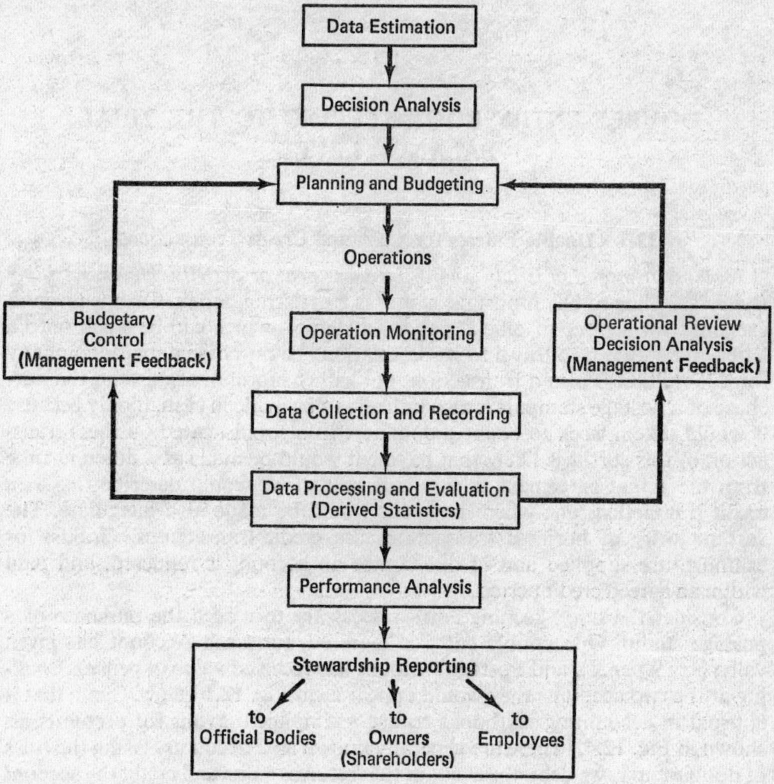

Fig. 11.7. The pattern of accounting activities.

Notes

(i) This diagram shows the more difficult accounting activities; all the elementary financial accounting in this book would be carried out in the three boxes 'data collection and recording', 'data processing and evaluation' and 'performance analysis'.

(ii) Accounting begins in the planning stage when information about the likely costs of any proposed business activities begins to be assembled (data estimation).

(iii) On the basis of these data, decisions which might be made are analysed and the best decisions arrived at in the light of this analysis.

(iv) Planning and budgeting follows, so that operations can begin.

(v) Once started, operations are monitored, a host of data about costs incurred, sales achieved, transactions engaged in, etc., are collected, recorded and processed. From the activities feedbacks are instituted to modify the plans and budgets in the light of real events. These modify the operations to correct unfavourable trends and take advantage of favourable ones.

(vi) At suitable intervals performance is analysed and reports are made to the parties interested. This is the stewardship function.

12

DOUBLE-ENTRY BOOK-KEEPING TO THE TRIAL BALANCE LEVEL

12.1 Double Entries for Cash and Credit Transactions

A business transaction is any sort of business deal or activity, however trifling it may be. Thus to buy a postage stamp is a **cash transaction**. Cash is given in exchange for a piece of official paper—a stamp—which can be stuck onto a letter and entitle it to travel to its destination. To purchase a major company for £25 million is also a transaction, but rather more involved than the purchase of a postage stamp. It is also unlikely to be made in cash, if only because it would take a week to count the money. In a sophisticated business transaction of this sort it is likely that payment would be made at a different time from the actual agreement to buy and sell, so we would describe this as a **credit transaction**, one where payment would be made at a later date. The vast majority of business transactions are credit transactions. Goods, for example, are supplied and in due course an account is rendered, and paid within an agreed credit period.

Consider the book-keeping entries necessary to record the purchase of a postage stamp. One double entry is required, for Cash Account has given value (say 9 pence), and Postage Account has received value (9 pence). Looking at the two accounts they would appear as in Fig. 12.1 below. (Note that it is usual in accounting textbooks to use a simplified layout for accounts, as shown in Fig. 12.4.) These are generally known as T accounts. Using the rules of double entry, we debit the account that receives value and credit the account that gives value. So we must debit Postage Account and credit Cash Account. Now look at Fig. 12.1 and the notes below it.

Now consider what entries would be necessary for the sale of goods on credit. Suppose we sell T. Robinson goods value £500 on July 1st, but he pays for them only on August 3rd, when he receives our monthly account. *We now need two double entries.* First we have to debit T. Robinson when he receives the goods, and credit Sales Account, which gave them to him. Later, at the end of the credit period, he pays us for the goods, and we credit him as the giver of the money and debit Bank Account because it has received the money. (He would be most unlikely to pay in cash, so Cash Account would not be affected.)

The first double entry is shown in Fig. 12.2, and the second double entry in Fig. 12.3.

Every single business transaction has to be recorded in the accounts by a double entry. If it is not, then the books will not balance and a Trial Balance cannot be extracted. Of course, there are systems of book-keeping which do not use double entry, like the 'Butcher's Book' method. When Mrs Brown took a joint without paying for it the butcher would write her name and the amount in his Day Book, which was really just a 'List of Debtors'. When she came in to pay the bill he would find the entry and cross it out to show that the debt was settled. Any system of book-keeping of this type is called 'single entry', and it is totally inadequate for any real 'accounting' purpose.

In order to make the principles of double entry clear we have to keep records involving quite a number of different types of transaction, and it is usual to do the first few exercises by what is called 'direct double entry'. This means that we ignore the day books, like the Journal, the Sales Day Book and the Purchases Day Book, and make the entries directly into the Ledger accounts themselves. This is dealt with in the next section. It involves keeping the

POSTAGE ACCOUNT — L.15

19..	Details	F	£	19..	Details	F	£
Jan. 1	Cash	L.1	0.09				

CASH ACCOUNT — L.1

19..	Details	F	£	19..	Details	F	£
				Jan. 1	Postage	L.15	0.09

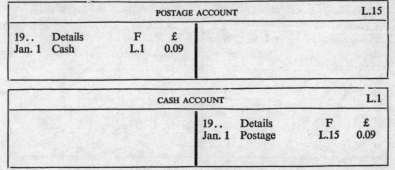

Fig. 12.1. Ledger entries for a simple cash transaction.

Notes

(i) The year has been written as 19.. to avoid appearing out of date.

(ii) Each account has its folio number written in the top right-hand corner. Postage Account is Ledger Page 15, and Cash Account is Ledger Page 1.

(iii) Postage Account has been debited, because it has received value (£0.09).

(iv) Cash account has been credited, because it has given value (£0.09).

(v) In the 'details' column the name of the account where the other half of the double entry is to be found is written in.

(vi) In the folio column (F), next to the money column, the cross-reference number of the other half of the double entry is written. So when looking at the Postage Account we can see that the other half of the double entry is on Page 1 of the Ledger, which is the Cash Account, whilst when looking at the Cash Account we can see that the other half of the double entry is on Page 15 of the Ledger, which is the Postage Account.

accounts for a short period, making all the double entries, and then taking out a Trial Balance to see if the books do balance and have been kept in a proper manner. Usually a month is chosen as a suitable period.

12.2 Types of Double Entry

First let us note the types of transaction which we are likely to meet in such an exercise, and in everyday life. They are:

(*a*) *Contributions of money or goods by the proprietor*. This is a contribution of capital, which brings assets (either cash or other useful things) into the business, given by the owner (the capitalist). Hence we must *debit the asset accounts* which are receiving value, and *credit Capital Account*, which is giving value.

(*b*) *Spending money from Cash Account* (*in cash*) *or from Bank Account* (*paying by cheque*). Since these accounts are giving value we credit them: *Credit Cash Account* if we spend cash, *Credit Bank Account* if we pay by cheque. The next question is, 'What did we spend the money on?' If we spent it on an asset, like furniture, we *debit the asset account*. If we spent it on something with a very short life, like a postage stamp, we regard the thing purchased not as an asset, but as a loss of the business. The account to be debited is the Nominal Account where we record such losses. So the rule is *Debit the Loss Account*. Examples are Postage Account, Repairs Account, Office Cleaning Account, etc.

(*c*) *Paying money to creditors*. These are suppliers to whom we owe money. We usually pay by cheque, or perhaps by credit transfer (bank giro). This means we *credit Bank Account*, which is giving money and *debit the creditor's*

T. ROBINSON ACCOUNT L.126

		F	£			F	£
19..							
Jul. 1	Sales	L.8	500.00				

SALES ACCOUNT L.8

		F	£			F	£
				19..			
				Jul. 1	T. Robinson	L.126	500.00

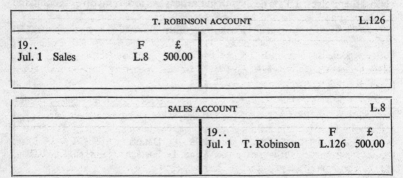

Fig. 12.2. Ledger entries for a sale on credit.

T. ROBINSON ACCOUNT L.126

		F	£			F	£
19..				19..			
Jul. 1	Sales	L.8	500.00	Aug. 3	Bank	L.2	500.00

BANK ACCOUNT L.2

		F	£			F	£
19..							
Aug. 3	T. Robinson	L.126	500.00				

Fig. 12.3. Ledger entries for payment for goods supplied earlier.

Notes
(i) In Fig. 12.2 T. Robinson was a debtor for £500.
(ii) In Fig. 12.3 he settles his debt by giving a cheque for £500, and his account is then clear (of any outstanding balance).

account, for he is receiving the money. The account of the creditor is of course a Personal Account.

(*d*) *Receiving money from debtors*. These are customers who owe us money for goods supplied earlier. This time the debtor is giving and we are receiving. *Debit Cash Account* if they pay in cash; *debit Bank Account* if they pay by cheque. *Credit the Personal Account* of the debtor who has given the money.

(*e*) *Sales on credit*. When we sell on credit, payment for the goods is postponed until later. The double entry records the giving of the goods (by Sales Account) and their receipt by the customer (who becomes a debtor of the business). So the rule is *debit A. Customer, credit Sales Account.*

(*f*) *Purchases on credit*. When we buy on credit the entry is the opposite of the one above. This time we are receiving goods (*debit Purchases Account*) and the supplier is giving them (*credit A. Supplier*).

(*g*) *Returns inwards*. A. Customer is dissatisfied with goods and returns them. We receive back the goods (*debit Sales Returns Account*) and he gives them (*credit A. Customer*).

(*h*) *Returns outwards*. The reverse of what is happening in (*g*) above. This time we are dissatisfied and return goods. The supplier receives them. *Debit A. Supplier* and *credit Purchases Returns Account*.

(*i*) *Withdrawal of money by the proprietor*. When this happens we call it 'Drawings' because the proprietor is drawing out some of his capital, or perhaps it would be better to say some of the profits he hopes he has made. The rule is: *debit Drawings Account* (which is receiving money) and *credit Cash Account* or *Bank Account*, whichever is giving it.

You might say that the wide variety of entries above are the everyday entries that we meet again and again. All sorts of other entries occur and require us to use our commonsense to decide what to do: for example, if we have a loan from the bank, who is giving the money (our friendly bank manager) and who is receiving it (we are, in the Bank Account). So *debit Bank Account* and *credit Loan Account* (*Generous Bank Ltd.*).

Let us now turn to explaining the double entries in the Model Exercise below.

12.3 A Model Exercise in Direct Double Entry

When doing an exercise of this sort it is usual to imagine a business that is just starting, for an established business would have a great many accounts already open, and it would be difficult to use an established set of accounts as many of them would have balances on them. In the details given below we have the starting position, and the first month's transactions of Abel Craftsman, who sets up in business with £1 000.00 cash on October 1st. The details of his transactions are as follows.

ABEL CRAFTSMAN'S TRANSACTIONS FOR OCTOBER

Oct.	1	Commenced business with a capital of £1 000.00 in cash
	1	Banked £850.00 of the cash
	1	Purchased goods for resale: £420.00 by cheque
	1	Sold goods on credit to M. Castle: £400
	2	Cash sales: £90.00
	3	Paid office expenses in cash: £5.00
	5	Purchased furniture for office use by cheque: £180.00
	8	Paid wages in cash: £35.00
	10	Sold goods on credit to R. Brown: £40.00
	12	M. Castle settled his account by cheque, less $2\frac{1}{2}$ per cent cash discount
	14	Received a loan from A. Banker £250.00. The bank charged interest at 10 per cent for one year
	16	Paid for repairs to garage lock: £4.80 in cash
	20	Bought goods on credit from J. Harper: £40.00
	24	Paid rates by cheque: £124.75
	26	Withdrew from bank for private use: £50.00

28 Cash sales: £120.00
29 Bought goods on credit from J. Horne: £85.55
30 Paid office-cleaning expenses: £16.25 in cash
31 Paid into bank from office cash: £100.00. Paid salaries by cheque: £124.00

Make the necessary entries in the Ledger and extract a Trial Balance.

The actual entries in the accounts for all these transactions are given in Fig. 12.4. The reader should follow the entries with the help of the explanations given below.

Explanation of Abel Craftsman's double entries

Oct. 1. Craftsman gave the business £1 000 in cash. This would mean that the Cash Account received £1 000, so we debit Cash Account, and we credit Craftsman's Capital Account because he gave the money (credit the giver).

Oct. 1. He banked £850; which means that Cash Account gave £850 to the Bank, which received it. Debit the receiver (Bank Account) and credit the giver (Cash Account).

Oct. 1. Craftsman purchased goods for resale by cheque. Bank Account gave £420 (credit Bank Account) and Purchases Account received £420 of goods (debit Purchases Account).

Oct. 1. Craftsman sold goods in credit to M. Castle for £400. This means that Castle receives the goods, and must be debited, thus becoming a debtor of the business. Sales Account is the giver of the goods, and is credited. Of course, Sales Account is a nominal account, the entry is just a record of the goods sold. Later the money paid for them will be received, but as the goods are sold on credit it will be some time before this happens.

Oct. 2. Cash Sales £90.00. Of course this entry is the result of 'cashing up' the till. In most shops this is done every day, or even every few hours, but here it is not a very frequent occurrence. Debit the Cash Account which has received the money, and credit Sales Account which has given the goods.

Oct. 3. When we pay for office expenses in cash, the Cash Account gives the money (credit the giver) but the Office Expenses Account has received this amount of value. Debit Office Expenses Account with £5.00; one of the losses of the business.

Oct. 5. This is the purchase of a fixed asset. When we buy furniture and pay by cheque Bank Account gives the money (credit Bank Account) and Furniture Account receives this amount of value, so debit the Furniture Account with £180.00.

Oct. 8. When we pay wages in cash, Cash Account gives the money £35.00 and Wages Account receives it. Of course, really the worker receives the money, but it is a loss of the business and it is recorded in the Wages Account, one of the nominal accounts. Debit Wages Account and credit Cash Account.

Oct. 10. When goods are sold on credit to R. Brown he receives the goods (debit R. Brown with £40.00) which are given by the Sales Account. Credit the Sales Account with £40.00.

Oct. 12. When M. Castle settles his account, which we see from October 1st above is £400, less 2½ per cent discount, he actually gives us £390 and Bank Account receives it. Debit Bank Account £390. Of course, because of the discount we allowed him, the full £400 has been settled. We must therefore credit Castle with both £390 and £10 discount allowed. This must be debited in Discount Allowed Account, as a loss of the business.

Oct. 14. If a bank lends us £250.00 and charges interest at 10 per cent for one year, the amount to be repaid is £275.00 (£250.00 + £25.00 interest). We receive the £250.00 as a debit entry in the Bank Account, but the Loan Account (A. Banker) has to be credited with £275.00. The other £25.00 is debited to Interest Payable Account as one of the losses of the business.

Oct. 16. We must credit Cash Account with £4.80, because it has given the cash to the locksmith, and debit Repairs Account which is one of the 'loss' accounts of the business.

Oct. 20. This is the purchase of goods from J. Harper. He gives the goods (credit Harper's Account with £40.00) and we record their receipt on the debit side of the Purchases Account.

Oct. 24. When rates are paid by cheque the Bank Account gives the money (credit Bank Account with £124.75) and Rates Account is debited (one of the 'loss' accounts of the business).

Oct. 26. The Bank Account gives the owner of the business £50.00 (credit Bank Account) and Drawings Account is debited. Remember 'Drawings' is what the owner draws out in expectation of profits earned.

Oct. 28. When goods are sold for cash, the money is received by Cash Account (debit Cash Account with £120) and Sales Account gives the goods, so credit Sales Account.

Oct. 29. J. Horne gives goods (credit J. Horne Account £85.55) and debit Purchases Account which receives them.

Oct. 30. Credit Cash Account with £16.25, and debit Office-Cleaning Account (one of the losses of the business).

Oct. 31. When money is paid into the Bank from office cash Bank Account receives the money (debit Bank Account with £100.00) and Cash Account gives it (credit Cash Account with £100.00). The second entry requires Bank Account to be credited with £124.00 as it is giving the money, and Salaries Account is debited with £124.00.

The reader who makes these entries on typical ledger paper (obtainable from most stationers) will find that they finish up as shown in Fig. 12.4 (pages 145–147). Note, however, that at the end of the month, in order that a Trial Balance can be prepared, the accounts have to be tidied up a little. This tidying up process has not been done in Fig. 12.4. To help the reader this process is explained in the next section.

CASH ACCOUNT L.1

			F	£				F	£
19..					19..				
Oct.	1	Capital	L.2	1 000.00	Oct.	1	Bank	L.3	850.00
	2	Sales	L.6	90.00		3	Office Expenses	L.7	5.00
	28	,,	L.6	120.00		8	Wages	L.9	35.00
						16	Repairs	L.14	4.80
						30	Office Cleaning	L.19	16.25
						31	Bank	L.3	100.00

CAPITAL ACCOUNT L.2

			F	£				F	£
					19..				
					Oct.	1	Cash	L.1	1 000.00

BANK ACCOUNT L.3

19..		F	£	19..		F	£
Oct. 1	Cash	L.1	850.00	Oct. 1	Purchases	L.4	420.00
12	M. Castle	L.5	390.00	5	Furniture	L.8	180.00
14	Loan Account (A. Banker)	L.12	250.00	24	Rates	L.16	124.75
				26	Drawings	L.17	50.00
31	Cash	L.1	100.00	31	Salaries	L.20	124.00

PURCHASES ACCOUNT L.4

19..		F	£	19..		F	£
Oct. 1	Bank	L.3	420.00				
20	J. Harper	L.15	40.00				
29	J. Horne	L.18	85.55				

M. CASTLE ACCOUNT L.5

19..		F	£	19..		F	£
Oct. 1	Sales	L.6	400.00	Oct. 12	Bank	L.3	390.00
				12	Discount Allowed	L.11	10.00

SALES ACCOUNT L.6

19..		F	£	19..		F	£
				Oct. 1	M. Castle	L.5	400.00
				2	Cash	L.1	90.00
				10	R. Brown	L.10	40.00
				28	Cash	L.1	120.00

OFFICE EXPENSES ACCOUNT L.7

19..		F	£	19..		F	£
Oct. 3	Cash	L.1	5.00				

FURNITURE ACCOUNT L.8

19..		F	£	19..		F	£
Oct. 5	Bank	L.3	180.00				

WAGES ACCOUNT L.9

19..		F	£	19..		F	£
Oct. 8	Cash	L.1	35.00				

R. BROWN ACCOUNT L.10

19..		F	£	19..		F	£
Oct. 10	Sales	L.6	40.00				

DISCOUNT ALLOWED ACCOUNT L.11

19..		F	£	19..		F	£
Oct. 12	M. Castle	L.5	10.00				

LOAN ACCOUNT (A. BANKER) L.12

19..		F	£	19..		F	£
				Oct. 14	Bank	L.3	250.00
				14	Interest Payable	L.13	25.00

INTEREST PAYABLE ACCOUNT L.13

		F	£			F	£
19..				19..			
Oct. 14	Loan Account	L.12	25.00				

REPAIRS ACCOUNT L.14

		F	£			F	£
19..				19..			
Oct. 16	Cash	L.1	4.80				

J. HARPER ACCOUNT L.15

		F	£			F	£
19..				19..			
				Oct. 20	Purchases	L.4	40.00

RATES ACCOUNT L.16

		F	£			F	£
19..				19..			
Oct. 24	Bank	L.3	124.75				

DRAWINGS ACCOUNT L.17

		F	£			F	£
19..				19..			
Oct. 26	Bank	L.3	50.00				

J. HORNE ACCOUNT L.18

		F	£			F	£
19..				19..			
				Oct. 29	Purchases	L.4	85.55

OFFICE CLEANING ACCOUNT L.19

		F	£			F	£
19..				19..			
Oct. 30	Cash	L.1	16.25				

SALARIES ACCOUNT L.20

		F	£			F	£
19..				19..			
Oct. 31	Bank	L.3	124.00				

Fig. 12.4. Ledger entries for the Model Exercise (Books of Abel Craftsman).

12.4 Tidying up Accounts For a Trial Balance

When we test the accuracy of the book-keeping records by extracting a Trial Balance it is necessary to draw up a list of all the accounts which have balances on them. A Trial Balance is prepared at regular intervals, usually monthly. There are three possible situations:

(*a*) An account might have no balance on it at all, when we say it is clear.
(*b*) An account may have a debit balance, like Office Expenses Account in Fig. 12.4.
(*c*) An account may have a credit balance, like Capital Account in Fig. 12.4

However, with some accounts it is not easy to see what the balance is until we tidy up that account. Thus the Cash Account and Bank Account in Fig.

12.4 are in a very unclear state, with a great many entries on each side. Even the Sales Account in Fig. 12.4 is not too clear; it obviously has a credit balance, but we need to add it up to find the total.

To tidy up accounts for a Trial Balance we take the following types of action:

(*a*) Where an account has only one item on it, as in the case of Capital Account, Office Expenses Account and several others, no action at all is required. We can see at once whether the account has a debit balance or a credit balance, and how much the balance is. Such balances can be taken straight away to the Trial Balance.

(*b*) Where an account has several entries, all on the same side, it is usual simply to add them up and write the total on the page very faintly in pencil. This total will be the debit balance or credit balance as the case may be, to be taken to the Trial Balance. Thus the total of Sales Account is £650.00, and the total of Purchases Account is £545.55. The totals would be written faintly in pencil on the accounts and carried to the Trial Balance as credit and debit items respectively.

(*c*) The accounts with entries on both sides now have to be balanced off. To do this we add up the debit side and then the credit side to see what is the

M. CASTLE ACCOUNT — L.5

19..		F	£	19..		F	£
Oct. 1	Sales	L.6	400.00	Oct. 12	Bank	L.3	390.00
				12	Discount Allowed	L.11	10.00
			£400.00				£400.00

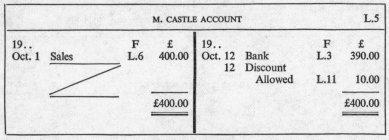

Fig. 12.5. An account which is 'clear'.

difference between the two. In the case of M. Castle's Account there is no difference. M. Castle's Account would therefore be balanced off as shown in Fig. 12.5. Since this account is clear, it will not need to appear on the Trial Balance at all. Note that a Z is drawn in on the lines where the debit side is shorter than the credit side. This is to prevent anyone at a future date from making a debit entry on that line, which has already been balanced off.

(*d*) Where accounts are not clear but a balance is outstanding, the balance has to be brought down to the new month. Thus in Cash Account the balance of cash in hand is £198.95. This figure is written in on the credit side (which of course makes both sides the same—the account is now balanced), but then the figure is brought down to the debit side at the start of the next month to show the balance of cash in hand on the first day of November. This is shown in Fig. 12.6. Note that the Z is once again used to fill in the spare lines on the debit side.

(*e*) The same procedure for the Bank Account reveals that the bank balance on October 31st, 19.., is £691.25, as shown in Fig. 12.7.

Mechanised or Computerised Accounts. The accounts shown in Figs. 12.5, 12.6 and 12.7 are of the traditional type. In these days of mechanised and

CASH ACCOUNT							L.1
19..		F	£	19..		F	£
Oct. 1	Capital	L.2	1 000.00	Oct. 1	Bank	L.3	850.00
2	Sales	L.6	90.00	3	Office Expenses	L.7	5.00
28	"	L.6	120.00	8	Wages	L.9	35.00
				16	Repairs	L.14	4.80
				30	Office Cleaning	L.19	16.25
				31	Bank	L.3	100.00
				31	Balance	C/d	198.95
			£1 210.00				£1 210.00
19..		F	£				
Nov. 1	Balance	B/d	198.95				

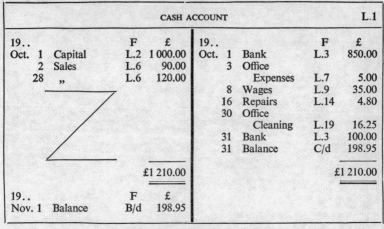

Fig. 12.6. Balancing off the Cash Account.

computerised accounting the 'balancing-off' method shown in these three illustrations is not necessary, because the machine or the computer is programmed to produce a running balance after every entry is made. At any time when a debit entry is made it is printed in a debit column and the running balance is adjusted. Similarly, a credit entry is printed in a credit column, and the running balance is adjusted. This is illustrated in Fig. 12.8. (*Note.* The computer also adds up the sales to date to inform the sales manager how trade with this customer is developing.

12.5 Extracting a Trial Balance

In extracting a Trial Balance all that is necessary is to look at each account in the ledger, tidy it up if necessary by the balancing process and bring the balance down. The balances are then listed on a sheet of paper, with the debit balances in a debit column on the left, and next to them the credit balances in

BANK ACCOUNT							L.3
19..		F	£	19..		F	£
Oct. 1	Cash	L.1	850.00	Oct. 1	Purchases	L.4	420.00
12	M. Castle	L.5	390.00	5	Furniture	L.8	180.00
14	Loan A/c	L.12	250.00	24	Rates	L.16	124.75
31	Cash	L.1	100.00	26	Drawings	L.17	50.00
				31	Salaries	L.20	124.00
				31	Balance	C/d	691.25
			£1 590.00				£1 590.00
19..		F	£				
Nov. 1	Balance	B/d	691.25				

Fig. 12.7. Balancing off the Bank Account.

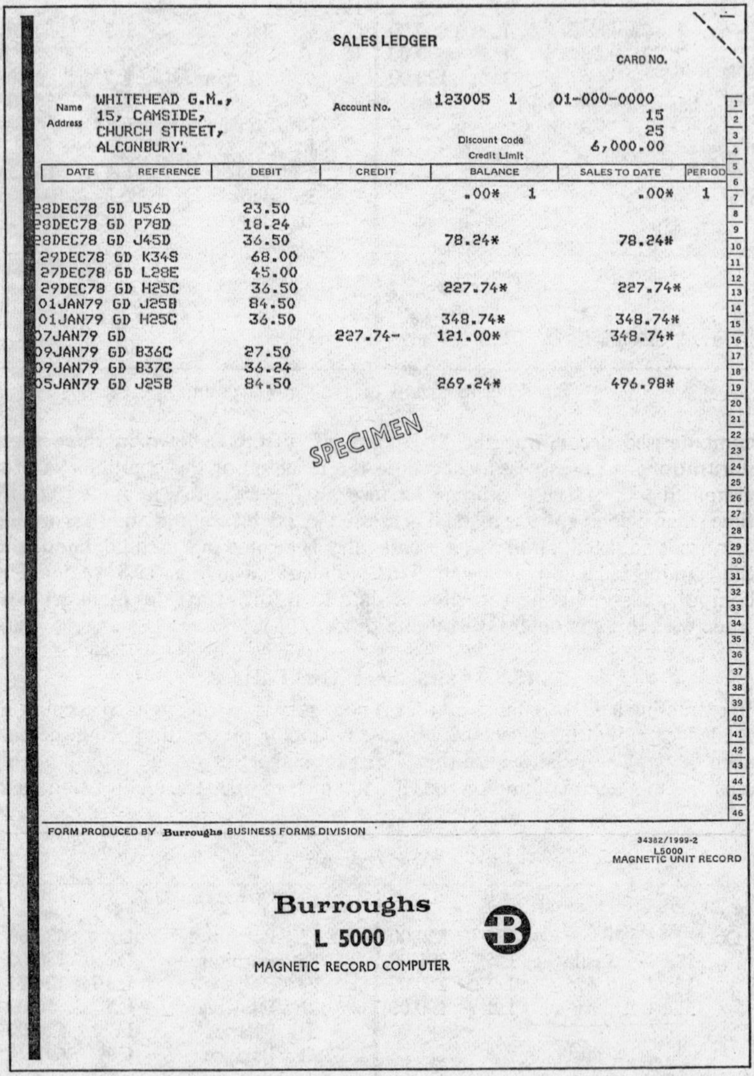

SALES LEDGER

CARD NO.

Name / Address: WHITEHEAD G.M., 15, CAMSIDE, CHURCH STREET, ALCONBURY.

Account No. 123005 1 01-000-0000

15

25

Discount Code

Credit Limit 6,000.00

DATE	REFERENCE	DEBIT	CREDIT	BALANCE	SALES TO DATE	PERIOD
				.00* 1	.00*	1
28DEC78	GD U56D	23.50				
28DEC78	GD P78D	18.24				
28DEC78	GD J45D	36.50		78.24*	78.24*	
29DEC78	GD K34S	68.00				
27DEC78	GD L28E	45.00				
29DEC78	GD H25C	36.50		227.74*	227.74*	
01JAN79	GD J25B	84.50				
01JAN79	GD H25C	36.50		348.74*	348.74*	
07JAN79	GD		227.74-	121.00*	348.74*	
09JAN79	GD B36C	27.50				
09JAN79	GD B37C	36.24				
05JAN79	GD J25B	84.50		269.24*	496.98*	

SPECIMEN

FORM PRODUCED BY Burroughs BUSINESS FORMS DIVISION

34382/1999-2

L5000

MAGNETIC UNIT RECORD

Burroughs

L 5000

MAGNETIC RECORD COMPUTER

Fig. 12.8. A mechanised account with running balance.

a column to the right. It is usual to list the names of the accounts, because it is helpful later in drawing up the 'Final Accounts' of the business. Just listing the folio numbers of the accounts is therefore not helpful. We have already seen that the Final Accounts, which are shown in the chart on page 131, are the Trading Account and the Profit and Loss Account. The preparation of these Final Accounts leaves us with a residue of accounts called the Balance Sheet. All this is explained in Chapter 14. The student should now study Fig. 12.9 carefully and note how it has been drawn up from the accounts shown in Figs. 12.4–12.7.

TRIAL BALANCE (BOOKS OF A. CRAFTSMAN)

(as at October 31st, 19. .)

		Dr. £	Cr. £
Cash A/c	L.1	198.95	
Capital A/c	L.2		1 000.00
Bank A/c	L.3	691.25	
Purchases A/c	L.4	545.55	
Sales A/c	L.6		650.00
Office Expenses A/c	L.7	5.00	
Furniture A/c	L.8	180.00	
Wages A/c	L.9	35.00	
R. Brown A/c	L.10	40.00	
Discount Allowed A/c	L.11	10.00	
A. Banker (Loan A/c)	L.12		275.00
Interest Payable A/c	L.13	25.00	
Repairs A/c	L.14	4.80	
J. Harper A/c	L.15		40.00
Rates A/c	L.16	124.75	
Drawings A/c	L.17	50.00	
J. Horne A/c	L.18		85.55
Office-Cleaning A/c	L.19	16.25	
Salaries A/c	L.20	124.00	
		£2 050.55	£2 050.55

Fig. 12.9. The Trial Balance of Abel Craftsman's Ledger.

12.6 What to Do if a Trial Balance Does Not Agree

If a Trial Balance does not agree there is a systematic procedure for discovering the error. Some of the steps in this procedure are rather complex and the reader will not yet fully understand them; they are discussed in detail later. The stages of the work in tracing errors are as follows:

(*a*) Add up the Debit and Credit columns again. It is easy to make a slip in addition, and a recheck is advisable.

(*b*) If the Trial Balance still does not agree take the total of one side from the other and find the difference. Imagine it is £27.56. Someone in the office may now have a bright idea, like '£27.56—that's what we paid for the second-hand duplicator we bought at the auction'. This kind of happy thought may save hours of work. When we check the item we find that it has been left off the Office Machinery Account.

(*c*) If no one has a happy thought like that, the next thing is to halve the difference and look for something on the wrong side of the Trial Balance. Half of £27.56 is £13.78. If a figure of £13.78 appears on the Trial Balance check to see if it is on the proper side: £13.78, for example put on the debit side when it should be on the credit side will make the debit side £13.78 too large and the credit side £13.78 too small, making a difference of £27.56.

(*d*) If we cannot correct the Trial Balance this way then our problem is more serious, but before we go on to other possibilities let us notice two more simple things. First, if an error is 1, or 10, or 100, or 1 000, or 0.10, or 0.01, it is probably due to a slip in addition. Somewhere we may have made a mistake in arithmetic that has put a balance out. For mistakes of this type a systematic check of all additions and subtractions is desirable.

Secondly, if an error divides by 9 it may be due to the transposition of figures. For instance, if a book-keeper writes 72 instead of 27 the error will be 45, which divides by 9. If an error divides by 9, then this is a possible cause of the trouble. Some people are very prone to make this kind of error because they are 'crossed laterals'—people whose dominant eye is not the same as their dominant hand. They may be right-handed and left-eyed, or left-handed and right-eyed. If you find that one book-keeper repeatedly makes this kind of mistake warn him to be especially careful about it.

(*e*) The next step is to check the extractions from the accounts into the Trial Balance. It is easy to make a slip here, and a quick 'calling over' of the Ledger Accounts to see if they have been extracted correctly will discover the error.

(*f*) If this has been done properly and the Trial Balance still does not agree, then we may be able to isolate certain sections of the work and prove that they are right by taking out Control Accounts. This is an important process which requires a whole chapter to itself, and the student is advised to disregard it for the present. It is fully explained in *Book-keeping Made Simple*.

(*g*) We must now check the entire month's activities, going over every single item and checking that a perfect double entry has been made in every case. This means checking all the additions, carrying forward, etc. It is a great labour, but to find the mistake it may be necessary.

(*h*) Finally, if we cannot find our mistake, we can open a **Suspense Account.** This means we take a new page in the Ledger and open up an account with the difference on the books. In the case we imagined earlier we would put £27.56 on the Suspense Account on the side where it was needed to make the books balance. The books will now agree, for the debits balance the credits; but, of course, sooner or later the mistakes are going to be discovered. The Suspense Account is a last-resort solution to the problem.

The student should now work through the exercises given below, and make sure he is thoroughly familiar with double entry and the extraction of Trial Balances to test the accuracy of the book-keeping.

12.7 Exercises: Direct Double Entry

1. On April 1st L. Hexham started in business as a dressmaker with capital of £2 500.00 which she banked in her Bank Account, except for £100.00 which she placed in her Cash Box. She then paid rent £80.00 and a telephone connection charge of £35.00, both by cheque. Open her accounts by direct double entries with

these entries and then enter the following further entries for April. At the end of the month extract a Trial Balance to check the accuracy of your accounting.

Apr. 1 Purchased materials, cottons, etc., for resale for £48.50 paying by cheque
1 Purchased sewing machine £140 and typewriter for office use £136, both by cheque. Purchased supply of stationery in cash £8.50
2 Purchased dresses, etc., for resale from Readymades Ltd on credit, £325.00
6 Cash sales for week £198.50. Banked £200.00 from cash box
6 Sold goods on credit to B. Wilfer £32.80 and Mrs A. Lammle £84.50. Purchased materials for resale for cash £38.30
8 Purchased postage stamps £3.25 in cash. Paid for dress patterns for resale by cheque £18.50
13 Cash sales for week £284.50. Banked £250.00 for safe-keeping
17 Paid Readymades Ltd Account by cheque, after deducting 5 per cent cash discount (Discount Received)
18 Purchased goods for resale on credit from Lingerie Ltd valued at £148.00
19 B. Wilfer settled her account for £32.80 in full in cash
20 Cash Sales £214.20
24 Purchased goods for resale by cheque £42.80
26 Sold garments to B. Wilfer on credit £42.20. Purchased dresses on credit from Readymades Ltd £185.00
27 Cash Sales £326.50. Banked £400 for safe-keeping
30 Paid rates by cheque £108.00

2. On April 1st W. Prescott started in business as a stationer with capital of £5 000.00 which he banked in his Bank Account, except for £50.00 which he placed in his Cash Box. He then paid rent £100.00 by cheque, and a telephone connection charge of £40.00 by cheque. Open his accounts by direct double entry with these entries and then enter the following further entries for April. At the end of the month extract a Trial Balance to check the accuracy of your accounting.

Apr. 1 Purchased goods for resale from H. Pizarro on credit value £450.00
1 Purchased goods for resale from H. Brown on credit, value £800.00 and typewriter for office use £85.00 by cheque. Purchased postage stamps £3.50 (cash)
4 Sold goods on credit to M. Lorrimer for £200.00
5 Paid salaries by cheque £164.00
10 M. Lorrimer returns goods, value £30.00
11 Paid wages £48.00 by cheque
13 Settled H. Pizarro's account in full, by cheque
15 Purchased goods on credit from M. Jordan £125.00
18 Cash Sales £380.00
20 Banked £100.00 from cash box
21 Drew from bank for private use £60.00
22 Refunded cash to a customer for goods returned £6.00
23 Sold goods on credit to R. Toyne £84.00
24 Purchased goods on credit from M. Nickolay £240.00
25 Paid for minor repairs £14.50 in cash
26 Returned goods to M. Nickolay £60.00 (not up to specification)
27 M. Lorrimer is in difficulties; agreed to accept £100.00 cheque in full settlement—rest treated as a bad debt (Debit Bad Debts Account with unpaid amount)
28 Paid wages in cash £48.00
30 Cash Sales £426.50

3. On May 1st T. Gray started in business as a butcher with capital of £3 500.00 which he banked in his Bank Account, except for £100.00 which he placed in his Cash Box. He then paid by cheque, rent £85.00 and a telephone connection charge of £48.00. Open his accounts by direct double entry with these entries and then enter the following further entries for May. At the end of the month extract a Trial Balance to check the accuracy of your accountancy.

May 1 Purchased shop-fittings for £1 650 by cheque and meat for resale from Market Traders Ltd on credit worth £240
1 Purchased dairy produce for cash £50 and office stationery, for cash £17.50
1 Cash Sales £164
4 Purchased machine by cheque £80.00 (Shop Fittings Account)
5 Paid wages in cash £65
9 Paid office expenses by cash £5.50
10 Gray settled his account by cheque less 2½ per cent cash discount with Meat Traders Ltd (put the discount in Discount Received Account)
13 Sold goods to A. Caterer on credit £45.50
14 Purchased meat on credit from Market Traders Ltd, £195
16 Received a loan from A. Banker £500.00. Interest for one year charged at 10 per cent
19 Paid cheque in full settlement less 5 per cent cash discount, to Market Traders Ltd
22 Withdrew from bank for private use £80.00
23 Cash Sales £524.00. Banked £400
24 Bought goods on credit from Savoury Foods Ltd, £65.50
27 Paid rates by cheque £76.00
28 Bought by cheque dairy produce for resale £68.50
29 Cash Sales £308.75
31 Paid into bank from tills £250.00; paid salaries by cheque, £260.00

4. On January 1st, 19. ., Paul Ross started up in business as a furniture dealer with capital of £8 000.00 which he put into his Bank Account, except for £250.00 which he used as a cash float. On the same day he took out a mortgage for £20 000 with his bank, which enabled him to buy premises valued at £15 000.00, stock (debit Stock Account) valued at £6 250.00, and fittings valued at £1 000.00. All of these sums were paid by cheque. He paid a celebrity £100 by cheque (debit Office Expenses Account) to open the shop, and the following transactions took place during January. Record the opening transactions, the transactions during the month, and take out a Trial Balance as at January 31st, 19. .

Jan. 5 Purchased on credit furniture for resale valued at £2 750 from Brighter Bedrooms Ltd
6 Cash Sales for week £2 350.00. Banked £2 000.00 from tills
12 Sold goods on credit to A. Coleman £185.00
13 Cash Sales for week £2 954.00. Banked £2 600.00
15 Paid for office stationery in cash £26.50
16 Paid wages in cash £545.20
20 Cash Sales for week £2 327.50. Banked £2 000.00
23 Purchased furniture on credit from New Homes Ltd, £4 250.00
24 Paid Brighter Bedrooms Ltd Account in full by cheque less 5 per cent cash discount
27 Cash Sales for week £2 840.50. Banked £2 500.00
31 Paid salaries by cheque £585.50. Paid wages in cash £532.30

5. On January 1st, 19.., R. Croydon started up in business as an office equipment dealer with capital of £6 250.00 which he put into his Bank Account, except for £250.00 which he used as a cash float. On the same day he took out a mortgage for £6 000 with his bank, which enabled him to pay by cheque for stock (debit Stock Account) valued at £8 000.00 and fittings valued at £1 000.00. He paid a month's rent on premises, £120, by cheque. The following transactions took place during January. Record the opening transactions, the transactions during the month, and take out a Trial Balance as at January 31st, 19..

Jan.	2	Cash Sales £240, of which £200 was banked
	4	Sold goods on credit to R. Branch £380.00
	6	Purchases office equipment for resale from Star Products Ltd on credit value £480
	9	Cash Sales £390, of which £350 was banked
	10	Bought second-hand motor vehicle for business use, £650.00 by cheque
	11	Paid for repairs to damaged window £27.50 in cash
	13	Purchased stationery for resale by cheque £165.50
	16	Cash Sales £984 of which £950 was banked
	17	Paid wages in cash £84.20
	18	Sold goods on credit to R. Tomlinson £420.00
	19	Paid Star Products by cheque for goods supplied on January 6th, less 5 per cent cash discount
	23	Cash Sales £785, of which £700 was banked
	25	Tomlinson settled his account by cheque, less 5 per cent cash discount
	27	Paid rates by cheque £146.50
	30	Cash Sales £1 240, of which £1 200 was banked
	31	Paid wages in cash £84.20

13

BOOKS OF ORIGINAL ENTRY

13.1 Principles of Original Entry

The student of Accountancy today has a bewildering variety of things to learn. In attempting to cover them many teachers and lecturers are forced to cut corners, and can justly claim that they are only doing what the modern technology does anyway. In Chapter 12 we learned how to do book-keeping to the Trial Balance by the 'direct double-entry' method, ignoring the books of original entry altogether. This is a laborious way to do accounting. For example, if we had 100 customers buying goods, 100 sales invoices would need to be entered. This would require separate entries in 100 different debtors' accounts, and 100 entries in the Sales Account. Clearly this is a great waste of time. We cannot avoid debiting each debtor's account separately, but if we use a book of original entry—the Sales Day Book—only the total of the book needs to be posted to Sales Account, thus saving 99 entries in the Sales Account. Books of Original Entry were therefore devised to save hundreds of entries in the nominal accounts like the Sales Account, Purchases Account, Sales Returns Account and Purchases Returns Account. The modern computer, however, does not find a few hundred entries any trouble at all. At 5 million bits a second a few hundred entries, even if each one requires several bits, are not going to take even one second. Direct double entry is therefore the basis on which computer ledgers are updated.

Another reason for understanding books of original entry is that in many firms, particularly smaller firms, they are still used, and the simplicity of the system, particularly for audit purposes, means that good control can be maintained by management.

However, the student's problems are not fully discovered even now, for it is also necessary to add that ways of saving time on the more laborious books of original entry—the Sales Day Book, Purchases Day Book, Sales Returns Book and Purchases Returns Book—have also been devised. These include (*a*) the filing of documents in post binders and (*b*) 'three-in-one systems'. An explanation of these methods is given in *Book-keeping Made Simple*.

What then are the principles of original entry?

(*a*) *The original entry is made from a document.* Every transaction starts with a document, as we saw in Fig. 11.4 (see page 130). When this document is recorded in the book of original entry appropriate to it, a permanent record of the document exists on the books of the firm. From that time on the document itself ceases to be useful, though it is usually filed away. Documents can act as evidence in the event of a dispute, and they are sometimes required to be presented in court.

(*b*) *Entries are made as they arise, in chronological order*. This is always helpful, for we can turn back to find the starting point of a particular event. As the original entry always includes a 'narration'—a continuous written account of the event—it is easy to follow what happened. Granted some of these entries become shortened to well-known phrases, but they still tell the whole story. Thus the narration 'Being cheque dishonoured at this date' tells us all we need to know, and so does 'Being payment of 50p in the £1 by R. Jones' trustee in bankruptcy'.

(*c*) *The original entry is then posted to the Ledger*. When posting to the Ledger a certain saving can be achieved in the double entries because, as explained above, only the total of a book like the Sales Day Book or the Purchases Day Book needs to be posted. Imagine a firm supplying drugs to practically every chemist's shop in the United Kingdom. Every day two or three hundred sales invoices will be sent off and the duplicates will be entered into the Sales Day Book. It will be important to post this Day Book to the ledger every day, to prevent an enormous backlog of postings building up. However, only the debit entries need be made (debiting every customer who has received a supply of drugs). The credit entry, in the Sales Account, need only to be made on the last day of the month, when the total sales for the month will be credited.

Clearly, such entries are very easy to follow. The original record replaces the document, and gives a permanent record in the books of account of the firm. The entry is then posted to the ledger, and a quick check of the appropriate account establishes that it has been done.

We must now look at each type of original entry.

13.2 Original Entries for the Sale of Goods—the Sales Day Book

When a businessman supplies goods to a customer, he makes out a document called an invoice. Originally there were two copies of this document, a top copy called the 'Customer's copy' and a duplicate called the 'Sales Day Book copy'. Today four copies are quite common, and in some nationalised industries as many as 20 copies are used. The invoice is one of the key documents in business, on which many other documents are based. For example, in export trade the invoice may be used as a Master Document from which Bills of Lading, Certificates of Origin, Certificates of Insurance, etc., are produced. Let us first consider this document in detail.

The Invoice

Definition: *an invoice is a business document which is made out whenever one person sells goods to another*. It can be used in courts of law as evidence of a contract for the sale of goods. It is made out by the person selling the goods, and in large businesses it will have at least four copies of different colours.

Fig. 13.1 shows the usual form of invoice in use in large firms. It must have the following information:

(*a*) Names and addresses of both the interested parties to the sale.

(*b*) The date of the sale.

(*c*) An exact description of the goods, with quantity and unit price, and details of the trade discount (if any) given. (This invoice is not one for branded articles, so no trade discount appears.)

(*d*) The terms on which the goods are sold, i.e. the discount that may be taken and the credit period allowed. The words 'Terms Net' means no discount is allowed. The words 'Prompt Settlement' means no credit period is allowed.

What Happens to the Four Copies?

Customer's: This is sent by post or by hand to the person buying the goods, and he uses it to enter in his Purchases Day Book. He then keeps the invoice as his copy of the contract of sale.

Sales Day Book Copy: This is usually the second copy, which is kept by the seller, entered in his Sales Day Book, and then filed to be kept as his copy of the contract of sale.

Third and Fourth Copies: These are sent together to the Stores Department of the seller, where the storekeeper takes the goods out of store. The third copy, often called the **Delivery Note,** is given to the carman to take with him to the buyer's warehouse, where he presents it with the parcel of goods, and gets a signature on it to prove that the goods arrived safely. This copy is then taken back by the carman to the storekeeper and is filed in the store after being entered in the Stores Record Book. The fourth copy is wrapped up in the parcel before it is given to the carman. It is often called the **Advice Note** and it enables the buyer's storekeeper to check the contents of the parcel and record the stores that have just arrived in his Stores Record Book. Neither of these documents shows the money value of the goods.

In countries where value added tax is used, as in the United Kingdom, some method of recording VAT is required. As can be seen in Fig. 13.1, the insertion of extra columns is necessary to show the tax rate and the actual tax added to the invoices. Accounting for VAT is fully explained in Chapter 15.

The Debit Note—A Document Very Like an Invoice

Definition: A debit note is a document which is made out by the seller whenever the purchaser has been undercharged on an invoice, or when he wishes to make some charge on a debtor which increases the debtor's debt.

Suppose that an invoice has been sent to a purchaser of a typewriter value £100.00, but by mistake the typist had typed £10.00 as the purchase price. Clearly the seller will want to correct this undercharge, but another invoice would not be appropriate since no 'goods' are being delivered. A debit note for £90.00 treated exactly like an invoice and put through the Day Books in exactly the same way as an invoice will put this matter right.

In the same way charges for carriage, or insurance, which were not known at the time the invoice was made out, could be charged to the debtor by means of a debit note.

Original Entries in the Sales Day Book

Having sent the top copy of the invoice to the customer, the supplier now records the second copy in his Sales Day Book. Since many orders are received every day, the invoice typists will be busy typing the invoices and each day a reasonable collection of the 'second copies' will find its way to the Sales Day Book clerk.

Imagine you are going down the corridor at your office and you meet Charlie, the office boy, carrying the bunch of invoice second copies to the young lady who keeps the Sales Day Book. He is holding this bunch of invoices tightly because he doesn't want to lose any. Scattering sales invoices like confetti is a great nuisance; they have to be picked up and put in order, and there is always the chance that one will fly down the back of a radiator and

Advice Note	**SALE INVOICE**
Delivery Note	**SALE INVOICE**
Sales Day Book Copy	**SALE INVOICE**
Customer's Copy	**SALE INVOICE**

SIMPLEX **SPECIALISED ACCOUNT BOOKS**

A. Stationer & Co. Ltd.,
43 Foremast Street,
Buxmoor
Hants.

GEORGE VYNER LTD
P.O. BOX No. 1
HOLMFIRTH
HUDDERSFIELD
HD7 2RP
Tel. No. HOLMFIRTH (048-489) 5221

VAT. Reg. No. 183 8619 27

DATE & TAX POINT	YOUR ORDER No. & DATE	DESPATCHED BY	LEDGER FOLIO	PLEASE QUOTE THIS REFERENCE WHEN MAKING PAYMENT
14 Feb. 19..	2174 12 Feb. 19..	B.R.S.	S.129	

QUANTITY	GOODS	Rate per 100 Copies	COST		VAT RATE	VAT AMOUNT	
250	Simplex D Account Books @	£100	250	00			
250	Simplex VAT Record Books @	£150	375	00			
50	Simplex Wages Books @	£ 50	25	00			
100	Simplex Licensees Account Books @	£200	200	00			
100	Simplex Everall Farm Account Book @	£150	150	00			
50	Simplex No. 2 Parcel Post Receipt Books @	£ 40	20	00			
50	Simplex No. 3 Parcel Post Receipt Books @	£ 80	40	00			
			1060	00	8%	84	80
		VAT	84	80			
			1144	80			
E. & O.E.	PAYMENT TERMS - NETT CASH 30 DAYS	INVOICE No.	02487				

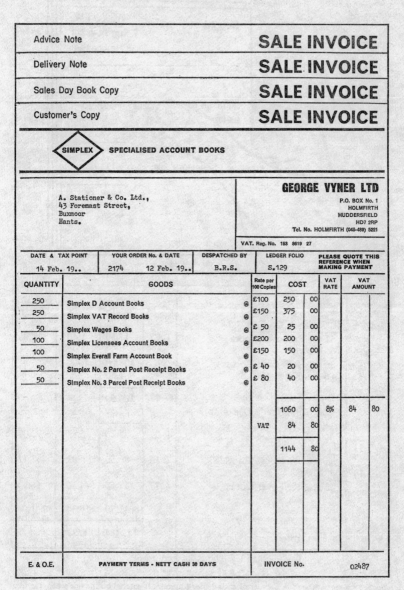

Fig. 13.1. A four-copy invoice system.

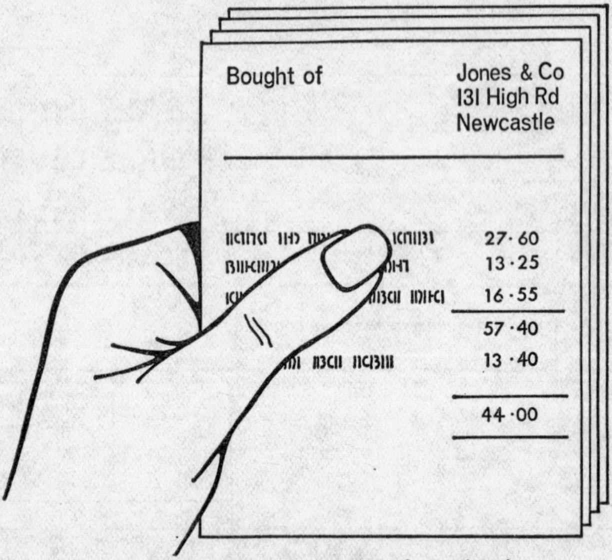

Fig. 13.2. This morning's collection of sales invoices.

19..			Details	VAT	S.D.B.1 Total
Jul. 1	R. Smith & Co. Ltd.				
	1 set Roll-over Doors	L.27	17.50	1.40	18.90
4	M. Brown				
	6 sets Roll-over Doors		105.00		
	6 sets Keys		1.50		
			106.50		
	Less 20% Trade Discount		21.30		
		L.3	85.20	6.82	92.02
11	R. Jones				
	1 set Lift Doors 2m wide	L.15	86.50	6.92	93.42
19	M. Luce				
	3 sets Roll-over Doors	L.17	52.50	4.20	56.70
			241.70	19.34	261.04
			L.46	L.37	

Fig. 13.3. The Sales Day Book.

Notes

(i) The debtor will have to be debited with the full amount payable, as shown in the total column opposite his entry. The folio number of each debtor's account is entered on the line where the total figure is to be found, not on the other lines (for example M. Brown's entry above). This prevents errors in posting.

(ii) The total of the details column is posted to the credit side of Sales Account, which thus represents the Sales net of VAT.

(iii) The total of the VAT column is posted to the credit side of the VAT Account (see Chapter 15).

(iv) We thus have a perfect double entry, for the various debit entries in the debtors' accounts will exactly balance the credits in Sales Account and VAT Account.

be lost. What is the bunch of invoices like? As shown in Fig. 13.2, it is a neat collection of invoices all exactly alike.

If this collection of Sales Day Book copies is compared with Fig. 13.5, which is of invoices from suppliers, to be entered in the Purchases Day Book, the difference will at once be clear. Sales Day Book copies are all similar, they are *our invoices* typed by *our invoice typists* yesterday. The Purchases Day Book invoices of Fig. 13.5 by contrast are the top copies sent to us by many different firms. They are all shapes, colours and sizes.

The ruling of the Sales Day Book is basically as shown in Fig. 13.3. The notes below explain how the postings are done, to achieve a double entry. The actual entries are shown in Fig. 13.4.

The reader should now try the exercises below.

13.3 Exercises: The Sales Day Book

In each of the exercises below enter the invoices in a Sales Day Book (it must have three columns as VAT has to be recorded). At the end of the month total the book and post the necessary figures into the ledger accounts.

1. 19..

Mar. 1 R. Giles purchases from us a Snifter 51 pencil case at £2.30. VAT £0.18

2 D. Shooter purchases a pen and pencil set at £2.50 and six cigarette lighters at £4.40 each. VAT added £2.31

13 R. Goode purchases 6 Snifter 51 pencil cases at £2.30 each. VAT added £1.10

14 W. Atkins purchases from us 2 cigarette lighters at £4.40 each, a silver pencil at £0.85, and 2 dozen ballpoint pens at £0.10 each. VAT added £0.96

25 R. Deal purchases 24 silver pencils at a special price of £0.60 each. VAT added £1.15

31 D. Shooter purchases 3 cigarette lighters at £4.40 each. VAT added £1.06

2. 19..

July 3 J. Rover bought from us 3 refrigerators 'Nanook' type at £65.00 each, £195.00. VAT at 12½%, £16.25

7 M. Humber bought from us 4 typewriters 'Tapitout Standard' type at £54.25 each, £217.00. VAT at 8%, £17.36

19 R. Grover purchased from us goods as follows: 3 standard 'Tapitout' typewriters at £54.25, £162.75; 2 portable 'Tapitout' typewriters at £28.50, £57. VAT at 8%, £17.58

27 M. Grudge purchased from us goods as follows: 3 'Nanook' type refrigerators (wall model) at £38.75 each, £116.25. VAT at 12½%, £14.53

3. 19..

June 1 R. Brown bought from us coloured silk worth £27.60. VAT charged £2.21

3 M. Smith bought from us coloured silk valued at £13.45 and linen goods at £7.65. VAT charged £1.69

11 Sold to R. Farmer cottons at £4.10, needles at £3.80, and pins at £2.25. VAT charged £0.81

17 Sold to M. Lucas cotton sheeting £45 and linen goods £12.50. VAT charged £4.60

24 Sold to R. White cotton goods £42.50 and linen goods at £17.75. VAT charged £4.82

30 Sold to M. Thomas goods; white fabric value £13.60 and blue fabric value £47.50. VAT charged £4.89

4. 19..

Apr. 9 M. Sketchley bought furniture valued at £846.50. VAT charged £67.72

13 A. Southgate purchased bedroom furniture £625.25 and lounge furniture £386.50. VAT charged £80.94

19 Terry & Co purchased office furniture £1 786.50. VAT charged £142.92

29 L. Waller and Co. purchased office furniture £3 726.20. VAT charged £298.10

R. SMITH AND CO. LTD L.27

19..		F	£	19..		F	£
Jul. 1	Sales	S.D.B.1	18.90				

M. BROWN L.3

19..		F	£	19..		F	£
Jul. 4	Sales	S.D.B.1	92.02				

R. JONES L.15

19..		F	£	19..		F	£
Jul. 11	Sales	S.D.B.1	93.42				

M. LUCE L.17

19..		F	£	19..		F	£
Jul. 19	Sales	S.D.B.1	56.70				

SALES ACCOUNT L.46

19..		F	£	19..		F	£
				Jul. 31	Sundry Debtors	S.D.B.1	241.70

VAT ACCOUNT L.37

19..		F	£	19..		F	£
				Jul. 31	Sundry Debtors	S.D.B.1	19.34

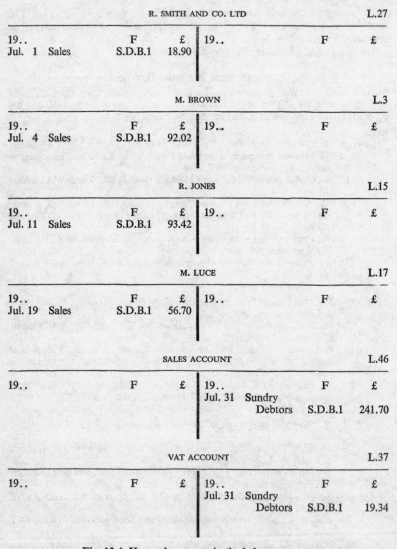

Fig. 13.4. How sales appear in the ledger accounts.

13.4 Original Entries for Purchases—the Purchases Day Book

When any businessman sells goods and makes out an invoice the top copy of that invoice is sent to the purchaser. This document is entered in the Purchases Day Book, as a permanent record of the transaction, just as the seller entered his copy in his Sales Day Book. The reader should note, however, that a collection of invoices to be entered in the Purchases Day Book looks quite different from a collection of 'sales' invoices. There may be several of these invoices arriving every day, possibly as many as a hundred. They will all be *the top copies of other firms' invoices,* and since they may have come from a hundred different firms the bundle of invoices will look like that shown in Fig. 13.5.

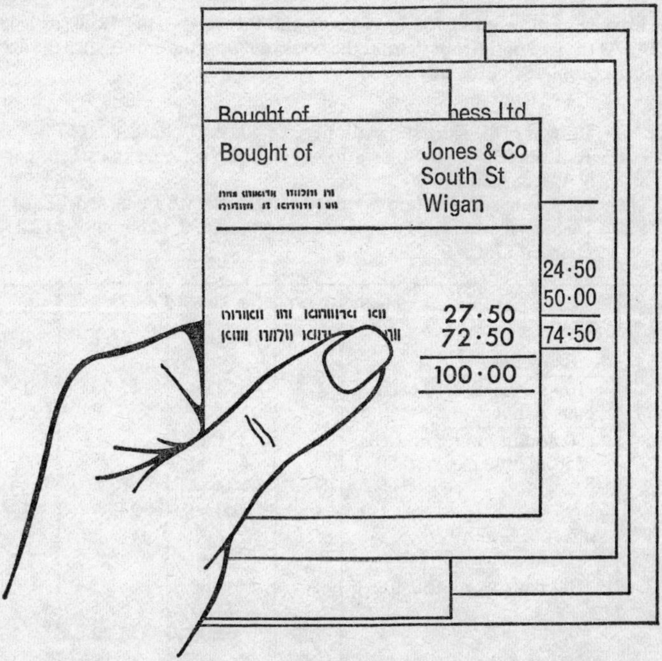

Fig. 13.5. This morning's collection of purchases invoices.

These invoices would now be recorded in the Purchases Day Book. The ruling of the Purchases Day Book is basically the same as the Sales Day Book already studied. In actual practice a firm might have a ruling specially devised to suit its own needs, with many 'analysis' columns to give separate figures for different classes of purchases and sales, but these analytical columns would be extra to the three basic columns shown, which are for 'net' purchases, VAT and total invoice value.

In posting these entries to the ledger we would of course expect the entries in many ways to be the opposite of the entries made in Fig. 13.4. Instead of sales, where the goods are being given to customers who receive them and consequently become debtors of the business (debit the receiver of goods), we now are dealing with purchases. When we purchase goods we receive them (debit the nominal account, Purchases Account). The supplier is giving them, so we must credit the giver, who becomes a creditor of the business. The actual entries are shown in Fig. 13.7. Note that this time VAT Account is debited, for the tax we have paid to our supplier must be refunded by the VAT officer, who thus becomes a debtor of the business. In fact, of course, the difference between the debit entries and the credit entries in the VAT Account will decide whether we must pay VAT, or receive a refund from the VAT officer (see Chapter 15).

The student should now try the exercises below.

13.5 Exercises: The Purchases Day Book

In the exercises below enter the invoices in the Purchases Day Book as shown in Fig. 13.6. At the end of the month total the book and post the entries into the accounts to obtain a complete double entry.

1. 19..

Apr. 1 Bought of G. Emerson stationery £8.40. VAT charged £0.67

3 R. Longfellow sold us stationery as follows: envelopes £50, paper £5. VAT charged £4.40

14 M. Twain supplies books valued at £285.50. VAT charged £22.84

30 H. Melville sends us goods: stationery £85.50, paper clips £12.25. VAT charged £7.82

19..			Details	VAT	P.D.B.1 Total
Jul. 1	R. Brown & Co.				
	100 sheets at 1.50 each	L.1	150.00	12.00	162.00
17	Peter Young Ltd.				
	50 counterpanes at 3.50		175.00		
	250 pillowcases at 0.50		125.00		
		L.2	300.00	24.00	324.00
21	Ambrose Smith Ltd.				
	100 balls wool at 0.25		25 00		
	100 balls wool at 0.40		40.00		
		L.3	65.00	5.20	70.20
31	Major & Co. Ltd.				
	10 'Bettawear' machines at 57.50 each	L.4	575.00	46.00	621.00
			1 090.00	87.20	1 177.20
			L.37	L.28	

Fig. 13.6. The Purchases Day Book.

Notes

(i) The creditor will be credited with the full amount payable, as shown in the total column.

(ii) The total of the details column will be posted to the debit side of Purchases Account, which thus shows the purchases, net of VAT.

(iii) The total of the VAT column is posted to the debit side of the VAT Account (see Chapter 15).

(iv) We thus have a perfect double entry, for the various credit entries in the accounts of our creditors exactly balance the debits in the Sales Account and the VAT Account.

R. BROWN AND CO. L.1

19..		F	£	19..		F	£
				Jul. 1	Purchases	P.D.B.1	162.00

PETER YOUNG LTD L.2

19..		F	£	19..		F	£
				Jul. 17	Purchases	P.D.B.1	324.00

AMBROSE SMITH LTD L.3

19..		F	£	19..		F	£
				Jul. 21	Purchases	P.D.B.1	70.20

MAJOR AND CO. LTD L.4

19..		F	£	19..		F	
				Jul. 31	Purchases	P.D.B.1	621.00

PURCHASES ACCOUNT L.28

19..		F	£	19..		F	£
Jul. 31	Sundry Creditors	P.D.B.1	1 090.00				

VAT ACCOUNT L.37

19..		F	£	19..		F	£
Jul. 31	Sundry Creditors	P.D.B.1	87.20				

Fig. 13.7. Ledger entries for purchases.

2. 19..

May 1 M. Tozer sold us table cloths £45. VAT charged £3.60

12 H. Bartlett sold us household linen £19.20. VAT charged £1.54

23 J. Broomfield sold to us craftwork £85. VAT charged £6.80

31 S. Burch sold to us fancy table linen £25.50. VAT charged £2.04

3. 19..

May 2 Bought from D. Whitcombe plants for resale £234. VAT added £18.72

13 Received from R. Wyatt shrubs £76.50 and trees £75.00. VAT added £12.12

25 Bought from Garden Units Ltd garden furniture £528.00. VAT added £42.24

31 Bought from D. Whitcombe plants £258. VAT added £20.64

4. 19..

Aug. 1 Bought of R. Carr floral decorations £85.00. VAT added £6.80

12 Bought of M. Darwood material £36.00, trimmings £14.50. VAT added £4.04

23 J. Fielding sold us decorative items value £16.80. VAT added £1.34

31 F. Ford sold us clothing for resale £264. VAT added £21.12

13.6 Invoices for Services—The Expenses Journal or Day Book

Very similar to the invoices described in the last section which are issued whenever one person sells goods to another, are invoices for services supplied, sometimes called Expense Invoices. These are sent out by gas companies, water boards, electric power authorities, local councils, and Government departments of various sorts. Garages send invoices for fuel supplied and repairs carried out to vehicles. All such invoices must be recorded in day books very similar to the Sales Day Book and the Purchases Day Book. However, they are not recording goods sold and bought, but services supplied. These are expenses, or losses, of the business. The Personal Account of the suppliers will be credited since that person is now a creditor to whom our firm owes money for services rendered. The other half of this double entry will be in the nominal account, i.e. loss account—for example, Light and Heat Account, Motor Vehicle Expenses Account, and so on.

Where a firm is only in business in a small way and the volume of work would not merit the trouble of having a separate Expenses Day Book such invoices would be dealt with through the Journal Proper, which is discussed later in this chapter.

13.7 The Return of Goods—Credit Notes

We must expect in the course of business that some of our customers will return goods for valid reasons. A purchaser is not entitled to return something just because he has changed his mind about having it; but occasionally we may oblige a client by accepting this type of return. The usual reasons for returning goods are:

(*a*) The purchaser holds that the goods are unsatisfactory for some reason—e.g. wrong colour; wrong size; not up to sample; not up to specification; imperfectly finished; damaged in transit, etc.

(*b*) The purchaser returns goods which he is entitled to return—for example, goods sent on approval.

In these circumstances the document used is the credit note.

Definition. A credit note is a business document made out whenever one person returns goods to another. A credit note is usually printed in red, to distinguish it from an invoice, and like an invoice is made out by the seller of the goods, who is now receiving them back again. Usually there are only two copies. The credit note should show:

(*a*) The names and addresses of both parties to the transaction.
(*b*) An exact description of the goods being returned.
(*c*) The unit price, the number, the total value of the goods returned, and details about VAT if applicable.
(*d*) The original invoice number and date, or other relevant details.

An example of a credit note is given in Fig. 13.8. Usually credit notes are made out in duplicate. The top copy is sent to the purchaser who has returned the goods, and is recorded in his Purchases Returns Book. The duplicate is kept by the seller and is recorded in his Sales Returns Book.

Other reasons for sending a credit note. Sometimes goods that are unsatisfactory for some reason are not returned because of the inconvenience and cost. A piece of furniture that has been damaged by rain in transport may only need repolishing. The purchaser may be perfectly prepared to have this repolishing carried out by one of his own employees, provided the seller will make him an allowancc to cover the cost. This will be done by sending a credit note for the agreed amount. This is called an **Allowance.**

We saw, in Section 13.2 above, that when an undercharge is made on an invoice a document called a debit note was sent to increase the original invoice to the proper figure. Invoice typists can make errors which result in overcharges instead of undercharges. Supposing the typewriter valued at £100.00 was invoiced at £1 000.00. Clearly a credit note for £900.00 will be required to correct the overcharge.

Credit notes may therefore be sent for three reasons:

(*a*) To credit a debtor with returns.
(*b*) To credit a debtor with an allowance.
(*c*) To credit a debtor to correct an overcharge.

13.8 Entering Credit Notes—The Sales Returns Book

When the buyer of goods returns them, or when for any other reason the seller makes out a credit note, the document must be recorded in the seller's book of original entry, which is the Sales Returns Book. As shown in Fig. 13.9, the collection of credit notes about to be entered into the Sales Returns Book is a neat collection of documents (the second copies of several credit notes issued to our customers who returned goods yesterday).

When entered in the Sales Returns Book, these credit notes will appear as shown in Fig. 13.10. The ruling of this book is exactly the same as the other day books already considered, but the student will note the following points:

(i) It is not usual to have more than one item on a credit note, for it is unlikely that several items will be returned (although this may of course happen).

(ii) The debtor has given back the goods, so the debtor's account will need to be credited in each case (see Fig. 13.11), but the Sales Returns Account will be debited as it has received the goods returned. The VAT Account will also be debited, for the VAT on these returned items will not be collected from the customers and consequently our liability to pay tax to the VAT officer, one of the firm's creditors, is reduced.

SALES CREDIT NOTE

SIMPLEX SPECIALISED ACCOUNT BOOKS

A. Stationer & Co. Ltd.,
43 Foremast Street,
Buxmoor
Hants.

GEORGE VYNER LTD
P.O. BOX No. 1
HOLMFIRTH
HUDDERSFIELD
HD7 2RP
Tel. No. HOLMFIRTH (048-489) 5221

VAT. Reg. No. 183 8619 27

DATE & TAX POINT	YOUR ORDER No. & DATE	DESPATCHED BY	LEDGER FOLIO	PLEASE QUOTE THIS REFERENCE WHEN MAKING PAYMENT
20 Feb 19..	2174 12 Feb 19..	B.R.S	S.129	

QUANTITY	GOODS		Rate per 100 Copies	COST		VAT RATE	VAT AMOUNT	
20	Simplex D Account Books	@	£100	20	00			
	Simplex VAT Record Books	@						
	Simplex Wages Books	@						
	Simplex Licensees Account Books	@						
	Simplex Everall Farm Account Book	@						
	Simplex No. 2 Parcel Post Receipt Books	@						
	Simplex No. 3 Parcel Post Receipt Books	@						
				20	00	8%	1	60
				1	60			
				21	60			
	"Damaged in Transit"							
E. & O.E.	PAYMENT TERMS - NETT CASH 30 DAYS		CREDIT NOTE No. 17					

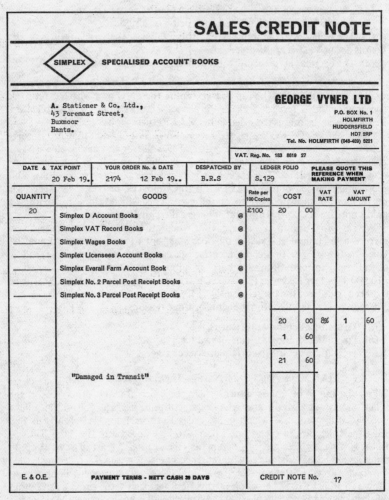

Fig. 13.8. A credit note; the original document for returns. *Note:* Credit notes are always printed in red.

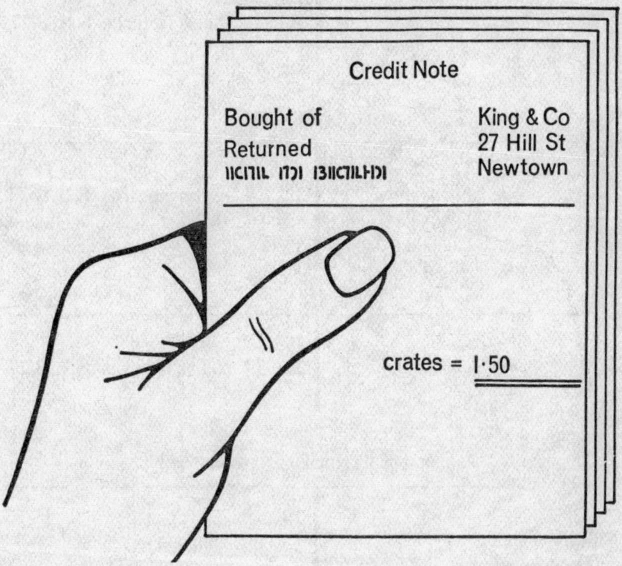

Credit Note
Bought of
Returned
King & Co
27 Hill St
Newtown
crates = 1·50

Fig. 13.9. This morning's collection of credit notes for sales returned to us. (The second copies go from the typist to the Accounts Department.)

19..			Details	VAT	S.R.B.27 Total
Jul. 3	Brown & Co.				
	2 crates at 0.50 each	L.1	1.00	0.08	1.08
7	Smith & Jones				
	4 chairs (wrong pattern)	L.2	17.60	1.41	19.01
19	Hook & Co.				
	1 bedroom suite		47.50		
	1 mirror		2.50		
		L.3	50.00	4.00	54.00
			68.60	5.49	74.09
			L.47	L.37	

Fig. 13.10. The Sales Returns Book.

BROWN AND CO. L.1

19..		F	£	19..		F	£
				Jul. 3	Sales Returns	S.R.B.27	1.08

SMITH AND JONES L.2

19..		F	£	19..		F	£
				Jul. 7	Sales Returns	S.R.B.27	19.01

HOOK AND CO. L.3

19..		F	£	19..		F	£
				Jul. 19	Sales Returns	S.R.B.27	54.00

SALES RETURNS ACCOUNT L.47

19..		F	£	19..		F	£
Jul. 31	Sundry Debtors	S.R.B.27	68.60				

VAT ACCOUNT L.37

19..		F	£	19...		F	£
Jul. 31	Sundry Debtors	S.R.B.27	5.49				

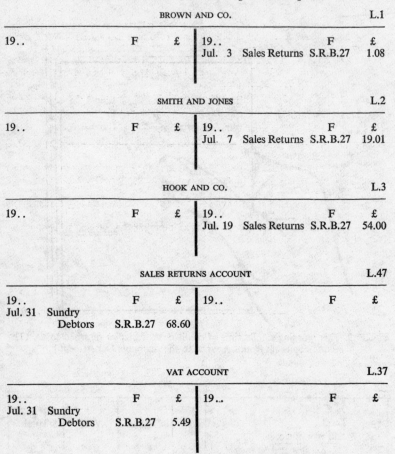

Fig. 13.11. Ledger entries for the sales returns.

13.9 Exercises: The Sales Returns Book

In the following exercises enter the credit notes in each exercise in the Sales Return Book. At the end of the month total the book and post it to the appropriate ledger accounts so as to achieve a correct double entry.

1. 19..

Jan. 4 Sent M. Smith a credit note for 2 steam irons at £9.85 each (heating element faulty). VAT £2.46

15 Sent R. Thompson a credit note for 3 electric fires at £8.50 each (switches faulty). VAT £2.04

17 Sent R. Leighton a credit note for a 'Washette' dishwater (faulty motor) at £137.50. VAT £17.19

18 Sent M. Kehu a credit note for an overcharge on an invoice (typing error), £10.00. VAT £0.80

2. 19..

July 12 Sent R. Day a credit note for goods returned as follows: 1 table (leg broken) at £87.50; 2 containers for Zahl polish valued at £5.50 each. VAT added £7.88

17 Sent M. Grossmith credit note for goods returned as follows: 20 mirrors valued at £38.50 altogether; 1 chair (not glued in manufacture) at £34.75. VAT £5.86 altogether.

29 Sent R. Thorpe credit note for goods as follows: 1 imitation Chesterfield suite (not up to quality of sample) £248.50. VAT £19.88

3. 19..

Aug. 4 M. Seager returned to us goods valued at £14.50 (picnic outfit crushed in transit). VAT £1.16

11 R. Loiter returned to us goods as follows: 1 camp bed (joints insecurely riveted) at £12.00; 2 camp tables (painting inferior) at £3.25 each. VAT added £1.48

17 M. Shoreditch returns goods valued at £37.25 (tent damaged in proofing process). VAT £2.98

29 M. Leman sent back goods as follows: 1 kit bag (eyelets torn) at £5.50; 2 sleeping bags (mildewed due to bad storage) at £7.50 each. VAT added £1.64

4. 19..

Aug. 7 Sent M. Team a credit note value £5.40 for containers returned empty. VAT £0.43

13 Sent R. Jorgensen a credit note value £58.00 (for 2 tile fireplaces—concrete frame not at right-angles to base). VAT £4.64

27 Sent M. Stevens a credit note as follows: 1 wrought-iron gate (hinges defective) at £17.50; 1 wrought-iron lampholder (insecure welding) at £15.50. VAT added £2.64

13.10 Entering Credit Notes—The Purchases Returns Book

Finally in this group of books of original entry concerned with the purchase, sale and return of goods we have to consider what happens to the top copy of the credit note which the seller of goods sends to anyone who returns goods for some reason. This time the purchaser will enter the credit note in his Purchases Returns Book. As can be seen in Fig. 13.12, the day's collection of top copies of credit notes is a rather mixed collection of different sized and coloured pieces of paper, but they will at least be similar in one respect, that credit notes are always printed in red to distinguish them from invoices.

When entered into the Purchases Returns Book, the entries will look as shown in Fig. 13.13, whilst the postings to the Ledger Accounts would be as shown in Fig. 13.14 (see page 173). Each of the suppliers to whom goods have been returned will be debited (debit the receiver). The Purchases Returns Account is credited with the total given back, and the VAT Account is also credited because our liability to the VAT authorities will have increased now that the input tax formerly claimed on these purchased items is disallowed and can no longer be deducted from our tax payable (see Chapter 15).

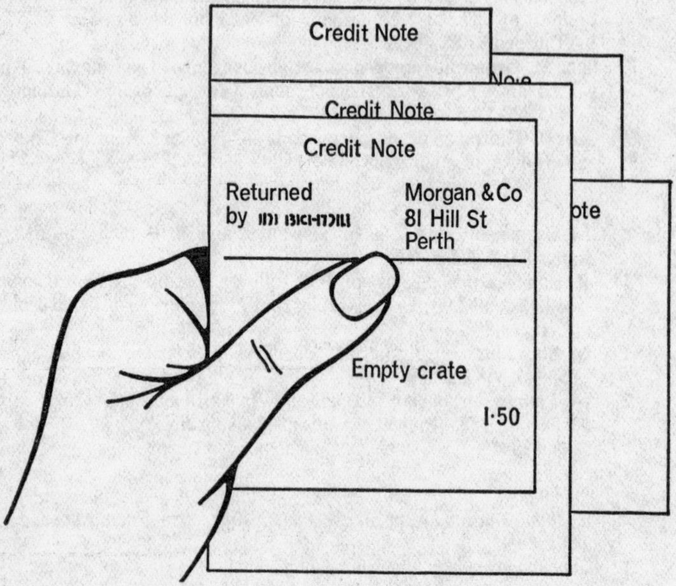

Fig. 13.12. This morning's postbag of credit notes for purchases we have returned. *Note:* Credit notes are usually printed in red.

			Details	VAT	P.R.B.14 Total
19..					
Jan. 7	R. Miles				
	1 packing crate	L.5	3.00	0.24	3.24
11	M. Joynson				
	2 boxes address cards (incorrectly displayed)	L.7	14.00	1.12	15.12
29	R. Brown				
	1 box ledger cards (on approval—not required)	L.11	8.50	0.68	9.18
			25.50	2.04	27.54
			L.49	L.37	

Fig. 13.13. The Purchases Returns Book.

R. MILES L.5

19..		F	£	19..		F	£
Jan. 7	Purchases Returns	P.R.B.14	3.24				

M. JOYNSON L.7

19..		F	£	19..		F	£
Jan. 11	Purchases Returns	P.R.B.14	15.12				

R. BROWN L.11

19..		F	£	19..		F	£
Jan. 29	Purchases Returns	P.R.B.14	9.18				

PURCHASES RETURNS ACCOUNT L.49

19..		F	£	19..		F	£
				Jan. 31	Sundry Creditors	P.R.B.14	25.50

VAT ACCOUNT L.37

19..		F	£	19..		F	£
				Jan. 31	Sundry Creditors	P.R.B.14	2.04

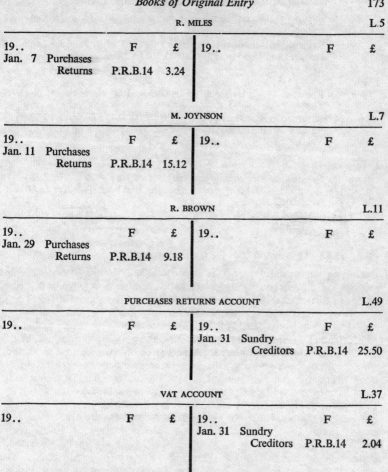

Fig. 13.14. Ledger entries for purchases returns.

13.11 Exercises: The Purchases Returns Book

In each of the exercises below enter the credit notes given into the Purchases Returns Book, total the book at the end of the month and post the entries to the Ledger to achieve a correct double entry.

1. 19..
   - Apr. 5 Returned to H. White & Co. containers valued at £12.00. VAT £0.96
   - 12 Returned to R. Robertson containers valued at £15.50. VAT £1.24
   - 17 Returned to M. Smith 2 copies of textbooks at £8.50 each. No VAT.
   - 24 Returned to R. Jones 1 picture (definition poor) at £32.00. VAT £2.56
2. 19..
   - July 3 Returned to H. Jones & Co. crates valued at £6.50. VAT £0.52
   - 15 Received a credit note from M. Lomax for goods returned to him as

follows: 1 white leather-covered dining suite and table at £402.50. VAT £32.20

17 Returned to M. Norrish goods as follows: 1 whitewood kitchen set at £65.00; 1 rosewood suite at £280.00. VAT £27.60

3. 19..

Sep. 4 Returned to M. Haddock goods damaged by rainwater £18.50. VAT £1.48

14 Returned to R. Plaice 1 packing case charged at £5.00. VAT £0.40

27 Returned to B. Harlow 2 mattresses £24.00 each (not up to sample) £48. VAT £3.84

4. 19..

Oct. 3 Returned to M. Venables woollen goods value £28.50. VAT £2.28

14 Returned to M. Spurgeon 2 tablecloths, best linen (faded) at £5.80 each. VAT £0.93

17 Received a credit note from H. Morton for garments returned £45.00. VAT £3.60

13.12 Original Entries for the Payment of Money—Documents

Recording payments of money is the second major field of book-keeping records, resulting from the supply of goods and services already described earlier in this chapter. Payment may be made in money (legal tender) or in some way which is as effective in transferring funds but does not require actual money to be handled. The commonest of these is the **cheque system**, but today the credit transfer and the direct debit are almost as important. With a **credit transfer** the debtor orders the bank to debit his own account and credit the account of the creditor. With a **direct debit** the creditor orders the bank to debit the debtor's account and credit his own account. The latter method is most frequently used by firms with a sound business link, like breweries and their tied public houses or oil companies and their tied garages.

Whatever method is used to settle indebtedness these are matters requiring two accounts, the Cash Account and the Bank Account, to be debited or credited as required.

Before entries can be made there must be an original document. This original document is the **statement**, and a typical modern example is illustrated in Fig. 13.15.

A statement is sent out by the creditor requiring payment to be made, usually at the end of the month, though some firms operate a system known as **cyclical billing**, by which about 4 per cent of the statements to be sent out each month are sent out each working day. This smooths out the work, preventing a rush of work at the end of the month, followed by another rush as the payments are received.

If the payment is made by cheque, the cheque may be regarded as a separate document accompanying the statement when the payment is made. Fig. 13.16 shows the two sets of procedures. It is self-explanatory. Under the Cheques Act, 1957, a cheque which has been cleared through a bank is a receipt, so that receipts are frequently not sent these days (though the creditor is obliged to send them if asked to do so). The reader should follow the illustration through and note the neat package of one document and the mixed package of the other document in each case.

STATEMENT

Burroughs Machines Ltd.

Anytown

WHITEHEAD G.M., 123005 1
15, CAMSIDE,
CHURCH STREET,
ALCONBURY.

DATE	REFERENCE	DEBIT	CREDIT	BALANCE
		BALANCE BROUGHT FORWARD		
		BROUGHT FORWARD		121.00*
09JAN79	GD B36C	27.50		
09JAN79	GD B37C	36.24		
05JAN79	GD J25B	84.50		269.24*

SPECIMEN

THE LAST ITEM IN THIS COLUMN IS THE AMOUNT DUE

L. 4001

Burroughs

Burroughs SERIES L VISIBLE RECORD COMPUTER SYSTEM

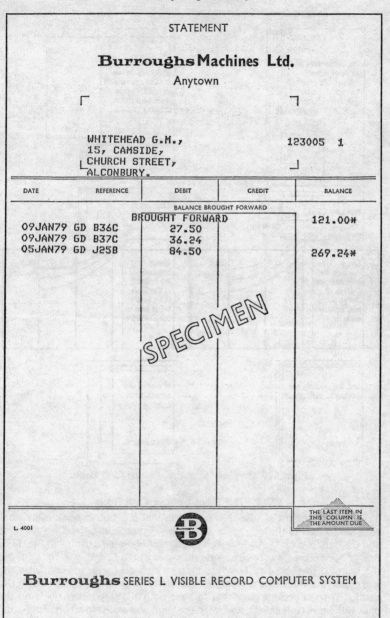

Fig. 13.15. A mechanised statement of account.
(Courtesy of Burroughs Machines Ltd)

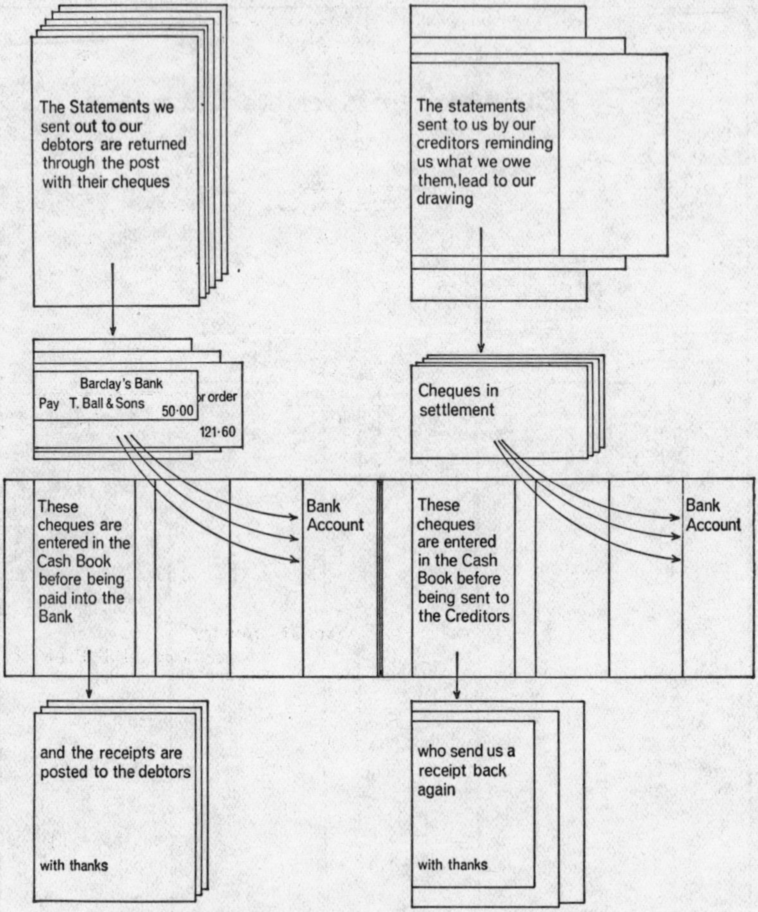

Fig. 13.16. Original documents and the Cash Book.

13.13 The Three-Column Cash Book

The Three-Column Cash Book is unique in that it is both a book of original entry and a part of the ledger, for it contains two accounts, the Cash Account and the Bank Account. As described in Chapter 11, and illustrated in Fig. 11.3, one of the easiest ways to subdivide the work in the Ledger was found to be the removal of these two busy accounts, which deal with money, from the ledger and put them into a separate Cash Book, kept by a specialist clerk, the cashier. It soon became clear that to have both accounts side by side on the page was a great advantage, and later a column was added to record discounts. On the debit side of the book, where money is being received, the discount would have been deducted by the debtor before he paid the money, and this was called Discount Allowed. On the credit side, where the cashier was giving the money away to the firm's creditors, he would deduct the discount and only send out the net payment. The discount was called Discount Received. These points can be most easily followed by looking at Fig. 13.17 and considering the notes opposite it on page 179.

13.14 Contra Entries in the Cash Book

In any account you can have only one half of a double entry. An account cannot receive and give both at the same time; but in the Three-Column Cash Book we have two accounts, the Cash Account and the Bank Account. It is possible to have both a debit entry and a credit entry at the same time. The two halves of the double entry on January 15th in Fig. 13.17 both appear on opposite sides of the Three-Column Cash Book, but not on opposite sides of the same account. The debit entry is in the Cash Account but the credit entry is in the Bank Account. Such entries are called **contra entries**, from the Latin prefix **contra** meaning 'opposite or against'. The folio column has a small 'c' in it, or an accountant might use the sign $\surd$.

The kind of contra entry we have in this specimen Cash Book is one in which cash has been taken out of the Bank Account on the credit side (the Bank Account has given) and has been put into the Cash Box (the Cash Account has received). This drawing of cash from the bank is a frequent occurrence; whenever we run short of cash we have to go to the bank and draw some money out.

It is possible to have a contra entry that is the exact reverse of this. If we sell a great many goods for cash the amount of cash in the till will increase and must be banked for safety. This involves a credit entry for the Cash Account, which is giving, and a debit entry for the Bank Account, which is receiving an increase of deposits.

Contra entries are a very important part of the Three-Column Cash Book; they can occur only because there are two accounts side by side, and it is quite untrue to say, as thoughtless students often do, that the Cash Book is the only account that can have a debit entry and a credit entry on it at the same time. *The Cash Book is not an account; it is two accounts, laid side by side for the greater convenience of the Cashier.*

13.15 Posting the Three-Column Cash Book to the Ledger

When we removed the Cash Account and the Bank Account from the Ledger and put them into the Cash Book they did not cease to be accounts. We now have two accounts which are not in the Ledger. Only one half of the double entries in these accounts has already been done. The other half is done when we post the Cash Book to the Ledger. Every item on the debit side of the Three-Column Cash Book requires a credit entry on the credit side of some other account. Similarly, every item on the credit side of the Cash Book requires a debit entry on the debit side of some other account. There is also a rather difficult little matter of the discounts to deal with. These are the *only entries that do not change sides*, as shown in Fig. 13.18.

The Ledger Accounts connected with the Three-Column Cash Book shown in Fig. 13.17 will therefore appear as in Figs. 13.19 and 13.20. To save space only the first personal account on each side has been shown; the others will be exactly the same. Note that it would be *absolutely wrong to post the contra entries*, both halves of the double entry being already done in the Cash Book.

Date 19..		Details	F	Discount Allowed	Cash	Bank	Date 19..		Details	F	Discount Received	Cash	Bank
Jan.	1	Opening Balances	J.1		24.50	17 035.35	Jan.	2	Postage	L.49		5.00	
	2	Cash Sales	L.7		42.25			4	R. Leverhulme	L.27	1.25		128.75
	3	H. Kemp	L.3	1.35		52.65		5	R. Morgenthal	L.28	0.35		7.35
	4	R. Robot	L.11			1.63		7	Wages	L.50		50.65	
	7	Cash Sales	L.7		34.40			12	Drawings	L.38			12.50
	11	M. Starr	L.14	0.65		17.35		13	L. Amaranth	L.5	0.15		5.65
	13	North London Rail (Refund)	L.29			0.65		14	J. Jarvis	L.12	0.35		7.95
								14	P. Heron	L.26	0.85		17.25
								14	F. Fish	L.23		0.65	
	15	M. Jordan	L.42	0.75		15.35		15	Cash	c			20.00
	15	Bank	c		20.00			15	Rates	L.55		17.63	
	15	R. Peters	L.15	1.20		17.80		15	Wages	L.50		40.90	
	15	H. Kemp	L.11			12.24		15	Balances	C/d		6.32	16 953.57
				3.95	121.15	17 153.02					2.95	121.15	17 153.02
Jan.	16	Balances	B/d	L.9	6.32	16 953.57					L.80		

Fig. 13.17 The Three-Column Cash Book.

Notes

(i) The book is used opened out to give a double page. The left-hand page is the debit side of the book, and has the debit side of the Cash Account, the debit side of the Bank Account and the Discount Allowed Column, which is not an account but just a Memorandum Column. The right-hand page is the credit side of the book, and has the credit side of the Cash Account, the credit side of the Bank Account and the Discount Received Column, which is again a Memorandum Column.

(ii) When cash is received it is entered on the debit side of the Cash Account. When cheques are received they are entered on the debit side of the Bank Account. Any discount allowed to the debtors (e.g. H. Kemp, M. Starr, M. Jordan and R. Peters) is put in the Discount Allowed Column, but this is not the debit side of an account, only a memo.

(iii) When cash is paid out it is entered on the credit side of the Cash Account. When cheques are made out and sent off to creditors they are entered on the credit side of the Bank Account. Any discount taken before paying these bills is entered in the Discount Received column.

(iv) When any item has been entered the entry is then posted to the Ledger. For example, cash sales is posted to Sales Account and H. Kemp's payment is posted to H. Kemp's Account. As these items have been debited in the Cash Book they will be credited in the Ledger Accounts. Similarly, the credit item 'Postage' on January 2nd will be debited to Postage Account, and the payment to R. Leverhulme will be debited to Leverhulme's Account in the Ledger, for he is receiving the money. Every entry therefore is posted over to the opposite side in the Ledger.

(v) The entry on January 15th is a special type of entry called a contra entry. This is explained in detail in the main text (see page 177).

(vi) *The total of the 'Discount Allowed' column* is posted to the *debit side* of the Discount Allowed Account (it is a loss of the business) and *the total of the 'Discount Received' column* is posted to the *credit side* of the Discount Received Account (it is a profit of the business). These are the only two figures which do not post over to the opposite side. This is explained in the main text (see page 182).

(vii) At the end of each day, or perhaps each week, the book is balanced off and the balances on the accounts carried down ready for the start of the next period.

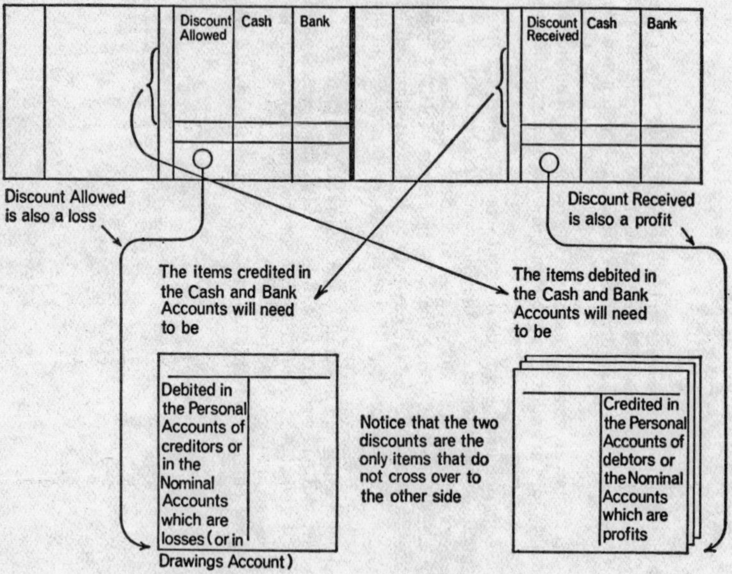

Fig. 13.18. How to post the Three-Column Cash Book.

SALES ACCOUNT L.7

					19..				
					Jan. 2	Cash		C.B.1	42.25
					7	,,		C.B.1	34.40

H. KEMP ACCOUNT L.11

19..				19..				
Jan. 2	Balance	B/d	54.00	Jan. 3	Bank		C.B.1	52.65
12	Goods	S.D.B.1	12.24	3	Discount		C.B.1	1.35
				15	Bank			12.24

(These are invented to make sense—a debtor must owe money before he pays it.)

(Note that both the cheque and the discount are entered.)

All the other debtors' accounts will look the same as H. Kemp's Account.

DISCOUNT ALLOWED ACCOUNT L.79

19..			
Jan. 15	Sundry Discounts	3.95	

(Note that discount is the only entry that does not cross over to the credit side.)

Fig. 13.19. Postings to the Ledger from the Cash Book—debit side.

POSTAGE ACCOUNT L.49

19..							
Jan. 2	Cash	C.B.1	5.00				

R. LEVERHULME ACCOUNT L.27

19..				19..			
Jan. 4	Bank	C.B.1	128.75	Jan. 1	Balance	B/d	130.00
4	Discount	C.B.1	1.25				

(All the other personal accounts of creditors will appear exactly like the one above.)

WAGES ACCOUNT L.50

19..							
Jan. 7	Cash	C.B.1	50.65				
15	„	C.B.1	40.90				

DRAWINGS ACCOUNT L.38

19..							
Jan. 12	Bank	C.B.1	12.50				

RATES ACCOUNT L.55

19..							
Jan. 15	Cash	C.B.1	17.63				

DISCOUNT RECEIVED ACCOUNT L.80

				19..			
				Jan. 15	Sundry Discounts	C.B.1	2.95

(Note that this account is the only one that does not cross over to the debit side.)

Fig. 13.20. Postings to the Ledger from the Cash Book—credit side.

Why Do the Discount Figures, When they are Posted, Not Cross Over to the Other Side?

Consider the double entry for the payment by H. Kemp on January 3rd. Remember every debit entry must be balanced up by a corresponding credit entry. In this case we have a double entry as follows:

Debit Side	*Credit Side*
52.65 in the Bank Account	52.65 in H. Kemp's Account
(see Fig. 13.17)	1.35 in H. Kemp's Account

Clearly this does not balance and we cannot count the 1.35 in the Discount column of the Cash Book because the Discount column is not an account, but only part of the layout of a 'Book of Original Entry'.

If we do post this 1.35 into the Discount Allowed Account it must not go over to the credit side; to do so would unbalance the double entry even more. The 1.35 must go on the debit side of the Discount Allowed Account, to record the loss and get the double entry correct.

The student should now develop a similar line of argument to explain why the Discount Received Account does not change over sides.

Bank Overdrafts

Sometimes the local bank manager will permit us to draw cheques to a greater value than the money that we have in the bank. Such overdrafts represent a loan to us of the outstanding balance. Of course, the bank will charge interest on the sum borrowed in this way, and if it exceeds a purely nominal amount the bank may even ask for collateral security. This is a security lying alongside the debt, which gives the bank a chance to recover its money should we not repay it when asked.

When a Bank Account is overdrawn in this way the account ceases to be an asset and becomes a liability. In these circumstances it cannot have a debit balance, like an asset account; the balance will be a credit balance.

In these circumstances our Three-Column Cash Book has a debit balance on the Cash Account, but a credit balance on the Bank Account: Bank Overdraft. It is impossible to have a credit balance on the Cash Account, since, unlike a Bank, you cannot get more out of a cash box than you put into it.

The student is now ready to try some entries in the Three-Column Cash Book. The first three exercises in Section 13.16 merely involve recording the entries in the Three-Column Cash Book. The remainder involve posting the Cash Book to the Ledger when the entries have been made and putting in the folio numbers.

13.16 Exercises: The Three-Column Cash Book

1. Enter the following items in the Three-Column Cash Book, and balance off the book on January 5th:

19..		
Jan.	1	T. Brophy commences business with cash £1 000.00; he pays £900.00 into the Bank Account from the cash book (contra entry); he buys goods (cash purchases) by cheque £230.00
	2	He pays rent £45.00; pays legal costs £7.35, both by cheque
	3	He settles a debt of £25.00 due to H. Jones by cheque, deducting discount at 5 per cent

4 P. Brown pays Brophy a debt of £10.60 by cheque, less 5 per cent discount
5 Pays wages £27.50 in cash; draws £30.00 for personal use (Drawings) from the cash box

2. Enter the following items in B. Jorgensen's Three-Column Cash Book and balance off at October 26th:

19. .
Oct. 1 Balances in hand, cash £55.50 and bank £795.50
2 Paid to R. Jones by cheque £212.50, discount £10.50
4 Received from B. Meths cheque for £41.00. Allowed him discount £1.00
5 Paid water rate £8.50; paid for repairs to office safe £5.65; paid office cleaner £5.00. All these payments made in cash
6 Drew £30.00 from bank for office cash (contra entry)
7 Paid R. Tompkins cash £12.35, received discount £0.65
9 Received from E. Lyne cash £15.95; gave him discount £0.80
10 Paid to F. Acomb cheque £360.10, discount £7.95
17 Received cheque from Dockerty & Sons £21.00; they were allowed discount £1.10
25 Paid cheque to F. Handsome £11.19
26 Drew cheque for wages £46.50; drew cheque for personal use £25.00 (Drawings)

3. Enter the following in R. Jollyboy's Cash Book and balance off on May 7th:

19. .
May 1 Balances: cash box £67.25; bank £1 300.26; paid R. Brown by cheque £5.50, discount £0.50
2 M. Slow paid by cheque £24.56; allowed him discount £0.74
3 Paid postage in cash £1.26; rent £40.00 in cash; paid T. Brownjohn by cheque £42.10, receiving discount £1.05
4 Drew cash from bank for office use £50.00
5 R. Little sent us a cheque for £128.73 in full settlement of his account of £135.50
6 Cash sales for week £875.00; Banked £800.00 from cash box
7 Bought machinery at auction for cash £95.10; paid wages in cash £37.50; paid for stamps in cash £3.50

4. L. Lewis's cash book is a Three-Column Cash Book. Make the following entries in it for the first week of July, 19. .

July 1 Balances in hand: cash £59.69, bank £1 650.15
2 Bought goods for resale for cash £42.60
3 Drew cash from bank for office use £40.00; R. Long paid cash £5.70, allowed him discount £0.30
4 Paid J. Robertson cheque £37.76
5 Paid telephone account £62.50 by cheque; sundry expenses £3.75 and postage £3.50, both in cash
6 Paid R. Matthias £38.00 by cheque; received discount £2.00
7 Received from T. Jonah £3.55 cash
8 Paid salaries £46.50 in cash; paid office cleaner £11.50 cash; paid for goods to be resold, by cheque £64.50; cash sales £235.50. Banked £200.00

Balance off the Cash Book and post it to the Ledger.

The following two questions require special care. They have bank overdrafts to begin with.

5. On May 1st R. Lunnis has the following balances on his Cash Book: cash £127.60, bank overdraft £175.45. Enter these balances (*the bank overdraft goes on the credit side*) and record the following in his Cash Book. Post to the Ledger.

19..		
May	1	R. Brown paid £126.75 by cheque; Lunnis allowed him discount of £3.25; bought stamps for £2.40 cash
	2	M. Jones sent a cheque for £112.56; no discount given as it was overdue Sent P. Robinson a cheque for £42.75; discount received £2.25; paid wages £24.50 in cash; paid for repairs £6.65 in cash
	3	R. Thompson paid £32.00 in cash; cash sales £414.50
	5	Paid carriage on parcel £1.65 in cash; paid £450.00 into the bank from the cash box

6. On May 1st John Brown had £27.50 in his cash box and was overdrawn at the bank by £270.65. Enter these opening balances in his Cash Book, enter the following items, balance off the Cash Book and post it to Ledger:

19..		
May	2	Paid for postage stamps £2.60 in cash; paid for repairs £5.47 in cash; paid to R. Jones a cheque for £28.50. Jones gave discount £1.50
	3	R. Wich paid in cash £5.00 to Brown; paid travelling expenses £2.75 in cash
	4	Cash sales £187.70; paid £150.00 out of the cash box into the bank
	5	Bought goods by cheque at an auction £17.50; paid rent for month £129.50 by cheque; paid wages £40.00 in cash
	6	R. Libbey paid by cheque £97.50 in full settlement of £100.00 which he owed us
	7	Rates paid by cheque £120.00; drew for personal use from bank £45.00

13.17 Original Entries for Petty Cash

The word 'petty' means 'small', from the French word *petit.* Many small payments in business, for such items as postage, refreshments for visitors and even the purchase of minor assets like staplers and date stamps, would be made to local shops and paid for by the petty cashier. The post of petty cashier is a responsible one for a junior member of staff, who acquires accounting experience while at the same time relieving the chief cashier of many small matters which are too trivial for his attention. A special system of record-keeping, the **Imprest System,** has been devised for these records.

The Imprest System

An imprest is a certain sum of money which has been set aside for a particular purpose. It is an advance of cash, with an implied promise that there is more to come later whenever it is needed and when the present imprest has been accounted for by the petty cashier. The main cashier starts the petty cashier off with a sum deemed to be sufficient for her needs for a limited time, say one week. Since postage is the commonest use for this system, the post girl is often the petty cashier. Given an imprest of £20.00, she will buy the stamps, pay for the telegrams, etc., and she will also pay out petty cash to anyone who needs it. The office boy may need petty cash for bus fares or to buy odd items required in a hurry, like string, cellulose tape or similar office sundries.

When the petty cashier begins to run short of money, she makes up her book in the way shown in Fig. 13.24 (page 188) and goes with it, and the petty cash box, to the cashier. The cashier then checks the book, agrees that the record has been properly kept, counts what is left in the till, and restores the imprest. This means he gives the petty cashier the amount of money spent, *so that she finishes up with the original imprest again, ready to start the next week.*

This is the really important point about the imprest system; the petty cashier is not given a further sum of £20.00 because with what she has left over she would have more than the agreed imprest. She is simply given enough money to bring the total to £20.00 again, thus *restoring the imprest position.*

Advantages of the Imprest System

(*a*) It saves the main cashier being endlessly bothered for trifling sums of money, and enables him to get on with his work.

(*b*) It trains young and inexperienced staff and develops their sense of responsibility.

(*c*) The sum of money chosen for the imprest is not large enough to present much of a temptation either to the petty cashier or to other employees. This does not mean that care should not be taken with petty cash. In most cities the majority of crimes connected with offices involves thefts of petty cash, usually at lunch-time. The petty cashier should always lock the till before she leaves her desk, and should lock it away in a safe as well when she goes to lunch.

(*d*) Even if it is stolen the loss does not represent a serious one to the firm.

(*e*) There is a very great saving in the posting of expenses to the nominal accounts, because of the analysis system. This is explained below.

(*f*) At any time the till can quickly be checked, for the cash left + the value of the payment vouchers = the original imprest.

Original Documents—The Petty Cash Voucher

Every transaction in business starts off with its original document and in the case of petty cash items the document concerned is the petty cash voucher. 'To vouch' is to certify the honesty of something, and the petty cash voucher certifies the honesty of the petty cash disbursement made. Petty cash vouchers may be receipts obtained from someone outside the business or may be an internal voucher. The former are preferable since they give less opportunity for dishonesty to the employee. Thus if an employee buys stationery for office use in cash he should obtain a bill from the shopkeeper. This bill becomes the petty cash voucher for that particular transaction. In circumstances where a proof of payment is not available (London Underground tickets, for example, are collected as the traveller leaves the station) the making out of an internal petty cash voucher, countersigned by an appropriate manager or head of department, will enable the employee to be reimbursed by the petty cashier. Typical external and internal petty cash vouchers are shown in Fig. 13.21 and 13.22.

Petty cash vouchers may be very small—bus tickets are an example. Such tickets may be stuck in books, or on larger sheets of paper, but they are proof of money spent and are therefore valid as vouchers. All petty cash vouchers

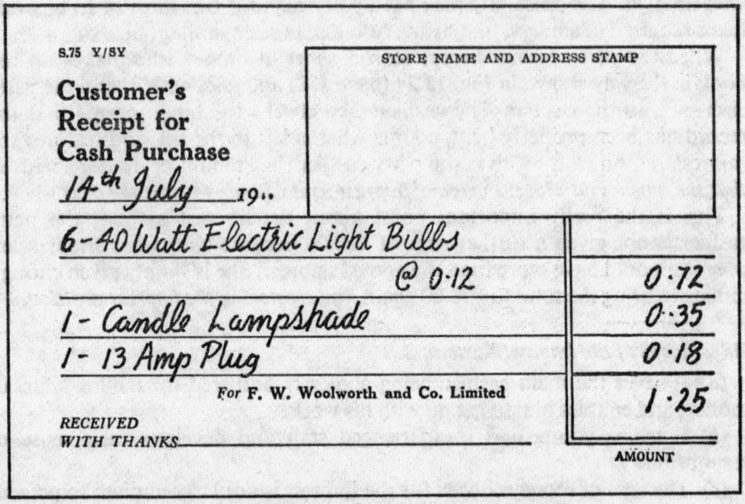
S.75 Y/SY

STORE NAME AND ADDRESS STAMP

Customer's Receipt for Cash Purchase

14th July 19..

	AMOUNT
6-40 Watt Electric Light Bulbs @ 0·12	0·72
1- Candle Lampshade	0·35
1- 13 Amp Plug	0·18
	1·25

For F. W. Woolworth and Co. Limited

RECEIVED WITH THANKS

Fig. 13.21. An 'external' petty cash voucher.

are numbered, and the numbers are recorded in the P.C.V. column in the petty cash book. They are then filed away in numerical order, so that if required the auditors may inspect them.

13.18 The Petty Cash Book

Fig. 13.24 gives an example of a petty cash book, and the notes opposite explain in detail how the entries are made.

Fig. 13.23 shows how the petty cash book is posted to the Ledger. The petty cash book may be regarded as a subsidiary Cash Book; the imprest having

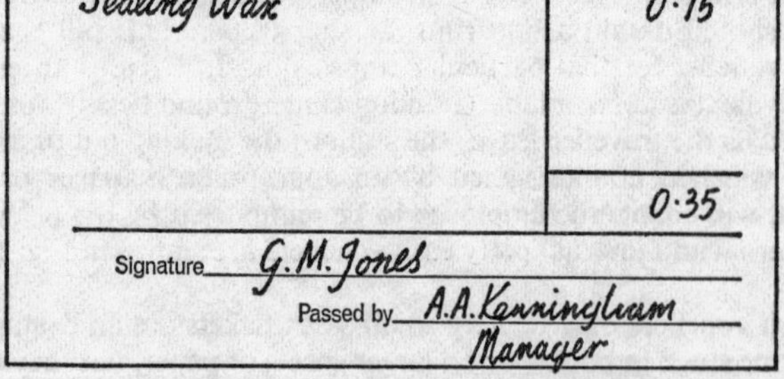
Petty Cash Voucher

Folio PCV27

Date May 15th 19..

For what required	AMOUNT
Methylated spirit	0·20
Sealing Wax	0·15
	0·35

Signature G. M. Jones

Passed by A. A. Kenningham Manager

Fig. 13.22. An 'internal' petty cash voucher.

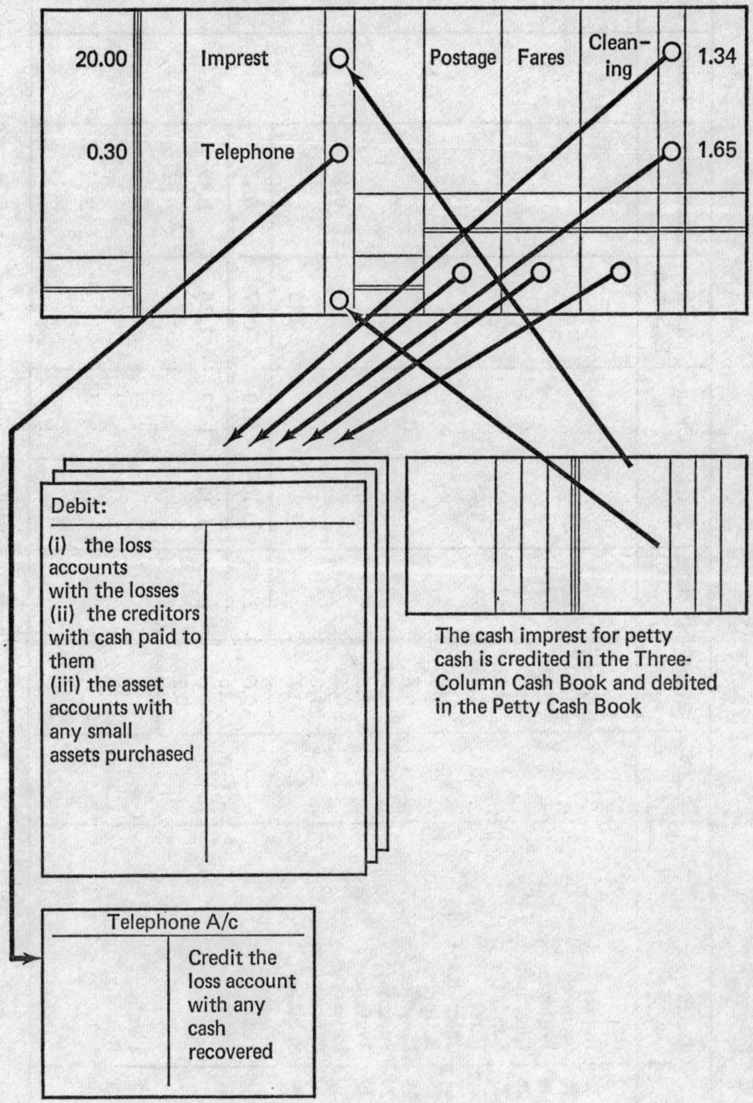
20.00
Imprest
Postage
Fares
Clean-ing
1.34
0.30
Telephone
1.65
Debit:
(i) the loss accounts with the losses
(ii) the creditors with cash paid to them
(iii) the asset accounts with any small assets purchased
The cash imprest for petty cash is credited in the Three-Column Cash Book and debited in the Petty Cash Book
Telephone A/c
Credit the loss account with any cash recovered

Fig. 13.23. Posting the petty cash book.

Dr.	Date	Details	P.C.V.	Total	Postage	Fares	Clean-ing	Sundry Expenses	Stationery	Folio	Ledger A/cs Cr.
	19..										
20.00	Mar. 25	Imprest	C.B.9								
	25	Stamps	1	1.50	1.50						
	26	Postage	2	0.65	0.65						
	26	Cleaning	3	0.45			0.45				
	27	Sundries	4	0.32				0.32			
	27	Fares	5	1.45		1.45					
0.30	28	Telephone Call	L.3								
	28	R. Jones	7	1.34						L.19	1.34
	29	Cleaning	8	0.65			0.65				
	29	Sundries	9	0.40				0.40			
	29	Travelling	10	1.65		1.65					
	30	Envelopes	11	0.45					0.45		
	30	Office Equipment	12	1.65						L.15	1.65
	30	Sundries	13	0.15				0.15			
	31	Totals	—	10.66	2.15	3.10	1.10	0.87	0.45		2.99
	31	Balance	C/d	9.64							
					L.5	L.11	L.27	L.36	L.49		
20.30				20.30							
9.64	Apr. 1	Balance	B/d								
10.36	1	Restored Imprest	C.B.11								

Fig. 13.24. The Petty Cash Book.

Notes

The following points will explain the operation of the petty cash imprest system shown above:

(i) The page is divided into two parts, debit and credit, but the 'centre' of the book is offset towards the extreme left of the page. This gives only a very small amount of debit side, whilst the credit side is expanded to make room for a series of analysis columns.

(ii) The details are written on the credit side, since there is no 'Details' column on the debit side.

(iii) The chief source of cash received is the cashier, who provides the original imprest, but other small sums may be received from staff, for telephone calls, etc. All receipts are debited.

(iv) On the credit side, money spent is first entered into the total column, but is then extended out into one of the analysis columns. This enables the total postage, fares, etc., to be collected together. A special column at the end is used to extend out any items which cannot be mixed with other items—for example, the payment to R. Jones can only be posted eventually to R. Jones' account.

(v) At the end of the week, or when the imprest is nearly all used, the petty cashier rules off the page in such a way as to total the 'Total' column and the analysis columns. These are then cross-totalled to ensure accuracy. The balance is found; the book is closed off and the balance is brought down.

(vi) The cashier then checks the petty cashier's work and restores the imprest by providing enough cash to raise the balance to the original imprest figure.

(vii) The book is now posted to the Ledger accounts, using the totals of the analysis columns and the individual special items in the end column. Folio numbers are entered as shown.

(viii) The petty cash vouchers, which authorise the payments made, are arranged in order, numbered and the P.C.V. numbers are entered in the column provided. The petty cashier is now ready for a further week's business.

been taken out of the Cash Book (credit the Cash Book) and debit the petty cash book which is receiving the money. The various payments out of the petty cash book are then credited in the petty cash book. The double-entry posting, as shown in Fig. 13.23, requires debit entries to be made in the 'Loss' Accounts, such as Postage Account and Fares Account; or in the Creditors' Accounts if any small payments were made to them (such as R. Jones in Fig. 13.25); or in the 'asset' accounts if we purchased small items of equipment.

The student should now try several petty cash exercises. It is possible to buy petty cash paper from a stationer, but as in examinations one usually has to rule up paper for petty cash exercises it is better to prepare a few sheets, even though this is rather laborious. Another way is to rule up one sheet and photocopy it if you have access to a photocopying machine.

13.19 Exercises: The Petty Cash Book

1. Rule up a petty cash book for five columns; Sundry Expenses, Fares, Stationery, Postage and Ledger Accounts. Enter the following items:

19..
Jan. 1 Drew imprest £30.00 from the chief cashier; paid for office teas £0.65; postage stamps £1.35; fares £0.55
2 Paid for envelopes £2.28; paid P. Jones £2.73
3 Paid fares £0.32; cleaning materials £0.63
4 Paid stationery £1.33; paid P. Brown £1.16
5 Paid for cleaning materials £1.25; paid fares £0.53
6 Paid for ball of string £0.78
7 Paid for sundry items for office use £0.86

Balance off the petty cash book and restore the imprest.

2. Enter the following items in a petty cash book which is kept on the imprest system. At the end, balance off the book and restore the original imprest. Use analysis columns for Fares, Postage, Sundry Expenses, Stationery, and Ledger Accounts, and invent appropriate folio numbers and petty cash voucher numbers.

19..
Oct. 1 Drew imprest from cashier £50.00
2 Paid fares £6.53; bought postage stamps £3.50
3 Paid for office teas £0.95; paid for stationery £0.66; paid for ball of string £0.45
4 Paid fares £5.15; paid for gum for office £0.90
5 Postage stamps £3.45; paid General Insurance Co. Ltd £4.85; paid J. Thomas £1.08
6 Paid fares £1.15; paid cleaner £12.50; paid dustman £1.00

3. M. Larkin employs a cashier who keeps a petty cash book on the imprest system. It has five analysis columns for Postage, Travelling, Stationery, General Expenses and Ledger Accounts. Rule special petty cash paper and record the following week's transactions, inserting appropriate folio numbers and petty cash voucher numbers:

19..
Jan. 1 Drew imprest of £40.00 from cashier; paid postage £2.50; paid R. Jones' account £2.25

2 Paid fares for office boy £1.42; paid for envelopes £0.55; collected from staff for private telephone calls £1.68
3 Paid for tea and cakes for typist's birthday £1.65
4 Paid postage £1.22; paid L. Smith's account £2.28
5 Paid fares (chauffeur) £4.50

Rule off the book, bring down the balance in hand, and restore the imprest to £40.00.

4. Enter the following in a petty cash book with five columns, for Postage, Fares, Office Sundries, Cleaning, and Ledger Accounts. Invent appropriate folio numbers and petty cash voucher numbers.

19..
Oct. 15 Drew petty cash imprest £50.00; paid postage £3.50
16 Paid fares £0.48; paid window-cleaner £3.50 and a creditor, T. Brown, £5.65
17 Paid postage £1.55; bought envelopes £2.50; bought cleaning materials £3.25
18 Paid R. Johnson £1.65; member of staff paid £0.45 for private telephone call; paid fares £0.90
19 Paid fares £2.75; paid cleaner's wages £6.35; paid M. Smith £4.15; paid postage £2.50

Balance the book and restore the imprest.

13.20 Journal Entries—Original Entries for All Other Items

We have now seen how to do original entries for purchases, sales, returns in and out, payments in cash and by cheque, and petty disbursements through the petty cashier. All other entries of every sort are dealt with through the Journal Proper, the original medieval Day Book, though it is still true to say that a business which deals in a particular field, such as the export field, might develop special day books to meet its requirements. For example, Bills of Exchange may be recorded in Bill Books, for Bills Payable and Bills Receivable.

It is quite impossible to give a full list of possible Journal Entries, for every conceivable event that occurs is the subject of a journal entry—from the opening up of a set of accounts on the first day the business commences to trade (opening entries) to the final moment when the proprietor dies, or the partnership is dissolved, or the limited company is wound up (closing entries). A detailed explanation of all the different types of journal entry is not possible here, but a table of journal entries is included (see Table 13.1 on page 196). First let us consider the importance of journal entries.

The Importance of Journal Entries

It is so important to have a clear grasp of journal entries that for centuries elementary examinations in Principles of Accounts have insisted that entrants to the accountancy profession must be well drilled in them. Today there is a tendency for those studying accountancy as a non-specialist subject to skip over this important topic, which can be difficult and may be tedious too. The result is that journal entries are not as well understood as they should be. This point has already been made with reference to double entry, in Chapter 11 (see page 124). Since journal entries are simply a process in which we decide what double entry to do for the particular problem that has arisen the student who can *think in journal entry form* will never be at a loss about double entry. Twenty years from the time he reads this section the reader will still be thinking back to it, and remembering it whenever a problem arises. We are giving the Chairman a golden handshake—what is the journal entry? Bill Bloggs has regrettably to be made redundant, and the agreed payment is £1 150—what is the double entry? We are issuing one million £1 shares at a premium of 50 pence (i.e. £1.50 each) payable in full on application—what is the journal entry? Clearly, these are important matters.

Journal Proper Paper

Journal paper can be purchased at any reputable stationers, and the ruling is given in Fig. 13.25 below. Its use is explained in the notes below the figure.

19..					
Date	Account to be Debited	Dr.	F	20.55	
	Account to be Credited		F		20.55
	Being, etc.				

Fig. 13.25. Paper for journal entries.

Notes

(i) The two money columns indicate which account is to be debited and which account is to be credited when the journal entry is posted to the Ledger. To make it quite clear the abbreviation Dr. (for debtor) is written on the line which is to be debited.

(ii) The name of each account is given and to separate off the debits from the credits those accounts which are to be credited (there may be more than one in some entries) are indented a little towards the right.

(iii) There follows a *narration*, which usually begins with the word 'Being . . .'. This explains what the entry is all about. For example, it might read 'Being office machinery purchased at this date'.

(iv) When the entry is posted to the Ledger the account to be debited is debited, and the folio number inserted at F in the layout above. The account to be credited is credited and its folio number is inserted at F on the correct line.

The most common types of journal entry are listed below. Some of them are clearly related to one another, and have been bracketed together. As explained above, the list could be made much longer, by including the issue of shares and debentures, transfers between partners' accounts, goodwill valuations and many other matters. It is easier to introduce such journal entries as they are reached during an accountancy course. The commonest journal entries therefore are:

{ (*a*) Opening entries
{ (*b*) Closing entries

{ (*c*) Purchase of assets
{ (*d*) Depreciation of assets
{ (*e*) Sale of worn-out or obsolete assets

(*f*) Bad debts entries
(*g*) Correction of errors
(*h*) Dishonoured cheques
(*i*) Bank loans, interest and charges

A Typical Journal Entry

Imagine that John Brown, a master carpenter, decides to set up in business on his own account on January 1st, 19. . . He has £3 000.00 in the bank, which he is prepared to bring in as working capital, and also £100 in cash. He decides to use half his present home as business premises. The value of the property is £16 000.00. He has tools worth £800, a motor vehicle worth £1 800.00 which is to be shared equally for business and domestic use, and a stock of wood worth £200.00. Half of this wood has not been paid for, so that he owes £100.00 to Wood Supplies Ltd. We have to open the books of the new new business. This is an 'Opening entry', (*a*) in the list given above.

First we must decide what Brown is actually bringing in to the business, because that will be his capital. It is often thought that capital is money, but capital can be contributed both in money and in 'kind', as stock, tools and equipment, etc. Everything he contributes is an asset of the business, and he may also, as in this case, bring in a liability which the business will honour in due course.

Listing the assets and liabilities at the start of business on January 1st, 19.., and being very careful to apportion any shared assets which are part 'business' and part 'domestic', we have:

	Assets (£)	*Liabilities* (£)
Land and buildings (half only)	8 000.00	
Tools	800.00	
Motor vehicles (half only)	900.00	
Stock	200.00	
Cash at bank	3 000.00	
Cash in hand	100.00	
Wood Supplies Ltd		100.00

It is a rule in accounting that the assets and liabilities of a business must always equal one another in value, a point which is explained in detail later when we come to consider balance sheets. Clearly this list of the business assets and liabilities does not balance. The assets total £13 000.00 and the liabilities only £100.00. The explanation is that we have left out one of the liabilities. The business now owes John Brown £12 900.00, the amount of capital he has contributed to the business. This is a liability of the business to the proprietor, and when Capital Account is credited with £12 900.00 the assets and liabilities will balance at £13 000.00. This illustrates a point which students frequently find confusing. They tend to think that the proprietor and the business are the same thing. That is quite wrong. *The accounts are kept from the point of view of the business and the owner is just one more creditor*. Of course, unlike ordinary creditors, he does not expect to be repaid at the end of the month. Should he dispose of the business to someone else he will expect to have all this capital returned to him, and perhaps extra for the goodwill of the business, whilst if he dies his heirs will expect to receive their inheritances and the Government will certainly expect its share of Capital Transfer Tax.

The journal entry can now be made (see Fig. 13.26) and posted to the Ledger, to open up all the accounts of the business (see Fig. 13.27). Note that the narration 'Being assets and liabilities at this date' simply explains in a few words exactly what the entry is about.

					J.1
19..				£	£
Jan. 1	Land and Buildings	Dr.	L.1	8 000.00	
	Tools	„	L.2	800.00	
	Motor Vehicles	„	L.3	900.00	
	Stock	„	L.4	200.00	
	Cash at Bank	„	C.B.1	3 000.00	
	Cash in Hand	„	C.B.1	100.00	
	Wood Supplies Ltd.		L.5		100.00
	Capital		L.6		12 900.00
	Being assets and liabilities at this date		£	13 000.00	13 000.00

13.26. An opening journal entry.

How to do Other Journal Entries

To conclude this section on journal entries the wide variety of entries that may be necessary cannot be fully explained, but Table 13.1 explains the commoner types (see page 196).

The student should now try some of the journal entries given below.

13.21 Exercises: Journal Entries

1. Elmer Ridge sets up in business as a music dealer, with the following assets: cash £100.00; cash at bank £2 500.00; stocks of instruments £480.00; records £185.00; musical manuscripts £65.00; furniture and fittings £80.00. Work out the total capital he has invested in the business and do the opening journal entry on May 1st. Post it to the Cash Book and the Ledger.
2. B. Irving is in business as a ladies' dressmaker and on March 1st has the following assets and liabilities: cash £270.00; cash at bank £4 300.00; stock £5 800.00; machines and equipment £2 106.00; furniture and fittings £840.00; debtors, B. Morgan £36.70, T. Slow £72.60, and M. Jordan £50.68; creditors, T. Young £505.70 and M. Smith £65.00; mortgage on property £6 000.00. Work out the capital and do the opening journal entry.
3. On August 24th at a bankruptcy sale, we purchased for cash goods value as follows: weighing machine £40.00; shelving and cupboards £25.00; goods for resale (purchases) £220.00; motor vehicle £120.00. Do the journal entry necessary to record the purchase of these items and post to the Ledger. (Clearly there will be several accounts to be debited in this exercise.)
4. On August 1 K. Khamis sets up in business. Next day he purchases on credit the following from Business Supplies Ltd: 1 office desk £68.50; 2 filing cabinets at £65.50 each; 1 electric typewriter, Serial No. 72/69310, £245.00; and a letter-folding machine £184.50. These items are to be kept on his books in two Asset Accounts only. Do the journal entry for the purchase of these assets.
5. My furniture and fittings are valued at £880.00, of which £600.00 is furniture. Do the journal entry for depreciation at 20 per cent on furniture and 10 per cent on fittings. Post to the Ledger.
6. Plant and machinery for Peter Cross is valued at £3 800.00 at June 30th. At December 31st he depreciates it by 10 per cent per annum. (Careful, this is only a half-year.) Show the journal entry and both Ledger Accounts.
7. On July 30th we sell a motor vehicle valued on our books at £300.00 for £580.00

LAND AND BUILDINGS ACCOUNT L.1

		F	£			F	£
19..		F	£	19..		F	£
Jan. 1	Capital	J.1	8 000.00				

TOOLS ACCOUNT L.2

		F	£			F	£
19..		F	£	19..		F	£
Jan. 1	Capital	J.1	800.00				

MOTOR VEHICLES ACCOUNT L.3

19..		F	£	19..		F	£
Jan. 1	Capital	J.1	900.00				

STOCK ACCOUNT L.4

19..		F	£	19..		F	£
Jan. 1	Capital	J.1	200.00				

BANK ACCOUNT C.B.1

19..		F	£	19..		F	£
Jan. 1	Capital	J.1	3 000.00				

CASH ACCOUNT C.B.1

19..		F	£	19..		F	£
Jan. 1	Capital	J.1	100.00				

WOOD SUPPLIES LTD ACCOUNT L.5

19...		F	£	19..		F	£
				Jan. 1	Sundry Assets	J.1	100.00

CAPITAL ACCOUNT L.6

19...		F	£	19..		F	£
				Jan. 1	Sundry Assets	J.1	12 900.0

13.27. Posting an opening entry to the Ledger.

Table 13.1. How to do Journal Entries

Type of entry	*Account to be debited*	*Account to be credited*
1. Opening entries	See full explanation in text	
2. Closing entries	These are explained in Chapter 17	
3. Purchase of an asset	Asset Account and VAT Account (if applicable)	Cash Account (if paying in cash)
or	Asset Account and VAT Account (if applicable)	Bank Account (if paying by cheque)
or	Asset Account and VAT Account (if applicable)	Creditor's Account (if paying later)
4. Depreciation of an asset	Depreciation Account (this is a Loss Account)	Asset Account (asset declines in value)
5. Sale of a worn-out asset	Cash Account (if sold for cash)	Asset Account (with book value)
or	Bank Account (if buyer pays by cheque)	Asset Account (with book value)
Note. If sold below book value debit Sale of Asset Account with the loss If sold above book value credit Sale of Asset Account with the profit		
6. Bad debt	Bad Debts Account (this is a Loss Account)	Debtors' Account (to remove the debt from the books)
7. A bad debt recovered	Bank Account (this is the money received)	Bad Debt Recovered Account (this is a Profit Account)
8. Correction of errors	Here you have to do what is necessary to correct the error. Think hard about it and make up your mind what the double entry will look like	
9. Dishonoured cheques	Debtor's Account (restore the debt to the debtor)	Bank Account (remove the cheque which has been dishonoured) Discount Allowed Account (remove the discount, if any, allowed to the debtor when he paid)
10. Bank loans	Bank Account (with the agreed loan) Interest Payable Account (with the interest payable; this is a Loss Account)	Loan Account (with the total repayable; including interest)
11. Bank charges	Bank Charges Account (this is a Loss Account)	Bank Account (to remove the money the bank has deducted)

to Rex Garages Ltd. Do the journal entry for the sale of this asset and post it to the Ledger.

8. On November 30th we sell a machine, valued on our books at £3 800.00, at auction. It fetches £1 500.00. Record the sale of this asset.
9. On July 19th a debtor, Anne Alien, who owes £100.00, informs us that in view of difficult economic circumstances the government of her country will only sanction the payment of half the money. It is decided to clear the whole debt in view of the political situation in the country concerned. Do the journal entry.
10. J. Houston was written off as a debtor some time ago for £300.00. On November 5th he sends us a cheque for £315.00 representing the complete payment of the debt and interest thereon for the intervening time. Do the journal entry.
11. Prepare journal entries to correct the following errors:

    (*a*) The purchase of a typewriter, value £75.50, has been wrongly included in purchases.

    (*b*) A credit note issued to R. Morgan for goods returned to the value of £60.00 has been posted to the account of R. Morton.
12. Show by means of journal entries how the following errors would be corrected in the books of C. Careless:

    (*a*) Machinery valued at £500.00 purchased on credit from Excel Engineering Company had been debited to the Purchases Account.

    (*b*) When paying J. Johnson, a creditor, Careless had deducted £5.00 discount. Johnson had disallowed this discount.

    (*c*) Depreciation of £200.00 on motor vehicles had been credited to the Fixtures and Fittings Account.
13. On May 19th a cheque for £52.50 received two days earlier from R. Thomas was returned marked 'refer to drawer'. Restore the debt to the debtor.
14. On July 11th two cheques are returned marked 'refer to drawer'. One was for £50.95 from L. Jones and the other £26.45 from T. Peterson. Do the journal entry restoring these debts to the Debtors' Accounts.
15. R. Jowett, who paid us £56.55 in full settlement of a debt of £59.50 on May 8th, dishonours his cheque. It is returned 'refer to drawer', on May 11th. Restore the debt to the debtor with a journal entry.
16. Steady Bank Ltd lend Overdrawn Ltd £10 000.00 secured on the plant and machinery of the firm. Record the journal entry as it would appear in the books of Overdrawn Ltd on March 31st. Interest will be charged at a later date.
17. On September 30th Steady Bank Ltd charge Overdrawn Ltd £575.00 interest on the loan described in question 16. Record this interest charge in the Journal of Overdrawn Ltd.

[*Note:* For those who find Journal entries difficult a fuller explanation is available in a companion volume, *Book-keeping Made Simple*.

14

ACCOUNTING TO THE TRIAL BALANCE, WITH BOOKS OF ORIGINAL ENTRY

14.1 Introduction

Now that the reader knows how to make original entries for all types of transactions (purchases, sales, purchases returns, sales returns, payments in cash and by cheque and the various types of infrequent entries recorded in the Journal Proper), it is time to do accounting to the Trial Balance level with a full set of books.

Advertisements will often be seen in the press offering employment to persons who can keep books to the Trial Balance level. This is the first stage of accounting and the student who approaches this chapter with a good sense of achievement on the work of earlier chapters is about to make a breakthrough to the point where he can call himself a 'Book-keeper to the Trial Balance'. Such a student should not feel too disappointed if his Trial Balances do not come out first time. It is a lucky accountant who does not make some slip in his month's work, and it takes a good level of experience to get even a textbook exercise right first time. The important thing is to persevere; by the time you have done three or four of these major exercises you will begin to know what you are doing.

14.2 What is Involved in Accounting to the Trial Balance?

Trial Balances in small offices are usually done once a month, on the last day of the month. They cannot be done more frequently because the work involved is too great, nor should they be done less frequently. The purpose of the Trial Balance is to discover any mistake; if there is one, it may be a long task finding it, even if there is only one month's work to look through. To delay making a Trial Balance for five or six months would mean Herculean labour if a mistake were discovered.

During any month we have been recording a wide range of transactions:

(*a*) Opening the books, with an opening journal entry, unless of course they were already open from last month, in which case we start with last month's balances already on the books.

(*b*) Recording a great many purchases, sales, purchases returns, and sales returns in the Day Books, and posting them to the Ledger.

(*c*) Recording in the Cash Book cash received and paid, and posting it to the Ledger Accounts.

(*d*) Recording petty cash received and paid, and posting it to the Ledger Accounts.

(*e*) Recording several less common items like the purchase of assets and the correction of errors in the Journal Proper and posting them to the Ledger. It may also be necessary to use the Journal to adjust VAT on cash sales, cash purchases and cash returns.

The final result of all these activities is a set of Ledger Accounts which have been entered accurately on the double-entry method, so that every debit entry has a corresponding credit entry. If everything has been done correctly, a list of the debit balances will exactly equal a list of the credit balances. Just as in Chapter 12 we were able to extract a Trial Balance from the accounts which we had prepared by direct double entry, we are now able to prepare a Trial Balance from the Ledger Accounts we have posted up from the Sales Day Book, Purchases Day Book, Cash Book, etc. In order to show how the whole process is carried out a specimen exercise using all the books is given below in Section 14.3. An explanation of each stage is given, but for typographical reasons the layout of the next few pages requires the student to turn as required to the display he is considering. The exercise, and the notes on the facing page, can be conveniently read, but this has required other parts of the display to be arranged to suit the printer's needs.

					J.1
19..				£	£
Jul. 1	Cash in Hand	Dr.	C.B.1	85.00	
	Cash at Bank	”	C.B.1	1 846.50	
	Stock A/c	”	L.1	3 214.60	
	A. Smith A/c	”	L.2	85.50	
	P. Rose A/c		L.3		160.00
	M. Jordan A/c		L.4		87.00
	Capital A/c		L.5		4 984.60
	Being assets and liabilities at this date		£	5 231.60	5 231.60
25	Shop Fittings	Dr.	L.13	240.00	
	VAT A/c	”	L.14	30.00	
	Electronic Weighing Co.		L.15		270.00
	Being purchase of electronic scale Serial No. 2F 17804 at this date				
31	Sales A/c	Dr.	L.9	200.00	
	VAT A/c		L.14		200.00
	Being VAT payable to H.M. Customs at this date				
31	VAT A/c	Dr.	L.14	4.33	
	Travelling Expenses A/c		L.6		0.53
	Motor Expenses A/c		L.7		2.86
	Petrol and Oil A/c		L.8		0.94
	Being VAT on inputs for month of July				

Fig. 14.1(*a*). The journal entries for the specimen exercise on page 200.

14.3 A Specimen Exercise to the Trial Balance

Robert Morgan started in business with the following assets and liabilities on 1 July, 19..:

Cash in hand £85.00. Cash at Bank £1 846.50. Stock £3 214.60. Debtor A. Smith £85.50. Creditors P. Rose £160.00, M. Jordan £87.00.

Open the accounts by means of an opening journal entry. Post the entry to the Ledger and the Three-Column Cash Book. Then enter the following transactions in the appropriate Book of Original Entry, post them to the Ledger, and extract a Trial Balance to prove the accuracy of your work.

19..

July 1 Sold goods on credit to A. Smith for £320.00 + VAT £25.60 = £345.60 in total

3 Paid travelling expenses £4.80 in cash

4 Paid for motor expenses by cheque £35.80. Paid for petrol and oil by cheque £8.50

5 Cash takings for sales totalled £650.00. Banked £550.00.

10 Purchased goods on credit from P. Rose £325.00 + VAT £26.00 = £351.00 in total

11 Paid postage £3.50 in cash

13 Cash sales totalled £480.00. Banked £400.00

15 Paid wages £85.00 in cash. Paid postage £2.50 in cash

18 Sold goods on credit to A. Smith for £420 + VAT £33.60 = £453.60 in total

20 Cash sales totalled £720.00. Banked £650.00. Paid P. Rose's account as at July 1st less 5 per cent discount, by cheque

21 Paid travelling expenses £1.80 in cash. A. Smith paid his account as July 1st in full by cheque

22 Paid postage £7.28 in cash

23 Sold goods on credit to J. Walker £128.50 + VAT £10.28 = £138.78 in total

24 A. Smith returned goods £40.00 + VAT £3.20 = £43.20 in total

25 Bought scales for shop use from Electronic Weighing Co. on credit £240.00 + VAT £30.00 = £270.00 in total (Serial No. of scales 2F 17804)

27 Cash sales totalled £650.00. Banked £400.00. Paid M. Jordan's account as at July 1st in full by cheque

28 Purchased goods on credit from P. Rose £480.00 + VAT £38.40 = £518.40 in total

30 Paid wages £85.00 in cash. Paid salaries £185.00 in cash. Paid National Insurance Contributions by cheque £45.50

31 The following VAT adjustments had to be made at the end of the month by journal entries. Debit Sales Account with £200.00 and credit VAT Account for VAT on cash sales. Debit VAT Account with £4.33, and credit the following accounts with the amounts shown: Travelling Expenses Account £0.53; Motor Expenses Account £2.86; Petrol and Oil Account £0.94.

Notes on Specimen Exercise to the Trial Balance

July 1 An opening journal entry is required, which must then be posted to the Ledger and the Cash Book. Then the sale to A. Smith is a Sales Day Book entry

3 A Cash Book entry

4 Two more entries in the Three-Column Cash Book

5 A Cash Book entry, followed by a contra entry to take £550.00 out of the Cash Account and into the Bank Account

10 A Purchases Day Book entry

11 A Cash Book entry

13 A Cash Book entry, followed by a contra entry

15 Two more Cash Book entries

18 A Sales Day Book entry

20 A Cash Book entry; a contra entry and another Cash Book entry

21 Two more Cash Book entries

22 A Cash Book entry

23 A Sales Day Book entry

24 A Sales Returns Book entry

25 This is the purchase of an asset and requires a journal entry.

27 A Cash Book entry; a contra entry and then another Cash Book entry

28 A Purchases Day Book entry

30 Three Cash Book entries

31 These journal entries are really explained fully in the instructions given in the specimen exercise. They result in the sales figure being reduced to the 'Net of VAT' figure, and the expenses named, i.e. Travelling Expenses, etc., being reduced also since the VAT is being claimed as a refund (or rather as a set-off against VAT payable). In a real business of course some convenient method of capturing VAT data would be devised for receipts and expenses such as those mentioned here.

Final Note: It is now necessary to post all the books of original entry to the ledger and extract a Trial Balance. After looking through this model exercise the reader should try to work several of the exercises given on page 205.

		F	Details	VAT	S.D.B.1 Total
19..			£	£	£
Jul. 1	A. Smith				
	Goods	L.2	320.00	25.60	345.60
18	A. Smith				
	Goods	L.2	420.00	33.60	453.60
23	J. Walker				
	Goods	L.12	128.50	10.28	138.78
		£	868.50	69.48	937.98
			L.9	L.14	

Fig. 14.1(*b*). The Sales Day Book for the specimen exercise on page 200.

		F	Details	VAT	P.D.B.1 Total
19..			£	£	£
Jul. 10	P. Rose				
	Goods	L.3	325.00	26.00	351.00
28	P. Rose				
	Goods	L.3	480.00	38.40	518.40
		£	805.00	64.40	869.40
			L.18	L.14	

Fig. 14.1(*c*). The Purchases Day Book for the specimen exercise on page 200.

		F	Details	VAT	S.R.B.1 Total
19..			£	£	£
Jul. 24	A. Smith				
	Goods	L.2	40.00	3.20	43.20
			L.19	L.14	

Fig. 14.1(*d*). The Sales Returns Book for the specimen exercise on page 200.

Date 19..		Details	F	Discount Allowed	Cash	Bank	Date 19..		Details	F	Discount Received	Cash	C.B.1 Bank
Jul.	1	Balances	J.1		85.00	1 846.50	Jul.	3	Travelling Exp.	L.6		4.80	
	5	Sales	L.9		650.00			4	Motor Exp.	L.7			35.80
	5	Cash	c			550.00		4	Petrol and Oil	L.8			8.50
	13	Sales	L.9		480.00			5	Bank	c		550.00	
	13	Cash	c			400.00		11	Postage	L.10		3.50	
	20	Sales	L.9		720.00			13	Bank	c		400.00	
	20	Cash	c			650.00		15	Wages	L.11		85.00	
	21	A. Smith	L.2			85.50		15	Postage	L.10		2.50	
	27	Sales	L.9		650.00			20	Bank	c		650.00	
	27	Cash	c			400.00		20	P. Rose	L.3	8.00		152.00
								21	Travelling Exp.	L.6		1.80	
								22	Postage	L.10		7.28	
								27	Bank	c		400.00	
								27	M. Jordan	L.4			87.00
								30	Wages	L.11		85.00	
								30	Salaries	L.16		185.00	
								30	Nat. Insurance	L.17			45.50
								31	Balances	C/d		210.12	3 603.20
			£		2 585.00	3 932.00				£	8.00	2 585.00	3 932.00
Aug	1	Balances	B/d		210.12	3 603.20					L.20		

Fig. 14.1(*e*). The Three-Column Cash Book for the specimen exercise on page 200.

Stock A/c — L.1

Op. Bal.	3214.60		

A. Smith A/c — L.2

Op. Bal.	85.50	Bank	85.50
Sales	345.60	Sales Ret.	43.20
"	453.60	Balance	756.00
	£884.70		£884.70
Balance	756.00		

P. Rose A/c — L.3

Bank	152.00	Op. Bal.	160.00
Discount	8.00	Purchases	351.00
Balance	869.40	"	518.40
	£1,029.40		£1,029.40
		Balance	869.40

M. Jordan A/c — L.4

Bank	87.00	Op. Bal.	87.00

Capital A/c — L.5

		Op. Bal.	4984.60

Travelling Expenses A/c — L.6

Cash	4.80	VAT	0.53
"	1.80	Balance	6.07
	£6.60		£6.60
Balance	6.07		

Motor Expenses A/c — L.7

Bank	35.80	VAT	2.86
		Balance	32.94
	£35.80		£35.80
Balance	32.94		

Petrol and Oil A/c — L.8

Bank	8.50	VAT	0.94
		Balance	7.56
	£8.50		£8.50
Balance	7.56		

Sales A/c — L.9

VAT	200.00	Cash	650.00
Balance	3,168.50	"	480.00
		"	720.00
		"	650.00
		"	868.50
	£3,368.50	Sun. Debtors	£3,368.50
		Balance	3,168.50

Postage A/c — L.10

Cash	3.50		
"	2.50		
"	7.28		

Wages A/c — L.11

Cash	85.00		
"	85.00		

J. Walker A/c — L.12

Sales	138.78		

Shop Fitting A/c — L.13

Electr. Weighing	240.00		

VAT A/c — L.14

Electr. Weighing	30.00	Sales	200.00
Expenses	4.33	"	69.48
Purchases	64.40		
Sales Returns	3.20		
Balance	167.55		
	£269.48		£269.48
		Balance	167.55

Electronic Weighing Co A/c — L.15

		Shop Fitt.	270.00

Salaries A/c — L.16

Cash	185.00		

National Insurance A/c — L.17

Bank	45.50		

Purchases A/c — L.18

Sun. Creditors	805.00		

Sales Returns A/c — L.19

Sun. Debtors	40.00		

Discount Received A/c — L.20

		Sun. Creditors	8.00

Fig. 14.1(*f*). Ledger entries for the specimen exercise on page 200.

TRIAL BALANCE OF R. MORGAN'S BOOKS
(as at July 31st, 19..)

	Dr. £	Cr. £
Cash A/c	210.12	
Bank A/c	3 603.20	
Stock A/c	3 214.60	
A. Smith A/c	756.00	
P. Rose A/c		869.40
Capital A/c		4 984.60
Travelling Expenses A/c	6.07	
Motor Expenses A/c	32.94	
Petrol and Oil A/c	7.56	
Sales A/c		3 168.50
Postages A/c	13.28	
Wages A/c	170.00	
J. Walker A/c	138.78	
Shop Fittings A/c	240.00	
VAT A/c		167.55
Electronic Weighing Co. A/c		270.00
Salaries A/c	185.00	
National Insurance A/c	45.50	
Purchases A/c	805.00	
Sales Returns A/c	40.00	
Discount Received A/c		8.00
	£9 468.05	9 468.05

Fig. 14.1(*g*). The Trial Balance for the specimen exercise on page 200.

14.4 Exercises: Accounting to the Trial Balance

1. Alfred Watkins started in business with the following assets and liabilities on February 1st, 19..: cash in hand £48.00; cash at bank £1 320.50; stock £2 346.55; land and buildings £8 400.00; debtors R. Wick £27.50, J. Newley £45.80; and a creditor H. Tumptop to whom he owed £185.95.

Open the accounts by means of an opening journal entry, post it to the Ledger and Cash Book to start off the accounts of the business and then enter the following transactions in the appropriate Books of Original Entry. At the end of the month post all the entries to the Ledger and extract a Trial Balance.

19..

Feb. 1 Purchased goods for resale from H. Tumptop to the value of £350. This included VAT of £25.93

3 Sold goods on credit to R. Wick £38.40. This included VAT of £2.84

5 Cash sales £680.00, of which Watkins banked £650.00. Paid casual wages £8.50, in cash

9 Purchased ladder for shop use £13.50 in cash. This included VAT of £1.00

12 Cash sales £520.00 of which £500.00 was banked. Paid the balance owing on February 1st to H. Tumptop less 5 per cent discount, by cheque

14 R. Wick settled his account as at February 1st, paying in full by cheque. Paid for van hire £24.51 in cash (Motor Expenses Account)
19 Cash sales £840.00, of which £800 was banked
20 Sold to J. Newley on credit goods valued at £84.50. This included VAT of £6.26
22 J. Newley paid his account as at February 1st in full by cheque
24 Paid postage in cash £1.25
26 Cash sales £750.00, of which £720.00 banked
28 Paid wages in cash £54.00. Paid salaries by cheque £120.00. Drew from bank for personal use £200.00. The following adjustments for VAT had to be put through the Journal: debit Sales Account with £206.67 and credit VAT Account (VAT on cash sales); debit VAT Account with £1.82 and credit Motor Expenses Account (VAT on van hire)

2. J. Gretchen started in business with the following assets and liabilities on January 1st, 19. . : cash in hand £50.00; cash at bank £1 650.00; stock £3 500.00; furniture and fittings £840.00; debtors R. Board £27.50 and J. Newcombe £275.55; and a creditor M. Longshore to whom he owed £48.50

Open the accounts by means of an opening journal entry, post it to the Ledger and Cash Book to start off the accounts of the business and then enter the following transactions in the appropriate Books of Original Entry. At the end of the month post all the entries to the Ledger and extract a Trial Balance.

19. .
Jan. 2 Purchased goods for resale from M. Longshore to the value of £760.00. This included VAT of £56.30
3 J. Newcome paid his account by cheque less 5 per cent cash discount £13.78. Sold goods on credit to M. Taylor for £85, including VAT of £6.30
5 Cash sales £550, of which £500.00 was banked for safe-keeping
9 Purchased goods for resale at bankrupt's sale £84.00 in cash
12 Purchased fittings for shop on credit from New Look Ltd, £285.50. This included VAT of £31.72
R. Board was declared bankrupt and it was decided to write the whole debt off as bad. £2.04 could be reclaimed from VAT. Cash sales £900 of which £800 banked for safe-keeping. Paid postage £3.85 in cash
19 Cash Sales £850.65 of which £800 banked for safe-keeping. Paid for packing materials and paper bags £56 in cash. Paid postage £4.80 in cash
22 Settled M. Longshore's account as at January 1st in full by cheque
26 Cash sales £460.00 of which £300.00 banked. Paid wages for month £126 in cash
29 Sold goods on credit to J. Newcombe for £485.50, of which £35.96 was VAT
31 Adjustments for VAT had to be made as follows: debit Sales Account with £204.49 and credit VAT Account (VAT on cash sales); debit VAT Account with £4.15 and credit Packing Materials Account; debit VAT Account with £6.22 and credit Purchases Account (VAT on goods purchased at bankrupt sale)

3. C. Gordon started in business with the following assets and liabilities on April 1st 19. . : cash in hand £245.00, cash at bank £842.50, stock £3 253.50, premises £8 000.00 and fittings £800.00. He had one debtor, T. Lawson, who owed him £378.50 and creditors R. Miller, £250.00 and K. Lake £380.00.

Open the accounts by means of an opening journal entry, post it to the Ledger and the Cash Book and then enter the following transactions on the dates shown using the appropriate books of original entry. At the end of the month post all these entries to the Ledger and extract a Trial Balance to check the accuracy of your work.

19. .

Apr. 1 Bought goods for resale from T. Elliot on credit £400.00; £29.63 of this VAT. Bought postage stamps £12.50
- 3 T. Lawson paid his account less 2½ per cent cash discount, by cheque
- 4 Bought at auction goods for cash (for resale at a later date) value £132.80, of which £9.84 was VAT
- 6 Cash sales £524 of which £500 was banked
- 9 T. Lawson cheque was returned marked 'Refer to Drawer'. The debt was restored to his account. (Careful—don't forget the discount he can no longer be allowed.)
- 11 Paid for packing materials in cash £28.50
- 13 Cash sales £636.50 of which £600 was banked. Paid for repairs to window £5.80 in cash
- 15 Sold goods on credit to M. Grainger £385.00 of which £28.52 was VAT
- 18 Purchased goods on credit £480.00 from L. Miller of which £35.56 was VAT
- 20 Cash sales £632.50 of which £600 is banked
- 25 Paid R. Miller's Account as at April 1st, by cheque less 5 per cent discount
- 27 Paid K. Lake's Account as at April 1st, by cheque in full. Cash sales £480.00, of which £450 was banked
- 28 Bought by cheque, filing cabinet (Serial No. 2164/F) from local office equipment suppliers £75.30. VAT included was £5.58
- 30 T. Lawson wrote to say that his bank had now agreed to honour his cheque, and it was accordingly paid in again. Discount was still allowed.

At the end of the month the following VAT entries had to be made: debit Sales Account with £168.37 and credit VAT Account (VAT on cash sales); debit VAT Account with £2.11 and credit Packing Materials Account; debit VAT Account with £0.43 and credit Repairs Account.

4. J. Payne started in business with the following assets and liabilities on January 1st, 19. .: cash in hand £84.00, cash at bank £1 720.00, stock £4 950.00 and premises £10 000.00, and fittings £5 000.00. He had two debtors, R. Brown £78.85 and T. Leggatt £276.40. He also owed £1 500.00 to G. Leyside.

Open the accounts by means of an opening journal entry, post it to the Ledger and the Cash Book, and then enter the following transactions on the dates shown using the appropriate books of original entry. At the end of the month post all these entries to the Ledger and extract a Trial Balance to check the accuracy of your work.

19. .

Jan. 1 R. Brown paid his account by cheque in full
- 2 Sold goods on credit to R. Brown £126.00 of which £9.33 was VAT
- 3 Purchased goods for resale on credit from G. Leyside £520.00 of which £38.52 was VAT
- 4 Cash sales £825.00 of which £800 was banked.
- 6 Bought furniture for office use from Comfichairs Ltd, £148.00, on credit, of which £10.96 was VAT
- 9 T. Leggatt paid his account by cheque, less 5 per cent discount
- 11 Paid carriage charges in cash £4.84. Cash sales £685.00 of which £650.00 was banked

13 Paid G. Leyside's Account as at January 1st, 19. ., by cheque less 5 per cent discount. Paid wages in cash £42.50
16 Sold goods on credit to T. Leggatt valued at £694.00 of which £51.41 was VAT
19 Cash sales £728.50 of which £720.00 was banked
20 T. Leggatt returned goods valued at £36.00 of which £2.67 was VAT
25 Cash sales £645.00 of which £600 was banked
27 Paid wages in cash £42.50
31 Cash sales £640.00 of which £625 was banked

The following VAT adjustments had to be made. Debit VAT Account with £0.36 and credit Carriage Charges Account (VAT on carriage). Debit Sales Account with £261.00 and credit VAT Account (VAT on Cash Sales).

15

VALUE ADDED TAX

15.1 What is Value Added Tax?

On April 1st, 1973, a new taxation system was introduced in the United Kingdom, replacing two other forms of taxation, purchase tax and selective employment tax, which were abolished on that date. This tax was designed partly to bring the United Kingdom taxation system into closer alignment with Common Market systems, but it has also spread taxation over a wider range of consumer products, making taxation fairer than before. The disadvantage of the new tax system is that it requires about 1 500 000 businesses, many of them quite small, to keep VAT records. This means that VAT routines have become part of office practice for every firm in the country.

The principle of VAT is that tax is levied on the value added to goods at every stage as they pass from the natural raw material stage to the finished product, and then onwards to the final consumer. Every middleman along the way buys goods and uses services which have already had some tax levied upon them. When he in turn sells goods or provides services, he levies tax on the price he charges his customers. The amount he is liable to pay over to Customs is the difference between his 'output tax' levied on customers and the 'input tax' levied upon him by his suppliers. It is directly related to the value he has added.

Imagine an oak tree cut down in a farmer's field, taken to a sawmill and cut into planks, sold to a manufacturer and turned into 500 coffee tables eventually retailed at £11 each including tax. The list of values added shown in Table 15.1 might be calculated. Tax has been levied at 10 per cent. The notes below explain in detail how the tax is calculated.

15.2 Office Activities Made Necessary by Value Added Tax

A businessman must perform the following activities to comply with the regulations for Value Added Tax:

(*a*) Complete and send off to the Customs and Excise authorities a registration form VAT 1, which registers the business as a 'Taxable Person' (provided the turnover exceeds £10 000 per annum).

(*b*) Record his outputs. These are the charges for goods and services which he makes to his customers, and to which he adds the tax payable to the customer. This enables him to calculate his **output tax** for any tax period. We have seen in Section 13.2 how this is done in the Sales Day Book.

(*c*) Record his inputs. These are the charges made to him by his suppliers of goods and services. The tax charged to him by these suppliers is called his **input tax**. We have again seen how this is done in the Purchases Day Book in Section 13.4.

(*d*) Complete his VAT return (Form VAT 100) at intervals, and account for the tax due.

Table 15.1. Calculations—Value Added Tax

Business	*Cost price free of tax*	*Sale price free of tax*	*Value added*	*Final charge to customer (incl. 10% tax)*	*Input tax*	*Output tax*	*Tax payable*
	£	£	£	£	£	£	£
1. Farmer	0	200 (tree trunk)	200	220	0	20	20
2. Sawmill Co.	200	500 (sawn planks)	300	550	20	50	30
3. Furniture manufacturer	500	3 000 (coffee tables)	2 500	3 300	50	300	250
4. Retailer	3 000	5 000	2 000	5 500	300	500	200

Notes

(i) In each business the final charge to the customer includes 10 per cent tax. This means that $\frac{1}{11}$ of the final charge is output tax, for which the businessman is accountable.

(ii) With the exception of the farmer, who is cutting down a gift of nature (a tree), the cost of the businessman's input is the price he pays to the previous businessman in the chain that leads to the final consumer. This again includes $\frac{1}{11}$ of the price as tax. This is his input tax.

(iii) The tax payable to Customs and Excise Department is the difference between output tax and input tax.

(iv) The effect of the tax is that the final consumers pay a total price of £5 500, of which £5 000 is the true value of the coffee tables they bought and £500 is tax. This £500 will be accounted for as shown in the *Tax payable* column above. It is not the businessman who pays the tax—that is paid by the consumer—but the businessman becomes an unpaid collection agent of H.M. Customs responsible for collecting the tax and paying it over to the Customs and Excise Department.

(*e*) Keep records and accounts that are adequate for these purposes. These records will now be explained in a little more detail.

15.3 Output Records

Every 'taxable person' must keep records of the goods and services he supplies to his customers, and must add to the charges made the correct rate of tax. Tax was originally chargeable at 10 per cent but is now charged at 8 per cent (the standard rate) and 12½ per cent on certain 'luxury' items such as petrol, television sets, hi-fi, furs, jewellery, etc. Certain goods and services are taxable, but at a zero rate. These include food, water, books and newspapers, items for the blind, fuel and power, building work, export services, transport and drugs supplied on prescriptions. It might seem pointless to say an item is taxable and then tax it at a zero rate, but in fact this enables a businessman who is not charging his customers tax on his outputs to reclaim the tax on his inputs that he has paid to suppliers.

There is a class of exempt goods and services which are not taxed at all. These include the leasing of land and buildings, insurance, banking, finance, postal services, and lotteries. The suppliers of these services do not need to register or keep records, but they are unable to claim back any tax paid on inputs.

For the ordinary businessman keeping records by means of a Sales Day Book recording the invoices sent out to his customers, the output tax will be found from the VAT column on the Sales Day Book and will be credited to VAT Account as already explained (see page 160).

For other businessmen, chiefly retailers, selling goods for cash, a series of Special Retailers' Schemes is in operation. These are explained later in this chapter.

The final effect of keeping 'output records' is that the businessman is able to calculate the total tax which he has added to his customers' statements, and which he must account for to the Customs and Excise authorities.

15.4 Input Records

A taxable person who is collecting tax from his customers as in paragraph 15.2(*b*) above does not have to pay the full amount over to the Customs and Excise. He is entitled to deduct from the sums collected as 'output tax' the total sums paid to his own suppliers. These are revealed by keeping 'input records', which show the value of goods and services supplied to him by other firms and the tax that these firms have charged—his 'input tax'.

We have already seen how VAT on purchases is collected together in the Purchases Day Book (see page 164) and posted to the debit side of the VAT Account. We have also seen how VAT on such capital items as assets purchased is taken into account in the journal entry for the purchase (see page 196).

15.5 The VAT Account

VAT fits very easily into the double-entry system; it is just one more account that we have to deal with. In the case of an ordinary trader the Customs and Excise Department is a creditor to whom the trader owes money. In the case of the zero-rated trader the Customs and Excise Department is a debtor, who owes the trader money. Figs. 15.1 and 15.2 illustrate the two types of account. The standard-rate account is cleared up every three months by paying the tax due to H.M. Customs. The zero-rate account is cleared up each month by a refund from H.M. Customs. In the Trial Balance at the end of any particular month the VAT Account will appear either as a creditor (standard-rate trader owing money to H.M. Customs) or as a debtor (H.M. Customs owing money to the zero-rated trader).

H.M. CUSTOMS AND EXCISE DEPARTMENT (VAT)

Dr.							C.L.163 Cr.
19.. Mar 31	VAT on Purchases	P.D.B.33	295.20	19.. Mar. 31	VAT on Sales	S.D.B.9	498.70
Apr. 17	Capital Item	J.72	36.80	Apr. 30	VAT on Sales	S.D.B.13	786.50
Apr. 30	VAT on Purchases	P.D.B.42	387.50	May 31	VAT on Sales	S.D.B.17	1 295.27
May 19	Capital Item	J.74	47.20				
May 31	VAT on Purchases	P.D.B.47	462.65				
May 31	Balance	C/d	1 351.12				
			2 580.47				2 580.47
Jun. 8	Bank	C.B.57	1 351.12	Jun. 1	Balance	B/d	1 351.12

Fig. 15.1. A standard-rated VAT Account.

Dr.		H.M. CUSTOMS AND EXCISE DEPARTMENT (VAT)					D.L.77 Cr.
19..				19..			
Mar. 1	Balance	B/d	167.25	Mar. 14	Refund from H.M. Customs	C.B.8	167.25
18	Capital Item	J.53	47.16	31	Balance	C/d	155.91
19	Capital Item	J.54	23.45				
31	Services	J.62	48.20				
31	M.V. Expenses	M.63	37.10				
			323.16				323.16
Apr. 1	Balance	B/d	155.91				

Fig. 15.2. A VAT Account in a zero-rated trade.

15.6 Special Retailers' Scheme

Because many retail traders do not issue invoices when they supply goods, VAT for small retailers is arranged under special schemes. These are described in Notice No. 727, *Special Schemes for Retailers*, which are available free from local VAT offices of H.M. Customs and Excise Department. These are very interesting to read, but are not usually recorded in ordinary book-keeping records. Students who are interested should look at such books as the *Simplex VAT book*—to be found at stationers or obtainable from George Vyner Ltd, Holmfirth, Huddersfield.

The essential feature of such systems, and the general principle behind the Special Schemes for Retailers, is that the shopkeeper cannot be expected to issue invoices for the sale of thousands of small items. We do not want an invoice every time we buy a bar of chocolate or a box of matches. Therefore the amount of VAT which the shopkeeper has collected in his daily takings must be arrived at by the use of VAT fractions. To consider these VAT fractions, and referring back to Section 2 of this book (Business Calculations) we may note the following fractions: $\frac{2}{27}$ for the standard-rate items charged at 8 per cent; $\frac{1}{9}$ for the higher-rate items charged at $12\frac{1}{2}$ per cent. There is of course no VAT with zero-rate items. How are these fractions arrived at?

First of all the retailer keeps a record of Daily Takings on paper ruled similarly to the paper shown in Fig. 15.3. The total of the Daily Takings includes the VAT the retailer has collected.

Calculations for VAT at the Standard Rate

Let us imagine that the total takings are £27 258.50 and the rate of tax is 8 per cent—the standard rate at the time of writing.

The figure of £27 258.50 includes 8 per cent VAT, so it is 108 per cent of the net-of-tax takings figure. The VAT element is therefore $\frac{8}{108}$ of the total: $\frac{8}{108} = \frac{2}{27}$ and this explains why the VAT fraction for standard-rate items is the awkward figure of $\frac{2}{27}$. Therefore the calculation is

$$\frac{2}{27} \times £27\,258.50$$
$$= \frac{£54\,517.00}{27}$$
$$= £2\,019.15 \text{ (Tax due to H.M. Customs)}$$

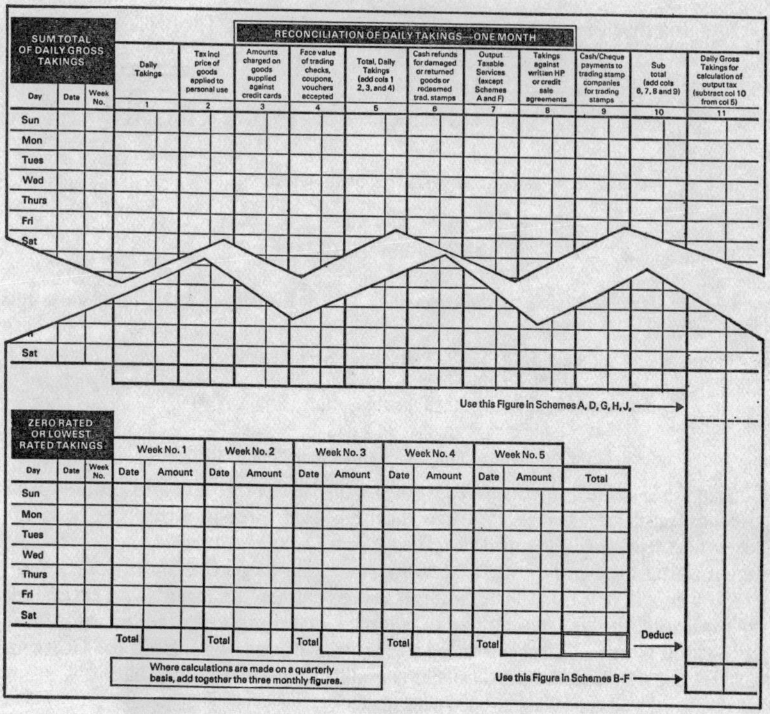

Fig. 15.4. Daily takings for the Small Retailers' Schemes.

(Courtesy of George Vyner Ltd, Huddersfield)

The sales figure (net of tax) is therefore

£27 258.50 − £2 019.15
= £25 239.35 (Sales, net of tax)

Check: To check the correctness of this calculation take the Sales (net of tax) and add 8 per cent to it

= £25 239.35 + 8% of £25 239.35
= £25 239.35 + 2 019.15
= £27 258.50 (Takings, including VAT)

Calculations for VAT at the Higher Rate

This time the fraction is simpler. The present higher rate is $12\frac{1}{2}$ per cent, so the takings (including VAT) will be $112\frac{1}{2}$ per cent of the selling price. The VAT element is therefore $\frac{12\frac{1}{2}}{112\frac{1}{2}}$ of the total takings and this cancels down to $\frac{1}{9}$.

Imagine that the higher-rate takings were £8 725.50. The VAT element is $\frac{1}{9}$ of this.

VAT element = £8 725.50 ÷ 9
= £969.50 VAT due to H.M. Customs

This means that the sales of higher-rate goods were

£8 725.50 − £969.50
= £7 756.00 (Sales, net of tax)

Check: To check this calculation take the Sales (net of tax) figure and add 12½ per cent to it

£7 756.00 + 12½% of £7 756.00
= £7 756.00 + £969.50
= £8 725.50 (Takings, including VAT)

15.7 The Tax Return (Form VAT 100)

The taxable person must render a return of the tax outputs and inputs of his business and pay tax every three months. The three-monthly intervals are known as 'tax periods' and the return and any tax due must be sent in within one month of the end of the tax period. A special tax period of only one month is allowed where a taxable person feels sure that his 'tax inputs' will exceed his 'tax outputs' in the usual course of events. For example, a small grocer selling zero-rated goods might be entitled to regular refunds of tax from the Customs and Excise. It would be hard on such small businessmen if they had to wait for three months to recover tax paid on inputs.

The tax return form is an official document sent to the 'taxable person' each quarter (or month if necessary) by a central computerised mailing service. Once the 'taxable person' has added up his VAT figures he is able to complete the VAT form. For many firms the form will simply be prepared from the VAT Account. For retailers the records of daily takings from the Special Scheme for Retailers will be included as well. A composite VAT Account, which incorporates both elements of output tax and includes all the items required on the official form, is reproduced in Fig. 15.4.

15.8 Exercises: Value Added Tax

1. A shopkeeper's takings (all his goods being charged to consumers with VAT at 8 per cent) were as follows: Monday £89.50, Tuesday £46.60, Wednesday £15.45, Thursday £86.60, Friday £176.70, Saturday £195.45. Calculate: (*a*) his total takings; (*b*) his output tax; (*c*) his net-of-tax takings.

2. A small businessman is supplied with goods valued at £780 in a given tax period. This figure is increased by 8 per cent VAT. His sales during the same period totalled £1 760 according to his till rolls, and this figure included VAT at 8 per cent charged to customers. Calculate the tax payable to Customs and Excise.

3. A grocer only deals in goods charged at the zero rate, but pays VAT on many items supplied to him. During the month of July he pays tax on goods supplied to him worth £4 800, net of tax. The rate of VAT is 8 per cent. What sum will pass between the grocer and the Customs and Excise in respect of these transactions and who will pay whom?

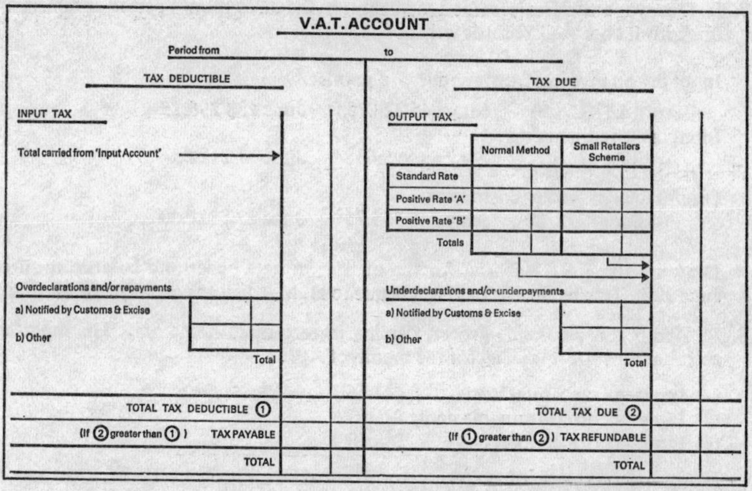
V.A.T. ACCOUNT
Period from to
TAX DEDUCTIBLE
TAX DUE
INPUT TAX
Total carried from 'Input Account'
OUTPUT TAX
Normal Method
Small Retailers Scheme
Standard Rate
Positive Rate 'A'
Positive Rate 'B'
Totals
Overdeclarations and/or repayments
a) Notified by Customs & Excise
b) Other
Total
Underdeclarations and/or underpayments
a) Notified by Customs & Excise
b) Other
Total
TOTAL TAX DEDUCTIBLE ①
TOTAL TAX DUE ②
(If ② greater than ①) TAX PAYABLE
(If ① greater than ②) TAX REFUNDABLE
TOTAL
TOTAL

Fig. 15.3. A VAT Account based on the Form 100 VAT Return.

(Courtesy of George Vyner Ltd, Huddersfield)

4. A professional man is told by the Customs and Excise authorities that his profession is exempt from VAT. What are the likely effects of this upon him? In your answer mention the following matters: (*a*) charges to be made for VAT to his customers; (*b*) registration on form VAT 1; (*c*) charges made to him by his suppliers.

5. M. Lawrence is a wholesale furniture dealer. In the three-month period commencing on March 1st, VAT records were as follows:

   Input tax on invoices from suppliers of goods:
   March £19 726.25 April £27 328.40 May £45 726.65
   Input tax on other items:
   March £3 506.25 April £4 712.35 May £5 816.42
   Output tax charged to customers:
   March £33 726.54 April £35 297.62 May £47 263.52
   Draw up the VAT Account for the quarter in date order, and balance it off on May 31st. This balance is paid by cheque to H. M. Customs on June 27th.

6. R. Hardy is a wholesale hardware merchant. In the three-month period commencing on October 1st his VAT records were as follows:

   Input tax on invoices from suppliers of goods:
   October £14 976.54 November £15 812.63 December £12 724.95
   Input tax on other items:
   October £256.25 November £817.14 December £245.32
   Output tax charged to customers:
   October £19 726.30 November £23 954.74 December £17 654.36

   Draw up the VAT Account for the quarter in date order and balance it off on December 31st. This balance is paid by cheque to H.M. Customs on January 7th.

7. R. Dovey is a wholesale fashion merchant. In the three-month period commencing on April 1st his VAT records were as follows:

   Input tax on invoices from suppliers of goods:
   April £37 256.50 May £45 328.75 June £38 296.25
   Input tax on other items:
   April £4 175.30 May £3 895.60 June £7 212.45

   Output tax charged to customers:
   April £60 275.45 May £65 385.75 June £72 726.30

   Draw up the VAT Account for the quarter in date order and balance it off on June 30th. This balance is paid by cheque to H. M. Customs on July 29th.

8. R. Kemp is a wholesale grocer, dealing in zero-rated items only. His input tax records show the following for the month of April:

   (*a*) Input tax on capital items £47.56
   (*b*) Input tax on consumable items £75.65
   (*c*) Input tax on services £48.50

   His output tax was, of course, zero. The balance owing by H. M. Customs to Kemp on April 1st was £138.50, and this sum was duly received on April 17th. Show the VAT Account for the month of April, and bring down the balance due from H. M. Customs on April 30th.

9. P. Burns is a wholesale fishmonger dealing in zero-rated items only. His input tax records show the following for the month of July:

   (*a*) Input tax on capital items £147.36
   (*b*) Input tax on consumable items £38.48
   (*c*) Input tax on services £15.75

   His output tax was, of course, zero. The balance owing by H. M. Customs to Burns on July 1st was £236.25, and this sum was duly received on July 14th. Show the VAT Account for the month of July and bring down the balance due from H. M. Customs on July 31st.

SECTION 5
ACCOUNTING TO FINAL ACCOUNTS LEVEL

16

FUNDAMENTAL ACCOUNTING CONCEPTS

16.1 Theory and Practice in Accounting

Accounting records have always developed pragmatically, to meet business needs as they arose. Thus the recording of amounts due from debtors, or to creditors, led to the development of double-entry book-keeping long before any real 'theory of accounting' was proposed. Even the calculation of profit was unnecessary to men who judged the profitability of their activities by the gradual accumulation of material wealth around them. The close of a particular venture, or even of a particular life, was the time to strike a profit. The last part of double-entry book-keeping to be invented was the Balance Sheet, yet many of today's textbooks stand Accounting on its head by beginning with the Balance Sheet. There are nice points of theory which can be demonstrated from the Balance Sheets, but trade, even international trade, was carried on for two or three thousand years without an appreciation of such points. Indeed, the inventor of the Balance Sheet wrote it down back to front, so poor was his understanding of accounting theory. Regrettably, United Kingdom accountants still follow his incorrect lead, though more rational nations like the Dutch, the Americans, the Germans and the French realised the error long ago and write it down correctly. This is one aspect of accounting practice which is overdue for harmonisation (see page 245).

The development of the capitalist system—particularly the modern egalitarian mixed economy—required a general agreement about basic accounting procedures. The need to meet taxation requirements forced businessmen to keep careful accounts, so that the portion of the profit accruing to the State could be accurately determined. The whole operation of a modern economy, with the necessity to make the best choice between alternative employments of capital and other resources, calls for a careful examination of costs and benefits. Accounting theory therefore is a relatively late arrival on the scene, though the basic principles on which it is founded have gained a general acceptance over the last two or three centuries. Only as recently as 1969 did the Institute of Chartered Accountants in England and Wales set up an Accounting Standards Steering Committee, which later embraced all the national accounting bodies. The result of their deliberations is a body of Statements of Standard Accounting Practice (SSAP) which constitute definitive statements of what is agreed to be the best practice to follow on particular aspects of accounting.

16.2 The Four Fundamental Concepts

The four fundamental concepts of accounting, which have achieved general recognition over the last two or three centuries and which are now enshrined in SSAP2 *Disclosure of Accounting Policies*, are as follows:

(*a*) The 'going concern' concept
(*b*) The 'accruals' concept

(*c*) The 'consistency' concept
(*d*) The 'prudence' concept

These four concepts, which are explained below, underline the preparation of the periodic accounts of firms—that is, the preparation of the Trading Account, the Profit and Loss Account and the Balance Sheet. Strictly speaking there are only two actual accounts: the Trading Account and the Profit and Loss Account. The Balance Sheet is not an account, but a list of all the balances left on accounts at the end of the financial year. The term 'periodic accounts' refers to the fact that these accounts are prepared at regular intervals. The 'year' is the period chosen, so that we talk of the 'Annual Accounts', but of course many firms prepare accounts quarterly in order to keep track of developments.

The preparation of annual accounts is explained later, in Chapters 17 and 18, but a preliminary discussion of these concepts helps us to understand how the 'final accounts' or 'annual accounts' emerge from the mass of ordinary accounts like the personal accounts, nominal accounts and real accounts mentioned already in Chapters 11–14.

Let us, then, look at these four basic concepts of accounting.

(*a*) **The 'Going Concern' Concept.** It is taken for granted when a set of final accounts is prepared by the accountant and presented to the owners—or the board of the company and its shareholders—that he has prepared the accounts of a 'going concern'. If the firm were about to go out of business, or a company were about to be wound up, a quite different set of considerations would enter into the picture of the firm's affairs. In those circumstances it would be necessary to sell off the assets, and turn them into cash. This is called liquidating the assets, and it often can be achieved only by selling the assets at considerably less than their value to the business as a going concern. Frequently serious 'losses on realisation' would be suffered in such circumstances, at other times 'profits on realisation' would be made.

Therefore the basic principle is that the accounts are prepared in the belief that the enterprise will continue to exist as a going concern in roughly its present form, and the accountant has no reason to believe that any major change is envisaged in the near future. On this understanding he is entitled to value the assets of the business at their value to the business as a going concern. They are valued according to rules well known to accountants, which will be explained later in this book. On the other hand, if the accountant knows that the business is shortly to cease trading he must declare this in a statement accompanying the accounts. If it has already ceased trading he will not prepare the accounts on a 'going concern' basis, and will make it clear which basis he has chosen, and why.

(*b*) **The 'Accruals' Concept.** The term 'accruals' means 'falling to one as a natural result of some activity'. Thus if we perform certain work or go to some expense in a particular period it ought to be rewarded by a revenue in that same period. Even if we do not actually get paid at once, the revenue that has accrued should be brought into the account. An example will explain the point.

Suppose a shopkeeper's financial year runs from January 1st to December 31st. Goods bought in January for £100 and sold in February for £150 clearly involve a profit of £50. If the customer does not pay until March it will not matter, for the transaction is completed long before the financial year ends in December. The expense, £100, set against the revenue earned £150, leaves a profit of £50. But what if a similar series of events takes place at the end of the year? Goods are bought for £100 in November, and sold in December for £150, although the money is not paid until January. When the accountant does the final accounts on December 31st he faces a difficulty. The £150 has not been paid, and it is quite possible it never will be paid, for 'bad debtors' are common enough. What should he do?

The 'accruals concept' tells him that he must include in his accounts all the expenses incurred in the year, and all the revenue that follows naturally from the expense (even if it has not been received). So long as it has accrued, and will on present expectations be received, it must be included.

Similarly, with any expense, such as wages, or rent, any amount due to be paid must be included because it has 'accrued due', even though the actual payment has been deferred for the moment because the employee is absent on an assignment abroad, or the landlord is spending the winter in North Africa.

The important points are whether the expenditure has been incurred or the earnings have been earned, not whether they have been paid or received.

An understanding of the accruals concept is not easy, and the reader must achieve a real grasp of the 'adjustments' necessary to take account of this concept. These are explained later (see pages 254–284).

(*c*) **The 'Consistency' Concept.** This concept holds that the accountant will deal consistently with similar items in the same accounting period, or from one period to another. Thus if 'work-in-progress'—sometimes called partly manufactured goods—is valued in a certain way this method of valuation should be applied consistently throughout. Suppose the basis is chosen that 'work-in-progress' should be valued at raw material cost plus half the labour cost for a fully manufactured unit. This seems to be a reasonable basis. Work entering the production line consists of the raw material only. By the time one or two processes have been done it is worth the raw material cost plus some labour cost. Up at the far end of the production line where the last few processes are being carried out the work-in-progress is worth the raw material cost plus almost all the labour cost. To average the valuation out at raw material cost plus half the labour cost seems a fair valuation. Now, suppose this basis is applied to component A but some different basis is applied to component B. This will be inconsistent and anyone studying the accounts will not know what the true value is.

Similarly, if we are told that the profits of a firm in a particular year were £100 000 and next year they were £120 000, we would naturally conclude that the firm has performed better this year than last. However, if the work-in-progress had been valued on a different basis (at cost plus full labour cost instead of cost plus half labour cost) this changed valuation would appear to raise the profits—as we shall see when we learn how to keep a Trading Account. Over-valuation of stock leads to over-valuation of profits and work-in-progress is one of our types of stock. Clearly we must be consistent from year to year if the results are to be compared with one another in a meaningful way.

(*d*) **The 'Prudence' Concept.** In the days before taxation was an onerous burden on businessmen the 'prudence' concept laid down that accounts should be prepared in a 'conservative' way. The prudent businessman does not count a profit as actually earned unless he has really received the payment for it, or established some other asset which is as good as cash in hand. Thus a totally reliable debtor is as good as money, but where a debtor is not deemed absolutely sound some 'Provision for Doubtful Debts' would be made. How this is done is explained later (see page 264).

Whilst a profit is therefore not taken if it is at all uncertain, a loss is accepted as soon as it occurs, or even where it is feared it may occur. Thus depreciation is written off assets at some agreed rate, and bad debts are written off if they appear to have occurred. If payment is eventually received the loss can always be reversed and taken in as a 'Bad Debt Recovered'—a fortuitous profit at long last, which the businessman gratefully accepts.

In these days of heavy taxation there is some danger that businessmen will use the 'prudence' concept to reduce profits, by being over-cautious in their provisions for depreciation, etc. This will reduce their tax liability. To avoid this, the Inland Revenue has certain scales of depreciation which it allows in particular trades and industries. Even so, disputes do arise and legal cases are reported almost daily where judges have upheld or rejected a taxpayer's concept of 'prudent behaviour'.

Departure from the Four Fundamental Concepts

The Statement of Standard Accounting Practices No. 2 (SSAP2) lays it down that if accounts are prepared on a different basis from those laid down in the four fundamental concepts described above, the facts should be explained. If this is not done, and there is no clear account giving the reasons for adopting different concepts, it will be assumed that the four concepts have been followed.

16.3 Accounting Bases

One or two fundamental starting points, or bases, must be known before financial accounts can be prepared. The most important of these are:

(*a*) The basic accounting period for which revenue and costs are to be brought into account.

(*b*) The basis on which Balance Sheet items are to be valued.

Looking at these in turn the following points need to be made:

(*a*) **Accounting Periods.** In general the accounting period will be one year, since this aligns with the Inland Revenue requirements for sole traders and partnerships, whilst for Limited Companies the 1976 Companies Act now requires companies to notify the Registrar of Companies of the annual date (called the **Accounting Reference Date**) to within seven days of which accounts will be made up. Thus a company which declared December 31st as its Accounting Reference Date could actually work out its final accounts to January 2nd if this was more convenient because it preferred to keep its financial year as a complete number of weeks.

Because the tax year traditionally ends on March 31st, companies who fail to notify an Accounting Reference Date will automatically have to adopt March 31st as the end of the financial year. Many companies prefer to align their financial Accounting Reference Dates with the tax year anyway, but it is not compulsory and the end of the calendar year and the anniversary of the company's incorporation are possible alternatives.

The interval between two successive Accounting Reference Dates is called the **Accounting Reference Period** and in most circumstances it will be a 12-month period. It is possible to give notice of a change of reference date—for example, where one company takes over another and wishes to align the subsidiary with its own accounting system—but in no circumstances may the period exceed 18 months.

(*b*) **Valuation of Assets.** The reader may not appreciate yet—since we have not yet dealt with the preparation of Final Accounts—that there is a link between the valuation of assets and the profits of the business. For example, suppose I purchase a heavy-goods vehicle for £8 000. During the year's use it will depreciate to some extent, but to what extent is not certain. If it is used heavily, for 18 hours per day, seven days a week, it will depreciate more than if it is used for eight hours a day five days a week. Suppose I decide that in the first case it will have a working life of two years, but in the second case it will last for five years. By the very simplest calculations this means it depreciates by £4 000 or £1 600 respectively. Thus in the first case I shall write off £4 000 against my profits (reducing the profits earned by £4 000) and £4 000 off the asset account, Heavy Goods Vehicles Account, reducing the value of this asset on the Balance Sheet. By contrast in, the second case it will only be necessary to reduce the asset by £1 600 and only £1 600 will therefore be taken out of the profits for depreciation.

There are in fact about ten different methods of calculating depreciation, and the 'consistency' rule holds that once a particular basis has been adopted it will be followed consistently year after year. Any departure from the established practice must be disclosed in a special note to the accounts, so that those interested can understand the reasons for the changed basis.

Other bases which affect the way in which profits are calculated are recognised for such matters as those listed below. The reader pursuing his studies to higher levels will find there are many more, and it is for the firm's accountant to recommend a basis for any new valuation problems that arise in the course of the year.

(*a*) Depreciation of fixed assets.

(*b*) Valuation of stocks of raw materials, work-in-progress and finished goods.

(*c*) Writing off of such items as goodwill and preliminary formation expenses. These are known as intangible assets.

(*d*) Hire purchase or instalment transactions.

(*e*) Property valuations.

(*f*) Foreign currency transactions.

A full list is given in SSAP2.

16.4 Inflation Accounting

One problem that has presented accountants with the greatest difficulties in recent years is the problem of **inflation accounting**. The difficulties have by no means been solved at the time of writing and in any case are too advanced for a full discussion in an elementary book of this type. Here it is perhaps sufficient if some mention is made of the terms used in the debate, which the student reader will surely meet in everyday conversation, and hear on the serious media programmes.

The underlying difficulty is that ordinary accounting as described in this book in Chapters 17–19 is **historical cost accounting**. This means that as we purchase goods or assets we record what they cost us. However, in inflationary times the costs that we have recorded soon become ancient history—hence the term 'historical cost accounting'. If I purchase a machine in year 1 for £10 000, with an expected life of five years, and no residual value, the straight line depreciation on the machine is £2 000 per annum. Each year I shall be permitted to write off £2 000 from the profits—and if I am wise I shall put this sum away to buy a new machine in due course. In inflationary times, with inflation at, say, 15 per cent per annum, by the time I get to the end of the five years the new machine will be costing £20 000, but I shall not have accumulated anywhere near enough to pay for it. If I try to anticipate the difficulty and push up my prices to customers to make extra profits to meet the need that is going to arise, I may lose customers or face actual controls from departments like the Department for Prices and Consumer Protection. Even if I slip through the price controls net, the extra profits made which should be siphoned off into the new investment will lead employees (themselves suffering inflation) to demand a 'fair' share, and shareholders will equally clamour for an increased dividend. It will help reduce these demands if accountants can produce a scheme which permits new investment to take place whilst eliminating an appearance of high profits. The various schemes of *inflation accounting* have been attempts to do just this.

The first scheme was called **Current Purchasing Power (CPP)**, which tried to rearrange the accounting procedures to take account of the falling value of the pound (in other words, its current purchasing power year by year). Then the Sandilands Report proposed an alternative system, which it called **Current Cost Accounting (CCA)**. This sought to adjust accounts to take note of the higher cost of replacing assets. It should really have been called **CRCA (Current Replacement Cost Accounting)**. The involved procedures it suggested resulted in such loud alarm calls from the accountancy profession that a watered-down version of the system was introduced instead. The Hyde Guidelines take their name from the chairman of the subcommittee which drew them up. The recommendations amount to a system of **Price Level Accounting (PLA)**, as an interim measure, to be used by all major companies. The suggestion is that the accounts should be prepared in the traditional way using historical costs, but should be accompanied by a prominent separate statement which adjusts the financial results in the light of inflation, under three main headings. These are:

(*a*) A *Depreciation Adjustment*—to take account of current replacement costs of assets.

(*b*) A *Cost of Sales Adjustment*—to take account of the rising cost of stock purchased.

(*c*) A '*Gearing*' *Adjustment*. This is an adjustment for changes in the value of monetary items such as amounts owed creditors (whose claims on the company are decreasing day-by-day in real terms).

Clearly such considerations are quite involved, and outside the scope of the present volume. The debate on inflation accounting seems likely to continue for some time.

16.5 Accounting Policies

When a particular basis is adopted for one of the bases mentioned in Section 16.3 above it then constitutes part of the '*Accounting Policy*' of the firm, and should be consistently followed from year to year. The basis represents, in the view of the management, the best basis for the enterprise's circumstances, and the one most likely to present a 'true and fair view' of the firm's financial results and its current financial position. The phrase 'true and fair view' was introduced in the Companies Act, 1948, and is designed to place a responsibility on the boards of companies to produce accounts which are not only true, but also fair. They are thus required to obey not only the law, but also the spirit behind the law, which was enacted to give those who invest in companies a reasonable chance of knowing the full facts about any company's results and its current financial situation.

Any departure from agreed policies must be covered by an explanatory statement attached to the published accounts drawing attention specifically to the changes which are being made.

This short description of the background concepts in accounting can only be amplified by describing in detail the preparation of the final accounts of various types of business. For simplicity's sake the basic activities will be described with references to the books of a sole trader. These will then be extended to cover the other main types of enterprise: partnerships, limited companies and non-profit making organisations. Finally the accounts of local government bodies and of central Government itself will be explained in simple form.

16.6 Exercises: Fundamental Concepts

1. 'Any company may give notice in the prescribed form to the registrar of companies specifying a date in the calendar year as being the date on which in each successive year an accounting reference period of the company is to be treated as coming to an end . . .' (Companies Act, 1976). Explain the term 'accounting reference period' and why it is desirable that a precise period should be specified for company accounts.
2. What are the 'four fundamental concepts' of accounting? Explain any one of them in detail.
3. What is an 'accounting policy'? In a limited company who decides such policies and what are the implications for the accountant of the adoption of such a policy?
4. In the Middle Ages it was only necessary to strike a Balance Sheet at rare intervals —for example, at the end of a particular venture or at the death of the owner of a business. Today the preparation of annual accounts is normal. What has happened to change accounting practice in this respect?

17

ACCOUNTING TO SIMPLE FINAL ACCOUNTS LEVEL

17.1 What are Final Accounts?

Final Accounts are the final stage in the accounting process. It is here that we work out the profit or loss of the business over the trading period. There are only two accounts: the Trading Account and the Profit and Loss Account. A Balance Sheet is finally drawn up of all the assets and liabilities to be carried over into the next accounting period. The starting point for the preparation of Final Accounts is the Trial Balance on the last day of the last month in the accounting period. The reader might like to look back to page 131 and recall the general layout for double-entry accounting. The notes that follow review all we now know about double-entry book-keeping and emphasise seven points of vocabulary which are of great importance.

Recapitulation of Double Entry

We have already seen that the accounts of a business consist of a very large number of entries made in **books of original entry** such as Cash Books, Sales Day Books, Purchases Day Books, etc. These original entries are then posted into the **Ledger**, which is the main book of account. Every page of the Ledger is called an **Account** and is headed with the name of the account. This may be the name of the person being dealt with (a debtor or a creditor). It may be a real thing, like premises or office equipment (an asset of the business). Finally it may be an expense account, like Wages Account (a loss of the business), or a receipt of revenue, like Commission Received Account, or Bad Debts Recovered Account (a profit of the business). These few words, **losses, profits, assets, debtors** and **creditors**, with two more, are the keys to accounting, for they tell us all we need to know to prepare the Final Accounts of any business, or other form of enterprise.

One other word is **liability**. The last thing we need to know is a phrase—**Trading Account Items**. These are certain accounts which for convenience are dealt with in the Trading Account, rather than the Profit and Loss Account.

The Vocabulary of Final Accounts

Let us pause to define each of these seven terms:

(*a*) **Losses.** A loss is an expense of the business, incurred in the course of pursuing the normal activities of the enterprise. Thus wages, postal expenses, rent, rates and motor-vehicle expenses are all losses of the business. Bad debts are a rather different type of loss, for it was not our intention to suffer them, but since some losses of this type are a feature of any business we are entitled to deduct them as losses in the Profit and Loss Account of the business.

(*b*) **Profits.** The main profit of a business is the difference between the cost price of the goods it deals in and their selling price. This is worked out in the Trading Account (see *Trading Account Items* below). In this paragraph we are referring to any other profits that arise in the course of business activity, such as Discount Received, Commission Received, Rent Received, Bad Debts Recovered, etc. These items are brought into the Profit and Loss Account.

(*c*) **Assets.** An asset is an item purchased for use in the business, often on a long-term basis. Such assets have lives greater than one year and are called **fixed assets.** Anything with a life of less than one year—such as a postage stamp—is regarded as an expense of the business and would be treated as a loss (see (*a*) above) unless it happened to be in stock on the last day of the year. Now the point about long-term assets is that they are handed on from year to year to be used in the business over their full life-time. This also applies to **current assets,** such as debtors, stock, etc. They are therefore not brought into either the Trading Account or the Profit and Loss Account. Instead they go in the Balance Sheet, to be carried over into next year.

There is one important point though. If an asset wears out (depreciates) it is necessary to write off the amount of depreciation, and that does go in the Profit and Loss Account as a loss. The asset is reduced in value because of the depreciation written off. This year hands on to next year a less valuable asset than it received at the start of the year. The reader who remembers Chapter 16 will see that the *accounting period* referred to in that chapter is the 'year' referred to above. Each accounting period receives a certain gift of assets from the previous period. During the year they will depreciate, but on occasions we shall replace them by new equipment, etc. This accounting period will then hand on a more valuable set of assets to next year. The Balance Sheet is a basket of assets (and liabilities—see below) handed on from one accounting period to another.

(*d*) **Debtors.** Debtors are persons who owe the business money. The word 'persons' means 'legal persons'. They may be real people, like Tom Smith, a sole trader, or Mary and Bill Jones, who are partners. They may be 'incorporations'. Incorporations are legal persons set up by Act of Parliament or by Royal Command. Such bodies as limited companies, nationalised corporations and chartered companies may be our debtors even though a real individual cannot be isolated as the individual responsible for the debt. The point about debtors is that they also go on into the next trading period, when in due course they settle the account and cease to be debtors. So debtors appear on the Balance Sheet and are treated as one of the assets of the business (see (*c*) above).

One rather unusual debtor is 'Drawings Account'. This is the account where the accountant collects together all sums drawn out of the business by the proprietor. This makes the proprietor a debtor, and therefore the Drawings Account should appear on the assets side of the Balance Sheet. In fact, for reasons which will be explained later, it is better to show it as a deduction from the calculated profits, for the owner is really drawing money out in expectation of profits made.

(*e*) **Creditors.** Creditors are persons to whom the business owes money, usually for goods or services supplied by the creditor. The proprietor is of course a creditor, in that the business owes him the capital he originally supplied to the firm, plus any sums earned as profit during the course of the trading period, plus any extra profits 'ploughed in' from previous years. Since these items are rather different from the ordinary creditors we keep them separate from other creditors, whom we call **external** creditors. External creditors are of two types, 'trade' creditors and 'expense' creditors. Creditors, like debtors, are carried over from one accounting period to the next, when of course we pay the creditor according to the terms of our contract with him. Most creditors are paid in the first month of the new accounting period, but long-term items like loans and mortgages might be repaid over several years. Creditors appear therefore on the Balance Sheet as a liability.

(*f*) **Liabilities.** Liabilities are the sums owed by a firm to its creditors. They are the opposite of 'assets' and appear on the opposite side of the Balance Sheet. They consist of *current liabilities* (those due to be paid very soon), *long-term liabilities* (those which by agreement are to be repaid over several years) and capital items, which will only be paid back when the business ceases to trade.

(*g*) **Trading Account Items.** This group of items is the group which tells us what is the result of our trading. The two chief items are Purchases Account and Sales Account, for if we take the purchase price of our goods away from the selling price, the difference must be the profit. Unfortunately, it is not quite as easy as that, because we do return some purchases (Purchases Returns), and our customers do send back a few sales (Sales Returns). We also have to take into account the **opening stock** at the start of the accounting period, and the **closing stock** at the end of the period.

It is also customary to bring in certain items, such as warehouse wages and other trading expenses into the Trading Account rather than the Profit and Loss Account. This is rather a grey area, where the accountant must decide what to do to give a 'true and fair view' of the trading activities.

(*h*) **Adjustments.** One final piece of vocabulary is the word **adjustments.** Although most of the figures in our Trial Balance are correct and ready to use in the Final Accounts it frequently happens that the figures on the accounts are not absolutely correct. The reader will remember the basic principle of accounts called the 'accruals' concept. We have to bring into our Final Accounts the correct figures for the accounting period, whether we have paid them or not, and whether we have received them or not. Suppose we pay salaries monthly, on the 26th of each month. Suppose our *Accounting Reference Date* is registered with the Registrar of Companies as December 31st. This year we intend to prepare accounts up to Friday, January 2nd (remember we must choose a date within seven days of the Accounting Reference Date). Now at this date the Salaries Account tells us that we have paid £21 740.60 in salaries during the year—but of course this is only up to December 26th—the last pay-day. Because of the 'accruals' concept we must now make an *adjustment* to take account of the salaries payable between December 26th and January 2nd. We must increase the salaries figure by an amount equal to one week's salaries—say £492.40. Although these salaries will not actually be paid until January 26th we must bring in the correct figure into the Final Accounts.

Readers must pay careful attention to adjustments, which are explained fully in Chapter 18. Here we are dealing with simple Final Accounts, and we shall disregard adjustments for the moment.

We are now ready to look carefully at a Trial Balance, and note how all these matters are to be found in every Trial Balance.

17.2 The Trial Balance from which Final Accounts are Prepared

Opposite we have a typical Trial Balance of the books of a sole trader. As usual, the accounts are listed and we have a debit column and a credit column.

R. JONES TRIAL BALANCE
(as at December 31st, 19..)

Ledger Accounts	Notes	Dr.	Cr.	Notes
Premises Account	Asset	12 980		
Capital Account			32 400	Liability
Debtors:				
R. Johnson Account	Asset	4 000		
M. Thompson Account	Asset	3 012		
Creditors:				
R. Lupin Account			480	Liability
M. Chuzzlewit Account			720	Liability
Plant and Machinery Account	Asset	15 000		
Office Furniture Account	Asset	3 200		
Cash Account	Asset	300		
Bank Account	Asset	2 900		
Bad Debts Account	Loss	450		
Carriage In Account	Loss	200		
Commission Paid Account	Loss	664		
Discount Allowed Account	Loss	400		
Discount Received Account			360	Profit
Rent and Rates Account	Loss	2 200		
Carriage Out Account	Loss	240		
Salaries Account	Loss	5 360		
Warehouse Wages Account	Loss	6 080		
Rent Received Account			800	Profit
Stock at January 1st, 19..	Trading Account Item	8 400		
Purchases Account	Trading Account Item	24 600		
Sales Account			62 160	Trading Account Item
Purchases Returns Account			360	Trading Account Item
Sales Returns Account	Trading Account Item	2 094		
Drawings	Special Item	5 200		
		£ 97 280	97 280	

Note

In abbreviated form these notes can be condensed into the following groups:

TRIAL BALANCE	Dr.	Cr.
	(*a*) Assets	Liabilities
	(*b*) Losses	Profits
	(*c*) 3 Trading Items	2 Trading Items
	(*d*) Drawings	

Fig. 17.1. A typical Trial Balance.

Accounts with debit balances are listed in the debit column and next to them is a note of the type of account they are. There are asset accounts, loss accounts, three Trading Account items and a special item, Drawings Account, which has been referred to in Section 17.1.

Accounts with credit balances are listed in the credit column. The notes alongside explain that these are either liabilities (the opposite of assets) or profits (the opposite of losses) and there are two Trading Account items. Why aren't there three Trading Account items, the same as on the debit side? The explanation is very simple. One of the Trading Account items is the opening stock on the first day of the year—the stock which this trading period inherited from the previous period. We must also know the closing stock at the end of the year—but we cannot find out what it is until the doors are shut on the last day of the old year. Then we have to do a 'stocktaking', counting all the stock and valuing it. This is hard work, but at the end it gives up the missing Trading Account item.

Study the Trial Balance given in Fig. 17.1 and the short note below it, and you will quickly see the pattern of assets, liabilities, losses, profits and Trading Account items. The unusual asset, Drawings Account, is listed as a special item.

17.3 Exercises: Preparation of a Trial Balance

A complete understanding of the various types of account to be found in a Trial Balance is best achieved by preparing one or two. The information in the following exercises should enable you to draw up a correct list of debit and credit balances in each case.

1. A. Jaffa extracts the following balances from his Ledger on December 31st. Present them in the form of a Trial Balance.

	£
Cash in hand	25.00
Cash at bank	625.00
Sales	7 265.00
Purchases	2 350.00
Motor vehicles	1 250.00
Rent and rates	125.00
Light and heat	60.00
Carriage in	50.00
Carriage out	35.00
Opening stock at January 1st	1 825.00
Commission received	135.00
Capital	8 000.00
Drawings	850.00
Returns outwards	160.00
Returns inwards	165.00
Warehouse wages	1 520.00
Office salaries	980.00
Debtors	2 365.00
Creditors	565.00
Furniture and fittings	800.00
Land and buildings	4 600.00
Loan from bank (borrowed on December 30th)	1 500.00

2. M. Lucas extracts the following balances from his Ledger on December 31st. Present them in the form of a Trial Balance.

	£
Capital at July 1st	18 000.00
Rent and rates	350.00
Purchases	15 500.00
Audit fee	250.00
Sales	25 500.00
Stock at July 1st	5 000.00
Telephone	100.00
Bank overdraft	550.00
Returns inward	250.00
Returns outward	500.00
Cash in hand	50.00
Machinery	5 000.00
Salaries	1 250.00
Factory wages	1 900.00
Discount received	250.00
Creditors	1 550.00
Debtors	2 700.00
Carriage outwards	100.00
Bad debts	150.00
Commission received	50.00
Furniture	5 600.00
Premises	5 000.00
Goodwill	3 200.00

3. From the following prepare B. Perkin's Trial Balance, as at December 31st:

	£
Capital	300 000.00
Rates and insurance	2 200.00
Light and heat	2 000.00
Purchases	186 000.00
General factory expenses	3 000.00
Sales	342 000.00
Stock at beginning of year	60 000.00
Postage	700.00
Office expenses	500.00
Bank loan	6 600.00
Returns in	3 000.00
Returns out	6 000.00
Cash in hand	600.00
Machinery	50 000.00
Office salaries	15 000.00
Warehouse wages	22 800.00
Discount received	3 000.00
Creditors	18 600.00
Debtors	32 400.00
Carriage in	1 200.00

(cont'd)

Bad debts	1 800.00
Commission received	600.00
Motor vehicles	3 700.00
Furniture	40 200.00
Premises	180 000.00
Goodwill (asset)	38 400.00
Cash at bank	3 300.00
Investment in Harrow Ltd	30 000.00

4. The following is a list of a trader's accounts at March 31st. Take out a Trial Balance.

Bad debts £1 080.00
Bank account £638.60
Discounts received £750.90
Travelling expenses £190.60
Machinery £11 000.00
Motor vehicles £1 600.00
Purchases £18 450.50
M. Jones's Capital £18 144.00
Stock at April 1st last £3 962.00
Creditor: A. Richards £2 500.50
Returns outwards £860.50
Light and heating £654.50
Repairs to plant £1 052.00
General expenses £190.20
Redecorations £960.50
Factory wages £5 850.50
Salaries £1 200.50
Rent Account £3 800.00
Sales Account £32 404.00
Drawings £750.00
Debtors: R. Thomas £1 240.00, B. Brown £2 000.00
Postage Account £40.00

17.4 Final Accounts—The Trading Account

We have seen in Section 17.2 that there are five Trading Account Items in the Trial Balance. They may be listed as follows:

Dr.	Cr.
Purchases	Sales
Sales returns	Purchases returns
Opening stock	

The point was also made that a sixth figure, the closing stock, was not on the Trial Balance, but would need to be found before the Final Accounts could be prepared, by doing the stocktaking. Let us deal with this point first.

Stocktaking. At the end of the financial year it is essential to 'take stock'. This means we must count the stock in hand, value each item and add up the total to give us the 'closing stock' figure we require for the Trading Account.

A few points about stocktaking should be noted. They are:

(*a*) Stock is sometimes stolen by staff. Frequently it is passed out over the counter to friends, or taken home at the end of the day. Stocktaking should therefore be done by someone other than the normal staff, either by a special team of stocktakers or by an outside agency specialising in such matters. If stocktaking is performed by the ordinary staff they have the opportunity to cover up deficiencies which they know exist. This will postpone the discovery of the shortage until next stocktaking time comes round.

(*b*) Stocktaking time is a useful time to appraise stock, to detect outdated lines, slow-moving items, bad buying by purchasing staff, etc. If the appraisal can be done a few weeks before the end of the year it may be possible to hold a stocktaking sale to clear many of these items—obviously at smaller profit margins. This reduces the physical effort of checking stock at the end of the financial year.

(*c*) Stock must be counted carefully, then each item must be valued, the value multiplied by the number of units in hand to give a total for that item, and finally a grand total must be prepared. The valuation is very important. Overvaluing stock makes the profit appear greater than it really is. Undervaluation makes the profit appear smaller than it really is. The rule for valuing stock is: 'Stock is valued at cost price or current selling price, whichever is the lower.' Thus if an item of stock cost £2.50 it would normally be sold at more than that—so that a profit is made. Such an item would be valued at cost price. However, if for some reason the item has declined in value—perhaps by becoming shop-soiled—and was now only likely to sell at £1.25 it would be valued at this 'current selling' figure. Remember this in accordance with the 'prudence' concept already discussed.

In any accounting exercise where the student is required to prepare a Trading Account the closing stock figure must be given, usually as a note below the Trial Balance from which the student is to prepare the Trading Account.

In order to demonstrate the preparation of the Trading Account it is proposed to use the Trial Balance given in Fig. 17.1 (see page 229) but it is necessary to add to the information given there the closing stock figure. This is found, on 'taking stock', to be £4 560.00.

Before preparing the Trading Account there are a number of special points to be made. These must now be explained.

(*a*) *Heading*. A Trading Account and a Profit and Loss Account are Final Accounts of a particular accounting period. It is essential to include this information in the heading, which is therefore written as follows:

TRADING ACCOUNT
(*for year ended December 31st, 19..*)

(*b*) *Making entries in the Trading Account clears other accounts*. When we use the six Trading Account items (Sales Account, Purchases Account, Sales Returns Account, Purchases Returns Account, Opening Stock and Closing Stock) to prepare the Trading Account we must of course do proper double entries. Let us consider the entry for the Sales Account in detail. On Fig. 17.1 we see that the figure on the Sales Account for the year was £62 160. When this figure is transferred from the Sales Account to the Trading Account a journal entry is required. This type of journal entry is called a **closing journal entry**. It is only made at the end of the financial year to transfer items into the Trading Account and the Profit and Loss Account. In this case the entry requires us to debit the Sales Account and credit the Trading Account. Note that this has the effect of closing off the Sales Account, which is now left with no balance on it. The Sales Account consequently disappears from the Trial Balance. In its place the Trading Account now has a credit entry to the same value. Figs 17.2–17.5 show these entries being made.

SALES ACCOUNT L.49

		Jan., Feb., Mar., etc., for 12 months totalling	62 160

Fig. 17.2. A Sales Account before closure.

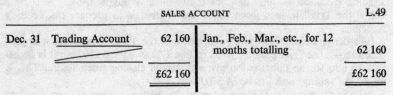

19..			£	£
Dec. 31	Sales Account Dr.	L.49	62 160	
	Trading Account	L.186		62 160
	Being transfer of Sales figure to Trading Account to determine gross profit			

Fig. 17.3. A closing journal entry.

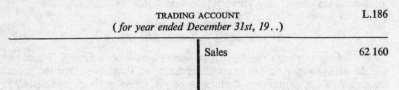

SALES ACCOUNT L.49

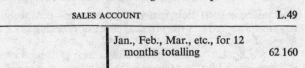

Dec. 31	Trading Account	62 160	Jan., Feb., Mar., etc., for 12 months totalling	62 160
		£62 160		£62 160

Fig. 17.4. The Sales Account closed off for the year.

Note
The result of this closing entry is that the Sales Account no longer has a balance on it; it is clear, and therefore vanishes from the Trial Balance. Its place has been taken by the entry in the Trading Account, which now reads:

TRADING ACCOUNT L.186
(*for year ended December 31st, 19..*)

		Sales	62 160

Fig. 17.5. Starting the Trading Account.

If we do similar closing entries with the other accounts which appear on the Trial Balance (the Purchases Account, the Sales Returns Account, the Purchases Returns Account and the Stock Account), these will also be cleared off and disappear from the Trial Balance, the figures on these accounts appearing in the Trading Account instead. To save space the journal entries, etc., have not been shown here, but the effect will be to bring the Trading Account into the position shown in Fig. 17.6. Before studying this the reader is warned that for reasons explained in section (*d*) below the final Trading Account looks quite different from Fig. 17.6. This is only the half-way stage.

(*c*) *Bringing the closing stock into account.* Whilst the entries in (*b*) above have cleared off all the Trading Account items on the Trial Balance into the Trading Account, the sixth item (the closing stock figure) is of course not on

TRADING ACCOUNT L.186
(*for year ended December 31st, 19..*)

19..		£	19..		£
Dec. 31	Purchases	24 600	Dec. 31	Sales	62 160
	Sales Returns	2 094		Purchases Returns	360
	Opening Stock	8 400			

Fig. 17.6. A first attempt at the Trading Account.

19..				£	£
Dec. 31	Stock Account	Dr.	L.37	4 560	
	Trading Account		L.186		4 560
	Being stocktaking figures for closing stock brought into account				

Fig. 17.7. Journalising closing stock.

the books at all. It consists of a figure derived from a mass of 'stock sheets'. This figure now has to be brought onto the Stock Account, which has only just been cleared of the opening stock balance by the closing entry to the Trading Account.

Since stock is an asset, it must, like all assets, be a debit entry on the Stock Account. When the journal entry to bring this stock on the books is made it will therefore mean debiting the Stock Account and crediting Trading Account. The entries will be as shown in Fig. 17.7, 17.8 and 17.9.

STOCK ACCOUNT L.37

19..		£	19..		£
Jan. 1	Balance B/d	8 400	Dec. 31	Trading Account L.186	8 400
Dec. 31	Trading Account (closing stock) L.186	4 560	31	Balance c/d	4 560
		£12 960			£12 960
19..		£			
Jan. 1	Balance B/d	4 560			

Fig. 17.8. Bringing the closing stock into account.

TRADING ACCOUNT L.186
(*for year ending December 31st, 19..*)

19..		£	19..		£
Dec. 31	Purchases	24 600	Dec. 31	Sales	62 160
	Sales Returns	2 094		Purchases Returns	360
	Opening Stock	8 400		Closing Stock	4 560
	Gross Profit	31 986			
		£67 080			£67 080

Fig. 17.9 An un-stylish (direct double-entry) Trading Account.

(*d*) *Style in the Trading Account.* We now come to the really important point about the Trading Account. Remember that this account is made out only once a year, and its purpose is to determine what profit we have made. However, the Trading Account is only the first part of the work, in which we find the Gross Profit (or over-all profit). The final 'Net' Profit is found in the Profit and Loss Account.

Since the purpose of this account is merely to discover the Gross Profit, and once that is done the Account is finished with and will not have any further entries, we might as well present it in good style to bring out exactly how the Gross Profit has been arrived at. The un-stylish Trading Account shown in Fig. 17.9 can be improved enormously if we take a few liberties with the double-entry system. For example, if we take the Sales Returns figure (which is on the debit side of the Trading Account in Fig. 17.9) over the credit side *and deduct it from the Sales*, we shall get a Sales less Sales Returns figure which tells the proprietor exactly what he did sell during the trading period. This is called the **Net Turnover** of the business and it is a very useful piece of information. Similarly, if we take the Purchases Returns figure from the credit side of the Trading Account in Fig. 17.9 over to the debit side *and deduct it from the Purchases* we find the Net Purchases figure. This again is a very useful figure to know—for it tells us how much we did actually purchase from suppliers during the year. (*Note.* Although we are taking liberties with the double-entry system we are not really doing anything wrong. To deduct something from the debit side is the same as adding it to the credit side, and to deduct something from the credit side is the same as adding it to the debit side.)

We can now take our argument one stage further and improve the style of the stock entries. First of all, the year begins with the stock in hand, or opening stock, and it would be sensible always to put this item first. Then more goods are added to stock as we buy them (the Purchases) but of course we have to take away the returns so that it is really the 'Net Purchases' which is added to opening stock. This gives us the total stock available during the year—what we received as an endowment from the previous year and the extra that we purchased. But did we sell all this stock? The answer is: 'No, some of it was left in hand at the end of the year, as closing stock.'

If we now bring this closing stock, which is on the credit side of the Trading Account in Fig. 17.9, over to the debit side *and deduct it from Total Stock Available* we have the Cost of the Stock Sold. This figure is a very important one. We only have to deduct it from the Net Sales figure to give us the Gross Profit, because

Net Turnover − Cost of Stock Sold = Gross Profit for the period

We now have a Trading Account (see Fig. 17.10) in good style.

(*e*) *Some final points about stylish Trading Accounts.* To conclude this section on the Trading Account and carry our stylish Trading Account to a final pitch of perfection there are one or two items which are usually included in the Trading Account as being more appropriately placed there than in the Profit and Loss Account. Two of them are items which affect the cost of purchases. They are *Carriage In* and *Customs Duty on Imported Purchases.* When we purchase things on which we have to meet expenses, such as Customs duty or carriage charges, the goods do not just cost us the invoice price, but

L.186

TRADING ACCOUNT
(for year ending December 31st, 19..)

19..			£	19..		£
Dec. 31	Opening Stock		8 400	Dec. 31	Sales	62 160
	Purchases	24 600			*Less* Returns	2 094
	Less Returns	360				
					Net turnover	60 066
	Net Purchases		24 240			
	Total Stock Available		32 640			
	Less Closing Stock		4 560			
	Cost of Stock sold		28 080			
	Gross Profit		31 986			
			£60 066			£60 066

Fig. 17.10. A more polished Trading Account.

these extra charges as well. It so happens that in the Trial Balance we are using there is no mention of Customs duty but there is an item 'Carriage In'. This should therefore be added to Purchases, as shown in Fig. 17.11. Similarly, if there is an entry for 'Customs Duty on Imports' in any Trial Balance this should also be added at this point.

Another of these special cases is the warehouse expenses which are involved in handling goods whilst they are in stock. Here it is up to the accountant to decide what he will do with such entries but in this book, for illustrative purposes, they have been entered in the Trading Account. The Trading Account shown in Fig. 17.11 may be regarded as a model example of how a Trading Account should be prepared.

17.5 Exercises: Trading Accounts

1. From the following particulars prepare the Trading Account of J. Weaver for the year ended December 31st, 19..: Sales £27 056.50; Purchases £15 275.75; Sales Returns £156.50; Purchases Returns £175.75; Stock January 1st £1 765.50; Stock December 31st £1 854.40.

2. From the following particulars prepare the Trading Account of C. Cooper for the year ended December 31st, 19..: Stock January 1st £1 279.65; Purchases £47 326.55; Purchases Returns £1 306.55; Sales £75 263.25; Sales Returns £1 263.25; Stock December 31st £2 735.50; Factory Wages £2 746.50.

3. Prepare the Trading Account of A. S. Brewis for the year ended December 31st, 19..: Stock January 1st £525.65; Cash Purchases £3 725.50; Credit Purchases £7 256.40; Carriage In £275.65; Returns Outwards £426.50; Cash Sales £5 650.50; Credit Sales £9 672.50; Returns Inwards £72.50; Stock December 31st £675.75.

4. Prepare a Trading Account for the year ended December 31st, 19.. for J. Lyons from the following information: Opening Stock £1 706.50; Purchases £5 726.50; Carriage In £126.50; Customs Duty on Imported Purchases £586.50; Purchases Returns £276.25; Closing Stock £1 409.20; Wages of warehouse workers £1 479.50; Warehouse expenses £826.45; Sales £12 265.30; Sales Returns £205.50.

TRADING ACCOUNT
(*for year ending December 31st, 19..*)

L.186

19..			£	19..		£
Dec. 31	Opening Stock		8 400	Dec. 31	Sales	62 160
	Purchases	24 600			*Less* Returns	2 094
	Add Carriage In	200			Net turnover	60 066
		24 800				
	Less Returns	360				
	Net Purchases		24 440			
	Total Stock Available		32 840			
	Less Closing Stock		4 560			
	Cost of Stock sold		28 280			
	Warehouse Wages		6 080			
	Cost of Sales		34 360			
	Gross Profit (transferred to Profit and Loss Account)		25 706			
			£60 066			£60 066

PROFIT AND LOSS ACCOUNT
(*for year ending December 31st, 19..*)

				19..		£
				Dec. 31	Gross Profit	25 706

Fig. 17.11. A Trading Account in good style.

5. At December 31st, 19.., the Trial Balance of E. Randall contained the following items:

	£
Stock at January 1st, 19..	2 785 00
Purchases	6 908.00
Sales	7 642.00
Returns Outwards	195.00
Returns Inwards	262.00
Warehouse Wages	700.00
Wages Owing	20.00
Import Charges	126.00

Randall's Stock at December 31st, 19.., was valued at £4 440.00. Prepare the Trading Account for the year ending December 31st, 19..

(RSA—Adapted)

6. The following figures relating to a dressmaking business were extracted from the Trial Balance taken out on March 31st, 19... From them select those items you consider should be used in the Trading Account of the business and prepare this account for the quarter ended on that date.

	£
Sales for the quarter	8 000.00
Purchases of cloth, etc.	2 554.00
Purchases of sewing machines	380.00
Carriage on goods sold	47.00
Returns to and allowances from suppliers	54.00
Purchases of cardboard boxes, wrapping paper. etc.	30.00
Office heating and lighting	103.00
Heating and lighting of workrooms	212.00
Office salaries and expenses	872.00
Workroom wages	1 650.00
Advertising	200.00
Rent and rates (three quarters workroom, one quarter office)	480.00
Electric power for machines	150.00
Carriage on purchases	32.00
Discounts allowed	36.00
Discounts received	50.00
Stocks of cloth, etc.:	
January 1st, 19..	600.00
March 31st, 19..	766.00

(RSA—Adapted)

17.6 The Profit and Loss Account

A Revised Trial Balance

Consider what has happened to the Trial Balance drawn up in Fig. 17.1 (see page 229).

Because of the transfer of items to the Trading Account, a number of the balances shown on that Trial Balance have been cleared off completely, and, as a result, have disappeared from the Trial Balance. In their place, we now have a Gross Profit figure on the Trading Account which is the final result of setting the purchases, stock, etc., against the sales for the year. In addition to this one of the accounts shown on that Trial Balance has changed from one figure to another, and has also changed its character. This is the Stock Account, which formerly was a nominal account with a balance of £8 400. It was a nominal account because the £8 400 was there 'in name only': in fact this stock had been sold and replaced by other stock purchased in the year. At first we transferred this £8 400 to the Trading Account, leaving the Stock Account clear for a short while, but then we reopened it with the closing stock. This closing stock is not a nominal figure, it is real. (Anyone who likes to check it can count the stock and value it.) It is therefore an asset, but, of course, tomorrow we begin a new year and we shall start selling our stock, so that the real figure today of £4 560 will soon become a nominal figure again. To be really clear about this is a vital part of understanding the stock. Our figure of £4 560 is an asset for today, but it will soon become a nominal account again, when dealings in stock change the real stock figure from £4 560 to some other figure.

Our revised Trial Balance now looks as shown in Fig. 17.12. The Trading Account items have disappeared, except for the Gross Profit, and we have only—in the debit column—Assets and Losses, while in the credit column we have only Liabilities and Profits.

R. JONES

TRIAL BALANCE

(*as at December 31st, 19..*)

Ledger Account	Notes	Dr.	Cr.	Notes
Premises Account	Asset	12 980		
Capital Account			32 400	Liability
Debtors:				
R. Johnson Account	Asset	4 000		
M. Thompson Account	Asset	3 012		
Creditors:				
R. Lupin Account			480	Liability
M. Chuzzlewit Account			720	Liability
Plant and Machinery Account	Asset	15 000		
Office Furniture Account	Asset	3 200		
Cash Account	Asset	300		
Bank Account	Asset	2 900		
Stock Account	Asset	4 560		
Bad Debts Account	Loss	450		
Commission Paid Account	Loss	664		
Discount Allowed Account	Loss	400		
Discount Received Account			360	Profit
Rent and Rates Account	Loss	2 200		
Carriage Out Account	Loss	240		
Salaries Account	Loss	5 360		
Rent Received Account			800	Profit
Drawings Account	Special Item	5 200		
Gross Profit (on Profit and Loss Account)			25 706	Profit
		£ 60 466	60 466	

Fig. 17.12. A revised Trial Balance.

Preparing a Profit and Loss Account

The preparation of the Profit and Loss Account is now a simple matter. It has opened with the Gross Profit from the Trading Account, on the credit side. We now have to transfer in, by closing journal entries exactly like those already described for the Trading Account, all the losses, such as Bad Debts Account and Commission Paid Account, and all the profits, such as Discount Received Account and Rent Received Account. The final result will be that all these accounts will be cleared off (and consequently disappear from the Trial Balance) whilst the Profit and Loss Account will reveal the true 'Net' Profit made in the trading period. This is shown in Fig. 17.13.

PROFIT AND LOSS ACCOUNT L.187
(for year ending December 31st, 19..)

19..		£	19..		£
Dec. 31	Bad Debts	450	Dec. 31	Gross Profit	25 706
	Commission Paid	664		Discount Received	360
	Discount Allowed	400		Rent Received	800
	Rent and Rates	2 200			
	Carriage Out	240			
	Salaries	5 360			
	Net Profit C/d	17 552			
		£26 866			£26 866
			19..		£
			Dec. 31	Balance (Net Profit) B/d	17 552

Fig. 17.13. The Profit and Loss Account.

Trading and Profit and Loss Accounts

Some accountants prepare these accounts, which are of course successive to one another, in the following manner. They simply insert a single heading, and then run the accounts on into one another, as two separate parts of the same piece of work. There is no objection to this at all. The whole piece of work then looks as shown in Fig. 17.14.

17.7 Exercises: Profit and Loss Accounts

1. From the following figures prepare T. Stebbing's Profit and Loss Account for the half year ended June 30th, 19..:

	£
Gross Profit	5 650
Discount Allowed	35
Discount Received	72
Bad Debts	124
Rent and Rates	430
Light and Heat	186
Packing and Delivery Expenses	68
Commission Received	272
Salaries	1 850

TRADING AND PROFIT AND LOSS ACCOUNT (*for year ending December 31st, 19..*) L.186

19..			£	19..		£
Dec. 31	Opening Stock		8 400	Dec. 31	Sales	62 160
	Purchases	24 600			*Less* Returns	2 094
	Add Carriage In	200			Net turnover	60 066
		24 800				
	Less Returns	360				
	Net Purchases		24 440			
	Total Stock Available		32 840			
	Less Closing Stock		4 560			
	Cost of Stock sold		28 280			
	Warehouse Wages		6 080			
	Cost of Sales		34 360			
	Gross Profit		25 706			
			£60 066			£60 066
	Bad Debts		450		Gross Profit	25 706
	Commission Paid		664		Discount Received	360
	Discount Allowed		400		Rent Received	800
	Rent and Rates		2 200			
	Carriage Out		240			
	Salaries		5 360			
	Net Profit		17 552			
			£26 866			£26 866
				19..		
				Dec. 31	Balance (Net Profit) B/d	17 552

Fig. 17.14. A Trading and Profit and Loss Account.

2. From the following particulars prepare M. Fletcher's Profit and Loss Account for the year ended December 31st, 19..:

	£
Gross Profit from Trading	7 246.50
Selling Expenses	1 245.50
Salaries	2 365.25
Discount Allowed	252.65
Discount Received	286.40
Rent, Rates, and Insurance	426.50

3. R. Dwyer's Trial Balance contains the following items other than assets and liabilities. From them prepare his Profit and Loss Account for year ending December 31st, 19..:

	£
Gross Trading Profit	11 260.00
Salaries	3 515.00
Selling Expenses	426.50
Package Materials	1 425.55
Rent, etc.	1 846.50
Discount Received	47.85
Discount Allowed	143.50

4. From the following particulars prepare the Trading Account and then the Profit and Loss Account of R. Mildred, for the month ending June 30th, 19..:

	£
Stock at start June 1st, 19..	1 760.55
Discount allowed	17.50
Insurance Premiums	4.15
Salaries	426.50
Purchases	4 550.50
Returns Outwards	12.14
Printing and Stationery	25.88
Rent and Rates	442.25
Sales	8 516.60
Returns Inwards	16.85
General Expenses	325.15
Telephone Account	25.50
Stock, June 30th, 19..	1 585.65
Discount Received	2.05
Interest paid on loans	30.55
Light and Heat	24.65

5. From the following list of balances you are required to prepare the Trading and Profit and Loss Accounts for the year ending March 31st, 19.., of Robert Dingley, a wholesale merchant:

	£
Returns Outwards	180.00
Carriage Outwards	210.00
Sales	47 810.00
Wages and Salaries (Half to Trading Account; half to Profit and Loss Account)	5 600.00
Returns Inwards	210.00
Commission Paid	1 800.00
Commission Received	220.00
Carriage Inwards	360.00
Motor Van Expenses	120.00
Stock, April 1st, 19..	5 500.00
Purchases	34 000.00
Bank Interest and Charges	115.00
Rent, Rates, and Insurance	1 140.00
General Expenses	1 850.00

(cont'd)

Bad Debts	210.00
Discount Allowed	120.00
Discount Received	680.00

In preparing your account you should note that stock on March 31st, 19.., was valued at £4 835.00.

17.8 The Appropriation of Profits

When the profits have been found, at the end of the Profit and Loss Account, they have to be allocated to the person or persons entitled to receive them. This is called **appropriating the profits.** In the case of a sole trader there is no real difficulty for he is entitled to the entire proceeds, which are his reward for showing enterprise. With other businesses, such as partnerships and limited companies, the profits have to be shared out in a proper manner, either between the partners or amongst the various classes of shareholders. This is usually done by transferring the profits to a special **Appropriation Account.** Here we need not be concerned with this account, which is dealt with more fully later in this book (see pages 286 and 294). We need only deal with the situation for a sole trader in this chapter.

Allocating Profit to the Sole Trader. Apart from the assets and liabilities and the Net Profit balance available on the credit side of the Profit and Loss Account, there is only one Account still present on the Trial Balance. This is the 'Special Item Drawings'. 'Drawings' is of course the money drawn out during the year by the owner of the business to live on whilst he is pursuing his business activities. What he is really drawing against are the profits he hopes he has made each week or each month, but he cannot be sure he really has been operating at a profit until he does his Final Accounts. We therefore say that he is drawing 'in expectation of profits'.

At the end of the year, when the profits are found by doing the Final Accounts, the sole trader is of course entitled to them, but if he has already drawn a large part of them in Drawings these must be deducted from the profits before he receives the residue as the final reward for his year's work.

19..			£	£
Dec. 31	Capital Account	L.11	5 200	
	Drawings Account	L.69		5 200
	Being drawings for year transferred			

Fig. 17.15. Closing off the Drawings Account.

We therefore need a closing journal entry to close off the Drawings Account into the Capital Account, before carrying the profits to the proprietor's Capital Account as well. These actions are illustrated in Figs. 17.15, 17.16 and 17.17. The final result of his year's activities is that the sole trader has enjoyed a reasonable standard of living (drawings of £5 200) and has also ploughed back into the growth of his business further profits in excess of £12 000. This looks a very satisfactory year's trading.

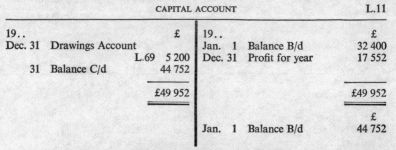

19..			£	£
Dec. 31	Profit and Loss Account	L.186	17 552	
	Capital Account	L.11		17 552
	Being residue of profit for year transferred to Capital Account			

Fig. 17.16. Closing off the Profit and Loss Account.

CAPITAL ACCOUNT L.11

19..		£	19..			£
Dec. 31	Drawings Account L.69	5 200	Jan.	1	Balance B/d	32 400
31	Balance C/d	44 752	Dec.	31	Profit for year	17 552
		£49 952				£49 952
						£
			Jan.	1	Balance B/d	44 752

Fig. 17.17. Appropriating the profit to the sole trader.

17.9 The Residue of the Trial Balance

We are almost at the end of the Final Accounts activities. We have found the net profit, and appropriated it to the sole trader's Capital Account. It remains to present the affairs of the business in a final statement called the Balance Sheet.

The Trial Balance, originally given in Fig. 17.1 (see page 229), has now been reduced to the point where it only contains the assets and liabilities. These accounts have not altered in any way, except that the Capital Account has changed because of the residue of profits added to it. The former figure of £32 400 has now been increased to £44 752.

As a result of these activities the Trial Balance now contains only the residual items which will continue into the next year's business—the assets and liabilities of the firm which will go on being used, or honoured, over the course of the next year. The problem now is to present these in such a way as to show 'a true and fair view' of the business to anyone interested in it. This means to the owner, the prospective buyer, should the owner be thinking of selling, or anyone else interested, like the tax authorities. Our Trial Balance now looks as in Fig. 17.18.

17.10 History Makes a Mess of Things—The Balance Sheet Reversed

In Chapter 16 reference was made to the fact that the Balance Sheet was overdue for harmonisation in that the United Kingdom and countries formerly associated with her prepare the Balance Sheet the wrong way round. The historical circumstances are worth noting.

Simon Stevin of Bruges invented the Balance Sheet in the sixteenth century. He called it a 'Statement of the Affairs' of the business, a phrase which we still use today in connection with single entry, dealt with in Chapter 19, page 322. Unfortunately, in taking the totals of the assets and liabilities out of the books he crossed them over and wrote them down with the assets on the right-hand side and the liabilities on the left. We don't quite know why he did this, probably he was thinking of it as if he were posting the Cash Book. It was quite wrong, but as the Balance Sheet is only a sheet of paper, not part of the real books, it doesn't make any difference, except that it is misleading to the student.

What made matters worse was that the British Parliament, not knowing its book-keeping, passed an Act which made this type of Balance Sheet the law of Great Britain. The Company Act of 1856 included, in Table B, a set of model

R. JONES

TRIAL BALANCE

(as at December 31st, 19..)

Ledger Accounts	Notes	Dr.	Cr.	Notes
Premises Account	Asset	12 980		
Capital Account			44 752	Liability
Debtors:				
R. Johnson Account	Asset	4 000		
M. Thompson Account	Asset	3 012		
Creditors:				
R. Lupin Account			480	Liability
M. Chuzzlewit Account			720	Liability
Plant and Machinery Account	Asset	15 000		
Office Furniture Account	Asset	3 200		
Cash Account	Asset	300		
Bank Account	Asset	2 900		
Stock Account	Asset	4 560		
		£ 45 952	45 952	

Fig. 17.18. The residue of the Trial Balance.

articles which referred to a Balance Sheet which 'shall be presented to the members at the Annual General Meeting in the form annexed to this table, or as near thereto as the circumstances permit' (Article 72). The Balance Sheet given was in Simon Stevin's form, with the assets on the right-hand side, and the liabilities on the left-hand side.

A British Act of Parliament, even when it makes absolute rubbish, is so revered a document that we all obey it. Other nations, which have less respect for formal nonsense, produce their Balance Sheets in the sensible form—as the accounts appear in the Trial Balance—with the assets on the left-hand side and the liabilities on the right-hand side. Fortunately, British policies do change in time, and harmonisation with the EEC countries may yet produce a British balance sheet in correct style. The author hopes that readers will play their part in promoting a more sensible approach. Remember, then, that although it makes no difference at all it is customary in Great Britain and associated countries to put the Balance Sheet with sides reversed: assets on the right, liabilities on the left.

17.11 The Order of Permanence and the Order of Liquidity

A Balance Sheet is a final statement of the affairs of a business, made out at a particular time, in this case at the end of the financial year. It shows what the present year's business is handing on to the following year as a factor endowment—in other words, a collection of resources to be used in the new financial period. These resources can be listed in any order, but it is usual to marshal the assets and liabilities in one of two methods, known as the **order of permanence** and the **order of liquidity.**

The **order of permanence** marshals the assets in that order which puts the most permanent asset first, with the others in descending order of permanence. Thus land, which lasts for ever, is very permanent, whilst cash—which is here today but gone tomorrow—is the least permanent (and therefore the most liquid of assets). In accounting, the word 'liquid' means 'in cash form', so that nothing is more liquid than cash itself. Money in the bank is almost as liquid as cash, but we do have to take steps to make it completely liquid and it is therefore the second most liquid item.

The **order of liquidity** is the reverse of the Order of Permanence. It has cash as its first item, bank moneys as its second item and so on, in decreasing order of liquidity or increasing order of permanence.

Which Order Should We Use? Traditionally banks (which are keen to impress depositors with the liquid nature of their assets and the consequent ease with which any depositor who wanted his money back could reclaim it) have always used the order of liquidity, though some of them display a poor appreciation of the principles of elementary accounting and publish badly marshalled Balance Sheets.

Industrial firms, anxious to impress prospective shareholders with the durable nature of their assets, have traditionally used the order of permanence.

At the moment there is a proposal under consideration to make the order of liquidity the standard method. Until some harmonisation and standardisation of procedure is agreed the author suggests that those referred to above be adhered to, i.e. *the order of permanence for industrial and commercial firms, but the order of liquidity for banks and financial institutions.*

The really important thing to achieve with a Balance Sheet is that the assets are well displayed, whichever order you choose. The two methods, the order of liquidity and the order of permanence, are simply the reverse of each other. The student should think seriously about where to place each asset and each liability. It has already been said that cash is the most liquid asset we have, and cash at bank is the second most liquid item. Which is more liquid, stock or debtors? This is debatable. Debtors have a contractual obligation to pay you. Has anyone a duty to buy your stock? Since the answer is 'No', we usually consider debtors as more liquid than stock. Similarly, the fixed assets are more, or less, easily convertible into cash, and become more fixed and permanent as we move through the list shown.

Subheadings on the Balance Sheet

One further point about marshalling the assets and liabilities on a Balance Sheet is that it is important to group certain items together. On the assets side we have two main groups: Fixed Assets and Current Assets. On the liabilities side we have three main groups: Current Liabilities, Long-Term Liabilities and the Capital. A word about each of these is desirable.

(*a*) **Fixed Assets.** Fixed assets are assets used to carry on the business. They cannot be sold without seriously interfering with the conduct of the business. They will be used to manufacture, warehouse, or sell the goods offered by the proprietor, or to provide the services hc makes available to the general public. The commonest fixed assets are:

Land and Buildings
Plant and Machinery
Furniture and Fittings
Motor Vehicles

(*b*) **Current Assets.** This name comes from the French word *courant*, which means running. These assets are continually running round as the business turns over; cash is used to buy stock which we sell to debtors who pay cash which is used to buy stock, etc. The commonest current assets are:

Cash in Hand
Cash at Bank
Debtors
Stock
Investments

Note. If investments are held as a useful way of earning money with idle cash not at present required in the business they are current assets.

(*c*) **Current Liabilities.** Just as 'current assets' are circulating in the course of business, current liabilities must be settled within a short while. Most accounts are payable monthly. The rather regrettable practice (especially by big firms) of paying later than the agreed period may shortly be corrected by legislation entitling the creditor to add interest when the credit period is exceeded. The usual distinction drawn between current liabilities and long-term liabilities is the one-year period. Liabilities which must be settled within the current financial year are viewed as current liabilities. Loans and mortgages do not usually fall into this class. The commonest types of current liability are:

Creditors (*Accounts Payable*)
Wages Due
Salaries Due
Commission Due
Bank Overdrafts (these are very short-term loans the bank can require us to repay at short notice)

(*d*) **Long-Term Liabilities.** These are usually a formal loan of money either from a bank or a building society or some other institutional investor like a finance company. These liabilities are evidenced by a formal agreement stating the amount of the loan, the terms of repayment, the rate of interest, and the **collateral security** provided. Collateral means 'lying alongside' and the security provided may be a mortgage on the deeds of the proprietor's property or a life assurance policy on his life. The commonest types of long-term liability are:

Bank Loans
Private Loans

Hire-Purchase Loans
Mortgages

(*e*) **Capital.** Finally, the capital invested in the business by the proprietor may be regarded as the longest-term liability of all. It is what the business owes to the owner of the business, and will normally be repaid only when he ceases to be interested in the firm, either because he sells it as a going concern, or closes down, or dies. The heirs will then have to decide how the capital is to be realised to pay the death duties (Capital Transfer Tax) and the inheritances provided for in the trader's Will.

For the sake of clarity the Balance Sheet has been displayed in Figs. 17.19

R. JONES

BALANCE SHEET
(*as at December 31st, 19..*)
Order of Permanence

CAPITAL		£	FIXED ASSETS		£
At Start		32 400	Premises		12 980
Add Profits	17 552		Plant and Machinery		15 000
Less Drawings	5 200		Office Furniture		3 200
		12 352			31 180
		44 752			
			CURRENT ASSETS		
			Stock	4 560	
LONG-TERM LIABILITIES		—	Sundry Debtors	7 012	
			Cash at Bank	2 900	
			Cash in Hand	300	
CURRENT LIABILITIES					
Sundry Creditors		1 200			14 772
		£45 952			£45 952

Fig. 17.19. A Balance Sheet in the order of permanence.

and 17.20 in both the order of permanence and the order of liquidity. In order to give a clear picture it is usual to show the profits at their full value, less Drawings, and thus demonstrate how the final figure on Capital Account was arrived at.

The student should now work a large number of exercises to the Final Accounts level. There are still many things to learn about Final Accounts, but we must first consolidate our present knowledge. Every time the student begins to prepare a set of Final Accounts from a Trial Balance he should be prepared to do it first in rough. He should then make a really neat set of Final Accounts, perfect in layout and style, from his rough copy. The student who acquires real facility at these exercises will find himself able to do the rough work, and get his Balance Sheet to balance, in about twenty minutes. A really neat fair copy then takes about ten minutes to write out. Headings and subtotals can be made to look attractive with suitable underlining in red (a ballpoint pen is best).

R. JONES

BALANCE SHEET
(*as at December 31st, 19. .*)
Order of Liquidity

			£			£
CURRENT LIABILITIES			£	CURRENT ASSETS		£
Sundry Creditors			1 200	Cash in Hand	300	
				Cash at Bank	2 900	
				Sundry Debtors	7 012	
LONG-TERM LIABILITIES			—	Stock	4 560	
						14 772
CAPITAL				FIXED ASSETS		
At Start		32 400		Office Furniture	3 200	
Add Profits	17 552			Plant and Machinery	15 000	
Less				Premises	12 980	
Drawings	5 200					
						31 180
		12 352				
			44 752			
			£45 952			£45 952

Fig. 17.20. A Balance Sheet in the order of liquidity.

17.12 Exercises: Simple Final Accounts

1. Here is the Trial Balance of A. Tacitus' books. From it prepare his Trading Account, Profit and Loss Account, and Balance Sheet.

TRIAL BALANCE
(*as at March 31st, 19. .*)

Stock at Start	5 560	
Debtors and Creditors	5 954	2 772
Freehold Land and Buildings	13 756	
Carriage In	398	
Purchases and Sales	16 722	32 394
Bad Debts	300	
Motor Vehicle Expenses	1 130	
Office Repairs Account	130	
Returns—In and Out	550	1 466
Fixtures and Fittings	6 500	
Motor Vans	1 600	
Office Expenses	750	
Capital at April 1st last year		22 730
Bank overdraft		1 038
Drawings	750	
Salaries and Commissions	5 650	
Depreciation	220	
Carriage Out	280	
Cash in Hand	150	
	£60 400	£60 400

Closing Stock on March 31st, 19. . : £4 500.00

2. Here is the Trial Balance of N. Carter's books on December 31st, 19... You are asked to prepare the Trading Account, Profit and Loss Account, and a Balance Sheet at this date for the year that has just passed.

	Dr.	Cr.
Debtors and Creditors	4 300	2 420
Plant and Machinery	9 500	
Purchases and Sales	8 500	25 000
Capital at January 1st, 19..		33 000
Premises	14 000	
Cash in Hand	500	
Bank Overdraft		600
Discount Allowed and Received	250	300
Bad Debts	340	
Motor Vehicles	2 000	
Commission Paid	1 300	
Insurance Premium	112	
Office Furniture	3 000	
Stock on January 1st, 19..	4 500	
Rent and Rates	320	
Fees to Lawyers for Debt Collection	180	
Returns—In and Out	150	62
Office Salaries	4 430	
Wages (to go in Trading Account)	4 500	
Drawings	3 500	
	£61 382	£61 382

Stock at the end of December: £3 900.00

3. Mr R. Teasdale is in business as a master tailor. On December 31st, 19.., he takes out his Trial Balance as shown below. Prepare his Trading Account, Profit and Loss Account, and Balance Sheet.

	Dr.	Cr.
Stock at January 1st, 19..	1 350	
Purchases and Sales	12 500	28 500
Returns—In and Out	25	41
Carriage In	22	
Carriage Out	40	
Factory Wages	1 250	
Factory Light and Heat	120	
Premises	14 000	
Plant and Machinery	12 800	
Motor Vehicles	1 800	
Debtors and Creditors	200	2 300
Office Expenses	2 164	
Office Salaries	6 200	
Commission Paid	200	
Bad Debts Recovered		25
Mortgage on Premises		10 800
Cash	10	
Balance at bank	2 300	
Capital		15 815
Drawings	2 500	
	£57 481	£57 481

Closing stock was valued at £1 900.00. Factory items are to be entered in the Trading Account.

4. Prepare a Trading Account, Profit and Loss Account, and Balance Sheet from the Trial Balance of P. Tyler's books below as at December 31st, 19..:

	Dr.	Cr.
Capital		36 000
Travellers' Salaries and Commissions	3 948	
Drawings	2 800	
Office Furniture	1 400	
Purchases and Purchases Returns	20 884	1 696
Sales Returns and Sales	728	59 936
Cash in Hand	884	
Cash at Bank	4 960	
Stock at January 1st, 19..	4 584	
Salaries	2 512	
Sundry Debtors and Creditors	14 788	6 792
Discount Received		72
Factory Wages	15 424	
Freehold Factory, January 1st, 19..	10 000	
Rent and Rates	2 776	
Carriage In	924	
Carriage Out	1 296	
Factory Expenses	2 896	
Factory Fuel	3 180	
Plant and Machinery	9 600	
Office Expenses	912	
	£104 496	£104 496

Closing stock was valued at £5 716.00. Factory items to be entered in the Trading Account.

5. Here is T. Lauder's Trial Balance as at December 31st, 19... You are asked to prepare his Trading Account, Profit and Loss Account, and Balance Sheet as at that date.

	Dr.	Cr.
Capital		45 720
Cash	550	
Cash at Bank	7 250	
Stock at January 1st, 19..	18 250	
Sales Returns and Sales	480	49 756
Purchases and Purchases Returns	16 248	1 248
Debtors and Creditors	9 312	8 268
Discount Allowed and Received	112	140
Factory Wages (Trading Item)	11 274	
Carriage Inwards	420	
Power and Heat for Office	380	
Rent and Rates	4 250	
Miscellaneous Expenses	385	
Salaries	4 260	
Drawings	4 500	
Office Expenses	840	
Freehold Premises	25 000	
Motor Vehicles	3 800	
Fixtures and Fittings	4 250	
Depreciation	780	
Interest and Commission Received		7 209
	£112 341	£112 341

The stock at the end of the year was valued at £12 500.

6. Mr Pinch's Trial Balance is as follows on December 31st, 19... Prepare his Trading Account, Profit and Loss Account, and Balance Sheet in good style.

	Dr. (£)	Cr. (£)
Opening Stock	5 800	
Capital		30 910
Carriage on Sales	420	
Sundry Expenses	840	
Purchases and Sales	16 248	38 726
Returns—In and Out	726	248
Salaries	4 284	
Cash	326	
Land and Buildings	17 250	
Plant and Machinery	12 250	
Office Furniture	4 000	
Commission paid to Travellers	1 856	
Cash at Bank	2 974	
Rent and Rates	880	
Factory Wages	4 260	
Mortgage on Property		4 000
Discount Allowed and Received	250	320
Debtors and Creditors	1 250	3 860
Light and Heat	450	
Drawings	4 000	
	78 064	78 064

Stock at the end of the year: £3 000.00.

18

ADJUSTMENTS IN FINAL ACCOUNTS

18.1 The Nature of Adjustments

In Chapter 17 we saw how to prepare a simple set of Final Accounts, and to arrive at the Net Profit for the year. In fact, most sets of final accounts require us to 'adjust' the figures on the various accounts before using them to prepare the Trading and Profit and Loss Accounts. This is because, as we saw in Chapter 16 (see page 220), accounts must be prepared on an 'accruals' basis.

The accruals basis really involves two ideas: **payments in advance** and **accrued expenses.** However, since these can arise both at the beginning of the year and at the end of the year, four situations have to be taken into account. Some illustrations will explain the point, but before considering actual cases let us repeat the principle of 'adjustments' in accounting. The principle is this:

In preparing final accounts the figures to be used for any profit of the business must be those that actually represent the earnings from the year's activities, and the expenses or losses of the business must be those actually incurred in earning the profits.

Now since the figures on any account, such as the Rent Account, might not actually be correct, because we may have paid rent in advance for next year (a payment in advance) or we may be behind with the rent (an accrued expense), it is necessary to 'adjust' the Rent Account figures to arrive at the correct expense for rent for the year. Since this can happen both at the beginning of the year and at the end of the year we have four possibilities to take into account. Usually one or two of these affect any particular account—for example:

Rent Account. If we usually pay rent in advance—say, on the 25th of each month to make sure it is paid before the 1st day of next month—then the figures for any year (let us call it Year 1) will include January's rent on December 31st—because we paid it in advance on December 25th. We must adjust the total of the Rent Account to leave out this figure. At the end of the next year we must make sure this January figure was included (it might be overlooked) and we must leave out the January figure for Year 3 (which was paid on 25 December Year 2).

Commission Payable. If commission is payable to our commercial travellers on sales to the end of each quarter, by the 15th of the following month, our Commission Paid Account on December 31st, Year 1, will not include a large figure for Commission Due. We must include this figure in the final accounts even though it will not actually be paid until January 15th, Year 2. At the end of Year 2 we must make sure this sum is left out of the figures for Year 2, but must include the Commission Due due for Year 2, which will not be paid until January 15th, Year 3.

This is the nature of adjustments. It is only by doing these adjustments that we can prepare accounts which are accurate and honest, to the satisfaction of the Inland Revenue authorities and (for companies) in compliance with the Companies Acts 1948–76, which require accounts to give a 'true and fair view' of the affairs of the business.

Moreover, since these adjustments must result in showing that the business has overpaid (an asset) or underpaid (a liability), every adjustment we do results in a modification of the Balance Sheet, which is the final statement of the affairs of the business at the end of the financial year. We may therefore say:

The purpose of adjustments is to produce a perfectly accurate set of Final Accounts for the period under review, and a perfectly honest Balance Sheet as at the date when the accounting period ended.

The main adjustments that are necessary are:

(1) Payments in advance by the firm.
(2) Payments in advance to the firm.
(3) Accrued expenses owed by the firm.
(4) Accrued receipts due to the firm.
(5) Bad debts.
(6) Provision for bad debts.
(7) Provision for discounts.
(8) Depreciation of assets.
(9) Depreciation of goodwill.

We must now look at each of these in turn.

18.2 Adjustments No. 1—Payments in Advance by the Firm

Certain expenses are nearly always paid in advance. The best example is insurance, since the insurance cover begins only on payment of the premium and then runs for a given period, usually one year. Rent is usually payable in advance, as are rates.

If we use insurance as an example, consider the following Insurance Account which we propose to close off into the Profit and Loss Account.

INSURANCE ACCOUNT L.61

19..		£	
Jan. 1	Balance	60.00	
June 30	Fire Insurance	18.00	
Sept. 30	Motor Vehicles	102.00	

Fig. 18.1. Expenses, some of which are in advance.

How much of these insurance expenses applies to the present year, assuming that they are all annual premiums? Clearly all the £60.00 on January 1st, 19.., has been used up by December 31st, 19.., and may fairly be treated as a loss. The fire insurance premium of £18.00 on June 30th, 19.., has only been half consumed; the insurance company has still to cover us for a further six months, £9.00 of this £18.00 has to be treated as an expense of the year, the other £9.00 is an asset at present—it will become an expense of next year.

The £102.00 paid for motor vehicle insurance on September 30th has only been one quarter used up by December 31st, 19.. : £76.50 of this is an asset; the insurance company owes us cover for this amount. The £25.50 is a loss for the present year.

Our adjustment now reads as follows: instead of £180.00 being transferred to the Profit and Loss Account as a loss, only £60.00 + £9.00 + £25.50 = £94.50 should be transferred, leaving £85.50 still on the Insurance Account as an asset of the business.

The journal entry for this will be:

19..			£	£
Dec. 31	Profit and Loss Account Dr	L.66	94.50	
	To Insurance Account	L.61		94.50
	Being Insurance Premiums for year transferred			

Fig. 18.2. Transferring the adjusted amounts.

and the Insurance Account now looks like this:

INSURANCE ACCOUNT L.61

19..		£	19..		£
Jan. 1	Balance	60.00	Dec. 31	Profit and Loss Account	94.50
June 30	Fire Insurance	18.00	31	Balance	85.50
Sept. 30	Motor Vehicles	102.00			
		180.00			180.00
19..		£			
Jan. 1	Balance	85.50			

Fig. 18.3. A nominal account that has become temporarily an asset account.

Notice that the Nominal Account, which has carried our losses on insurance for the year, is at present carrying a balance that is in effect an asset. It must appear on the assets side of the Balance Sheet, since the insurance company are virtually debtors for this amount of cover.

(*Note*. Some theoreticians argue that a nominal account cannot have a real balance, and say the correct thing to do is to transfer this balance to a Sus-

BALANCE SHEET
(*as at December 31st, 19..*)

	FIXED ASSETS	
	CURRENT ASSETS	
	Stock	
	Debtors	
	Cash	
	Insurance in Advance	85.50

Fig. 18.4. The most liquid asset.

pense Account for Balance Sheet purposes. This is a highly academic rule 'more honoured in the breach than in the observance'.)

The Balance Sheet will now have this balance on the assets side, under Current Assets. The best place is to put it as the most liquid item, since it is so liquid *you have already spent it*. This is shown in Fig. 18.4.

In examination work, where a student is working from a Trial Balance without the actual accounts, it is usual to show the adjustment on the Trading Account or Profit and Loss Account itself, by indenting the main figure. The Profit and Loss Account in this case would look as follows:

PROFIT AND LOSS ACCOUNT L.66
(*for year ending December 31st, 19..*)

Insurance	180.00		
Less Amount Paid in Advance	85.50		
		94.50	

Fig. 18.5. The best way to show adjustments for examination purposes.

The payment in advance must still be shown on the Balance Sheet as in Fig. 18.4.

18.3 Adjustments No. 2—Payments in Advance to the Firm

If payments in advance by the firm should not be counted as losses of the present year, but regarded as assets carried over to the next year for use in the coming months, it seems only logical that payments in advance to the firm for services not yet rendered should not be treated as profits, but carried forward to the next year as liabilities.

Taking the example of insurance used in Section 18.2 on page 255, from the insurance company's point of view the position will be the reverse of payments in advance by the firm. They have received premiums, of perhaps £1 000 000.00. Of this figure, let us imagine that £250 000.00 represents premiums received in advance. Clearly only £750 000.00 should be transferred to the Revenue Account, the rest remaining on the books as a liability to the policy-holders. It will become a profit in the course of the coming year. Such an account might look like this after closure:

PREMIUMS RECEIVED ACCOUNT L.195

Dec. 31	Revenue Account	750 000.00	Sundry Premiums	1 000 000.00
	Balance	250 000.00		
		1 000 000.00		1 000 000.00
			Balance	250 000.00

Fig. 18.6. A nominal account that has temporarily become a liability.

When the credit balance is taken into the Balance Sheet it will look like Fig. 18.7. Notice that because the Balance Sheet is the wrong way round the liability appears to change sides. Remember always that United Kingdom Balance Sheets are misleading.

BALANCE SHEET
(*for year ending December 31st, 19..*)

CURRENT LIABILITIES		
Premiums in Advance	250 000.00	

Fig. 18.7. A very current liability.

18.4 Exercises: Payments in Advance

1. Lomax's Rent Account shows payments made to his landlord on January 3rd, March 31st, June 26th, September 25th, and December 20th, 19.., of £400.00 each time. The rent is £400.00 per quarter. Show the Rent Account for the year, including the transfer to Profit and Loss Account on December 31st, 19...
2. Phillipson's Insurance Account shows annual insurance payments as follows: Fire Policy on January 1st, £26.50; Motor Vehicles on March 31st, £124.00; Life Assurance on June 30th, £36.00. Show the Insurance Account for the year, including the transfer to Profit and Loss Account on December 31st, 19...
3. The Swinging Hypnotists' Club had a credit balance on its Subscriptions Account of £225.00, which represented subscriptions in advance, on January 1st, 19... During the year subscriptions of £6 255.00 were received, but £255.00 of this was in advance for the next year. Show the Subscriptions Account, including the amount transferred to the club's Income and Expenditure Account (this is the same as the Profit and Loss Account, and is explained later, on page 312).
4. Robson & Co. receive commissions on the sales executed for Yamachita & Co.: 2½ per cent commission on cost price on accepting the authority to sell, and 2½ per cent on selling price when the sale is made. If they are unable to sell, the commission on cost price is returnable. They therefore do not count such commission as profit until they have made the sale.

   On January 1st, 19.., there was £326.00 of such commission outstanding as profit earned, but subject to the 'returnable' clause. During the year other commission came to £5 786.00 and on December 31st there was £525.50 outstanding again.

   Draw up the Commission Received Account and thus show how much was transferred as profit to the Profit and Loss Account.

18.5 Adjustments No. 3—Accrued Expenses Owed by the Firm

Sometimes we are not in advance with our payments but in arrears. Rent may be accrued due, or commission to travellers may be accrued due.

The word 'accrued' simply means 'collected' or 'built up' over the weeks. Any accruals must sooner or later be paid and settled. A common example is commission payable, referred to in Section 18.1 above.

Let us use this as an example. Our financial year ends on December 31st, 19.., but commission payable to our sales representatives is payable on the 15th day of each month for sales to the end of the previous month. On December 31st the Commission Paid Account looks as shown in Fig. 18.8. The sum due on January 1st is shown, and it was of course paid on January 15th to various representatives. Similar payments were made in February, March, etc., but at the end of the year the payment made in December was for sales up to the end of the previous month (November). We now have to adjust for this by carrying to the Profit and Loss Account the full figure (including the sum payable on January 15th for commission in sales during December; let us imagine this sum due to be £929.25). The resulting journal entry will mean that Profit and Loss Account is debited with £12 750.75, which is therefore credited to Commission Paid Account. This is shown in Fig. 18.9. This nominal (Loss) account now becomes temporarily a liability account, showing how much is owed to our sales representatives. It will therefore appear on the Balance Sheet shown as a Current Liability (see Fig. 18.10).

COMMISSION PAID ACCOUNT L.324

19..			£	19..		£
Jan. 15	Bank	C.B.17	956.50	Jan. 1	Commission due on Dec. 31st	956.50
Feb.–Dec.						
(Various payments) (shown this way to save space)			11 821.50			

Fig. 18.8. Commission Paid Account waiting to be adjusted.

COMMISSION PAID ACCOUNT L.324

19..			£	19..		£
Jan. 15	Bank	C.B.17	956.50	Jan. 1	Commission due on Dec. 31st	956.50
Feb.–Dec.						
(Various payments)			11 821.50	Dec. 31	Profit and Loss Account	12 750.75
Dec. 31	Balance C/d		929.25			
			£13 707.25			£13 707.25
				19..		£
				Jan. 1	Commission due on Dec. 31st	929.25

Fig. 18.9. A nominal account that has temporarily become a liability.

BALANCE SHEET
(*as at December 31st, 19..*)

Current Liabilities		
Commission due to Salesmen	929.25	

Fig. 18.10. An accrued expense appearing on the Balance Sheet.

As with all adjustments, we have achieved a double aim. We have brought the charge against the profits for Commission Paid to our representatives to the correct figure for the year, so that full account is taken for the loss suffered in this respect in the trading period. We have also produced a correct Balance Sheet which reveals the exact situation with regards to the firm's liabilities, since we have included the money owing to the representatives.

What effect does this credit balance have next year? On January 15th we shall pay the representatives £929.25, which will mean a credit entry in the Cash Account (or Bank Account) and a debit entry on the Commission Paid Account. This debit entry will be cancelled out by the balance carried down on

January 1st, so that the £929.25 will not be charged to the Profit and Loss Account next year. It has already been charged to Profit and Loss Account as shown above.

18.6 Adjustments No. 4—Accrued Receipts Due to the Firm

Expenses may have accrued that we owe to other firms, but clearly the reverse can also be true. Receipts that the firm should have received for goods or services supplied this year may still be outstanding at the end of the year. It would be unfair in principle to let next year receive the benefit of this year's work. We should include these profits, even if they have not actually arrived, as if they had done so. This means we must adjust our Final Accounts. Rent Received is a good example of this type of adjustment. Many firms sublet spare rooms in their buildings to smaller businesses and thus earn valuable rent. If such a subtenant is in arrears with his rent, and we feel quite sure he will pay, this rent should be included. What is needed in the Profit and Loss Account is a full year's rent from the subtenant, even if he has not paid in full.

Example 18.1. P. Brown sublet a room to Homeless at a rent of £195 per quarter, payable in arrears: Homeless paid rent on March 27th, June 29th, and September 30th, but had not paid his next quarter due December 31st. Show the Rent Received Account for the year, after transferring the year's rent to the Profit and Loss Account. Homeless is deemed to be reliable.

Clearly the profit for the year on this tenancy is £780 and this figure should be carried to the Profit and Loss Account. The Rent Received Account will therefore look as follows:

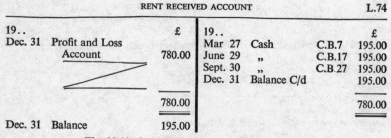

RENT RECEIVED ACCOUNT L.74

		£				£
19..			19..			
Dec. 31	Profit and Loss Account	780.00	Mar 27	Cash	C.B.7	195.00
			June 29	„	C.B.17	195.00
			Sept. 30	„	C.B.27	195.00
			Dec. 31	Balance C/d		195.00
		780.00				780.00
Dec. 31	Balance	195.00				

Fig. 18.11. A profit that has accrued as an asset.

This balance will appear as a current asset on the Balance Sheet.

18.7 Exercises: Accrued Expenses and Accrued Receipts

1. P. Carter, a retailer, sublets the flat over his shop at an annual rent of £800.00 payable quarterly in arrear. During the year the tenant paid rent due from him on March 23rd, June 25th, and September 30th, but at December 31st had not paid the quarter's rent due. Show the Rent Account in P. Carter's Ledger, after the preparation of his Profit and Loss Account for the year.

(RSA—Adapted)

2. From the following information prepare the Electricity Account in the Ledger of L. Welsh, a manufacturer:

Amount due at January 1st, 19..	64.35
Payments during the year	
January 15th	64.35
April 20th	54.25
July 17th	42.35
October 15th	47.55

The bill for electricity supplied during the three months ended December 31st was £82.50 and not paid until January 19th, 19... Balance the account on December 31st, 19...

(RSA—Adapted)

3. At January 1st, 19.., T. Tennant owed a quarter's rent, £200.00 in respect of business premises that he occupied. During the next twelve months he paid £200.00 by cheque on each of the following dates: January 4th, March 26th, June 25th, and December 27th.

(*a*) Prepare Tennant's Rent Account as it would appear after his Profit and Loss Account for the year ending December 31st, 19.., had been drawn up.

(*b*) What entry relating to rent should appear in his Balance Sheet dated December 31st, 19..?

(RSA—Adapted

4. H. & C. Ltd erect lifts and repair them. Their Repairs Revenue Account has a debit balance of £728.00 at January 1st, 19.., for repairs effected the previous year and not yet paid for. During the year £9 878.60 was paid by customers for repairs work, and at December 31st it was calculated that £1 020.45 was outstanding for repairs already executed. Show the Repairs Revenue Account for the year, after transferring the correct profit to the Trading Account.

Show also the entry in the Balance Sheet as at December 31st for the Repairs Account.

18.8 Exercises: Final Accounts Exercises including Payments in Advance and Accrued Expenses

1. Here is the Trial Balance of Gerard Eliasson on December 31st, 19... You are asked to prepare his Trading Account and Profit and Loss Account for the year, and his Balance Sheet as at this date, bearing in mind the adjustments given below the Trial Balance.

TRIAL BALANCE
(as at December 31st, 19..)

	Dr. £	Cr. £
Cash in Hand	27.50	
Cash at Bank	2 465.00	
Purchases and Sales	8 248.25	13 612.50
Returns—In and Out	112.25	48.25
Stock at January 1st, 19..	780.00	
Wages	450.00	
Salaries	580.00	
Light and Heat	420.00	
Commission Received		650.25
Rent Received		130.00
Carried forward	13 083.00	14 441.00

Brought forward	13 083.00	14 441.00
Telephone Expenses	120.50	
Insurance	250.00	
Motor Vehicles	1 250.00	
Land and Buildings	4 000.00	
Plant and Machinery	1 400.00	
Loan from Southern Bank		3 000.00
Interest Paid	150.50	
Capital		2 813.00
	£20 254.00	£20 254.00

Notes

(*a*) At December 31st, 19. ., stock was valued at £1 250.00.
(*b*) Insurance has been paid in advance for 19. . £50.00
(*c*) Interest is due on the loan from the bank £30.00

(East Anglian Examination Board—Adapted)

2. Prepare a Trading Account, Profit and Loss Accounts, and Balance Sheet from B. Murray's Trial Balance as at March 31st, 19. . .

	Dr. £	Cr. £
Capital (B. Murray)		5 000.00
Cash	25.00	
Bank	11 075.00	
Premises	2 000.00	
Motor Vehicles	850.00	
Plant and Machinery	1 270.00	
Factory Wages	866.50	
Office Salaries	735.25	
Factory Light and Heat	124.50	
Office Light and Heat	38.50	
Commission Received		594.00
Loan from R. Cambridge		2 406.00
Office Expenses	27.25	
Stationery	164.00	
Discount Allowed and Received	27.00	36.75
Purchases and Sales	7 246.00	18 294.75
Sales Returns and Purchases Returns	124.00	146.75
Drawings (B. Murray)	600.00	
Stock at April 1st, 19. .	1 320.00	
Debtors and Creditors	2 136.50	2 279.75
Carriage In	100.00	
Carriage Out	28.50	
	£28 758.00	£28 758.00

Stock at the end of the year was valued at £1 400.00. £43.50 is owing for factory wages and is to be included in the above accounts. Commission amounting to £26.00 has not yet been received, but is to be included as part of the year's profits.

3. Mrs Brown runs a small clothing factory and on December 31st, 19.., takes out the following Trial Balance. From it prepare her Trading Account, Profit and Loss Account, and Balance Sheet. There are some adjustments given below.

	Dr.	Cr.
	£	£
Stock at January 1st, 19..	1 800.00	
Purchases and Sales	42 300.00	58 725.00
Returns—In and Out	125.00	1 300.00
Carriage In	100.50	
Carriage Out	265.50	
Factory Wages	3 200.50	
Factory Light and Heat	400.75	
Land and Buildings	7 500.00	
Plant and Machinery	6 500.00	
Motor Vehicles	1 800.00	
Debtors and Creditors	2 400.25	1 800.50
Office Expenses	230.00	
Office Salaries	5 370.50	
Commission Paid	400.00	
Commission Received		40.50
Drawings	5 000.00	
Cash	850.00	
Cash at Bank	2 450.00	
Capital		13 827.00
Mortgage on Premises		5 000.00
	£80 693.00	£80 693.00

Closing stock was valued at £4 270.00.
Wages due amounted to £100.00.
An amount is owing for office expenses £30.00.
A sum is due to Mrs Brown for commission amounting to £26.50.

4. Prepare a Trial Balance from the following balances extracted from the books of R. Lasham on March 31st, 19.., and then produce a Trading Account, a Profit and Loss Account, and a Balance Sheet:

Discount Allowed	21.00
Discount Received	26.75
Returns Inward	55.75
Returns Outward	30.00
Purchases	700.00
Sales	1 200.00
Bank Overdraft	125.50
Creditors	140.00
Debtors	545.50
Cash in Hand	10.00

(cont'd)

Rent and Rates	80.75
Premises (Freehold)	2 500.00
Stock at April 1st, 19..	350.00
Machinery	1 000.00
Carriage Charges on Sales	69.25
Capital Account	4 850.00
Office Wages	1 263.00
Travellers' Salaries	500.00
Drawings Account	440.00
Commission Received	1 163.00

You should also take into account the following adjustments:

(*a*) Rent and rates due £16.25.
(*b*) Office wages due £17.00.
(*c*) Travellers' salaries paid in advance £50.00.
(*d*) Commission received in advance £17.00.
(*e*) The stock on hand at March 31st amounted to £467.00.

18.9 Adjustments No. 5—Bad Debts

One of the important figures on a Balance Sheet is the Sundry Debtors figure. This shows how much our debtors owe us, and naturally appears on the assets side of the Balance Sheet. At the end of the financial year, before the debtors' figure is brought into the Balance Sheet, all debts should be scrutinised to see whether they are in fact good debts. If we leave a bad debtor on our books, and pretend that the debt is good, we are breaking both our rules. Rule 1 said that we must admit and write off every loss that has been suffered in the year. Rule 2 says we must have an honest Balance Sheet. Neither rule will be observed if we allow a bad debt to persist in the new year.

Any debt revealed in our scrutiny as being bad should be written off to the Bad Debts Account as already described in Chapter 13 (see page 196). This will leave us with a true valuation of the debtors on our Balance Sheet, and the Bad Debts Account will be written off the profits, so that the full loss for the year has been accepted.

18.10 Adjustments No. 6—Provision for Bad Debts

We may have achieved a true debtors' figure, but is it also a 'fair' view? Even the best debtor can become a bad debtor if fate knocks unkindly on his door. Someone will die, or be maimed for life, or become seriously ill, and his affairs will deteriorate over the next few months. Every business suffers a percentage of bad debts, and the average businessman knows roughly what percentage of bad debts is normal for his type of business.

If we intend to be perfectly accurate in our figure for the debtors, we should adjust for this expected percentage of bad debts. This is one of the finer points of book-keeping and the student should follow this example with care.

Example 18.2. R. Brown's debtors total £4 260.00 and it is usual in his trade for 5 per cent of debts to prove to be bad. Brown decides to provide this amount out of his profits for the year.

Method: 5 per cent of £4 260.00 = £213.00. Brown must write off £213.00 from his profits as shown in Fig. 18.12.

PROFIT AND LOSS ACCOUNT L.198

Provision for Bad Debts	213.00	Gross Profit	8 194.00

Fig. 18.12. Providing for bad debts that have not yet occurred.

This means he must debit the Profit and Loss Account. But which account must be credited? Will Jones die, or Smith, or Bryant? Will Higgins get ill, or will it be Morris? Clearly Brown cannot tell, and yet he has to credit some account. The solution to the problem is to credit a nominal account, the Provision for Bad Debts Account. This account is best regarded as a liability to the proprietor. It is his profits that have been taken and tucked away in this Provision Account where he cannot spend them. When bad debts occur in the first few months of the year, the profits set aside from last year will offset the loss suffered, so that the new year is not suffering last year's bad debts.

The really ingenious part of this arrangement is the way it is dealt with on the Balance Sheet. We have charged the £213.00 to the Profit and Loss Account so that the current year has suffered the loss. We have this credit balance on the Provision for Bad Debts Account. As it is a credit balance, we should expect it to appear on the liabilities side of the Balance Sheet, as shown in Fig. 18.13.

BALANCE SHEET
(*as at December 31st, 19..*)

		CURRENT ASSETS	
Provision for Bad Debts	213.00	Debtors	4 260.00

Fig. 18.13. Provision for bad debts is a liability.

In fact, it is much better style to take it over to the assets side as a deduction from the asset, debtors. If we do this we make it perfectly clear to anyone reading the Balance Sheet that although the debtors' balances actually total £4 260.00, we expect to collect only £4 047.00. This gives a 'true and fair view' of the asset, debtors.

BALANCE SHEET
(*as at December 31st, 19..*)

	CURRENT ASSETS		
	Debtors	4 260.00	
	Less Provision	213.00	
			4 047.00

Fig. 18.14. The best way to display debtors.

18.11 What Happens to the Provision for Bad Debts in the Next Year?

Consider the present provision as shown in the last section. It has a credit balance. It represents a liability to the proprietor for profits earned, but retained in the business in case bad debts occur.

Next year we shall suffer some bad debts, and at the end of the year the provision we shall need will certainly not be £213.00. It would be a very rare chance that our debtors' figure for one year should be exactly the same as the

PROVISION FOR BAD DEBTS L.199

			19..		£
			Jan. 1	Balance	213.00

Fig. 18.15. The Provision for Bad Debts Account.

debtors' figure twelve months later. As the provision is tied to the debtors' figure it must vary from year to year.

Method 1

The simplest way to deal with this problem is to write the bad debts off the Provision Account and not off the Profit and Loss Account, on December 31st next. We can then make a new charge to profits for the new provision. There are three possibilities, one of which is highly improbable:

(*a*) The bad debts could be less than the provision at present of £213.00.
(*b*) The bad debts could be exactly £213.00.
(*c*) The bad debts could be more than the present provision.

Example 18.3. (*a*) The next year R. Brown suffers bad debts of £132.00 and on December 31st his debtors balances are £3 850.00.

If we write the bad debts off against the provision and not against the Profit and Loss Account we will debit them in the Provision Account as we close off the Bad Debts Account. This figure of £132.00 deducted from £213.00 leaves a balance of £81.00 still in the Provision Account.

This year we need 5 per cent of £3 850.00, which is £192.50. As we already have £81.00 in the provision for Bad Debts Account, we need to take only £111.50 from the profits in the Profit and Loss Account. When this sum is debited to Profit and Loss Account and credited to Provision Account we have an account which balances off with exactly the right provision.

PROVISION FOR BAD DEBTS ACCOUNT L.199

19..		£	19..		£
Dec. 31	Bad Debts	132.00	Jan. 1	Balance	213.00
31	Balance C/d	192.50	Dec. 31	Profit and Loss Account	111.50
		£324.50			£324.50
			Jan. 1	Balance B/d	192.50

Fig. 18.16. The old provision changed to the new provision figure (example (*a*)).

(*b*) Too unlikely to be worth illustrating.

(*c*) Going a further year with this account, R. Brown suffers serious bad debts due to an economic slump. The total bad debts are £426.50 and his roll of debtors totals £5 900.00. Brown decides to increase the provision to 10 per cent of the debtors' figure. This time the bad debts transferred to the Provision for Bad Debts Account use up the entire provision of £192.50 and leave an unsatisfied loss of £234.00. This will have to be written off the Profit and Loss Account. As we also need a new provision of £590.00 (10 per cent of the debtors), we have to write off £824.00 from the Profit and Loss Account into the Provision for Bad Debts Account. This will then have exactly the right balance for the new provision.

PROVISION FOR BAD DEBTS ACCOUNT L.199

19..		£	19..		£
Dec. 31	Bad Debts	132.00	Jan. 1	Balance	213.00
31	Balance C/d	192.50	Dec. 31	Profit and Loss Account	111.50
		£324.50			£324.50
Year 2		£	Year 2		£
Dec. 31	Bad Debts	426 50	Jan. 1	Balance B/d	192.50
31	Balance	590.00	Dec. 31	Profit and Loss Account	824.00
		£1 016.50			£1 016.50
			Jan 1	Balance	590.00

Fig. 18.17. The old provision changed to the new provision figure (example (*c*)).

Method 2

An alternative way to deal with the bad debts next year is to keep the Bad Debts Account and the Provision for Bad Debts Account quite separate. At the end of the year the total of the Bad Debts Account is written off to the Profit and Loss Account by a closing journal entry.

The Provision for Bad Debts Account is now adjusted to the new provision. In Fig. 18.16 the old provision was changed from £213.00 to £192.50. Since Bad Debts are being treated separately from the Provision for Bad Debts, we now have:

PROVISION FOR BAD DEBTS ACCOUNT L.199

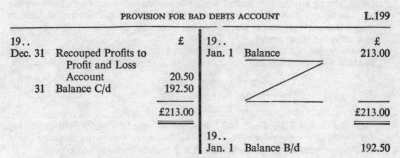

19..		£	19..		£
Dec. 31	Recouped Profits to Profit and Loss Account	20.50	Jan. 1	Balance	213.00
31	Balance C/d	192.50			
		£213.00			£213.00
			19..		
			Jan. 1	Balance B/d	192.50

Fig. 18.18. The old provision changed to the new figure (example (*a*)).

Note that the Profit and Loss Account will suffer the same burden as before, but in a different way, as shown in Fig. 18.19.

METHOD 1: PROFIT AND LOSS ACCOUNT L.175

19..		£			
Dec. 31	Provision for Bad Debts	111.50			

METHOD 2: PROFIT AND LOSS ACCOUNT L.175

19..		£	19..		£
Dec. 31	Bad Debts	132.00	Dec. 31	Recovered Provision for Bad Debts	20.50

Fig. 18.19. The effect on the Profit and Loss Account.

18.12 Exercises: Bad Debts and Provision for Bad Debts

1. (*a*) At January 1st, 19. ., the balance of the Provision for Bad Debts Account of J. Moore stood at £250.00. During that year bad debts amounting to £96.00 were incurred and at December 31st a balance of £280.00 was carried forward. In the next year £35.00 was received in respect of a debt previously written off and a loss of £122.00 for bad debts was suffered, but Moore decided to reduce his provision to £270.00.

   You are to prepare the Provision for Bad Debts Account for years 1 and 2.

   (*b*) Assuming that at the end of the second year Moore's debtors amounted to £5 400.00, give the entry in the Balance Sheet of that date in respect of them.

   (RSA—Adapted)

2. The balance sheet of J. Wilson, dated January 1st, 19. ., gave his total debtors as £6 500.00 and there was a provision of 8 per cent against bad debts. During the following year the bad debts written off amounted to £486.00, but a debt of £126.00 written off in a previous year was paid in full.

   At December 31st, a year later, Wilson's debtors were £7 000.00 and he decided to increase his provision to 10 per cent of that amount.

   You are to prepare the Bad Debts and Provision Accounts for the year 19. ., and to show the relevant entries in the Profit and Loss Account and in the Balance Sheet dated December 31st, 19...

   (RSA—Adapted)

3. The following information relates to the wholesale business of Tupman. Show the account or accounts which you would expect to find in his Nominal Ledger to record the information for the year ended December 31st, 19... (Note: Personal accounts are not required.)

   January 1st, 19. .. The provision for bad and doubtful debts amounts to £425.00. The following debts were written off as irrecoverable on December 31st, 19. .:

T. Wardle	27.50
W. Jingle	3.24
K. Trotter	18.75

   On September 18th, 19. ., £4.12 was received in respect of a debt previously written off as irrecoverable. When the Final Accounts were being prepared it was decided to increase the provision for bad and doubtful debts to £480.00.

   (RSA—Adapted)

4. At December 31st, 19. ., a firm's debtors totalled £2 600.00 and its Provision for Bad Debts Account amounted to £120.00. It was decided to write off as irrecoverable debts of £140.00, and to carry forward a provision of 5 per cent of the debtors.

   Prepare the Provision Account for bad and doubtful debts, the entries in the

Profit and Loss Account, and the entry for debtors on the Balance Sheet at December 31st, 19...

(RSA—Adapted)

5. On January 1st, 19.., the Sales Ledger of T. & Co. showed the following debtors:

Smith	£250.00
Brown	128.00
Jones	22.00
Robinson	230.00
Williams	140.00

T. & Co. had a Bad Debts Provision equal to 10 per cent of the total debts outstanding. Trading continued during the year 19.. with these and other customers, except that there were no sales to Jones and Robinson; the former made no payment in respect of the amount due from him, whilst Robinson paid only £200.00 during the year. On December 31st, 19.., (*a*) it was found that the Sales Ledger debit balances, including those due from Jones and Robinson, totalled £952.00; (*b*) it was decided to write off as bad debts the amounts then due from Jones and Robinson; and (*c*) it was decided to adjust the Bad Debts Provision to 8 per cent of the remaining debts.

You are asked to show the entries recording the above in the appropriate impersonal Ledger Accounts for the financial year ended December 31st, 19...., including the entries in the firm's Profit and Loss Account for the year.

18.13 Adjustment No. 7—Provisions for Discounts on Debtors

Another source of possible misconception about debtors arises from the discounts that may be taken by our debtors if they pay promptly. If we are allowing debtors to deduct discount, the valuation placed on debtors on the Balance Sheet will be misleading if we do not provide for this discount.

The provision for discount is very similar indeed to the provision for bad debts, but when calculating the amount to be provided we use the **Net Debtors** figure, that is **Debtors less Provision for Bad Debts.** Since we have provided for the bad debts these debtors will not qualify for discount, as they are not going to pay promptly.

Example 18.4. R. Brown's debtors total £4 260.00 on December 31st, 19... He provided for 5 per cent of possible bad debts and a further 2½ per cent of discount to be allowed to debtors.

Calculation: 5 per cent of Bad Debts = £213.00. This figure gives a net figure of £4 047.00

2½ per cent of £4 047.00 = £101.18

The journal entry will be:

19..			£	£
Dec. 31	Profit and Loss Account Dr.	L.175	101.18	
	Provision for Discount A/c	L.25		101.18
	Being 2½% of Net Debtors provided to cover discounts			

Fig. 18.20. Providing for discount on debtors.

The Balance Sheet entry for debtors will now be as shown in Fig. 18.21.

BALANCE SHEET (ASSETS SIDE ONLY)
(as at December 31st, 19..)

CURRENT ASSETS		
Debtors		4 260.00
Less Bad Debts Provision	213.00	
and Discount Provision	101.18	
		314.18
		3 945.82

Fig. 18.21. Providing a 'true' figure for debtors.

Provision for Discount on Creditors. It could well be argued that if we are reducing the sums due to the business from debtors by providing for discount on debtors, we should also reduce the amount due to creditors by adjusting for the discounts we shall ourselves receive when we pay them. If we intend to pay promptly, it seems certain that we shall receive these discounts in due course.

This is an example of an area which is neither black, nor white, but only grey. To refuse to take 'Discount Received' in advance as a profit when we have just taken 'Discount Allowed' in advance as a loss seems to offend against the *consistency concept* described in Chapter 16. On the other hand the *prudence concept* also described in Chapter 16 holds that the prudent businessman always accepts at once a loss which he knows he will suffer, but does not accept a profit he fully expects to make until he actually makes it. 'There's many a slip, twixt the cup and the lip' says the old proverb. The 'prudence concept' is so strongly ingrained in business experience that it over-rides the 'consistency concept' in this particular case.

18.14 Adjustments No. 8—Depreciation of Assets

Depreciation is the reduction in value of an asset as a result of fair wear and tear. As an asset loses value we reduce the book valuation of it in line with our estimate of the loss. This can be done in several different ways.

The accounting principle which motivates accountants to try different methods of depreciation is that we are seeking in our accounting to achieve a 'true and fair view' of the position of the business. As far as limited companies are concerned in Great Britain, this is positively required by law. The Companies Act requires all businesses to keep accounts in such a way as to give a 'true and fair view' of the company's affairs. This view requires two things:

(*a*) The assets must be valued on the books at a fair value so far as we can estimate it.

(*b*) If a loss has been suffered it must be charged against the profits—to do otherwise would overstate the profitability of the business.

Applying these two rules to the problem of depreciation, we see that if an asset wears out the loss suffered as a result of wear and tear must be written off the profits. At the same time the asset will be reduced in value to show only its present value now that it has been partly worn out.

There are about eight different methods of calculating depreciation, but we need consider only the three commonest methods. These are:

(*a*) The straight-line or equal-instalment method.
(*b*) The diminishing-balance method.
(*c*) The revaluation method.

Other points of interest are:

(*d*) The amortisation of leases.
(*e*) How to leave assets on the books at cost price.

(*a*) The Straight-Line or Equal-Instalment Method

The accountant first calculates the amount of the annual charge for depreciation necessary to reduce the asset to its scrap value, or residual value by equal annual amounts, over the lifetime of the asset. To do this we use the following formula:

$$\text{Annual charge} = \frac{\text{Cost price less Scrap value}}{\text{Estimated lifetime in years}}$$

Example 18.5. A motor vehicle is purchased for £2 750.00 on January 1st. It is estimated that it will need replacing in four years and will then fetch £750.00 on trade-in. Using the formula, we have

$$\text{Annual charge} = \frac{2\,750.00 - 750.00}{4}$$
$$= \frac{2\,000.00}{4}$$
$$= \underline{\underline{£500.00}}$$

The asset will be depreciated by four equal instalments of £500.00 and will then be reduced on the books to a value of £750.00.

The depreciation journal entry will appear each year as shown in Fig. 18.22. The effect of these entries on the Motor Vehicles Account is shown in Fig. 18.23.

19..			£	£
Dec. 31	Depreciation Account Dr.	L.271	500.00	
	Motor Vehicles Account	L.11		500.00
	Being depreciation written off at this date			

Fig. 18.22. A journal entry for depreciation.

From the point of view of the Final Accounts the Depreciation Account is a nominal account where all sorts of amounts for the depreciation of various assets will be collected together. At the end of the adjustment period, when all these items have been collected together, the total of the Depreciation Account will be cleared by a closing entry transferring the loss to Profit and Loss Account.

Advantages and Disadvantages of the Straight-Line Method

Advantages: (*a*) It is straightforward and easily understood. (*b*) It writes the asset down over a definite period to a predicted minimum value below which the business would not normally keep the asset.

MOTOR VEHICLES ACCOUNT L.11

Year 1			£	Year 1			£
Jan. 1	Rex Garages	J.1	2 750.00	Dec. 31	Depreciation	L.17	500.00
				31	Balance C/d		2 250.00
			£2 750.00				£2 750.00
Year 2			£	Year 2			£
Jan. 1	Balance B/d		2 250.00	Dec. 31	Depreciation	L.17	500.00
				31	Balance C/d		1 750.00
			£2 250.00				£2 250.00
Year 3			£	Year 3			£
Jan. 1	Balance B/d		1 750.00	Dec. 31	Depreciation	L.17	500.00
				31	Balance C/d		1 250.00
			£1 750.00				£1 750.00
Year 4			£	Year 4			£
Jan. 1	Balance B/d		1 250.00	Dec. 31	Depreciation	L.17	500.00
				31	Balance C/d		750 00
			£1 250.00				£1 250.00
Year 5			£				
Jan. 1	Balance B/d		750.00				

Fig. 18.23. Depreciation by the straight-line method.

Disadvantages: (*a*) Whenever new assets are bought or old assets are sold the depreciation for the asset must be recalculated. (*b*) There is an increasing charge to the Profit and Loss Account over the years, because the repairs on an old machine increase. As the depreciation charge is steady the total cost—depreciation plus repairs—must increase over the years. This offends against the 'consistency concept', which holds that we should try to even out the burden to Profit and Loss Account over the years from the use of the same asset. (*c*) There is no provision made for replacing the asset when it is worn out.

(*b*) The Diminishing-Balance Method

Under this method the asset is depreciated by a fixed percentage every year on the diminishing balance of the account. This is a very simple method since recalculation is not required when additions or sales take place during the year.

Example 18.6. A firm's depreciation policy for motor vehicles requires the book-keeper to write 25 per cent off the diminishing balance of the asset every year. Show the Depreciation Account for a motor vehicle valued at £2 750 bought on January 1st, 19. . (Calculation to nearest £1).

The Motor Vehicles Account will appear as follows:

MOTOR VEHICLES ACCOUNT L.11

Year 1			£	Year 1			£
Jan. 1	Rex Garages	J.1	2 750.00	Dec. 31	Depreciation	L.17	688.00
				31	Balance C/d		2 062.00
			£2 750.00				£2 750.00
Year 2			£	Year 2			£
Jan. 1	Balance B/d		2 062.00	Dec. 31	Depreciation	L.17	516.00
				31	Balance C/d		1 546.00
			£2 062.00				£2 062.00
Year 3			£	Year 3			£
Jan. 1	Balance B/d		1 546.00	Dec. 31	Depreciation	L.17	387.00
				31	Balance C/d		1 159.00
			£1 546.00				£1 546.00
Year 4			£	Year 4			£
Jan. 1	Balance B/d		1 159.00	Dec. 31	Depreciation	L.17	290.00
				31	Balance C/d		869.00
			£1 159.00				£1 159.00
Year 5			£				
Jan. 1	Balance B/d		869.00				

Fig. 18.24. Depreciation by the diminishing-balance method.

Advantages and Disadvantages of the Diminishing Balance Method

Advantages: (*a*) It is straightforward and recalculations are not required when new assets are purchased or old assets sold. (*b*) The charge against the profits for the use of the asset is more even over the years, since the diminishing charge for depreciation offsets the increasing charge for repairs.

Disadvantages: (*a*) The asset is never completely written off. (*b*) Where a very short life is normal for an asset the percentage method is unsatisfactory, since the percentage required to write the asset off is very high. For instance, to write off £100.00 completely over three years requires a 90 per cent depreciation rate, i.e. 90.00 the first year, 9.00 the second year, and 0.90 the next year. This charge is so uneven as to be unsatisfactory. (*c*) Again there is no provision for replacing the asset at the end of its useful life.

(*c*) The Revaluation Method

With some businesses it is quite impossible to treat depreciation by the normal method. For example, a farmer can hardly say with certainty, 'This old cow has declined by 20 per cent this year.' She may have had two fine calves. Where a firm has many loose tools—for example, shovels, spades, hoes, and rakes for a landscape gardening firm—it is often difficult to depreciate these items.

The sensible method in these cases is the revaluation method. This may result in a loss, a depreciation charge, or a profit—an appreciation in value caused by a rise in the asset's value.

Example 18.7. Farmer Giles's herd was valued at £12 725.00 on January 1st by the local valuer called in for the purpose. On December 31st the same valuer estimated the herd to be worth £12 065.00. Show the depreciation entry and the Herd Account.

These entries are shown in Figs. 18.25 and 18.26.

19..				
Dec. 31	Depreciation Account Dr.	L.7	660.00	
	Herd Account	L.5		660.00
	Being decrease in value of herd during year			

Fig. 18.25. Depreciation on revaluation.

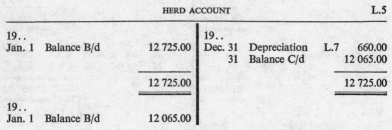

HERD ACCOUNT L.5

19..			19..				
Jan. 1	Balance B/d	12 725.00	Dec. 31	Depreciation	L.7	660.00
			31	Balance C/d		12 065.00
		12 725.00				12 725.00
19..						
Jan. 1	Balance B/d	12 065.00				

Fig. 18.26. An asset account that has been revalued.

(*d*) Amortising Leases—a Special Case of the Straight-Line Method

When we purchase the lease of a property, we purchase the right to live in that property for a given number of years, after which time it is returnable to the landlord. The commonest period for a long-term lease is 99 years, but some leases are now being given for 999 years. Short leases are very common too.

If we purchase a lease for £15 000.00 which has 20 years to run, we should write off one twentieth of its value every year, i.e. £750.00 each year. This is called *amortising the lease*—that is, writing off the dead part of the life of the lease. *It is a special case of the straight-line method of depreciation, but more advanced treatments are possible.*

(*e*) Leaving Assets on the Books at Cost Price

A change has come over the established methods of depreciation since the Companies Act of 1948, which introduced the requirement for companies that assets must be shown on the Balance Sheet at 'cost price less accumulated depreciation to date'. In Figs. 18.22 and 18.23 we saw that the depreciation is written off the asset, so that the book value of the asset quite rightly reduces as the years pass. In these circumstances with long-lived assets we may lose sight of what the asset originally cost and thus be unable to comply with the requirement of the Companies Act outlined above.

One way of overcoming this difficulty is to credit the depreciation, not in the

Asset Account, but in a separate Provision for Depreciation Account, which collects the depreciation over the years, leaving the asset on the books in the Asset Account at cost price. The two accounts would look like this at the end of the third year, using the example illustrated previously in Fig. 18.23. The result is shown in Fig. 18.27 below.

MOTOR VEHICLES ACCOUNT L.11

19..							
Jan. 1	Rex Garages	J.1	2 750.00				

PROVISION FOR DEPRECIATION ON MOTOR VEHICLES ACCOUNT L.12

				19..			
				Dec. 31	Motor Vehicles		500.00
				19..			
				Dec. 31	" "		500.00
				19..			
				Dec. 31	" "		500.00

Fig. 18.27. Leaving the asset on the books at cost price.

The value of the asset at any given time is therefore the book-value (i.e. cost price), less the accumulated depreciation to date. In this case it would be:

	£
Cost price	2 750.00
Less depreciation	1 500.00
Present value of asset	1 250.00

which is the same as the balance on the Asset Account shown in Fig. 18.23 at the end of the third year.

18.15 Adjustments No. 9—Goodwill and Writing off Goodwill

Goodwill is an extra valuation placed upon a going concern over and above the value of the assets forming it. It is paid by the buyer to the seller of a business in expectation of profits to be made, which result directly from the hard work of the former owner. It is sensible that the buyer should pay for the assets, premises, stock, etc., which he takes over. Why should he pay an extra sum for goodwill?

Imagine that Jones buys Smith's business and opens shop on January 1st. The doorbell rings as Roberts, a regular customer of Smith's, enters the shop. 'Twenty cigarettes please, Joe. Hullo—where is Joe?' Jones will explain that Joe has retired from business but that he will be very happy to serve him in future. The profit on that packet of cigarettes came from Smith's hard work and the goodwill extended him by the people in the area.

Goodwill—an Intangible Asset

Goodwill is often called an 'intangible asset'. You cannot actually touch this asset, but it really does exist. The people who had business relations with

Smith will continue to deal with Jones because they are used to the idea that this shop is efficiently run. It is for this intangible benefit that Jones pays a lump sum of money as compensation to the previous owner. The value of goodwill is a matter for negotiation between the parties when a business changes hands. The seller will demand a good price for the goodwill, the buyer will offer less, and by a process of haggling the bargain will finally be struck.

Writing off Goodwill

Since goodwill is not a real asset in the normal meaning of the word 'real', it is frequently written off over the first few years of the business's new lease of life. There is no necessity to write off goodwill if the business is making steady profits, since steady profits are a sign of public goodwill. The goodwill must therefore still be as valuable as, or more valuable perhaps than, the original purchase value.

If goodwill is to be written down, then it cannot be written off the Profit and Loss Account, because it is not a revenue loss. It is a decision by the proprietor to reduce the stated value of his assets. This must be met out of his own pocket by a 'capital' loss—in other words, the amount written off cannot be put with other depreciation and written off the Profit and Loss Account. To do so would reduce the profits of the firm, and consequently the Inland Revenue's share of those profits. *Accountants say that a decision to write off goodwill is not a charge against the profits, but an appropriation of profit.* This means that it is a way of using up the profits after the net profit has been found in the Profit and Loss Account. Instead of giving all the net profit to the proprietor(s) we use some of it to extinguish goodwill, or a part of the goodwill.

It will therefore be debited as a 'capital' loss either to Capital Account or, in the case of a partnership or limited company, to an account we have not yet met called Appropriation Account (see page 286).

The journal entry will be as in Fig. 18.28 below.

19..				
Dec. 31	Capital Account Dr.		400.00	
	Goodwill Account			400.00
	Being Goodwill reduced at this date			

Fig. 18.28. Writing down the value of goodwill.

The Paradox of Goodwill

Accountants sometimes speak of the paradox of goodwill. A paradox is an apparent contradiction. We have on our books, when we take over a business, an asset at a high valuation called goodwill. In fact, the public bears us no goodwill at all, for they do not even know that we exist. As the years go by, if we adopt the policy of writing off the intangible asset by a series of appropriations of profit, our goodwill gradually reduces until it is written off completely. At the same time, the public have now learned to know us; they realise our goods or services are reliable and they now bear us some goodwill. Here is the paradox of goodwill: it is valued at a high figure on the books when it is worthless, and at nothing on the books when it is very valuable.

18.16 Exercises: Depreciation

1. On January 1st a firm bought a machine for £1 800.00. Its probable working life was estimated at 10 years and its probable scrap value at the end of that time at £200.00. It was decided to write off depreciation by the fixed instalment method. Show the Machinery Account for the first two years.

   (RSA—Adapted)

2. L. Jericho has a machine on his books which he purchased on July 1st, 19.., for £3 000.00. He depreciates it at a rate of 10 per cent per annum on December 31st of every year. In 19.. this is based on cost price, but in subsequent years it is based on the value at the start of the year (i.e. he uses the diminishing-balance method). Show the Machinery Account for years 1, 2, and 3, bringing down the balance each year.

   (East Anglian Examination Board—Adapted)

3. A and B, who set up in partnership as builders on January 31st, 19.., had a motor van the value of which was £1 200.00. On February 1st, 19.. (next day), the firm bought (for cash) a further motor van for £800.00 and a car for £1 600.00.

   It is decided to write off depreciation at 20 per cent per annum on the reducing balance system. On January 31st, two years later, the car was sold for £450.00 (cash).

   You are asked to prepare the Motor Vehicles Account as it would appear in the partnership books for each financial year ended January 31st, Year 1 and Year 2, showing the amount written off as depreciation each year.

4. 'Elfreda', a hairdresser, pays £7 000 for a lease of premises which is to last five years. Amortise the lease at the end of the first year.

5. B. Popular, who is in business as a contractor, purchased the business one year ago. Part of the purchase price was £2 800 for goodwill. Popular decides to write this off over a four-year period, as an appropriation of part of the profits made. Show (*a*) the journal entry and (*b*) the Goodwill Account for the year.

6. A. Farmer has a herd valued at £15 750.00 on March 31st, 19... One year later, when he has the herd revalued, it is only valued at £13 275.00. Show the journal entry for the depreciation, and the 'Herd Account' for the year, balanced off and brought down.

7. Gardening Ltd use great quantities of small tools whose working life is fairly short. All purchases of such tools are entered in the Loose Tools Account, but the stock of loose tools is valued on December 31st of each year. On January 1st, 19.., they were valued at £415.00. New tools to the value of £277.00 were added in the year, on June 30th. On December 31st the stock of loose tools to be carried forward to the next year was valued at £440.00. Show the journal entry for depreciation and the Loose Tools Account for the year.

18.17 Specimen Exercise to Final Accounts, with Adjustments

To conclude this chapter, it only remains to show how adjustments are dealt with (*a*) in real life and (*b*) in examination conditions.

Adjustments in Real Life

As regards the former, the answer is simple. Adjustments are dealt with in real life in the way described in this chapter, which may be listed as follows:

(i) After preparing the final Trial Balance for the year, decide which of the accounts on the Trial Balance need adjustment.

(ii) Decide the amount of adjustment required in each case, and thus determine the true figures to be used in the Trading Account, Profit and Loss Account and Balance Sheet.

(iii) Do the closing journal entries for the preparation of the Final Accounts, taking the adjustment into account in the process.

(iv) Post these closing journal entries to the ledger, thus preparing the Trading Account and Profit and Loss Account, whilst at the same time clearing up most of the nominal ledger accounts, except for those involved with adjustments. These accounts will have debit or credit balances as a result of the adjustments and thus become temporary assets or liabilities. They will therefore need to appear on the Balance Sheet.

(v) Finally prepare the Balance Sheet, in good style.

Adjustments in Examinations

In examinations it is usual to present the student with a Trial Balance as at the end of the financial year, and a list of adjustments to be taken into account. The student then does the adjustments in the course of drawing up the Final Accounts, showing by a series of indented figures what the adjustment was and how he arrived at the true final figures. Every adjustment gives rise to an entry in one of the final accounts (either the Trading Account or the Profit and Loss Account) but also causes the account concerned to have a small balance on it which must appear on the Balance Sheet. We therefore say 'Every adjustment appears twice', once in the Final Accounts and once on the Balance Sheet.

The reader should now follow the adjustments in the specimen exercise given below.

Example 18.8. The following trial balance was extracted from the books of T. Leyside, a trader, as at 31st December, 19..:

	£	£
Capital Account		27 600
Freehold Land and Buildings	25 250	
Furniture and Fittings	1 450	
Purchases	39 275	
Sales		86 418
Debtors and Creditors	5 200	6 324
Rates	236	
General expenses	3 428	
Salaries	13 550	
Drawings	2 350	
Bad Debts	450	
Balance at bank	20 452	
Provision for Doubtful Debts at January 1st, 19..		720
Discounts Allowed	320	
Discounts Received		680
Stock in Trade, January 1st, 19..	9 456	
Insurance	325	
	£121 742	£121 742

The following adjustments are to be taken into account:

(i) Stock in trade, December 31st, 19.., £10 750.
(ii) At December 31st, 19.., rates paid in advance amounted to £64.
(iii) Salaries outstanding at December 31st, 19.., £520.
(iv) The provision for doubtful debts is to be reduced to 10 per cent of the debtors.
(v) On January 1st, 19.., Leyside purchased a motor van which was partly for business use for £3 000 and furniture for the business costing £200. He paid for both with cheques drawn on his private bank account. No entries have been made in the books of the company recording these transactions. The car is to be regarded as half business and half domestic.
(vi) Provide £165 for depreciation of furniture and fittings and allow for depreciation on the motor van at the rate of 20 per cent per annum on cost.

You are required to prepare a trading and profit and loss account for the year 19.. and a balance sheet at December 31st, 19...

Notes on Adjustments

(*a*) As far as adjustment (ii) is concerned the true figure for rates for the year will be £236 − £64 = £172.

(*b*) When the outstanding salaries are included the correct figure for salaries for the year will be £13 550 + £520 = £14 070.

(*c*) Since the debtors' figure is £5 200 the bad debts provision has to be reduced to £520. This means that £200 (£720 − £520) previously tucked away in this provision can be restored to Profit and Loss Account as a profit.

(*d*) Half the value of the car (£1 500) and the new furniture (£200) have to be brought onto the books as new assets. The £1 700 to pay for these came from Leyside's private funds. It is therefore new capital contributed and must be credited to Capital Account.

(*e*) The two depreciation items will come in the Profit and Loss Account and reduce the value of Fixtures and Fittings by £165 and of Motor Vehicles by £300.

The solution of the Example is given as Fig. 18.29.

TRADING AND PROFIT AND LOSS ACCOUNT
(*for year ending December 31st, 19..*)

	£		£
Opening Stock	9 456	Sales	86 418
Purchases	39 275		
Total Stock Available	48 731		
Less Closing Stock	10 750		
Cost of Stock Sold	37 981		
Gross Profit	48 437		
	£86 418		£86 418

(*cont'd*)

Rates	236		Gross Profit	48 437
Less In Advance	64		Reclaimed Provision	
		172	for Bad Debts	200
General Expenses		3 428	Discount Received	680
Salaries	13 550			
Add Amount due	520		Total Profits	49 317
		14 070		
Bad Debts		450		
Discount Allowed		320		
Insurance		325		
Depreciation:				
Fixtures	165			
Motor Vehicle	300			
		465		
Total Expenses		19 230		
Net Profit		30 087		
		£49 317		£49 317

BALANCE SHEET
(*as at December 31st, 19..*)

		£				£
Capital (at start)		27 600	*Fixed Assets*			
Additions		1 700	Freehold Land and Buildings			25 250
			Fixtures and Fittings		1 450	
		29 300	Additions		200	
Net Profit	30 087					
Less Drawings	2 350				1 650	
		27 737	*Less* Depreciation		165	
						1 485
		57 037	Motor Vehicles		1 500	
			Less Depreciation		300	
						1 200
						27 935
Current Liabilities			*Current Assets*			
Creditors	6 324		Stock		10 750	
Salaries due	520		Debtors	5 200		
		6 844	*Less* Provn.	520		
					4 680	
			Balance at Bank		20 452	
			Rates in Advance		64	
						35 946
		£63 881				£63 881

Fig. 18.29. Final Accounts with adjustments.

18.18 Exercises: Final Accounts with adjustments

1. From the following abridged Trial Balance of M. Montgomery dated December 31st, 19. ., prepare his Profit and Loss Account for the year, and his Balance Sheet at that date. You should note that:

(*a*) Rates £20.00 were prepaid, and £50.00 was owing by Montgomery's tenant.
(*b*) The machinery balance is to be depreciated by 10 per cent and the additions by 5 per cent.
(*c*) £100.00 is to be written off the goodwill (debit to Capital Account).

TRIAL BALANCE
(*at December 31st, 19. .*)

	Dr.	Cr.
	£	£
Rates	200.00	
Salaries	1 284.00	
Heating, Lighting, etc.	176.00	
Insurance	49.00	
Advertising	260.00	
General Expenses	137.00	
Drawings	2 010.00	
Cash in Hand	16.00	
Trade Debtors	1 104.00	
Stock at December 31st, 19. .	2 618.00	
Machinery	4 000.00	
Machinery Additions	500.00	
Land and Buildings	12 000.00	
Bank	1 000.00	
Goodwill	500.00	
Gross Profit		6 026.00
Discount Received		135.00
Rent from Subtenant		1 150.00
Loan from Helpful Bank Ltd		3 150.00
Trade Creditors		1 393.00
Capital Account (January 1st, 19. .)		14 000 00
	£25 854.00	£25 854.00

2. After his Trading Account has been prepared for the year ended December 31st, 19.., a trader's position is as follows:

	Dr. £	Cr. £
Trading Account, Gross Profit		15 250.75
Plant and Machinery	8 290.00	
Stock at December 31st, 19..	410.50	
Debtors	625.75	
Creditors		1 180.25
Capital at January 1st, 19..		7 965.50
Discount Allowed	223.25	
Discount Received		183.50
Salaries and Office Expenses	6 160.00	
Rent, Rates, and Insurance	1 865.50	
Carriage Outwards	120.00	
Bad Debts	85.00	
Goodwill	1 035.00	
Drawings	2 850.00	
Cash at Bank	2 895.00	
Petty Cash	20.00	
	£24 580.00	£24 580.00

Draw up the trader's Profit and Loss Account for the year, and a Balance Sheet as at December 31st, 19.., taking into consideration:

(*a*) Depreciation on Plant and Machinery which is to be provided for at 10 per cent of its original cost, £12 000.00.

(*b*) Rent £1 400.00 a year, of which the quarterly instalment due December 25th, 19.., is unpaid.

(*c*) £335.00 to be appropriated for the reduction of goodwill (debit to Capital Account).

3. The following Trial Balance was extracted from the books of Donald Haig. You are required to draw up the Trading Account and Profit and Loss Account of the business for the year ending September 30th, 19.., and a Balance Sheet as at that date.

TRIAL BALANCE
(at September 30th, 19..)

	Dr. £	Cr. £
Stock at start on October 1st	4 200.00	
Purchases and Sales	12 386.50	26 286.00
Returns	186.00	682.50
Wages (enter in Trading Account)	6 536.75	
Carriage on Purchases	580.25	
Salaries	3 570.00	
Advertising	706.50	
Carriage on Sales	320.00	
Rates	528.50	
Heating and Lighting	619.00	
Bad Debts	599.00	
Insurance	78.00	
Debtors and Creditors	3 500.00	4 750.50
Capital		21 050.00
Drawings	3 600.00	
Cash in Hand	28.50	
Cash at Bank	130.00	
Goodwill	1 200.00	
Land and Buildings	14 000.00	
	£52 769.00	£52 769.00

You should take the following into account:

(*a*) The stock in hand on September 30th, 19.., was valued at £5 221.00
(*b*) The land and buildings are to be depreciated by 5 per cent.
(*c*) Salaries £250.00 are owing.
(*d*) Rates have been prepaid to the extent of £40.00.
(*e*) Goodwill is to be reduced by £600.00 (debit to Capital Account).

(RSA—Adapted)

4. M. Martindale carries on business as a retailer. On December 31st, 19.., the following Trial Balance was extracted from his books:

TRIAL BALANCE
(*at December 31st, 19..*)

	Dr. £	Cr. £
Goodwill	343.00	
Premises	7 600.00	
Debtors and Creditors	1 600.00	2 755.00
Wages	4 296.00	
Rent Received		2 170.00
General Expenses	2 308.00	
Bad Debts	206.00	
Discount	175.00	
Commission	278.00	
Purchases and Sales	17 439.00	33 453.00
Capital at January 1st, 19..		13 500.00
Drawings	2 675.00	
Cash	126.00	
Bank	5 210.00	
Stock at January 1st, 19..	2 400.00	
Carriage Outwards	472.50	
Salaries	4 325.50	
Loan Interest	80.00	
Loan (Midland Bank Ltd)		2 000.00
Advertising	97.00	
Returns Inwards and Outwards	365.00	276.00
Carriage Inwards	158.00	
Furniture and Fittings	4 000.00	
	£54 154.00	£54 154.00

(*a*) On December 31st, 19.., the value of stock in hand was estimated at £2 300.00.

(*b*) Two thirds of the wages is to be charged to the Trading Account and one third to the Profit and Loss Account.

(*c*) The goodwill is to be written off in full (debit to Capital Account).

(*d*) A provision for bad debts of 5 per cent of the debtors' figure is to be made.

(*e*) A provision for discount of 2½ per cent of the net debtors is to be made.

(*f*) Only half the loan interest has been paid at December 31st.

You are to prepare the Trading Account and Profit and Loss Account for the year ending December 31st, 19.., and the Balance Sheet as at that date.

19

FINAL ACCOUNTS FOR VARIOUS TYPES OF BUSINESS UNITS

19.1 Types of Business Unit

In Chapters 17 and 18 we learned how to draw up the Final Accounts of a sole trader, including the commoner types of adjustment required. In this chapter we shall carry this further to deal with other types of business unit, including the following:

(*a*) Partnership Accounts
(*b*) Limited Company Accounts
(*c*) Club Accounts (Non-Profit-Making Organisations)
(*d*) Local Government Accounts
(*e*) Central Government Accounts

19.2 Partnership Accounts

A partnership is a type of business unit where two or more people agree to go into business with one another. The agreement may be informal, but it is better if a partnership deed is drawn up in which the parties set out the agreement they have reached on such matters as the provision of capital, the sharing of profits, the fields of responsibility, etc. An experienced lawyer will draw up such a document quite inexpensively and will raise many points the partners themselves might not have considered.

The *Partnership Act of 1890* is a short Act of Parliament which controls partnerships in all circumstances where the partners have not reached agreement on a particular matter. Naturally it covers the entire range of possible dispute between partners, but the main accounting features are contained in Section 24 and are briefly as follows:

(*a*) All the partners are entitled to contribute equally to the capital. They must share equally the profits of the business, and must contribute equally to the losses.

(*b*) No partner is entitled to a salary for his part in the activities of the firm.

(*c*) No partner is entitled to interest on his capital, before the profits are ascertained.

(*d*) Where a partner lends money to the firm over and above his capital he shall be entitled to interest at 5 per cent per annum.

(*e*) Any partner may see and copy the books of the partnership, which must be kept at the ordinary place of business.

(*f*) No new partner may be introduced without the general consent of all the partners.

The Act applies only in the absence of agreement between the parties on any particular point, so that most firms come to quite different arrangements about interest, sharing of profits, etc., from those listed above.

The Accounting Records of a Partnership

The Trading Account and Profit and Loss Account of a partnership business are exactly the same as those of a sole trader's business. It is only when it comes to the appropriation of the profits to those who are entitled to them that a difference creeps into the accounting records. Instead of transferring the profit to the Capital Account as was done with the sole trader (see page 244), the net profit is transferred to an **Appropriation Account** and this account is used to share the profits in an agreed manner. Before looking at this account one or two other explanations must be made. These concern:

(*a*) The Capital Accounts of the partners.
(*b*) The Current Accounts of the partners.
(*c*) The Drawings Accounts of the partners.

(*a*) *The Capital Accounts of the Partners.* Since every partner will contribute some capital it is necessary to have a Capital Account for each partner. It is also usual to keep this account fixed at the original amount contributed, unless a formal agreement is made to increase or decrease it by an agreed sum. Therefore the transfer into the Capital Account of any residue of profits ploughed into the business, as was done with the sole trader's accounts (see page 244), is not usual. Instead the capital account is kept fixed and these transfers are made into the partners' **Current Accounts.**

(*b*) *The Current Accounts of the Partners.* In order to collect together any profits to which the partner is entitled (such as interest on capital, partnership salary or share of the profits) each partner has a Current Account. As its name implies, this account does fluctuate, unlike the Capital Account which is fixed at the original capital contribution. Interest on capital, interest on loans, salaries and any share of the profits will be credited to the Account, for of course the business owes them to the partner. Deducted from the Current Account, on the debit side, will be any sums transferred from the Drawings Account.

(*c*) *The Drawings Accounts of the Partners.* Each partner has a Drawings Account which is used to collect together the drawings he makes in cash, or by cheque, or in kind (by taking home goods from the shop, etc.). At the end of the year total drawings will be transferred to the debit of the partner's Current Account.

The layout of these various accounts, and also the final Balance Sheet, can be followed in Figs. 19.1–19.4 and the notes below them. These accounts refer to the partnership of J. Justice and F. Fairplay, whose Profit and Loss Account reveals a profit for the year of £18 296.00. The capital originally contributed was £5 000 from J. Justice and £10 000 from F. Fairplay. At the start of the present year Justice was overdrawn on his Current Account by £160, but Fairplay had a credit balance on his Current Account of £650. The partnership agreement provides that Justice is to have a salary of £2 000 per year, and that each partner is to have interest on capital at 10 per cent per annum. This rate of interest is also to apply to the opening balances on the Current Account and be either payable or receivable by the partner according to whether he is overdrawn or in credit. The partners have agreed to write £500 off goodwill (remember goodwill reductions are an appropriation of profit as explained on page 276). After these matters have been dealt with the residue of profits is to be shared one third to Justice, two thirds to Fairplay. During the year Justice has drawn £4 000 and Fairplay £6 000. The notes below each figure explain the chief points of interest. (To save space the Trial Balance with the other figures in it has not been reproduced.)

APPROPRIATION ACCOUNT L.171
(*for year ending December 31st, 19..*)

19..		£	19..		£
Dec. 31	Goodwill	500	Dec. 31	Net Profit	18 296
31	Salary J	2 000	31	Interest on Current A/c J	16
31	Interest on Capital J	500			
	F	1 000			
31	Interest on Current A/c F	65			
31	Share of Residue J	4 749			
	F	9 498			
		£18 312			£18 312

Fig. 19.1. An Appropriation Account for a partnership business.

Notes
(i) On the credit side we have the Net Profit transferred in from the Profit and Loss Account. We also have interest of £16 as extra profit which Justice is obliged to contribute as interest on his overdrawn Current Account at the start of the year (see Fig. 19.2).
(ii) On the debit we see how the profit of £18 312 has been shared out. First it has been used to write £500 off the Goodwill Account. Then Justice has received his salary of £2 000. Then both partners have been awarded the interest due to them under the partnership agreement on their capital, while Fairplay gets the extra he is entitled to on the balance of his Current Account.
(iii) Finally the residue of the profit is shared, one third to Justice, two thirds to Fairplay.
(iv) Of course all these entries would require closing journal entries.

CURRENT ACCOUNT (J. JUSTICE) L.165

19..		£	19..		£
Jan. 1	Balance	160	Dec. 31	Salary	2 000
Dec. 31	Interest on Current A/c	16	31	Interest on Capital	500
31	Drawings	4 000	31	Share of Residue	4 749
31	Balance C/d	3 073			
		£7 249			£7 249
			19..		
			Jan. 1	Balance B/d	3 073

CURRENT ACCOUNT (F. FAIRPLAY) L.166

19..		£	19..		£
Dec. 31	Drawings	6 000	Jan. 1	Balance	650
31	Balance C/d	5 213	Dec. 31	Interest on Capital	1 000
			31	Interest on Current A/c	65
			31	Share of Residue	9 498
		£11 213			£11 213
			19..		
			Jan. 1	Balance B/d	5 213

Fig. 19.2. The partners' Current Accounts.

Notes

(i) At the start of the year Fairplay had a credit balance (i.e. the business owed him £650 besides the capital on his Capital Account). By contrast, Justice had a debit balance of £160. This means that in the previous year he drew out more than the profits he had earned, and consequently was in debt to the business for that amount.

(ii) The partners are credited with the various amounts due to them this year for salary, interest on capital and for Fairplay his interest on Current Account. The residue of the profit is also credited.

(iii) Justice, by contrast, has to be debited with £16 interest on the overdrawn Current Account at the start of the year.

(iv) Both partners' drawings during the year (see Fig. 19.3) are cleared into their Current Accounts, on the debit side.

(v) Since this was a very profitable year, both partners end up with favourable (credit) balances on their Current Accounts.

DRAWINGS ACCOUNT (J. JUSTICE) L.167

19..			£	19..			£
Jan. 31	Cash	C.B.1	360	Dec. 31	Current Account	L.165	4 000
Feb., Mar., Apr., etc.		C.B.7	3 640				
			£4 000				£4 000

DRAWINGS ACCOUNT (F. FAIRPLAY) L.168

19..			£	19..			£
Jan. 31	Cash	C.B.1	500	Dec. 31	Current Account	L.166	6 000
Feb., Mar., Apr., etc.		C.B.7, etc.	5 500				
			£6 000				£6 000

Fig. 19.3. The partners' Drawing Accounts.

Notes

(i) Throughout the year steady drawings have been made from cash, etc.

(ii) The accounts are cleared by transferring the totals to the partners' Current Accounts where the debit entries reduce the amounts due to the partners.

BALANCE SHEET
(*as at December 31st, 19. .*)

Capitals			**Fixed Assets**			
J. Justice		5 000	Land and Buildings			16 000
F. Fairplay		10 000	Plant and Machinery			8 000
			Furniture and Fittings			3 000
		15 000				
						27 000
Current Accounts			**Current Assets**			
J. Justice	3 073		Stock		5 210	
F. Fairplay	5 213		Debtors	280		
			Less Prov.	28		
		8 286				
Long-term liability					252	
Mortgage		4 000	Cash at Bank		1 052	
Current Liabilities			Cash in Hand		36	
Creditors	6 000					
Wages due	264					6 550
		6 264				
		£33 550				£33 550

Fig. 19.4. A partnership Balance Sheet.

Notes

(i) It is usual for the two (or more) Capital Accounts to be added together as shown.

(ii) Similarly, the two Current Accounts are added together, unless of course one is overdrawn and has a debit balance. In that case the partner is in the same position as a debtor of the business and the Current Account will be taken over to the assets side.

(iii) In other respects the Balance Sheet is the same as for sole traders.

The reader should now work through the exercises which follow. These give practice in making out Appropriation Accounts, Current Accounts and the full Final Accounts of partnership businesses.

Note. In working Final Accounts exercises for partnerships, it is always advisable to do the Appropriation Account and the Current Accounts so that the Balance Sheet figures can easily be derived from the available information, even though the question may not ask for them.

19.3 Exercises: The Final Accounts of Partnerships

1. Sybrandt and Cornelis are in partnership. They have a written agreement which says:

(*a*) Partnership capitals shall carry interest at 10 per cent per annum.
(*b*) Cornelis shall have a salary of £2 000 per annum.
(*c*) Goodwill shall be reduced each year by 20 per cent.
(*d*) Profits over and above those required for the first three clauses shall be shared two thirds to Sybrandt and one third to Cornelis.

Capitals are: Sybrandt £15 000, Cornelis £10 000. Goodwill is valued at £2 000. Show the Appropriation Account (i.e. the Appropriation Section of the Profit and Loss Account) if the profits at December 31st, 19. ., were £10 500.

(East Anglian Examination Board—Adapted)

2. Dickens, Kipling and Hardy are partners in carrying on a business under an agreement which provides that, after allowing interest on capital (but not on Current Accounts) at 5 per cent per annum, and partnership salaries of £2 000 to Dickens and £1 500 to Kipling, the remaining profit is to be shared one fourth to Dickens and three eighths each to Kipling and Hardy.

   The Net Profit for the year ended March 31st, 19.., was £16 350 before providing partnership salaries or interest on capital. The balances on the partners' capital accounts on April 1st, 19.., were: Dickens £14 000, Kipling £13 000 and Hardy £10 000, and there was no further contribution of capital during the year.

   You are required to prepare the Appropriation section of the firm's Profit and Loss Account for the year ended March 31st, 19...

3. The partnership agreement between L. Hemp, T. Wool, and M. Cotton contains the following provisions:

   (*a*) The partners' fixed capitals shall be: Hemp £12 000, Wool £10 000 and Cotton £8 000.
   (*b*) Wool and Cotton are to receive salaries of £2 000 and £1 000 respectively.
   (*c*) Interest on capital is to be calculated at 6 per cent per annum.
   (*d*) Hemp, Wool, and Cotton are to share profits and losses in the ratios 3 : 2 : 1.
   (*e*) No interest is to be charged on drawings or Current Accounts.

   On January 1st, 19.., the balances on Current Accounts were: Hemp Cr. £700, Wool Cr. £400 and Cotton Dr. £100.

   During the year the drawings were Hemp £4 500, Wool £2 800, and Cotton £2 200.

   The Profit and Loss Account for the year showed a profit of £18 900 before charging interest on capital, or partners' salaries.

   Show the Appropriation Account and the Current Accounts of Hemp, Wool, and Cotton, as at December 31st, 19.., after division of the profit.

   (RSA—Adapted)

4. At January 1st, 19.., G. Watson was running a business in which he had £10 000 capital. He also had a balance of £2 000 on the credit side of his Current Account. As from this date, S. Holmes came in as a partner on the following terms:

   (*a*) Watson's capital was to remain unchanged and Holmes' was to bring in £6 000, of which £1 000 was to be credited to his Current Account.
   (*b*) Interest at 10 per cent per annum was to be allowed on both capitals and current starting balances from the beginning of the partnership.
   (*c*) Holmes was to be credited with a salary of £2 500 per annum.
   (*d*) Profits, after charging interest and salary, were to be divided between Watson, two thirds, and Holmes, one third. Holmes withdrew £300 per month and Watson £400 per month. At December 31st, 19.., the Net Profit available for division before charging the partnership interest and salary was £9 400.

   You are required to prepare the Appropriation Account, and the Current Accounts of the partners.

5. Peele and Mellis conduct a merchanting business in partnership on the following terms:

   (*a*) Interest is to be allowed on partners' Capital Accounts at 10 per cent per annum.
   (*b*) Peele is to be credited with a partnership salary of £2 000 per annum.
   (*c*) The balance of profit in any year is to be shared equally by the partners.

After preparing their Trading and Profit and Loss Account for the year ended March 31st, 19.., but before making any provision for interest on capital or for Peele's partnership salary, the following balances remained on the books:

	Dr. £	Cr. £
Capital Accounts:		
Peele (as on April 1st previous year)		10 000
Mellis (as on April 1st previous year)		20 000
Current Accounts:		
Peele (as on April 1st previous year)		220
Mellis (as on April 1st previous year)		110
Drawings Accounts:		
Peele	3 000	
Mellis	4 000	
Profit and Loss Account—Net Profit for year		15 000
Stock at March 31st, 19..	8 400	
Goodwill Account	1 000	
Plant and Machinery, at cost	20 000	
Plant and Machinery, depreciation		6 000
Fixtures and Fittings, at cost	4 800	
Fixtures and Fittings, depreciation		950
Trade Debtors and Creditors	3 500	850
Loan from H. Oldcastle, £2 000, and accrued interest		2 120
Rent accrued due at March 31st, 19..		150
Insurance unexpired at March 31st, 19..	95	
Cash at Bank, Current Account	10 605	
	£55 400	£55 400

It is agreed by the partners to reduce the book value of goodwill by writing off £250 at March 31st, 19.. (to be charged to the Appropriation section of the Profit and Loss Account).

You are asked to prepare the Appropriation section of the firm's Profit and Loss Account and the partners' Current Accounts for the year ended March 31st, 19.., together with the Balance Sheet as on that date.

(RSA—Adapted)

6. The following Trial Balance was extracted from the books of Messrs Tree and Branch, wholesalers, who share profits and losses three quarters and one quarter respectively. Prepare the Trading Account and Profit and Loss Account for the year ending December 31st, 19.., and the Balance Sheet as at that date.

TRIAL BALANCE
(as at December 31st, 19..)

	Dr. £	Cr. £
Capital Accounts, January 1st, 19..:		
Tree		15 000
Branch		20 000
Drawings:		
Tree	3 000	
Branch	4 000	
Current Accounts, January 1st, 19..:		
Tree		1 200
Branch	800	
Trade Debtors and Creditors	4 520	6 130
Warehouse Wages	8 500	
Office Salaries	6 240	
Stock at January 1st, 19..	12 600	
Purchases and Sales	27 000	82 000
Returns In and Out	500	640
Bank Balance	7 750	
Cash in Hand	420	
Lighting and Heating:		
Warehouse (¾) Office (¼)	840	
Rates:		
Warehouse (¾) Office (¼)	600	
Freehold Premises	28 000	
Fixtures and Fittings	9 560	
Vehicles	8 000	
Stationery	320	
Sundry Expenses	650	
Postage and Telephone	450	
Insurance	480	
Discounts allowed and received	220	380
Provision for Bad Debts		400
Bad Debts incurred during year	450	
Vehicle Expenses	850	
	£125 750	£125 750

In preparing the accounts provide for the following items which have not yet been passed through the books:

(*a*) Stock at December 31st, 19. ., was valued at £9 600

(*b*) Fixtures and fittings are to be depreciated by 10 per cent and vehicles by 20 per cent.

(*c*) Rates prepaid amount to £64.00.

(*d*) Insurance unexpired amounts to £10.00.

(*e*) Provision for bad debts at December 31st, 19. ., to be 5 per cent of trade debtors' total.

(*f*) Ten per cent interest on the partners' capital and a salary of £2 000 for Branch are to be charged to the Appropriation section of the Profit and Loss Account.

19.4 The Final Accounts of Limited Companies

A limited liability company is a type of business organisation authorised by Act of Parliament, or by Royal Charter, whose capital is contributed by members who are accorded the privilege of limited liability. This means that they are liable for the debts of the company to the extent of the shareholding that they have contributed, or have agreed to contribute. Beyond that sum they are not liable for the company's debts.

The result of this is that persons who deal with a limited liability company on credit, supplying it with goods or services, run a certain risk; they may never be paid. Every person who engages in trade with a company ought to know he is running such a risk, and for this reason the word 'Limited' must appear as the last word of the name of the firm. It is a warning to all: this firm has limited liability. Many people think a limited company is safer and more reliable to deal with than a sole trader or partnership, but this is not necessarily so.

A few basic points about the accounts of limited companies may be listed as follows:

(*a*) **Capital.** The total capital which a limited company may issue to the general public is authorised by the Registrar of Companies when he grants the Certificate of Incorporation. This **Authorised Capital** must be stated on the Balance Sheet, so that those dealing with the company know the total amount which they can look to should any difficulties arise. It does not follow that all the capital will be 'called up' at once, since it may not be necessary at the start of the business.

(*b*) **Shares.** Shareholders may be invited to buy various classes of shares. **Ordinary Shares**, often called **equity shares**, share equally in the profits of the business. Ordinary shareholders are the most important shareholders. They also carry most of the risks. All profits which are not distributed to shareholders belong to the ordinary shareholders, and are called **reserves.** Therefore we use, in our accounts, the term **Ordinary Shareholders' Interest in the Company** to indicate what their total interest is—i.e. the capital originally contributed, plus profits ploughed back, including the balance out of the Appropriation Account, plus other profits resulting from the revaluation of assets such as premises, land, etc.

Preference shareholders are entitled to a fixed rate of dividend in preference to ordinary shareholders, but do not share in the residue of profits unless they are **participating preference shares.**

(*c*) **Loans to a Company.** Where a company borrows money from people other than the shareholders who are actually taking an active interest in its affairs by becoming members, it does so by means of a bond called a **Debenture.** A Debenture is a loan to a company usually secured on the assets of the firm. There are two main kinds, Fixed Debentures and Floating Debentures. Fixed Debentures are secured on the fixed assets, and if the interest is not paid regularly the Debenture holders may seize the fixed assets and sell them to regain their money. This naturally winds up the company. A Floating Debenture is secured on the circulating assets of the company, chiefly the stock, which can be seized if the interest is not paid. Debentures usually earn less than Preference Shares.

(*d*) **The Final Accounts.** Limited companies have the same sort of Final Accounts as all other businesses, but companies that appeal to the public for funds must publish part of these accounts so that the shareholders and creditors can see exactly how the company has prospered. These legal requirements differ from the accounts used for internal accounting so that the accountant must modify his ordinary accounts to comply with the regulations. A Manufacturing Account (for manufacturing companies), a Trading Account, a Profit and Loss Account, an Appropriation Account, and a Balance Sheet will be required in a full set of Final Accounts. At this stage students should observe the following points about the Appropriation Account and Balance Sheet.

19.5 The Appropriation Account of a Limited Company

A company is in some ways like a very large partnership, except that the shareholders have limited liability. Each shareholder hopes to receive an appropriation of profit, but the directors will decide this, and not even the preference shareholders can insist on being paid a dividend. The directors have the right to keep profits in reserve for a variety of purposes, and to be niggardly with their dividends—provided they are prepared to risk being dismissed at the Annual General Meeting of the shareholders.

One way in which the Appropriation Account of a company differs from that of a partnership is that the shareholders cannot be given every last penny of the profits. If you have 27 213 shareholders and you make £10 000 profit, it is impossible to give away the last penny. You cannot divide the profits equally. There must always be a balance left over and carried down to next year. An Appropriation Account for a company therefore usually starts with an opening balance on the credit side. Then the Net Profit is transferred from the Profit and Loss Account to the credit side, under the balance.

A typical Appropriation Account for a limited company is given in Fig. 19.5 and explained in the notes below it.

19.6 The Balance Sheet of a Limited Company

Schedule 2 of the Companies Act, 1967, lays down Parliament's rules for British companies with regard to the published Balance Sheet. The legislature rightly held that since companies appeal to the public for funds the published Balance Sheet should reveal as much information as possible to potential investors. The aim of a good book-keeper should be to produce a Balance Sheet giving as clear a picture of the affairs of the company as is possible, and many progressive firms go beyond the requirements of Schedule 2 of the Act.

The more important requirements of Schedule 2 are made clear in Example 19.1 which follows on page 298, with the Appropriation Account below it. For the sake of clarity the Balance Sheet appears on page 296 with explanatory notes on the facing page. The Balance Sheet is then shown in 'vertical style' on page 299. Please read page 298 first, then pages 296–7, and page 299. (The one feature of company accounts not illustrated here is the requirement to show the previous year's figures, for comparison purposes.)

THE X CO. LTD

APPROPRIATION ACCOUNT

(*for year ended December 31st, 19..*)

19..		£	19..		£
Dec. 31	Goodwill	500.00	Jan. 1	Balance B/d	427.50
	Plant and Machinery Reserve	1 000.00	Dec. 31	Net Profit	17 256.75
					17 684.25
	General Reserve	3 000.00			
	Preference Dividend	2 000.00			
	Ordinary Dividend	8 000.00			
	Balance C/d	3 184.25			
		£17 684.25			£17 684.25
			19..		
			Jan. 1	Balance B/d	3 184.25

Fig. 19.5. A company's Appropriation Account.

Notes

(i) On the credit side the account opens with a balance left over from the previous year. This may be quite large if the directors are pursuing a prudent policy of keeping strong reserves in hand.

(ii) Then the net profit is transferred in from the Profit and Loss Account.

(iii) On the debit side the directors started by reducing the value of the intangible asset 'goodwill'. A rather similar asset with companies is **Formation Expenses.** These are the legal and taxation costs of forming a limited company, which may be quite large (if underwriters had to be paid, for example, to cover the issue of shares). After all these expenses we are left with only an entry on the debit side of an expenses account 'formation expenses'. We have started the company, which is an asset of a sort. Like goodwill it is usual to write this asset off over the first few years of the company's life.

(iv) Prudent directors usually put away considerable parts of the profits as reserves. These may be for a specific purpose—like **Plant Replacement Reserves**—or for general purposes—like **General Reserves.** The chief reason for holding General Reserves is to *equalise the dividend.* It is a fact that shareholders become restless if dividends fluctuate: 42 per cent one year and 0 per cent the next year is better than 20 per cent each year, but most shareholders prefer the latter. The placing of surplus profits into General Reserve Account, from which they can be transferred back in subsequent years if required, is therefore sound policy.

(v) Finally the Preference Dividend is paid in full, and a reasonable Ordinary Dividend. Any balance left over is carried down to the credit of Appropriation Account.

Three further points:

(*a*) Remember that placing profits in a Reserve Account only stops the shareholders getting large dividends. It does not take the assets which the profits represent out of circulation. The extra net worth (see Section 19.13) is still in the firm and if it is in cash form it may be frittered away. To keep it safe it should be invested—at least put on Deposit Account—but sometimes it is better if it is actually invested in a Sinking Fund of shares and other investments.

(*b*) Reserves like those mentioned above are called **Revenue Reserves.** The directors are entitled to transfer revenue reserves back to Appropriation Account for distribution as profits in future years. Another type of reserves, **Capital Reserves,** are explained in the notes to Fig. 19.6. These *may not be* transferred back for distribution as dividends.

(*c*) Of course each of these entries is only half of a closing journal entry. The other half will either reduce an asset (goodwill) or create a liability (a credit entry in a reserve account or in a dividend account). The latter will be settled by sending out the dividend warrants. The former will be carried forward to the Balance Sheet as part of the ordinary shareholders' interest in the company.

BALANCE SHEET (*as at December 31st, 19..*)

ORDINARY SHAREHOLDERS' INTEREST IN THE CO.		
	Authorised	Issued
Ordinary Shares of 1.00 fully paid	100 000.00	60 000.00
RESERVES		
Capital Reserves		
Share Premium Account		1 000.00
Revenue Reserves		
General Reserves (at start)	20 000.00	
Add New Appropriation	4 000.00	
	24 000.00	
Balance on Approp. Account	5 551.00	
		29 551.00
		90 551.00
Less Fictitious Asset Prelim. Expenses (1 000.00—250.00)		750.00
Ordinary Shareholders' Equity		89 801.00
PREFERENCE SHAREHOLDERS' INTEREST IN THE COMPANY		
	Authorised	
Preference Shares of 1.00 fully paid	40 000.00	20 000.00
DEBENTURES		
$5\frac{1}{2}$% Debentures of 100.00 each		10 000.00
Reserve for Future Taxation		10 000.00
		£129 801 00

FIXED ASSETS			
Land and Buildings (at cost)			18 000.00
Plant and Machinery (at cost)		20 000.00	
Less Depreciation		12 000.00	
			8 000.00
Furniture and Fittings (at cost)		4 000.00	
Less Depreciation		1 500.00	
			2 500.00
Patent Rights Owned (at cost)		2 000.00	
Less Depreciation		1 000.00	
			1 000.00
Motor Vehicles (at cost)		14 500.00	
Less Depreciation		1 501.00	
			12 999.00
			42 499.00
TRADE INVESTMENTS (valued by Directors at 12 050.00)			12 000.00
CURRENT ASSETS			
Other Investments (Market value 34 750.00		33 000.00	
Stock (at cost)		27 500.00	
Debtors		4 700.75	
Bank		19 250.00	
Cash in Hand		1 750.25	
		86 201.00	
Less			
CURRENT LIABILITIES			
Ordinary Dividend	6 000.00		
Pref. Div.	1 200.00		
Creditors	3 699 00		
		10 899.00	
Net Working Capital			75 302.00
Net Value of Assets			£129 801.00

Fig. 19.6. The Appropriation Account and Balance Sheet of a company (see also Fig. 19.7—vertical style).

Notes

Assets Side. Schedule 2 requires that Fixed Assets, Current Assets and assets that are neither fixed nor current shall be distinguished from one another. The value of any Fixed Asset shall be its cost, less the total depreciation to date. This is made easier if the method of accumulating depreciation in a separate account, as described in Chapter 18, page 274, is adopted. In this example the assets have been listed in the order of permanence, less the depreciation to date. The chief advantage of the vertical-style balance sheet shown in Fig. 19.7 is the improved presentation of the depreciation.

Patent Rights Owned is an asset which is less common than most. Where a firm buys patent rights it buys the right to use an invention for a number of years. It is a Fixed Asset whose benefit to the business lasts for the length that the patent right has to run, and it will therefore be depreciated rather like a lease.

Trade Investments are one of the types of asset covered by the rule which says that 'assets neither fixed nor current' must be shown separately, under appropriate headings. They are shown here in an intermediate position between Fixed Assets and Current Assets. This is justified by their dual nature.

Trade investments are investments held by a company often for the sake of controlling, or attempting to achieve control of, a subsidiary firm in the same line of business. For a variety of reasons firms may wish to gain control of other firms in the same line of business as themselves: to reduce competition, or to ensure supplies of vital components, or to market their goods in a particular area. Control of 51 per cent of the voting shares gives effective control of such subsidiaries. Rules about such holding companies are complex, but it is enough to realise that these investments can be sold like any other investment, so that they are, in a way, Current Assets. On the other hand, if sold, the parent company will lose control of the subsidiary, so that the assets are Fixed Assets. The position shown on the Balance Sheet reflects this dual feature of trade investments; they are assets which are neither fixed nor current. The phrase 'valued by the directors at £12 050.00' implies that these are unquoted investments. They cannot be dealt with on the Stock Exchange, probably because the subsidiary is a private limited company, not a public limited company. It is therefore impossible to say what the market value is. Schedule 2 requires that *Quoted Investments* be stated separately from *Unquoted Investments*, and that the market price, or directors' valuation, be shown either in the Balance Sheet or by way of a note.

The **Current Assets** are listed in the order of permanence, but the style of presentation here is in advance of the present legal requirements. The Current Liabilities have been brought over to the assets side of the Balance Sheet, and have been deducted from the Current Assets figure. The student who understands **Working Capital** (see page 338) will realise that this style enables us to find the Net Working Capital and actually state the amount of this **Net Current Assets** figure. This is a very good method of presentation, enabling the investor to see at a glance the Working Capital position.

One asset which is not shown on the assets side at all in this presentation is the **Fictitious Asset, Preliminary Expenses** (Formation Expenses) which is taken to the liabilities side and deducted from the Ordinary Shareholders' Interest in the company. Preliminary Expenses are expenses involved in setting up a Limited Company.

Liabilities Side. *The Ordinary Shareholders' Interest in the Company.* Here the presentation is in advance of the requirements of the Companies Acts, and conforms to the very best ideas of accountants. The important feature here is the clear distinction between the ordinary shareholders' interest in the company as distinct from the *preference shareholders' interest*. So often on company Balance Sheets the Ordinary and Preference Capitals are added together, and Capital and Revenue Reserves are shown below. This is not at all helpful, because it does not make clear who owns what. The presentation shown here is being adopted by most progressive companies. It makes absolutely clear that the *Capital Reserves* and *Revenue Reserves* belong to the ordinary shareholders and form part of their interest in the company. Capital Reserves are profits made in an unusual way—for example, in this Balance Sheet the **Share Premium Account** is a sum of capital contributed by the preference shareholders as a premium on entry to the company. By paying more than the face value of the shares the preference shareholders are compensating the ordinary shareholders for their efforts in building up the company. A Debenture Premium Account is similar. These Capital Reserves therefore belong to ordinary shareholders, they must be left in the business as permanent capital: sometimes they are issued as bonus shares to the ordinary shareholders. Other Capital Reserves are **Profits Prior to Incorporation** and **Written-up appreciations on Fixed Assets** like **Revaluation of Premises Account.**

Revenue Reserves are reserves set aside out of profits, like the General Reserve used for equalising dividend over good and bad years. Such reserves may be taken out and distributed to the ordinary shareholders. Why do such reserves still belong to the ordinary shareholders only? Because the preference shareholders never leave any profits in the firm but always take their full fixed dividend out and enjoy it. It follows that the ordinary shareholders' interest in the company includes all the reserves.

Fictitious Assets. We can now see that the 60 000 Ordinary Shares in Enterprise Ltd are worth £90 551.00. But there is one point further to consider. One of the assets is a Fictitious Asset—Preliminary Expenses. These are the legal expenses incurred in floating a company. We spent money on them but what we got for the money was just permission to go ahead and trade. It is no sort of real asset at all, and the best way to show it is to deduct it from the ordinary shareholders' interest. This leaves the value of the 60 000 shares at £89 801.00.

Example 19.1. After taking out the Trading and Profit and Loss Accounts at December 31st, 19.., the revised Trial Balance of Enterprise Ltd is as follows:

	Dr. £	Cr. £
Cash	1 750.25	
Bank	19 250.00	
Stock at End of Year	27 500.00	
Balance from January 1st on Appropriation Account		894.50
Preliminary Expenses	1 000.00	
Net Profit for Year		26 106.50
Furniture and Fittings (cost £4 000.00)	2 500.00	
Patent Rights Owned (cost £2 000.00)	1 000.00	
Premium on Preference Shares		1 000.00
Ordinary Capital (authorised £40 000.00)		60 000.00
6% Preference Share Capital (authorised £40 000.00)		20 000.00
5½% Debentures of £100.00 each		10 000.00
General Reserve		20 000.00
Land and Buildings (at cost)	18 000.00	
Plant and Machinery (cost £20 000.00)	8 000.00	
Quoted Investments held (market value £34 750.00)	33 000.00	
Unquoted Trade Investments (valued by directors at £12 050.00)	12 000.00	
Motor Vehicles and Spares (cost £14 500.00)	12 999.00	
Debtors and Creditors	4 700.75	3 699.00
	£141 700.00	£141 700.00

You are to show the Appropriation Account and Balance Sheet after taking into account the following decisions of the Directors:

(*a*) A dividend of 6 per cent on the Preference Shares is to be paid.
(*b*) A dividend of 10 per cent is recommended on the Ordinary Shares.
(*c*) £4 000.00 is to be put to General Reserve Account.
(*d*) £250.00 to be written off Preliminary Expenses.
(*e*) £10 000.00 is to be appropriated as a Taxation Reserve.

A solution to this question is given in Fig. 19.6 and incorporates the main requirements of Schedule 2. These are explained in the notes opposite Fig. 19.6.

In Fig. 19.7 the same Balance Sheet is reproduced in vertical style, so that this method of presentation may be followed.

ENTERPRISE LTD
APPROPRIATION ACCOUNT
(*for year ending December 31st, 19..*)

Taxation Reserve	10 000.00	Balance	894.50
Preliminary Expenses	250.00	Net Profit	26 106.50
Transfer to General Reserve	4 000.00		
Preference Dividend	1 200.00		
Ordinary Dividend	6 000.00		
Balance	5 551.00		
	27 001.00		27 001.00
		Balance	5 551.00

ENTERPRISE LIMITED

BALANCE SHEET IN VERTICAL STYLE

(as at December 31st, 19..)

ORDINARY SHAREHOLDERS' INTEREST IN THE COMPANY			
		Authorised	Issued
Ordinary Shares of 1.00 each, fully paid		100 000.00	60 000.00
RESERVES			
Capital Reserves			
Share Premium Account		1 000.00	
Revenue Reserves			
General Reserves (at start)	20 000.00		
Add New Appropriation	4 000.00		
	24 000.00		
Balance on Appropriation Account	5 551.00		
		29 551.00	
			30 551.00
			90 551.00
Less Fictitious Asset			
Preliminary Expenses 1 000.00—250.00			750.00
Ordinary Shareholders' Equity			89 801.00
PREFERENCE SHAREHOLDERS' INTEREST IN THE COMPANY			
		Authorised	
6% Preference Shares of 1.00 each, fully paid		40 000.00	20 000.00
DEBENTURES			
5½% Debentures of 100.00 each			10 000.00
Reserve for Future Taxation			10 000.00
			129 801.00

REPRESENTED BY			
FIXED ASSETS	COST	*Less* DEPRECIATION TO DATE	VALUATION
Land and Buildings	18 000.00	—	18 000.00
Plant and Machinery	20 000.00	12 000.00	8 000.00
Furniture and Fittings	4 000.00	1 500.00	2 500.00
Patent Rights Owned	2 000.00	1 000.00	1 000.00
Motor Vehicles	14 500.00	1 501.00	12 999.00
			42 499.00
TRADE INVESTMENTS (valued by Directors at 12 050.00)			12 000.00
CURRENT ASSETS			
Other Investments (Market Value 34 750.00)		33 000.00	
Stock		27 500.00	
Debtors		4 700.75	
Cash at Bank		19 250.00	
Cash in Hand		1 750.25	
		86 201.00	
Less			
CURRENT LIABILITIES			
Ordinary Dividend	6 000.00		
Preference Dividend	1 200.00		
Creditors	3 699.00		
		10 899.00	
		Net Working Capital	75 302.00
		Net Value of Assets	£129 801.00

Fig. 19.7. A 'vertical style' Balance Sheet.

The Balance Sheet of Enterprise Ltd can be rearranged in vertical style. The advantage of this method is that it is easy to print, it gives plenty of room to print the depreciation, etc., and it at last does away with the mistakes Simon Stevin left us with over the reversal of the sides of the Balance Sheet. We now have a top and a bottom, but no sides at all. Many firms are adopting this style, and the student should compare it with the more traditional style in Fig. 19.6.

19.7 The Published Accounts of Limited Companies

Although a full set of accounts (i.e. Manufacturing Account, Trading Account, etc.) would be needed to ascertain the profits, the company needs to publish only certain information. The term 'publish' refers to the need to make certain documents available to the Registrar of Companies, which then become part of the company file at Companies House. These may be viewed by the public, on payment of a nominal charge. In practice most public companies, if they have a spare copy, will send them out free of charge to those members of the public who request them. The documents comprise:

(*a*) A Profit and Loss Account—but containing only certain items.
(*b*) A Balance Sheet.
(*c*) The auditor's report.
(*d*) The director's report.

Where a company is a **holding company**, i.e. it controls subsidiaries, it must prepare **Group Accounts.**

The items required to be shown in addition to those already mentioned in the notes to Fig. 19.6 and 19.7 may be listed as follows:

(*a*) The turnover, as a note to the Profit and Loss Account—but to protect small companies from aggressive takeovers turnover need not be declared if it is less than £250 000 per year.

(*b*) The net profit.

(*c*) Amounts charged for depreciation, renewals or diminution in value of fixed assets.

(*d*) Amounts paid out as interest on loans, debentures, etc.

(*e*) Amounts charged for Corporation Tax.

(*f*) Sums used to redeem share capital or loans.

(*g*) Sums set aside for reserves, or drawn from reserves.

(*h*) Dividends paid, or proposed.

(*i*) The remuneration of the auditors.

(*i*) The figures for the previous accounting period, for comparison purposes, shall be shown in the margin.

(*k*) The director's emoluments, including the emoluments of the chairman, the highest paid director if he receive more than the chairman, and the numbers of directors who earned less than £2 500, and in bands of £2 500 above that basic figure.

(*l*) **Contingent Liabilities.** Another requirement of Schedule 2 is that contingent liabilities should be stated as notes on the Balance Sheet. These are liabilities that may arise in certain contingencies. The commonest one is where Bills of Exchange are dishonoured by our debtors. In such cases we may become liable for them. Lawsuits pending also give rise to a possibility that the Court will find against us. A note on the bottom of the Balance Sheet stating the directors' valuation of likely contingent liabilities ensures that investors are aware of such possibilities, but we do not need to specify the matter because this would tell the Court we expected to lose the case.

Finally, it should be noted that because of the complex nature of the information required to be furnished by companies, the published accounts can be extremely difficult to present. To overcome the problems a set of notes is provided which simplify the briefer details in the accounts. Whilst this is no doubt a perfectly satisfactory way of providing the information it is a fact that some sets of published accounts are so abbreviated that they become almost meaningless. There is a great deal to be said for final accounts which show a reasonably clear picture of the company's affairs, without the need to investigate several pages of detailed notes. Otherwise the requirement to give a 'true and fair view' of the company's affairs may be defeated as far as ordinary (less knowledgeable) shareholders are concerned.

Full knowledge of the complete range of requirements is not necessary at this point, but the checklist which follows (reproduced by courtesy of *Accountants' Weekly*) is a good guide to them.

Table 19.1. A Checklist of Statutory Requirements for Companies

No.	*Profit and Loss Account*	*Reference in the Companies Acts*
1	Turnover (unless less than £250 000 and company not member of a group) and method by which it is arrived at	*2 Sch. 13A(5) 1967* *S. 1 1971, No 2044*
2	Rents received (less outgoings) if a substantial part of revenue	*2 Sch. 12(1) 1967*
3	Income from quoted/unquoted investments (shown separately)	*2 Sch. 12(1) 1967*
4	Auditor's remuneration including expenses	*2 Sch. 13 1967*
5	Interest payable on: (*a*) loans (if wholly repayable within five years) and all bank loans and overdrafts; (*b*) all other loans	*2 Sch. 12(1)(b) 1967*
6	Hire of plant and machinery	*2 Sch. 12(b) 1967*
7	Depreciation, method of provision and whether it is not provided for any fixed assets	*2 Sch. 12(1)* *2 Sch. 12(4)* } *1967* *2 Sch. 14(2)*
8	UK corporation tax/income tax and basis of computation	*2 Sch. 12(1)(c) 1967* *2 Sch. 14(3) 1967*
9	Amounts provided for redemption of share capital and loss	*2 Sch. 12(1) 1967*
10	Transfers to or from reserves	*2 Sch. 12(1) 1967*
11	Transfers to provisions (other than depreciation) and withdrawals therefrom for another purpose	*2 Sch. 12(1) 1967*
12	Aggregate dividends paid and proposed	*2 Sch. 12(1) 1967*
13	Prior-year items	*2 Sch. 12A 1967*
14	Unusual, exceptional or non-recurrent transactions	*2 Sch. 14(6) 1967*
15	Comparative figures	*2 Sch. 14 1967*
16	Aggregate directors' emoluments including pension scheme contributions	*S. 196 1948*
17	Aggregate directors' and past directors' pensions	*2 Sch. 19 1967*
18	Compensation paid to directors for loss of office	*S. 191 & 192 1948*

Table 19.1—*continued*

No.	*Profit and Loss Account*	*Reference in the Companies Acts*
19	(Except for those companies which are neither holding companies, nor subsidiaries, and the aggregate directors' emoluments less than £15 000)	*S. 6 (6) 1976*
	(A) the number (with comparatives) of directors whose emoluments fall within bands of £2 500 (B) the chairman's emoluments, or the emoluments as chairman of each person so acting (C) the emoluments of the highest paid director (or directors if equal) if in excess of the aggregate chairman's emoluments (D) the number (with comparatives) of directors who have waived rights to receive emoluments during the year and the amount thereof	*2 Sch. 19 1967*
	Note. (A), (B) and (C) exclude pension contributions	
20	Number of employees whose emoluments fall into each £2 500 bracket about £10 000	*2 Sch. 19 1967*

No.	*Balance Sheet*	*Reference in the Companies Acts*
A. Share capital and reserves		
1	Authorised and issued share capital	*2 Sch. 2 1967*
2	Amount of redeemable preference shares, earliest and latest dates of redemption, whether at company's option or in any event, premium payable (if any)	*2 Sch. 2(a) 1967*
3	The shares and the rate of interest, where interest has been paid out of capital	*2 Sch. 2(b) 1967*
4	Aggregate amount of reserves and classified under subheadings appropriate to company's business movement in reserves under each subheading	*2 Sch. 6 1967* *2 Sch. 7 1967*
5	Share premium account	*2 Sch. 2(c) 1967*
6	Capital redemption reserve fund	*S. 58(1)(d) 1948*
7	Name of company's ultimate holding company and its country of incorporation	*S 5(1) 1967*
B. Liabilities and provisions		
1	Redeemed debentures company has power to reissue	*2 Sch. 2(d) 1967*
2	State if any liability is 'secured' on assets otherwise than by operation of law	*2 Sch. 9 1967*
3	Aggregate amount of provisions (other than depreciation) classified into appropriate subheadings showing movement during year	*2 Sch. 6, 7, 27 1967*
4	Amounts due to subsidiaries, separately from all other liabilities	*2 Sch. 15(2) 1967*

Table 19.1—*continued*

No.	*Balance Sheet*	*Reference in the Companies Acts*
5	Amounts due to holding and fellow-subsidiary companies, distinguishing debentures	*2 Sch. 16 1967*
6	Aggregate amount of bank loans and overdrafts	*2 Sch. 8(1) 1967*
7	Other loans any part of which has more than five years to run, indicating repayment terms and rate of interest	*2 Sch. 8(1)(d)* *2 Sch. 30* *2 Sch. 8(4)*
8	Recommended dividends	*2 Sch. 8(1) 1967*
9	Basis of computing UK corporation tax	*2 Sch. 11(10) 1967*
10	Deferred taxation and any amount used from it for another purpose during period	*2 Sch. 7(a) 1967*
11	Comparative figures	*2 Sch. 11(11) 1967*
C. Assets		
1	Assets, summarised with such particulars as are necessary to disclose their general nature and classified under headings appropriate to company	*2 Sch. 2 1967*
2	Fixed, current and other assets identified as such	*2 Sch. 4(z) 1967*
3	Show separately long and short leasehold	*2 Sch. 11(6c) 1967*
4	Additions and disposals of fixed assets under each heading (comparatives not required)	*2 Sch. 11(6B) 1967*
5	Aggregate cost and valuation of fixed assets under any heading and aggregate amounts written off since acquisition. Exceptions for investments valued by directors and goodwill, etc.	*2 Sch. 5(3) 1967*
6	Aggregate amount of goodwill, patents and trade marks not written off	*2 Sch. 8(1b) 1967* *2 Sch. 8(2) 1967*
7	Shares in subsidiaries Amounts due from subsidiaries Shares in fellow subsidiaries Amounts due from holding and fellow-subsidiary companies	*2 Sch. 15(2) 1967*
8	Amount of quoted investments and market value	*2 Sch. 8(1)(a) 1967*
9	Amount of unquoted investments showing, if directors' valuation is not given, cost or valuation and aggregate amount written off. Also other stringent disclosure requirements	*2 Sch. 5(A) 1967*
10	Debentures of company held by nominee or trustee for company, nominal and book value	*2 Sch. 10 1967*
11	Loans to employees to purchase company's shares	*2 Sch. 8(1)(c) 1967*
12	Expenditure not written off in respect of each of preliminary expenses, issue expenses, share commission paid, discounts allowed on shares	*2 Sch. 3 1967*
13	Comparative figures	*2 Sch. 11(11) 1967*

Table 19.1—*continued*

No.	*Director's Report*	*Reference in the Companies Acts*
	A. Information to be stated regarding the company	
1	State of company's affairs	*157 (1948)*
2	Proposed dividend	*157 (1948)*
3	Proposed transfer to reserves	*157 (1948)*
4	Issue of shares or debentures during period, giving reasons, class and amount and consideration received	*16(1)(b) (1967)*
5	Any other matters 'material to appreciation of company's affairs by its members'	*16(1)(b) 1967*
6	Significant changes in fixed assets	*16(1)(a) 1967*
7	Indication of difference between book and market value of land and buildings if significant	*16(1)(a) 1967*
8	Principal activities and any significant changes	*16(1) 1967*
9	Average number of UK employees if 100 or more, and their aggregate remuneration. (If holding company disclose group totals. Wholly owned subsidiary of UK company exempt.)	*18 (1967)*
10	Totals of UK political and charitable contributions respectively of company (or, if any made by subsidiaries, of the group) unless together not more than £50. Amount and name of political party or person paid for each contribution for political purposes over £50. Wholly owned subsidiary of UK company exempt	*19 (1967)*
11	Analysis of turnover and profit before tax, between differing classes of business (unless turnover less than £250,000) required only on group basis for a holding company	*17 (1967)*
12	Value of goods exported or statement that no goods exported (unless turnover less than £250,000)	*20 (1967)* *S.I. 1971 No. 2044*
	B. Information to be stated regarding the directors	
1	Names of directors at any time in period	*16(1) 1967*
2	Directors' interests in shareholdings of company or group (with comparatives or date first appointed a director if later) Certain exemptions for wholly owned subsidiaries	*16(1)(e) 1967* *S. I. 1968 (1533)*
3	Details of interests of directors in contracts with the company	*16(i)(c) 1967* *16(3) 1967*
4	Details of directors' rights to acquire shares	*16(i)(d) 1967*

19.8 Exercises: The Final Accounts of Companies

1. A limited company has authorised capital of 200 000 Ordinary Shares of which 100 000 shares of £1.00 are issued and 50 000 Preference Shares of £1.00 of which 30 000 are issued. On March 31st, 19.., it was found that the Net Profit was £27 050.00 for the year. There was also a balance on the Appropriation Account of £1 150.00 from the previous year. Fixed assets total £138 200 and Current assets £20 000. The directors resolved:

   (*a*) To put £5 000.00 to General Reserve and £2 000.00 to Plant Replacement Reserve.
   (*b*) To reserve £4 500.00 for Corporation Tax.
   (*c*) To pay the 5 per cent Preference Dividend.
   (*d*) To recommend a 10 per cent dividend on the Ordinary Shares.

   Show the Appropriation Account and the Balance Sheet. There are no current liabilities other than any resulting from the appropriation.

2. Draw up the Appropriation Account and Balance Sheet of Trihard Ltd, whose Authorised Capital is £100 000.00 made up of 80 000 £1.00 Ordinary Shares and 20 000 £1.00 7 per cent Preference Shares. Details are:

	£
Balance on Appropriation Account, January 1st, 19..	725.00
Profits for Year	11 206.00
Ordinary Share Capital Fully Paid	60 000.00
Preference Share Capital Fully Paid	20 000.00
Profits prior to Incorporation	8 260.00
Revenue Reserves—General Reserve	10 000.00
5% Debentures 600 at £10.00 each, secured on the Land and Buildings of the company	
Land and Buildings (at cost)	32 000.00
Plant and Machinery (at cost)	24 000.00
Provision for Depreciation on Plant and Machinery	6 000.00
Provision for Bad Debts	2 000.00
Motor Vehicles	2 300.00
Stock	17 561.00
Investments (at Market Value)	6 390.00
Cash at Bank	7 250.00
Debtors	18 500.00
Creditors	1 860.00
Cash in Hand	50.00
Trade Investments (valued by Directors at £19 500.00)	18 000.00

   The directors decide:

   (*a*) To pay the Preference Dividend for the year.
   (*b*) To put £5 000.00 into the General Reserve.
   (*c*) To recommend a dividend of 8 per cent on the Ordinary Shares.

3. The following Trial Balance was extracted from the books of Strangford, Ltd., at December 31st, 19. . :

TRIAL BALANCE

(as at December 31st, 19. .)

	£	£
Share Capital: Authorised and Issued 30 000 shares of £1.00		30 000.00
Carriage In	100.00	
Provision for Bad Debts, January 1st		200.00
Stock-in-Trade, January 1st	7 350.00	
Purchases	81 400.00	
Sales		102 540.00
Trade Debtors	9 500.00	
Trade Creditors		3 800.00
Freehold Property at Cost	16 000.00	
General Expenses	7 240.00	
Wages and Salaries	6 130.00	
Rates	250.00	
Directors' Fees (Profit and Loss Account)	1 000.00	
Furniture and Fittings at Cost	4 000.00	
Provision for Depreciation of Furniture and Fittings, January 1st		600.00
Bad Debts Written Off	630.00	
Profit and Loss Account Balance, January 1st		2 050.00
Balance at Bank	5 590.00	
	£139 190.00	£139 190.00

The following matters are to be taken into account:

(*a*) Wages and salaries outstanding at December 31st £240.00.
(*b*) The Provision for Bad Debts required at December 31st is £370.00.
(*c*) Rates paid in advance at December 31st amounted to £60.00.
(*d*) Stock-in-trade December 31st was valued at £5 480.00.
(*e*) Provide for depreciation of furniture and fittings at the rate of 5 per cent of cost.
(*f*) The directors propose to pay a dividend of 10 per cent for 19. . on the issued capital as at December 31st, 19. .

You are required to prepare a Trading and Profit and Loss Account for 19. . and a Balance Sheet as at December 31st, 19. . .

(RSA—Adapted)

4. The following Trial Balance was extracted from the books of Pembroke Ltd as on December 31st, 19. . :

TRIAL BALANCE

	£	£
Share Capital, Authorised and Issued, 100 000 Ordinary Shares of £1.00 each		100 000.00
5% Debentures		25 000.00
Purchases	150 430.00	
Sales		188 590.00
Stock-in-trade at January 1st	15 325.00	
Provision for Bad Debts		225.00
Freehold Properties (at cost)	115 000.00	
Furniture and Equipment (at cost)	13 400.00	
Provision for Depreciation of Furniture and Equipment		5 360.00
Debenture Interest to June 30th, 19..	625.00	
Bank Overdraft		140.00
Trade Debtors	16 440.00	
Trade Creditors		9 870.00
Preliminary Expenses	1 800.00	
Wages and Salaries	19 200.00	
Rent and Rates	1 850.00	
General Expenses	3 950.00	
Bad Debts	1 360.00	
Profit and Loss Account: Balance at January 1st, 19..		10 195.00
	£339 380.00	£339 380.00

You are given the following information:

(*a*) Stock-in-Trade at December 31st, 19.., £18 220.00.

(*b*) The Provision for Bad Debts is to be increased to £295.00.

(*c*) Rates paid in advance at December 31st were £90.00.

(*d*) Provision is to be made for depreciation of furniture and equipment at the rate of 10 per cent per annum (on cost).

(*e*) One quarter of the balance on the Preliminary Expenses Account is to be written off.

(*f*) The directors have decided to recommend a dividend of 7 per cent (ignore taxation).

You are required to prepare a Trading and Profit and Loss Account, a Profit and Loss Appropriation Account for the year 19.., and a Balance Sheet as on December 31st, 19..

(RSA—Adapted)

19.9 Club Accounts (The Accounts of Non-Profit-Making Organisations)

People join together for a multitude of reasons in voluntary organisations: for mutual entertainment, for protection, or for professional reasons. There are sports clubs, trade unions, consumer cooperatives, political associations, automobile associations, and many more. The richness of any society lies partly in the variety of the voluntary organisations it promotes.

From the book-keeper's point of view the aim of such organisations is the pursuit of some interest other than financial gain, so that they may all be termed non-profit-making organisations. Yet associations of this sort must have funds to promote their activities, and these funds must be honestly accounted for. The official elected for this purpose is called the Treasurer, one of the key figures on the committee which is elected to run the club. The others are the Secretary, responsible for organising the club's activities, and the Chairman, or President, who controls the meetings.

The Treasurer's functions are to collect subscriptions, disburse such funds as are needed in the course of the activities, and report to the members when required, but especially at the **Annual General Meeting**—an important occasion in the club's life. At this meeting the activities of the club are reviewed, criticisms are voiced, or praise is accorded the Committee. The Treasurer submits suitable Final Accounts to the members, supported by an audited statement approved by two members who were elected as auditors at the previous Annual General Meeting. In this chapter we shall clarify the form of Final Accounts suitable for clubs. Before we do so we must first consider the ordinary records of club receipts and payments.

The Analysed Cash Book of a Club

Clubs rarely keep a full set of Ledger Accounts, but some clubs are very large indeed and need just as huge an organisation as any other large-scale business. For example, the Automobile Association of Great Britain has an annual budget in excess of £55 million. It employs patrolmen, inspection staff, legal advisers, and operates a chain of regional headquarters. The Co-operative Movement is one of the greatest voluntary organisations in the world. In Great Britain trade exceeds £1 000 million a year. Such huge organisations can hardly conduct their affairs with a penny notebook, yet many club treasurers in small clubs do exactly that, whilst bigger clubs usually have just a Cash Book with analysis columns. We shall see that even very small clubs must analyse their receipts and payments once a year for the Annual General Meeting, so that we may say *the analytical Cash Book is the basic club record, or book of original entry*. Such a book is shown in Fig. 19.8.

In this type of book the Treasurer keeps a record of all sums received and paid, and analyses them into various subheadings as he goes along. He can add up the columns and cross-tot each page of the book to check that he is doing the work correctly and at any given time the balance in hand can easily be found.

A Treasurer who has no such book but merely keeps a record of the cash received and paid in an ordinary cash notebook will have to analyse the notebook at the end of the year, to find the totals spent under various headings. In this way he arrives at the same result as the Treasurer with the more sophisticated ruled book. From either method the Treasurer can prepare the Receipts and Payments Account.

The Receipts and Payments Account

Definition. The Receipts and Payments Account is the simplest way a Treasurer can account for the funds of a non-profit-making organisation. It is a statement of receipts and payments, drawn up from an analysis of the club's Cash Book. At the end of the year the Treasurer will take the final figures for the year's receipts and payments from the summary at the back of the Club Accounts book illustrated in Figure 19.8. These will be arranged as shown in Fig. 19.9.

Receipts for the month *(in cash and by cheque)* Month of JANUARY Year 19••

Date	Details	P.C.V.	1 Subs. £ p	2 Donations £ p	3 Refr. Sales £ p	4 Raffles £ p	5 Theatre Visits £ p	6 £ p	7 £ p	8 Misc. £ p	9 Cash drawn from bank £ p	10 In Cash £ p	11 By Cheque £ p
			Analysis Columns — You may head the spare columns to suit your own club or school									Amount Received	
JAN 4	Subscriptions 5 members		10 00									10 00	
5	Gift – Mrs Clark			5 25									5 25
11	Refreshments				3 25							3 25	
12	Subs Jones + Family		6 00										6 00
18	Refreshments				3 55							3 55	
19	Theatre Visit						8 50						8 50
25	Refreshments				2 80							2 80	
26	Subs. Brown + Smith		4 00									4 00	
30	Refreshments				2 95							2 95	
30	Raffle + Refreshments				4 20	2 45						6 65	
31	Cash from Bank										10 00	10 00	
	Totals *(cross-tot to check)*		20 00	5 25	16 75	2 45	8 50				10 00	43 20	19 75

Payments for the month *(in cash and by cheque)* Month of JANUARY 19••

Date	Details	P.C.V.	1 Equipment £ p	2 Refreshments £ p	3 Stationery £ p	4 Theatre Visit £ p	5 Raffle Prizes £ p	6 £ p	7 £ p	8 Misc. £ p	9 Cheques for cash £ p	10 In Cash £ p	11 By cheque £ p
			Analysis Columns —you may head the spare columns to suit your own club or school									Amount Paid	
JAN 9	Table Tennis Table		24 50										24 50
10	Refreshments			1 40								1 40	
17	"			1 55								1 55	
19	Duplicating Paper				1 85							1 85	
20	Theatre Visits					9 25							9 25
25	Refreshments			1 42								1 42	
29	"			2 05								2 05	
30	Raffle Prizes						1 85					1 85	
30	Dart Board Lighting		15 00									15 00	
31	Cash From Bank										10 00		10 00
	Totals (Cross-tot to check)		39 50	6 42	1 85	9 25	1 85				10 00	25 12	43 75

If entries have been analysed correctly total of columns 1-9 will equal total of columns 10 and 11.

Fig. 19.8. The analysed Cash Book of a club (by courtesy of George Vyner Ltd).

QUEENSWOOD COMMUNITY ASSOCIATION

RECEIPTS and PAYMENTS ACCOUNT

Annual General Meeting

Year ending December 31st 19..

Receipts	£	p	Payments	£	p
Opening Balances at Start of Year:			Equipment	249	50
Cash in Hand	16	54	Refreshment materials	162	25
Cash at Bank	132	20	Stationery	38	45
Subscriptions 240 @ £2	480	00	Theatre visit	330	00
Donations	25	00	Raffle prizes	18	00
Refreshments Sales	383	65	Miscellaneous	127	60
Raffles	28	30			
Theatre visits income	347	50			
Miscellaneous items	23	50	Closing Balances at end of year:		
			Cash in Hand	18	12
			Cash at Bank	492	77
	£1436	69		£1436	69

Auditors' names and Signatures: __________

Treasurer's Name and Signature: __________

Fig. 19.9. A simple Final Account for a club.

Notes

(i) The end-of-year position of the club funds is given by the Closing Balances on the Receipts and Payments Account above. (The cash should be available for counting at the AGM. The bank statement and bank reconciliation statement should also be presented.)

(ii) Stocks in hand are valued at £14. (A valuation should be placed on any stocks of refreshments, stationery, etc., based on cost, or the current selling price if this is lower than the cost price.)

(iii) Assets available are valued at £152. (Where assets have been purchased some reasonable value should be placed upon them, and it may be necessary to say who looks after them.)

(iv) Creditors. (Any outstanding debts by the club should be listed showing the creditors' names and the amounts owed.)

(v) Debtors. If money is owed to the club the amount should be given, but the names of members who have not paid their subscriptions should not be revealed—only the total value of such debts.

Limitations of the Receipts and Payments Account

For a variety of reasons the Receipts and Payments Account is unsatisfactory as a record of the club's activities, and only very small clubs would produce their accounts in this way at the Annual General Meeting. The chief objections are:

(*a*) There is no record of the club's initial assets apart from cash in hand. Where a club had at the start of the year premises or equipment of value it is unsatisfactory to have no mention of this at the Annual General Meeting.

(*b*) Similarly, and more important, there is no record of the assets owned by the club at the end of the year. If a club has equipment it should be shown as a list of assets on a Balance Sheet.

(*c*) There is no mention of liabilities outstanding. The members must ask the Treasurer about outstanding bills, and payments in advance to the club.

(*d*) The members cannot see whether a profit or loss was made on the year's activities. In club accounts it is not usual to call profits and losses by these names. It is not the business of clubs to make profits out of the membership; the aim is rather to provide amenities with funds mutually subscribed, whether by subscription or by lotteries and similar harmless fund-raising techniques.

We therefore use the phrase **surplus** for profits, and **deficiency** for losses. Members have either contributed more than necessary, leaving a surplus, or less than necessary, leaving a deficiency of funds.

We are therefore faced with the usual Final Accounts problems—how to present a 'true and fair view' of the club's affairs. The solution is to present a more sophisticated set of Final Accounts than the Receipts and Payments Account. These are the **Income and Expenditure Account** and a **Balance Sheet** as at the date of the Annual General Meeting. Sometimes a Trading Account is also produced if sales of drinks, etc., are considerable.

The Accumulated Fund of a Club

Just as the phrase 'Profit and Loss' is not an appropriate one for non-profit-making organisations, so the word 'capital' is not really appropriate either. 'Capital' has acquired implications that are distasteful to many societies—co-operative societies, for example. So the gentler phrase **Accumulated Fund** has come to be used for the capital fund of a club. It describes exactly how the fund is collected over the years.

The calculation of the Accumulated Fund is one that gives many students difficulty, yet it is quite simple. The Accumulated Fund, like the Capital Fund of a sole trader, can be calculated by the formula:

Accumulated Fund = Total Assets − External Liabilities

What the club owned at the beginning of the year, less what is owed at the start of the year, gives the Accumulated (or Capital) Fund at the beginning. It is exactly like doing the arithmetic for an opening journal entry. The Accumulated Fund occupies the same position as the capital on the Balance Sheet. Like the Capital Account it is increased by the surplus (profit) which is added to it, or decreased by the deficiency (loss) which is deducted from it.

Example 19.2. The Space Exploration Society was set up some years ago to promote an interest in astronomy and space research. On January 1st, 19.., it had assets as follows: Premises £2 000.00; Telescopes, etc., £1 800.00; Furniture and Fittings £500.00; Cash at bank £380.50; Cash in hand £23.50; subscriptions were due from 15 members at £5.00 each, and 17 members had paid next year's subscriptions in advance at £5.00 each; a printer's bill for £15.75 was due. Calculations for the Fund would be set out as follows, and would appear on the Balance Sheet as Accumulated Fund at the beginning of the year:

Total Assets		£
Premises		2 000.00
Telescopes		1 800.00
Furniture and Fittings		500.00
Cash at Bank		380.50
Cash in Hand		23.50
Subscriptions due		75.00
Less Liabilities		4 779.00
Subscriptions in Advance	85.00	
Printing Bill	15.75	
		100.75
Accumulated Fund		£4 678.25

Trading Accounts of Clubs

It is quite common to prepare a number of Trading Accounts to show the results of a particular aspect of the club's activities. For instance, a Bar Trading Account for clubs with licensed premises is very common, especially since stocks would enter into the calculations. Similarly, a Trading Account on refreshments or on dances and socials might be presented as a preliminary account for Final Accounts.

The Income and Expenditure Account

This is the main account for the Final Accounts of a club. It is exactly like the Profit and Loss Account of a sole trader except that the final result is called a surplus, or a deficiency, not a net profit or net loss. Once again we must state the period 'for year ended, etc.' and we must be careful to make adjustments so that the revenue expenses and revenue receipts are those only for the period concerned. Capital items do not enter into a Revenue Account, so that any equipment purchased does not appear in the Income and Expenditure Account but goes straight to the Balance Sheet.

Example 19.3. The Woodlands Old Girls' Association was formed some years ago, and at January 1st, 19.., had assets and liabilities as follows: premises £250.00; games apparatus £50.00; cash at bank £50.00; cash £42.00; subscriptions were due from three members at £2.00 each and were paid in advance for next year by seven members, at £2.00 each. The treasurer produces the following Receipts and Payments Account for 19.. on December 31st.

RECEIPTS AND PAYMENTS ACCOUNT
(for year ending December 31st, 19..)

Receipts		*Payments*	
Balance of Cash in Hand	42.00	Rent of Ground	10.00
Subscriptions	250.00	Groundsmen's Tips	25.00
Profit on Dances	40.00	Purchase of Equipment	60.00
Hire of Pitches	5.00	Donation to School Funds	100.00
		Balance in Hand	142.00
	£337.00		£337.00

You are asked to prepare the Income and Expenditure Account and the Balance Sheet at December 31st, 19.., bearing in mind that (*a*) subscriptions in advance were £25 and (*b*) the groundsman was owed £5 for preparing new hockey posts.

The solution is given in Figs. 19.10 and 19.11, but the calculation of the Accumulated Fund at start is as follows:

	£
Total Assets	
Premises	250.00
Games Apparatus	50.00
Cash at Bank	50 00
Cash in Hand	42.00
Subscriptions Due	6.00
	398.00
Less Liabilities	
Subscriptions in Advance	14.00
Accumulated Fund at Start	384.00

Notice particularly that subscriptions in advance are a liability, since we owe the members one year's entertainment, etc., in return for their subscriptions.

The task is now to prepare the Income and Expenditure Account and the Balance Sheet, from the receipts and payments we have been given. Since the Receipts and Payments Account is an analysed Cash Book, and this Cash Book has never been posted to any Ledger Accounts, it follows that the profits are on the debit side. They have never been posted over to the credit side of the profit accounts as in an ordinary

WOODLANDS OLD GIRLS' ASSOCIATION

INCOME AND EXPENDITURE ACCOUNT

(*for year ended December 31st, 19..*)

Rent		10.00	Subscriptions	250.00
Groundsman's Tips	25.00		*Less* Subscriptions in Arrear	
Add amount due	5.00		on January 1st	6.00
		30.00		244.00
Donation to School Funds		100.00	*Add* Subscriptions in	
Surplus (transferred to			Advance on January 1st	14.00
Accumulated Fund)		138.00		
				258.00
			Less Subscriptions in	
			Advance on December 31st	25.00
				233.00
			Profit on Dances	40.00
			Hire of Pitches	5.00
		£278.00		£278.00

Fig. 19.10. An Income and Expenditure Account.

BALANCE SHEET

(*as at December 31st, 19..*)

ACCUMULATED FUND		£	FIXED ASSETS		£
At Start	384.00		Premises		250.00
Add Surplus	138.00		Games Apparatus	50.00	
			Add New Apparatus	60.00	
		522.00			
					110.00
					360.00
CURRENT LIABILITIES			CURRENT ASSETS		
Subscriptions in Advance	25.00		Cash at Bank	50.00	
Groundsman's Tip	5.00		Cash in Hand	142.00	
		30.00			192.00
		£552.00			£552.00

Fig. 19.11. A club's Balance Sheet.

business. Similarly, the losses are on the credit side, having never been posted to the debit side of expense accounts. The resulting Income and Expenditure Account and Balance Sheet are as shown on page 313. The figures for the Balance Sheet come from three places: (*a*) the opening Accumulated Fund calculation, (*b*) the capital expenditure in the Receipts and Payments Account, and (*c*) the surplus of the Income and Expenditure Account.

The student should note carefully how this improved set of Final Accounts clarifies the position to the members. We now have a clear picture of the surplus collected during the year. We can also see what the assets are, and whether there are any outstanding liabilities. We have adjusted the receipts and payments to the exact figures for the year, and have carried our surplus to the Accumulated Fund.

19.10 Exercises: The Final Accounts of Clubs

1. The following sums of money were received and paid by the Treasurer of the Coronation Croquet Club during the season April–September, 19... On April 1st the club had a cash balance of £40.65 brought forward from the year before.

Moneys received: Subscriptions £126.00; visitors' fees £16.00; refreshment sales £48.55; sales of ties and blazer badges £22.35; lottery receipts £38.95.

Moneys spent: Postage £4.65; refreshment expenses £31.15; gift to groundsman £10.50; treasurer's honorarium £5.25; prizes and trophies £32.55; lottery printing £0.65; lottery prize £25.00.

Draw up the Receipts and Payments Accounts for the year, for submission to the Annual General Meeting on September 30th; 19... Bring out clearly the Cash Balance on September 30th.

(East Anglian Examination Board—Adapted)

2. The following particulars relate to the Hole in the Road Club for the year ended December 31st, 19... The treasurer presents the information to the members in the form of a Receipts and Payments Account. You are required to draw up this account.

	£
Cash Balance:	
January 1st	10.50
December 31st	9.26
Bank Balance:	
January 1st	60.00
December 31st	28.72
Payments:	
Refreshments	141.10
New Games Equipment	19.00
Rent to September 30th	90.00
Rates	25.00
Printing	15.58
Stationery	28.12
Postage	17.00
Repairs to Games Equipment	12.10
Lighting and Heating	51.50
Wages	120.60
Dance Expenses	53.60
Competition Prizes	14.30
Receipts:	
Subscriptions	332.10
Sale of Dance Tickets	73.18
Competition Fees	20.00
Sale of Refreshments	130.10

(RSA—Adapted)

3. The Arthurian England Archaeological Society has the following Receipts and Expenses during the summer season 19..:

Receipts: Subscriptions £176.00; donations £250.00; collections at 'digs' £127.30; sale of refreshments £37.50; raffle (surplus artefacts) £27.80.

Payments: Rights to dig on land £50.00; hire of barrows, etc., £25.00; small tools £12.50; refreshment purchases £28.50; report printing £75.00; wages of student labour £25.50; transport costs £72.50; carbon-14 test charges £36.20.

Draw up the Receipts and Payments Account and calculate the balance in hand.

4. The New Town Association began activities on January 1st, 19.., and the following is a summary of its transactions for that year:

		£
Receipts:		
Subscriptions		2 750.50
Net Income from Dances and Whist Drives, etc.		1 120.50
Interest		15.00
		3 886.00
Payments:		
Rent of Premises	900.00	
Rates	120.00	
Lighting, Heating, etc.	480.00	
Purchase of Savings Certificates	500.00	
		2 000.00
Balance in Hand at December 31st, 19.. (including £1 800 in Trustee Savings Bank)		£1 886.00

One quarter's rent, £300.00, is due at December 31st, 19.., and a £160.00 heating bill is not paid; subscriptions received include £25.00 in advance for 19..; rates in advance at December 31st, 19.., were £15.00.

You are asked to prepare the Association's Income and Expenditure Account for the year and its Balance Sheet on December 31st, 19...

5. (*a*) Distinguish briefly between (i) a Receipts and Payments Account, (ii) an Income and Expenditure Account, and (iii) a Profit and Loss Account.

(*b*) The following is a summary of the receipts and payments of the Freshwater Angling Society for the period from the date of formation on January 1st, 19.., to December 31st, 19..:

	£		£
Subscriptions	780.00	Purchase of Clubhouse	1 500.00
Gate Money	1 154.00	Purchase of Refreshments	150.00
Sales of Refreshments	385.00	Equipment	125.50
Loan from Friendly Bank Ltd	1 000.00	Printing, Stationery, etc.	84.50
		Travelling Expenses	136.00
		Sundry Expenses	84.00
		Rent	500.00
		Balance (c/d) of which £700 is banked)	739.00
	£3 319.00		£3 319.00

Prepare a Trading Account for Refreshments, the Income and Expenditure Account of the club for the year ended December 31st, 19.., and the Balance Sheet at that date, taking into consideration the following:

(*a*) There is an unpaid account for printing amounting to £12.80.
(*b*) Subscriptions received included £10.00 paid in advance.
(*c*) The stock of refreshment materials on hand at December 31st was valued at £8.00.

6. After the passing of certain entries for the calculation of the profits or losses on the restaurant and bar, the Trial Balance of the Bluewater Sailing club on December 31st, 19.., is as follows:

	Dr. £	Cr. £
Club Motor Launch	1 850	
Members' Subscriptions Received		5 250
Accumulated Fund at January 1st, 19..		28 883
Club Sailing Boats	4 300	
Hiring Fees Received for Club Boats		1 550
Leasehold Premises	14 000	
Maintenance Expenses of Launch and Club Boats	850	
Furniture and Equipment	1 600	
Cash in Hand	184	
Balance at Bank	3 275	
Stocks of Wines and Spirits	1 785	
Racing Entrance Fees Received		330
Cost of Racing Prizes	250	
Salaries of Secretary and Office Assistant	5 950	
Sundry Creditors		866
Printing and Stationery	185	
Wages of Club Boatman	2 485	
General Expenses	230	
Rates	330	
Loss on Restaurant Catering	185	
Profit on Bar		760
Office Expenses, Postages and Telephone	180	
	£37 639	37 639

You are required to draw up the club's Income and Expenditure Account for the year, and a Balance Sheet as at December 31st, 19.., taking the following into account:

(*a*) The motor launch, the fleet of club boats, and the furniture and equipment should all be depreciated by 10 per cent.

(*b*) On January 1st, 19.., the club's lease had 20 years to run, and a proportionate amount for the current year should be written off the Leasehold Premises Account.

(*c*) Members' subscriptions for the current year, amounting to £60.00, were in arrear and unpaid on December 31st, 19..

19.11 Local Government Accounts

Local government bodies in the United Kingdom are organisations of enormous importance carrying out a wide range of activities in the fields of education, highways and transportation, leisure and amenity services, police and other protection services, welfare and social services, etc. Most of the major counties have budgets of more than £100 million annually; some of them far more than this. A specialist accountancy body, the *Chartered Institute of Public Finance and Accountancy*, whose members occupy all the major positions in this important sector of the economy, recommends appropriate forms of accounts and generally ensures that a high standard of professional behaviour is maintained throughout the service.

Clearly a full account of local government finance is impossible here, and is a specialist subject of study. For Business Statistics and Accounting we must limit ourselves to a general view of the Final Accounts presented to the public by a typical authority. The courtesy of Cambridgeshire County Council in permitting the use of the extracts given below from its Annual Accounts publication is greatly appreciated.

Revenue Accounts. 'Revenue Account' is a general term used in many fields of accountancy to describe an account where income is set against expenditure. In local government Revenue Accounts, although quite large sums are received as income for some of the services provided, expenditure heavily outweighs income on most of the services. For example, in Education considerable sums of income for such items as fees from evening institutes are still relatively insignificant when set against the vast costs of primary and secondary education.

The published accounts cannot possibly include much of the detailed accounting which goes into the day-to-day records of the Authority, and a summary alone is possible. Such a 'Summary Revenue Account' is reproduced on page 318, while the more important features are referred to in the notes opposite.

Balance Sheets. Once again the Balance Sheet of a local government body such as the Cambridgeshire County Council is a formidable document. There are countless premises in use, each with its own inventory of equipment, stocks and spares. Every department has its transport, creditors, debtors, cash in hand, etc. A Balance Sheet can only be presented in summary form, as a Consolidated Balance Sheet presenting the final totals for the assets and liabilities of all these wide-ranging facilities and services. The detailed figures must be looked at in the departmental records, which appear as annexes to the summary accounts in the body of the published 'Accounts'.

Fig. 19.13 shows the Consolidated Balance Sheet figures, and the notes below it explain some of the chief features.

19.12 The Accounts of Central Government

In Gladstone's day, when 'the chief preoccupation of Governments was the saving of candle-ends', the whole of the nation's public expenditure was only £67 million pounds. The present-day figures shown in the accounts of this section run into billions of pounds. It might be thought that an elementary book of accounting need not go into such massive sums, but in order to com-

SUMMARY REVENUE ACCOUNT

	Gross expenditure (£)	*Income* (£)	*Specific grants, recharges and reimbursements* (£)	19..–19.. *Net expenditure* (£)
Education	74 198 164	3 931 830	4 909 517	65 356 817
Highways and Transportation	12 129 433	871 017	3 972 098	7 286 318
Leisure and Amenities	1 872 251	56 267	1 620	1 814 364
Magistrates' Courts	600 338	2 272	473 404	124 662
Planning	514 173	5 011	—	509 162
Police	9 346 482	778 250	4 251 869	4 316 363
Policy and Resources	2 172 307	2 061 176	961 903	850 772 Cr.
Probation and After-Care	428 474	7 641	335 750	85 083
Public Protection	3 088 813	190 845	72 445	2 825 523
Small Holdings	1 139 876	778 050	94 885	266 941
Social Services	10 035 055	1 863 453	85 148	8 086 454
	115 525 366	10 545 812	15 158 639	89 820 915
Less Rate Support Grant—				
Needs Element				35 207 666
Resources Element				15 638 639
				50 846 305
NET EXPENDITURE from rates, balances, etc.				£38 974 610

Amount raised by precept	37 532 884
Loan in aid of rates*	416 000
Less transfer to balances	—
Add transfer from balances	1 025 726
	£38 974 610

Fig. 19.12. The Revenue Account of a local authority.

Notes

(i) The account is set by the printer in vertical style. The expenditure comes in the top half of the page and the receipts in the lower half of the page. However, this vertical style is modified, so that the Gross Expenditure has any income and specific grants, etc., set against it at once (in the top half of the page), thus revealing the Net Expenditure to the County Council in the end column.

(ii) How this net expenditure is financed is then shown in the further development of the end column of the accounts. Continuing the style adopted of deducting grants made by outside bodies, the Rate Support Grant from Government sources is deducted—a total of more than £50 million—leaving a final 'net expenditure' for the County Council to finance.

(iii) In the lower part of the page this expenditure is shown to have been financed chiefly by levying rates on the residents in the County (Amount raised by precept). A small loan in aid of rates, from a New Town Authority, contributed almost half a million pounds, and the final balance had to be transferred from reserves.

(iv) The whole presentation is neat, lucid and economical.

(v) The published accounts also included the figures for the previous year, for comparison purposes. These have been omitted for reasons of space.

* Loan in aid of rates from Peterborough Development Corporation towards expansion costs (repayable when New Town produces a surplus).

CONSOLIDATED BALANCE SHEET
(at March 31st, 19. .)

		31.3.19. . (£)
Assets		
Capital Outlay		101 914 699
Deferred Charges		1 553 554
Suspense Accounts		180 464
Stocks		524 679
Investments		62 340
Debtors		
Government Departments		1 302 600
Other		4 371 748
Deferred Debtors		1 331 298
		111 241 382
Liabilities		
Loans Outstanding	28 517 982	
Temporary Borrowing	2 035 244	
Sundry Creditors	8 880 357	
Cash Overdrawn	6 700 679	
		46 134 262
NET ASSETS		£65 107 120

Represented by:	
Capital Discharged	50 470 829
Capital Receipts Unapplied	1 047 134
Capital Fund	3 160 229
Repairs and Renewals Fund	1 112 604
Capital Grant Unapplied	600 000
Trust Funds	
Capital Balances	47 779
Revenue Balances	7 945
County Fund Balance	8 660 600
	65 107 120

NOTE: This Consolidated Balance Sheet excludes the Superannuation Fund.

Fig. 19.13. The Balance Sheet of a local authority.

Notes

(i) The assets are rather unusually displayed, the term Capital Outlay covering a huge total of capital assets purchased in the various cost centres whose accounts must be referred to in the annual accounts if details are required. They are valued at cost.

(ii) The term 'Suspense Accounts' refers to 'payments in advance' carried over to the next financial year.

(iii) The term 'Deferred Charges' refers to expenses incurred in the issue of stocks and loans over the years. Like 'Formation Expenses' in companies they are fictitious assets, and are being written down over the years.

(iv) The published accounts contain brief explanations of the bases on which the Balance Sheet has been prepared, but the reader will see that these accounts involve specialised arrangements more appropriate to an advanced book on public accountancy than the present introductory volume.

plete our picture of the book-keeping scene it is necessary to look at the accounts of Central Government.

Basically it is very simple. There are three main sections to be looked at. These are:

(*a*) The Consolidated Fund
(*b*) The National Loans Fund
(*c*) The National Loans Fund Balance Sheet

(*a*) **The Consolidated Fund.** A single account, the Consolidated Fund, ultimately receives all the moneys collected by taxation and pays out all the sums required to meet day-by-day expenditure in the spending departments (called 'Supply Services'). The difference between the receipts and payments must either be a 'surplus' or a 'deficiency'. If there is a surplus it is used to reduce the National Debt. In times of heavy public expenditure there is more likely to be a deficit and this will need to be borrowed. This forms the largest part of PSBR (Public Sector Borrowing Requirement) and in the first instance it is borrowed from the National Loans Fund.

The Consolidated Fund is shown in Fig. 19.14 and explained in the notes below it.

(*b*) **The National Loans Fund.** The second part of the nation's accounts is the National Loans Fund itself. Here we have the actual management of the nation's finances, where attempts are made to cover Government expenditure, supervise cash flows, borrow where necessary, etc. This Fund is illustrated in Fig. 19.15 and described in the notes below it.

(*c*) **The National Loans Fund Balance Sheet.** This is rather an unusual Balance Sheet. It has no fixed assets or current assets, since these would be recorded somewhere in the departments and ministries which actually control the property, machinery, etc. Instead its assets are the debts these bodies still owe to the National Loans Fund, whilst its liabilities are the National Debt itself.

The Balance Sheet is shown in Fig. 19.16 and described in the notes below it.

19.13 The Increased Net Worth Method of Finding Profits

We have learned how to calculate the profits of the three major types of private-sector business units: sole traders, partnerships and limited companies. We have also learned how to account for the funds of non-profit-making bodies such as clubs and societies, and public-sector institutions like local authorities and the Central Government. It remains to deal with one final method of discovering the financial results of an enterprise—the increased net worth method of finding profits.

Single Entry Book-keeping. Whilst all the final accounts already dealt with have assumed that businessmen keep financial records, it is a fact that many small businessmen do not. In the past the vast majority of businessmen kept no records at all, or used the 'Butcher's Book' method. The family butcher, supplying Mrs Jones with meat on credit, wrote her debt into a debtors' record of some sort, and crossed the entry through when she paid up at the end of the week or month. All such methods of book-keeping are called 'single-entry' book-keeping, since they do not carry out a proper 'double-entry' procedure.

Consolidated Fund
(in the year ended March 31st, 19..)

Receipts	£	£	*Payments*		£
Inland Revenue	20 709 965 000		Supply Services		37 066 246 967
Customs and Excise	10 900 122 000		Consolidated Fund Standing Services:		
Vehicle Excise Duty	845 884 000		Payment to the National Loans Fund in respect		
			of service of the National Debt		1 133 455 854
Total Tax Revenue		32 455 971 000	Northern Ireland: share of taxes, etc.		637 673 107
Broadcast Receiving Licences		246 714 647	Payments to the European Communities, etc.		548 736 444
Interest and Dividends		190 008 823	Other Standing Services:		
Miscellaneous Receipts		885 354 689	Civil List	1 360 200	
Contingencies Fund: Repayments		320 000 000	Annuities and pensions	1 612 735	
			Salaries and Allowances	90 230	
Total Receipts		34 098 049 159	Courts of Justice	7 612 168	
Deficit (*met from the National Loans Fund*)		5 594 242 536	Post-war credits (including interest)	973 272	
			Miscellaneous services	4 530 718	
					16 179 323
			Issues to the Contingencies Fund		290 000 000
		£39 692 291 695	Total Payments		£39 692 291 695

Treasury
October 17th, 19..

Fig. 19.14. The nation's accounts. Part I: The Consolidated Fund.

Notes

(*i*) The receipts come chiefly from taxation, television licences, and odd amounts of interest, repayments, etc.

(ii) Payments are largely made by the spending departments, and are called Supply Services. There are several other headings, like the Civil List which supports the monarchy and the sums paid to support the judicial system.

(iii) In the year in question the deficit was £5 500 million and was met by borrowing from the National Loans Fund.

National Loans Fund

(in the year ended March 31st, 19..)

Receipts		£	*Payments*	£
Balance at start of year		2 024 862	Service of the National Debt: Interest	4 449 341 629
Interest, etc.			Management and expenses	84 960 084
Interest on loans repayable to the National Loans Fund	2 554 631 335			4 534 301 713
Profits of the Issue Department of the Bank of England	845 822 974		Consolidated Fund deficit met from National Loans Fund	5 594 242 536
Miscellaneous Receipts	391 550		Issues in respect of loans	4 453 042 673
Service of the National Debt: Balance met by Consolidated Fund	1 133 455 854		Exchange Equalisation Account: Issues of sterling capital	3 000 000 000
			International Monetary Fund	309 963 665
		4 534 301 713	National Debt: sums repaid	163 175 758 491
Repayment of loans		3 512 670 811		
Exchange Equalisation Account: repayments of sterling capital		900 000 000	Total Payments	181 067 309 078
National Debt: sums borrowed		172 119 889 503	Balance at end of year	1 910 723
Other receipts: Death Duties Surrendered Securities Account: transfer of surplus		332 912		
Total Receipts		£181 069 219 801		£181 069 219 801

Fig. 19.15. The Nation's Accounts. Part II: The National Loans Fund.

Notes

(*i*) On the receipts side we have about £4 500 million coming in as interest on loans supplied to various public bodies in years gone by and in various other ways.

(ii) A further type of receipt is the actual repayment of loans. For example, New Town Development Corporations eventually start to make a profit and repay the loans borrowed while the town was under construction.

(iii) The chief item here is the receipt of huge sums borrowed by the Government, £172 000 million. This is mostly the National Debt rolling over. As old securities come to their payment date and are repaid the money is borrowed back by selling new securities to the public. But a glance at the payments side shows that borrowing (receipts) exceeded repayments by about £9 000 million.

(iv) On the payments side the huge sums needed to service the National Debt (i.e. pay the interest on it) are truly staggering; £4 500 million. This is four times as much as the total housing budget, for example.

Please send me ...... copy/ies of

Answer Book: Business Statistics and Accounting

Name ....

Address ....

....

....

Payment enclosed (95 per copy, postage included)

ANSWER BOOK

A booklet is available containing answers to all the Exercises sections in this book, and may be obtained *in the UK only* by filling in the other side of this card and returning it with payment of 95p to

Made Simple Books,
William Heinemann Ltd.,
10 Upper Grosvenor St.,
London W1X 9PA

Summary of National Loans Fund Assets and Liabilities

Assets at March 31st, 19..	£	*Liabilities at March 31st, 19..*	£
Advances outstanding	27 898 707 723	National Debt outstanding	67 165 824 431
Exchange Equalisation Account: sterling capital	2 500 000 000		
Subscriptions and contributions to international financial organisation: International Monetary Fund	1 759 192 915		
Other assets	899 858 027		
	33 057 758 665		
Balance being the liability of the Consolidated Fund under Section 19(1) of the National Loans Act, 1968	34 108 065 766		
	£67 165 824 431		£67 165 824 431

Fig. 19.16. The Nation's Accounts. Part III: The Balance Sheet of the National Loans Fund.

Notes

(*i*) Note that this Balance Sheet is done the correct way round, with the assets on the left and the liabilities on the right. Is it too much to hope that everyone else should copy the Treasury. (See page 245.)

(ii) The single liability is the National Debt—given in greater detail elsewhere in ghe published accounts.

(iii) The assets are the debts owed by countless Ministries, Departments, Local Authorities and other institutions to the Fund. There are also one or two other funds to which contributions have been made as a matter of policy, but one day the money might return to the National Loans Fund Authorities so it is technically a debt owed to the Fund by these bodies—notably the I.M.F.

Profit as an Increase in Net Worth. Imagine that a man starts business with £100 capital, which he uses to buy a second-hand motor vehicle. He then resells it during the day for £120 cash. He uses £5 to buy a meal during the day (drawings) and at the end of the day has £115. Clearly there has been an increase in his 'net worth' from £100 at the start of the day to £115 at the end of the day, which looks like a profit of £15. However, he has also lived through the day, by taking 'Drawings' of £5. The true profit is therefore:

$$\text{Profit} = \text{Increase in Net Worth} + \text{Drawings} = £20$$

The reader might argue that this is obvious, because it is the difference between the cost price and selling price of the car. This is true, of course, but if we substitute a year's activities for a day's activities, the range of purchases and sales would be much greater, and it would be impossible to arrive at a profit figure because the man has kept no records. What we can do is count up his 'net worth' at the end of the year and estimate his drawings during the year. We can then find out his increase in net worth, by taking initial net worth from final net worth and hence his profit for the year. In order to do this we draw up two **Statements of Affairs.**

Statements of Affairs. When Simon Stevin of Bruges invented the Balance Sheet he called it a 'Statement of Affairs'. This term is still used in single-entry and bankruptcy proceedings, where the exact financial situation of a businessman at a given date has to be determined. In finding the increase in a trader's net worth we need to know his state of affairs at the start and the end of the year. The change in his state then helps us find what profit he made in the year. The following example illustrates the matter.

Example 19.4. On January 1st A. Brown sets up in business with a capital of £100. At the end of the year he has assets as follows: Stock of motor vehicles for resale £4 280, Office equipment £135, Cash at Bank £5 250, Cash in hand £860. He estimates his drawings at £5 per day for 310 days, and he has given his wife £40 per week for 52 weeks. What are his profits for the year?

The Statement of Affairs at the start of the year reads as follows:

STATEMENT OF AFFAIRS
(*as at January 1st, 19..*)

	£		£
Capital	100	Cash in hand	100

The Statement of Affairs at the end of the year reads as follows:

STATEMENT OF AFFAIRS
(*as at December 31st, 19..*)

	£			£
Capital (Net Worth) of business to owner of business	10 525	*Fixed Assets*		
		Office Equipment		135
		Current Assets		
		Stock for re-sale	4 280	
		Cash at Bank	5 250	
		Cash in Hand	860	
				10 390
	£10 525			£10 525

Calculations

Drawings = £5 × 310 + £40 × 52
= £1 550 + £2 080
= £3 630

Increase in Net Worth = £10 525 − £100 (Capital at start)
= £10 425

Profit = Increase in Net Worth + Drawings = £10 425 + £3 630
= £14 055

The concept of profit as an increase in net worth is a most important one. Although the year's activities have involved many items of expenditure which do not appear in A. Brown's calculations (rent, rates, light and heat, etc.), he has clearly met all these expenses during the year out of the business takings. These payments have cancelled out some of the receipts during the year but the rest of the receipts have resulted in the increased wealth he now enjoys. Clearly he has established a nice little business during the year, for his wealth has grown from £100 to £10 525 and he has lived through the year as well by drawing £3 630.

Extra Capital Contributed. Sometimes a trader's increased wealth is caused partly by an injection of extra capital from private sources. For example, if A. Brown has benefited from a legacy of £5 000 during the year and had put this sum into the business, the increased net worth of £10 425 would be partly explained by this legacy, and not entirely be due to profit. Clearly any such increase would not be taxable as part of profits. In this case the increase in net worth is only £5 425, and the profit when drawings were added would be only £9 055.

Inland Revenue and the Increased Net Worth Method. This method of discovering profits is the one used by the Inland Revenue when a trader does not keep proper records. It is, of course, open to some abuse, for a trader might try salting profits away in odd corners and not declaring them. It is well known that the Inland Revenue Investigation Department follows closely all reports of robberies. The man who claims that thieves stole £7 000 from his bedroom wardrobe has suffered a severe loss. When the Inland Revenue have finished enquiring how he came to have £7 000 in his bedroom wardrobe in the first place he may find himself paying back tax on sums of money which the burglar has enjoyed.

19.14 Exercises: Finding Profits by the Increased Net Worth Method

1. The following Statements of Affairs have been drawn up to give the financial position as on January 1st, 19.., and December 31st, 19.., respectively, of A. Brogan, who keeps his books on a single entry basis:

STATEMENT OF AFFAIRS
(*as at January 1st, 19..*)

	£			£
Capital		*Fixed Assets*		
At Start	8 940	Fixtures		940
Current Liabilities		*Current Assets*		
Creditors	1 062	Stock	5 040	
		Debtors	3 511	
		Cash	511	
				9 062
	£10 002			£10 002

STATEMENT OF AFFAIRS
(as at December 31st, 19..)

		£			£
Capital			*Fixed Assets*		
At close		12 014	Fixtures		880
Current Liabilities			*Current Assets*		
Creditors	1 356		Stock	5 600	
Wages Due	50		Debtors	4 600	
			Cash at Bank	1 700	
		1 406	Cash in Hand	640	
					12 540
		£13 420			£13 420

Brogan has transferred £200 a month regularly from his business bank account to his private bank account by way of drawings, and has taken £50 of stock for his private use. The alteration in the value of the fixtures represents depreciation. Calculate Brogan's profits for the year.

2. A. Rover is in the entertainments profession. He has little time to keep books and relies solely on his memory for receiving fees and paying his way. Once a year he consults his accountant on his financial position. They draw up the following figures:

	January 1st	*December 31st*
	£	£
Cash in Hand	55	326
Cash at Bank	855	7 761
Instruments and Electronic Equipment	800	2 400
Motor Vehicles	560	1 700
Debts Due by A. Rover	126	641
Fees Due to A. Rover	25	461

Capital contributed during year (and partly responsible for his extra assets) as a result of a legacy and prize award, £2 000.00. Drawings for personal support during year, £1 240.

You are asked to draw up a Statement of Affairs as at December 31st, and to show your calculations of the profit made during the year.

3. On January 1st, 19.., T. J. Wise began business by paying £1 600 into a Bank Account. He did not keep complete books of account, and used the Bank Account for both his private and business expenses. On March 31st, 19.., Wise wished to ascertain his profit or loss for the quarter. On that date his cash in hand was £20 and the balance at the bank £550. Stock-in-trade was valued at £1 680 and a motor van at £900. Trade creditors were £992 and trade debtors £378. Rent of £50 was prepaid, and an account for electricity, £38, was outstanding

An examination of bank withdrawals disclosed that £516 of these were for private expenses. Wise had also taken £434 for private expenses out of the business takings before paying them into the bank. The motor van was brought into the business during the quarter at the same figure as its valuation on March 31st, 19..

Prepare a statement to show the profit or loss of the business for the quarter ended March 31st, 19...

4. On January 1st, 19.., A. Singleton decided to go into business. His only asset was

a bank balance of £2 000. For the next six months he kept no books except a Cash Book.

At June 30th, 19.., his cash balance was £90 and his bank balance £430. Singleton estimated his debtors at £1 280, stock-in-hand at £1 400, and he had a van worth £800. His creditors amounted to £1 900. During the half-year he had drawn £1 060 for his personal expenses.

Draw up a statement showing the profit or loss Singleton had made by June 30th, 19...

20

ACCOUNTING RATIOS

20.1 What are Accounting Ratios?

A ratio is a quantitative relationship between two similar magnitudes which shows how many times one goes into the other, either integrally or fractionally. If profits have doubled this year, the ratio of this year's profit to last year's profit is 2:1. If a Gross Profit of £10 000 has to be reduced by £1 000 because of rent, the *expense ratio* for rent is $\frac{1\,000}{10\,000} = \frac{1}{10}$. Since we usually express such ratios as percentages we multiply the fraction $\frac{1}{10}$ by 100 and say that the expense ratio for rent is 10 per cent.

The basic financial ratios are as follows:

(*a*) The gross profit percentage
(*b*) The net profit percentage
(*c*) Expense ratios
(*d*) The rate of stockturn
(*e*) The working capital ratio or 'current' ratio
(*f*) The 'acid-test' ratio or 'quick' ratio
(*g*) The return on capital employed

A short explanation of each of these is necessary.

20.2 The Gross Profit Percentage

This is the percentage of Gross Profit that we make upon Sales, or a better phrase is **Net Turnover.** The term Net Turnover means sales less returns, and the Net Turnover of the business is itself an important statistic about any enterprise. The formula for the Gross Profit Percentage is therefore:

$$\text{Gross Profit Percentage} = \frac{\text{Gross Profit}}{\text{Net Turnover}} \times 100$$

Consider the Trading Account as shown in Fig. 20.1.

The Gross Profit Percentage on this Trading Account is:

$$\frac{\text{Gross Profit}}{\text{Net Turnover}} \times 100$$

$$= \frac{12\,000}{27\,500} \times 100$$

$$= \underline{\underline{43.6\%}}$$

Supposing that next year the firm does twice as much business? Would it need to make twice as many purchases? Would it expect to pay out twice as many expenses? Would it expect to make twice as much profit? Of course we cannot answer a 'yes' with absolute confidence to all these questions, but

TRADING ACCOUNT
(for year ending December 31st, 19..)

Opening Stock		1 450.00	Sales	27 900.00
Purchases	13 800.00		*Less* Returns	400.00
Add Carriage In	450.00			
			Net Turnover	27 500.00
	14 250.00			
Less Returns	700.00			
Net Purchases		13 550.00		
Total Stock Available		15 000.00		
Less Closing Stock		2 000.00		
Cost of Stock Sold		13 000.00		
Warehouse Expenses		2 500.00		
Cost of Sales		15 500.00		
Gross Profit		12 000.00		
		£27 500.00		£27 500.00

Fig. 20.1. A Trading Account.

generally speaking the answer will be 'roughly yes'. If we sell twice as many goods we would expect to buy twice as many goods. For the sake of this argument we will assume that everything simply doubles. Next year the Gross Profit Percentage works out as follows:

$$\frac{\text{Gross Profit}}{\text{Net Turnover}} \times 100$$
$$= \frac{24\,000}{55\,000} \times 100$$
$$= 43.6\%$$

You will see that it is the same answer as we had before, and this is the vital thing about the Gross Profit Percentage: it is a constant. It ought to come out the same every year providing our business is running in the same way. If the Gross Profit percentage has fallen during the year there must be some explanation. The most likely ones are:

(*a*) The manager or staff are stealing the cash takings. This will reduce the sales figure and the profits will fall. The cash is being diverted into the manager's or someone else's pocket.

(*b*) Perhaps someone is stealing the stock? One of the things about stocktaking is that it discovers losses of stock. A lower stock than we should have means a higher cost of sales figure and a lower Gross Profit. Who takes the stock home? Two pounds of sugar and a quarter of tea every night for a year makes quite a big hole in the stock. A very common practice of dishonest shop assistants is to help their friends to free goods. A packet of cigarettes to each boyfriend soon stops the Gross Profit Percentage being constant.

(*c*) If neither (*a*) nor (*b*) is the cause, stock might be getting lost in other ways. For instance, breakages due to clumsiness in the crockery department transfer some of the stock to the dustbin. Bad buying of perishables has the same effect—we throw away the tomatoes that go bad, the cheese that gets stale, the cakes that go dry. If we don't actually throw them away we have to sell them cheaply and that still means the profit on them is lost.

(*d*) Another type of bad buying, in the clothing and footwear trades especially, concerns the out-of-touch buyer who is behind the times and buys lines that have to be reduced in the sales because we cannot get rid of them in any other way. We have to keep our fashion buyers young in heart or their work will adversely affect the Gross Profit Percentage.

(*e*) A quite legitimate explanation for the falling Gross Profit Percentage may be that the cost of goods to us has risen and we have been slow to pass this on to the public. It may be because we have poor control in our pricing department, or because competition from more efficient traders prevents us from raising prices. Sometimes governments regulate prices by law and force the trader to accept lower profit margins. A government tax may be levied but because of the demand in our particular market we are unable to pass the tax on and must suffer it ourselves. The astute businessman will at least be ready with his plans to recoup these losses as soon as the law, or the market situation, changes.

(*f*) The expense items on the Trading Account may be the cause of the trouble. Is the manager taking on more staff than he needs? Perhaps the light and heat bill has risen dramatically. Is it a hard winter? If it is, there is nothing we can do about it. If it is not, perhaps the staff have brought in electrical appliances without our knowledge and are eating hot buttered toast with our electricity. In this case we will order the bright fellow who thought of the idea to take his toaster home again.

(*g*) It may be that the stock is wrongly valued. An error in stock valuation affects the Gross Profit. If we overvalue our closing stock we overvalue the Gross Profit; but the next year, when that closing stock has become the opening stock, we undervalue our Gross Profit. This double action produces a drop in the Gross Profit Percentage compared with the previous year.

20.3 The Net Profit Percentage and Expense Ratios

The Net Profit is the clear profit left after the office and selling expenses have been deducted from the Gross Profit. If we wish to check on the efficiency of the office and sales sides of our business, the ratio that gives us a clear picture of the trends shown is the Net Profit Percentage. This is found by the formula:

$$\text{Net Profit Percentage} = \frac{\text{Net Profit}}{\text{Turnover}} \times 100$$

Consider Fig. 20.2, a Profit and Loss Account which follows from the Trading Account in Fig. 20.1.

The Net Profit Percentage here is calculated as follows:

$$\text{Net Profit Percentage} = \frac{6\,330}{27\,500} \times 100$$

$$= \underline{\underline{23.0\%}}$$

PROFIT AND LOSS ACCOUNT
(*for year ending December 31st, 19..*)

Salaries	1 450.00	Gross Profit	12 000.00
Light and Heat	1 300.00	Commission Received	1 180.00
Insurance	850.00	Rent Received	250.00
Advertising	2 400.00		
Depreciation	450.00		13 430.00
Bad Debts	650.00		
	7 100.00		
Net Profit	6 330.00		
	£13 430.00		£13 430.00

Fig. 20.2. A Profit and Loss Account.

Once again we would expect the Net Profit Percentage to be constant—that is, to remain roughly the same from year to year—provided we always prepare our Profit and Loss Account in the same way. It follows that any significant change in Net Profit Percentage, say 2 per cent or more, would be investigated to discover the cause.

Suppose that last year the Net Profit Percentage was 26.5 per cent and this year it has fallen to 23 per cent. This is a significant fall and we must find the reason.

What Can Have Caused a Fall in the Net Profit Percentage?

If the Gross Profit Percentage is steady but the Net Profit Percentage has fallen the fault must lie in the expenses or profits shown on the Profit and Loss Account. We should examine each expense item carefully, working out an **Expense Ratio to Turnover**, for this year and the previous year. This is quite simple and involves a calculation:

$$\text{Expense ratio} = \frac{\text{Expense}}{\text{Turnover}} \times 100$$

So for Salaries it would be:

$$\frac{\text{Salaries}}{\text{Turnover}} \times 100$$
$$= \frac{1\,450}{27\,500} \times 100$$
$$= 5.3\%$$

By comparing this with the similar figure for the previous year we may discover some increase in expense. Perhaps the manager has taken on more staff than are really necessary? Similar expense ratios may reveal other causes of the change. Perhaps the advertising has been excessive? An increased advertising budget has not yielded proportionately higher sales. Perhaps insurance rates have risen, and have not been passed on to the consumer in higher prices? The profits on the credit side may show some falling off from the previous year. Have we received less commission than previously, or less rent? These will also affect Net Profit Percentage.

When we discover the cause of the fall in Net Profit Percentage we must take the necessary action to correct the profitability of the business. This means we must reduce the expenses that are soaring, or increase the receipts that have been declining. If such action is impossible, we must pass the increased cost on to the final consumer.

Interim Final Accounts

Some firms find the annual check-up on Gross Profit and Net Profit Percentage too long a period to wait before correcting undesirable trends. The more quickly we can discover adverse variations, the quicker we can take steps to put them right. The best thing is to take out interim Final Accounts at six-monthly, or even three-monthly, intervals.

20.4 Exercises: Gross Profit and Net Profit Percentages

1. (*a*) State, briefly and clearly, what you understand by the term Net Turnover in relation to the business of a retailer.

   (*b*) A trader had in stock on July 1st 600 articles costing £2.00 each. During the month he bought 1 800 more of these articles at the same price and sold 2 020 at £3.00 each, of which 20 were returned. Draw up a statement showing the Gross Profit earned and express the Gross Profit as a percentage of the turnover.

2. On preparing the Trading Account of R. Lyons, a retailer, for the financial year ended March 31st, 19.., it was found that the ratio of Gross Profit to sales was 15 per cent, whereas for the previous financial year the corresponding ratio had been 25 per cent. State, with your reasons, whether or not the following may have contributed to cause the decline:

   (*a*) The stock at March 31st, 19.., was undervalued.

   (*b*) The cost of a new delivery van had been included in the purchases for the year ended March 31st, 19.., and charged to Trading Account.

   (*c*) The sales for the year ended March 31st, 19.., showed a decline compared with the previous year.

   (*d*) In both years R. Lyons and his family had been supplied with goods from the shop but the value of these goods had not been recorded in the books of the business.

   (*e*) On the last day of the financial year an employee was successfully convicted of dishonesty with regard to the theft of takings from the tills.

3. In making a comparison between two successive years of his business, R. Rogers notices the following matters:

	Year 1	*Year 2*
	£	£
Turnover	65 000.00	85 000.00
Gross Profit	25 900.00	27 560.00
Net Profit	8 800.00	11 600.00

   Present these two sets of results in such a way as to make a comparison, and state any conclusions you can draw.

4. M. Smith presents you with the following data about his business. In Year 2 he had appointed a dynamic young manager who has produced the increase in turnover shown. Comment upon these results, and on the manager's performance.

	Year 1	*Year 2*
	£	£
Turnover	27 000	68 000
Gross Profit	15 500	28 500
Net Profit	8 250	11 000

5. In Year 1 Brown's turnover was £165 000 and the following items appeared in his Profit and Loss Account, amongst others.

Occupation Expenses	£2 300
Heat and Light	£500
Telephone Expenses	£725

In Year 2 Brown's turnover, under a new manager, had risen to £225 000 but net profit percentage was down by 3 per cent. The above expenses had changed as follows:

Occupation Expenses	£3 600
Heat and Light	£725
Telephone Expenses	£2 430

Comment on the possible causes of the fall in Net Profit Percentage, offering support for your answers where possible from the calculation of helpful ratios.

20.5 Turnover, Rate of Turnover or Rate of Stockturn

The *turnover* of a business is the final sales figure, i.e. the sales less returns inwards. It is often called the **net turnover.** The chief accounting requirement affecting turnover is that limited companies with a turnover in excess of £250 000 per annum are required to declare their turnover in their published accounts.

Sales are of course achieved by buying, or manufacturing, stock in trade and selling it. As the stock is turned over profits are made, so that profitability reflects the rate of turnover of stock. Other things being equal, if the rate of stock turnover is increased profits will rise. It may even be worth lowering prices, and thus selling at less profit per unit, if the turnover rises more than proportionately.

The rate of stock turnover is always expressed as a number. To say that the rate of stockturn is six means that the stock turns over six times in a year. Is this a good rate of stockturn or is it a poor one? We cannot possibly say until we know the product we are discussing. If a grocer turned over his stock of eggs six times a year they would be in stock for an average of two months each. This hardly makes them new-laid eggs by the time they are consumed. On the other hand, grand pianos tend to be a slow-moving line and do not deteriorate if kept in stock two months. Some classes of goods are very 'perishable', like newspapers, which must be turned over every day if they are to be sold at all.

Calculating the Rate of Stock Turnover

Two formulae which give the same answer are:

$$1.\ \text{Rate of Stockturn} = \frac{\text{Cost of Stock Sold}}{\text{Average Stock at Cost Price}}$$

$$2.\ \text{Rate of Stockturn} = \frac{\text{Net Turnover}}{\text{Average Stock at Sales Price}}$$

Use formula 1 for the moment. If you find the average stock, and divide it into the amount of stock sold at cost price, you will find out how often the stock turns over in each trading period.

The average stock is found by taking Opening stock + Closing stock and dividing by 2. If quarterly stock figures are available we can add up the four quarterly figures and divide by 4.

Using the Trading Account of Fig. 20.1, we find that the average stock comes out to £1 725:

$$\frac{1\,450 + 2\,000}{2} = \frac{3\,450}{2} = 1\,725$$

As the cost of stock sold is £13 000 it follows that

$$\text{Rate of Stockturn} = \frac{13\,000}{1\,725} = \frac{520}{69} = 7.5 \text{ times per year}$$

Whether this is a good rate of stock turnover we cannot say, but it means that goods are in stock for roughly seven weeks on average. For some classes of goods this might be a good rate of stockturn. For fresh fish or spring flowers it would hardly do.

20.6 Exercises: Rate of Stock Turnover

1. A trader carries an average stock, valued at cost price, of £2 000.00 and turns this over five times per year. If he marks his stock up by 25 per cent on cost price, what is his Gross Profit for the year?
2. A trader carries an average stock valued at cost price of £6 250.00 and turns this over four times a year. If his mark-up is 20 per cent on cost, and his overheads came to £2 800.00, what is the Net Profit for the year?
3. A retailer carries an average stock valued at cost price of £600.00. His rate of stock-turn is 150, his average profit is 10 per cent on cost, and his overheads and running expenses come to £6 500.00. What is his Net Profit for the year?
4. H. J. is in business as a retailer and during the year ended December 31st, 19. ., the average value of his stock at cost price was £8 000.00. He turned this over four times, at an average mark-up of 50 per cent. His fixed expenses were £3 000.00 and his variable expenses 15 per cent of the turnover. Calculate H.J.'s profit or loss for the year. If he had turned over his stock only three times during the year, by how much would his profit or loss have been affected?
5. Marshall & Co. Ltd are a firm of wholesalers. Their average stock is valued at £42 000.00 at cost, and is turned over four times in each trading year at an average mark-up of 50 per cent on cost. The firm's fixed, or standing, charges are £18 000.00 and their variable expenses are 20 per cent of the turnover. Calculate (*a*) the firm's profit for the year and (*b*) the profit if the stock is turned over five times in a year. What conclusion would you draw from the difference in the amount of profit?
6. Peter Bird's financial year ended on July 31st, 19. . . His Trial Balance at that date included the following items:

	£
Sales	125 720
Sales Returns	2 140
Stock August 1st, previous year	5 250
Stock July 31st, 19. .	4 550
Gross Profit for year	35 500

You are required to calculate:

(*a*) Net purchases for the year.
(*b*) Cost of goods sold during the year.
(*c*) Rate of stock turnover for the year (correct to one decimal place).
(*d*) Gross Profit percentage to turnover (correct to one decimal place).
(*e*) Gross Profit percentage to cost of sales (correct to one decimal place).

20.7 Vocabulary for the Balance Sheet Ratios

Balance Sheets are not always well presented and the ratios which may be found from the Balance Sheet require the accountant to use figures which appear only when the Balance Sheet is in good style. These figures, which have been referred to in Section 17.11, are as follows:

Current Assets. Those assets which are held in the business with a view to their conversion into cash in the ordinary course of the firm's profit-making activities.

Fixed Assets. Those assets which are retained in the firm for use by the proprietor and his employees, because they permanently increase the profit-making capacity of the business.

Net Assets. In many sets of published accounts the current liabilities are brought over to the assets side of the Balance Sheet and deducted from the current assets. This gives the *net current assets*, also called the 'Working Capital' (see below). When the net current assets are added to the fixed assets they give the *net assets*, i.e. the total assets less the current liabilities. The net assets represents all the assets purchased by the firm, using its long-term funds (capital and profits ploughed back, plus any long-term borrowing).

Current Liabilities. Those liabilities which will fall due for payment fairly quickly, and certainly within less than one year.

Long-term Liabilities. Those liabilities which will not fall due immediately, but which will be repaid over an agreed period greater than one year.

Capital. The net worth of the business to the owner of the business; that portion of the owner's wealth which he has invested in the business either originally or by leaving past profits to accumulate in the service of the firm.

Fig. 20.3 shows a typical Balance Sheet which will serve as a basis for discussion. By careful consideration of this Balance Sheet and the ratios des-

M. ERASMUS
BALANCE SHEET
(*as at December 31st, 19..*)

CAPITAL				FIXED ASSETS		
At Start		24 000.00		Premises	7 400.00	
Add Net				Plant and		
Profit	4 500.00			Machinery	14 000.00	
Less				Motor Vehicles	3 800.00	
Drawings	6 000.00					
		−1 500.00				25 200.00
				CURRENT ASSETS		
			22 500.00	Stock	8 898.00	
LONG-TERM LIABILITIES				Debtors	3 704.00	
Bank Loan			10 000.00	Bank Moneys	650.00	
CURRENT LIABILITIES				Cash in Hand	48.00	
Creditors			6 000.00			
						13 300.00
			38 500.00			38 500.00

Fig. 20.3. A Balance Sheet for appraisal.

cribed below the reader may learn more phrases which are commonly used in business to help in the interpretation of Final Accounts. A mastery of these terms enables an accountant to make sound judgments about businesses whose affairs he is considering. The new terms are:

(*a*) **Fixed Capital.** This is capital tied up in fixed assets (which are shown on the assets side). In the case of M. Erasmus the fixed capital is £25 200.00. The significance of fixed capital is that it is sunk into the business and cannot be regained without seriously affecting the conduct of the business. If Erasmus tries to realise this fixed capital by selling motor vehicles or plant and machinery, the distribution or production of the firm's products will be hampered. If he tries to sell the premises he will be out in the street.

(*b*) **Floating Capital or Circulating Capital.** This is capital tied up in current assets (also shown on the assets side). These can be realised more easily and without interfering with the conduct of the business; indeed, that is what we are in business for—to turn over stock and make profits as the stock turns into cash.

(*c*) **Liquid Capital.** The term 'liquid' in economic matters means 'in cash form'. The liquid capital is that portion of the assets that are available as cash, or near cash. In this case it is £4 402.00, the total of cash, bank moneys and debtors.

(*d*) **Working Capital.** This is the most important of these four terms—one of the most vital concepts in business. It is that portion of the capital invested in the business which is left to run the business after providing the fixed capital. Once a firm has bought its premises, plant and machinery, etc., it still needs working capital to run the business, to pay wages and sundry expenses. One might really say that having met all the capital expenditure one still needs funds for revenue expenditure. The £13 300.00 that Erasmus has left after paying for his fixed assets is clearly something to do with working capital, but the real way to find working capital is as follows:

$$\begin{aligned}\text{Working Capital} &= \text{Current Assets} - \text{Current Liabilities}\\ &= £13\,300.00 - £6\,000.00\\ &= £7\,300.00\end{aligned}$$

(*e*) **External Liabilities.** These are liabilities owed to persons outside the business, and that means both current liabilities and long-term liabilities, in this case £16 000.00

(*f*) **Capital Owned.** This is the net worth of the business, the value of the business to the owner of the business. In this case it is £22 500.00.

(*g*) **Capital Employed.** This is a very important figure. It can be defined in a number of different ways and a table of them is presented later (see Table 20.1). A simple definition of the term is that it is the capital employed in the business no matter who provides it. Clearly this business is worth £38 500.00, because it has that many assets. Who has provided the capital to buy £38 500.00 worth of assets? The owner, Erasmus, has provided £22 500.00, but he is also employing the bank's money (£10 000.00) and his creditors' money (£6 000.00), making £38 500.00 in all.

In most investigations we are interested in a particular group and the capital they have personally employed in earning their share of the profits. That is why Table 20.1 shows a number of alternative ways to find the capital employed.

We must now turn to consider each of the ratios which can be found from the Balance Sheet.

20.8 The Working Capital Ratio (or Current Ratio)

The working capital ratio shows the relationship between Current Assets and Current Liabilities. Ideally a business should be able to meet all its current liabilities without hesitation. The ratio is therefore:

$$\text{Working Capital Ratio} = \frac{\text{Current Assets}}{\text{Current Liabilities}}$$

In the case of Erasmus's Balance Sheet this works out to:

$$\frac{13\,300}{6\,000} = 2.2$$

What is reasonably safe working capital ratio? It is generally agreed that 2:1 is a desirable working capital ratio. This means that the external debts can be met twice over from the available current assets.

So important is working capital considered to be that many accountants prefer to show the figure on the Balance Sheet itself. This is done by bringing the Current Liabilities over to the Assets side of the Balance Sheet and deducting them. This leaves a 'net current assets' figure (sometimes called a 'net working capital' figure) only to be added in with the Fixed Assets. For an example of this system the reader should turn back to Fig. 19.6.

20.9 The Acid-Test Ratio or 'Quick Ratio'

Even if the working capital ratio is adequate it can sometimes be unsatisfactory if the majority of the current assets are in Stock, an illiquid asset. We cannot pay our creditors with Stock, and so the acid-test of solvency is given by those assets which can *quickly* be turned into cash. There are Cash itself, money in the bank, Investments and Debtors (who have a legal obligation to pay). The quick ratio, liquid capital ratio, or acid-test ratio is found by the formula

$$\text{Liquid Capital Ratio} = \frac{\text{Current Assets} - \text{Stock}}{\text{Current Liabilities}}$$

$$= \frac{4\,402}{6\,000} = 0.73 \text{ times}$$

The name 'acid-test ratio' is used to show that this is the critical test of solvency. Can the firm, with its present cash and debtors (due to pay within the month) meet its current liabilities (due for payment within the month)? This is very interesting because it shows how weak this firm is as far as liquid assets go. Most of its current assets are stock.

The minimum acid-test ratio is 1:1, which means that a firm can pay its immediate debts at once from its immediately available assets.

20.10 Return on Capital Employed (or Return on Capital Invested)

The general formula for finding the return on capital employed is:

$$\frac{\text{Profit}}{\text{Capital employed}} \times 100$$

However, it is possible to vary each of these terms in a particular case—for example, should the capital employed be the capital at the start of the year, or the end of the year or an average figure, and should loans be included as capital (because although they are not strictly speaking capital they are certainly finances employed in earning the profits). It depends upon the purpose of the enquiry which we are pursuing how we define the terms 'profit' and 'capital employed'.

The basic rules for defining these terms are outlined below.

Capital Employed. The capital is employed in the business to buy the assets, which are then put to work to earn the profits of the business. The various definitions of capital employed are therefore related to the 'assets base' chosen for the purpose of the enquiry. A list of these is given in Table 20.1.

Table 20.1 Assets Bases for Capital Employed

Capital Employed defined as:	*Method of discovering the value of the assets for each definition*
(*a*) Total Assets	(*a*) Total asset figure as given on Balance Sheet
(*b*) Assets employed in *this* business	(*b*) Total asset figure — debtors (because the debtors are using our money in their businesses)
(*c*) Assets actively employed	(*c*) Total assets — debtors and also any other idle assets such as unoccupied premises, moth-balled plant and machinery, idle cash balances, etc.
(*d*) Assets provided by long-term funds	(*d*) Total assets — current liabilities
(*e*) Net worth to the owner(s)	(*e*) Total assets — current liabilities and loan funds.
(*f*) Ordinary Shareholders' interest in the company	(*f*) As in (*c*) above but also minus Preference Shares

Profit. The profit figure is found in the Profit and Loss Account, but this may need adjustment before it is used in the calculation for 'Return on Capital Employed'. The principle is that the profits earned should be those accruing to the 'assets base' which is being used, i.e. (*a*)–(*f*) in the 'Capital Employed' column of Table 20.1. The profits are appropriated in the Appropriation Account. As successive Appropriations reduce the profit available the residual profit is applicable to the next 'asset base' in the chain. These various definitions of 'Profit' are listed in Table 20.2.

Special Considerations for the Small Businessman

The proprietor of a small business would in normal events take a job with some firm if he were not self-employed. In judging how far he is benefiting from being in business he might well feel that he should deduct from his profit figure (the return he is earning from being self-employed) a substantial sum for loss of wages in some other opportunity. Similarly, if his capital were not tied up in this business it could be earning him a suitable dividend from a building

Table 20.2. Definitions of Profit for 'Return on Capital Employed'

Profit definition	*How it is obtained from the accounts*
(i) Earnings before interest and tax (applicable to bases (*a*), (*b*) and (*c*) in 'Capital Employed' column of Table 20.1)	(i) Net Profit figure + interest payments deducted in Profit and Loss Account
(ii) Earnings after tax (applicable to base (*d*) in Table 20.1)	(ii) Net Profit figure + interest added back as in (i) − Tax appropriations
(iii) Earnings after interest and tax (applicable to base (*e*) Table 20.1)	(iii) Net Profit figure − Tax appropriations
(iv) Earnings after interest, tax and Preference Dividends (applicable to base (*f*))	(iv) Net Profit figure − Tax and Preference Dividend appropriations
(v) For sole traders and partnerships special considerations apply. They are explained below (see page 340).	

society or other investment. The businessman might therefore discover his final profit in the following way.

$$\text{Profit} - \begin{pmatrix}\text{Opportunity Cost in}\\ \text{some other employment}\end{pmatrix} \text{ and } \begin{pmatrix}\text{Opportunity Cost of}\\ \text{capital invested elsewhere}\end{pmatrix}$$

Such a formula reduces the profit to the point where it shows him only the *net benefit from being self-employed.*

Since the best definition of capital employed for such a business is Asset base (*b*) in Table 20.1, we have the final formula

$$\text{Return on Capital Invested in the small business} = \frac{\begin{pmatrix}\text{Net Profit} - \text{Opportunity cost of employment and investment}\end{pmatrix}}{\text{Total assets} - \text{Debtors}} \times 100$$

In real terms, this means as follows:

Example 20.1. A is in business as a grocer. Total assets are valued at £21 500 of which £500 is debtors. Profits are found to be £4 935. A believes that if he ceased to be self-employed he would be able to obtain employment as a manager at £65 per week, and his capital invested (£12 000) would earn 6½ per cent. Calculate his Return on Capital Employed.

$$\text{Return on Capital Employed} = \frac{\text{Net Profit} - \text{Opportunity Costs}}{\text{Total assets} - \text{Debtors}} \times 100$$

$$= \frac{4\,935 - [(65 \times 52) + (£12\,000 \times 6\tfrac{1}{2}\%)]}{21\,500 - 500} \times 100$$

$$= \frac{4\,935 - (3\,380 + 780)}{21\,000} \times 100$$

$$= \frac{775}{21\,000} \times 100$$

$$= \underline{\underline{3.69\%}}$$

A is therefore earning an extra benefit of 3.69 per cent by being self-employed. He has to decide whether this increased earnings, plus the non-monetary advantages of being his own master, outweigh the risks run by being self-employed.

Calculating the Return on Capital Employed

Returning to the basic formula given at the start of Section 20.10, we have

$$\text{Return on Capital Employed} = \frac{\text{Profit} \times 100}{\text{Capital Employed}}$$

In any calculation referring to a particular firm, or an examination question about an imaginary firm, we have to select the appropriate asset base for the 'capital employed' figure (see Table 20.1) and the correct 'profit' definition to suit that asset base, and when substituted in the formula above they will give us the Return on Capital Employed.

20.11 Exercises: Balance Sheet Vocabulary and Ratios

1. Define the following terms:

   (*a*) Working capital
   (*b*) Current assets
   (*c*) Current liabilities
   (*d*) Fixed assets

   Why is it important to distinguish each of these items clearly?
2. (*a*) What do you understand by the term 'Working Capital'? (*b*) State, with reasons, whether the following transactions would increase or decrease the working capital of a business; or would they have no effect?

   (i) Machinery no longer required is sold for Cash, £1 250.
   (ii) £2 000 is paid for a lorry.
   (iii) £500 is received from a trade debtor.
   (iv) Stock costing £200 is sold on credit to a customer for £250.
   (v) Stock is exchanged for office furniture £160.
3. (*a*) It is not uncommon for current liabilities to be deducted from current assets in the published accounts of a company. What is the object of this form of accounting presentation?

   (*b*) It is not uncommon for 'Formation Expenses' to be deducted from the ordinary shareholders' interest in the company on a Balance Sheet. Why is this a sound accounting practice?
4. (*a*) How do you distinguish between short-term and long-term liabilities? Why is it important to make this distinction in practice?

   (*b*) What is the distinction between 'revenue reserves' and 'capital reserves'? Why do these items appear on the liabilities side of the balance sheet? If they are a liability, to whom are they owed?
5. What do you understand by the term 'net assets' and what is its significance for accounting procedures and calculations?
6. Here is the abbreviated Balance Sheet of Trihard Ltd.

BALANCE SHEET

(as at December 31st, 19..)

Ordinary Shares	100 000
Reserves ploughed back over the years	82 000
Preference Shares (7 per cent)	20 000
Debentures (6 per cent)	60 000
Current liabilities	18 000
	£280 000

Represented by	£
Formation Expenses	2 000
Fixed Assets	160 000
Trade Investments (in a subsidiary L. Ltd)	61 000
Stock	35 000
Debtors	5 000
Cash at Bank	15 000
Cash in Hand	2 000
	£280 000

Rearrange the Balance Sheet to bring out:

(*a*) The ordinary shareholders' interest in the company
(*b*) The Working Capital
(*c*) The 'net assets'

You are now told that *before* paying the Debenture interest and the Preference Dividend the profits had been £23 000. What was the Return on Capital Employed to the Ordinary Shareholders? If they were paid a 7 per cent dividend what additional sum was put away to reserves this year?

7. Here is the abbreviated Balance Sheet of Workwell Ltd.

BALANCE SHEET
(*as at December 31st, 19..*)

	£
Ordinary Shares	200 000
Reserves ploughed back in previous years	186 000
Preference Shares (7 per cent)	80 000
Debentures (5 per cent)	100 000
Current liabilities	104 000
	£670 000

Represented by	£
Preliminary Expenses not yet written off	2 500
Fixed Assets	560 000
Investments	64 500
Stock	25 000
Debtors	8 000
Cash at Bank	7 000
Cash in Hand	3 000
	£670 000

Rearrange the Balance Sheet to bring out:

(*a*) The ordinary shareholders' interest in the company
(*b*) The Working Capital
(*c*) The 'net assets'.

You are told that the investments are held to earn income from spare cash balances. Calculate the working capital ratio and the liquid capital ratio. Comment on their adequacy.

8. The balance sheets of Rovers Ltd at December 31st, Year 1, and December 31st, Year 2, are as follows:

		Year 1		*Year 2*
		£		£
Fixed Assets				
Plant at cost	60 000		60 000	
Less depreciation	20 000	40 000	25 000	35 000
Motor vehicles	15 000		18 000	
Less depreciation	5 000	10 000	8 250	9 750
Current Assets				
Stock	6 500		9 250	
Debtors	4 850		5 250	
Bank	3 965		4 580	
		15 315		19 080
		£65 315		£63 830
Ordinary Share Capital		25 000		25 000
Retained Profit		10 800		1 600
Debentures		20 000		20 000
Current Liabilities		9 515		17 230
		£65 315		£63 830

You are asked to redraft these two balance sheets to show the working capital and the capital employed by the ordinary shareholders at December 31st, Year 1, and at December 31st, Year 2.

Index